RELIGIOUS AND SPIRITUAL EXPERIENCES

What is the value of religious and spiritual experiences within human life? Are we evolutionarily programmed to have such experiences? How will emerging technologies change such experiences in the future? Wesley J. Wildman addresses these key intellectual questions and more, offering a spiritually evocative naturalist interpretation of the diverse variety of religious and spiritual experiences. He describes these experiences, from the common to the exceptional, and offers innovative classifications of them based on their neurological features and their internal qualities. His account avoids reductionalistic oversimplifications and instead synthesizes perspectives from many disciplines, including philosophy and natural sciences, into a compelling account of the meaning and value of religious and spiritual experiences in human life. The resulting interpretation does not assume a supernatural worldview but incorporates religious and spiritual experiences into a positive affirmation of this-worldly existence.

WESLEY J. WILDMAN is Associate Professor of Philosophy, Theology, and Ethics at Boston University, where he directs the doctoral program in Religion and Science. His previous recent publications include *Religious Philosophy As Multidisciplinary Comparative Inquiry* (2010) and *Science and Religious Anthropology* (2009).

RELIGIOUS AND SPIRITUAL EXPERIENCES

WESLEY J. WILDMAN

Boston University

CAMBRIDGE
UNIVERSITY PRESS

32 Avenue of the Americas, New York NY 10013-2473, USA

Cambridge University Press is part of the University of Cambridge.

It furthers the University's mission by disseminating knowledge in the pursuit of education, learning and research at the highest international levels of excellence.

www.cambridge.org
Information on this title: www.cambridge.org/9781107423459

© Wesley J. Wildman 2011

First published 2011
First paperback edition 2014

A catalogue record for this publication is available from the British Library

Library of Congress Cataloguing in Publication data
Wildman, Wesley J., 1961–
Religious and spiritual experiences / Wesley J. Wildman.
p. cm.
Includes bibliographical references and index.
ISBN 978-1-107-00008-7 (hardback)
1. Experience (Religion) 2. Technology. I. Title.
BL53.W 573 2011
210–dc22
2010037095

ISBN 978-1-107-00008-7 Hardback
ISBN 978-1-107-42345-9 Paperback

For Gay

Contents

Contents

Figures

ix

Preface

Religious and spiritual experiences (RSEs) are a puzzle. Some people receive them gratefully as reliable ways to discover the deepest truths about reality. Others approach them warily, as misleading side-effects of the human brain's spectacular virtual-reality processing system. Great passion surrounds such opposed convictions, because the stakes are high. The first group defends the very meaning of human life, after all, while the second group protects the world from dangerous fanaticism. The passion on all sides makes patient inquiry exceptionally difficult but that has not stopped intellectuals from trying. As a result, endless streams of reflection on the puzzle, most promising impartial handling of evidence and judicious interpretation, pour into the present from all of the world's literate philosophical and religious traditions. In our own time, studies of the social psychology and neuroscience of these experiences join the confluence of wisdom, sometimes naively claiming to offer the last word on the subject.

No approach, no researcher, no writer, and no book will speak the last word on RSEs. Advance in understanding occurs at the margins, to be sure, but the central puzzle remains because there are no knock-down refutations of the best versions of competing interpretations. The first challenge facing the interpreter of RSEs is therefore to avoid simple-minded thinking on the subject. This is more difficult than it may seem at first glance. It involves committing to working carefully across the relevant disciplines and traditions, thereby properly preparing the interpreter to avoid pitfalls into which less diligent inquirers routinely fall. Elementary traps include thinking that RSEs are self-authorizing, that they must be delusions because they have neural representations and causal conditions, and that it is sufficient to take account of wisdom on the subject from one religious tradition or one discipline. People fall into such traps so often that the overall picture is somewhat tragicomic – pitfalls becoming pratfalls. There are many less obvious traps as well. Awareness of many disciplines and many religious and philosophical traditions may not force a resolution of the puzzle but, by helping the interpreter avoid mistakes that by now should feel more embarrassing than they do, multidisciplinary and multireligious competence makes inquiries more difficult to dismiss and far more interesting.

The second challenge facing the interpreter of RSEs is to acknowledge that the task is to evaluate the overall plausibility of *entire systems of interpretation*. Supposing simple arguments will defeat the interpretations of sophisticated opponents is a fool's hope. Presuming that evidence (however construed) can neatly clinch the case one way or another is vulgar; every sophisticated interpretative framework can assimilate the same evidence in basic ways. Simple arguments and basic evidence can eliminate fundamentally inadequate interpretations, which can be extremely useful. But the best interpretations of RSEs, no matter how opposed, eagerly sop up evidence like a hungry worker consumes the remains of a bowl of warm soup. These are large-scale systems of interpretation that read the entire world in creative and compelling ways; RSEs merely ride on the impressive coattails. Such large-scale systems of interpretation are robust and adaptive to an exceptional degree.

The inquiry presented in this book fully accepts these two challenges, refuses shortcuts, and attempts to take responsibility for the interpretation offered. The approach to inquiry is described more fully in *Religious Philosophy As Multidisciplinary Comparative Inquiry: Envisioning a Future for the Philosophy of Religion* (Wildman 2010), so I won't dwell on methodological questions in this volume.

The resulting interpretation is not only scientifically and philosophically informed; it is also theological in character. In this respect, as the subtitle indicates, it is a spiritually evocative yet naturalist theological interpretation of RSEs – a combination that can seem passing strange to some and a welcome relief to others. Naturalism is so closely allied with materialism and anti-religiousness for some that the term seems lost for spiritually and religiously positive uses. Impressive traditions of religious naturalism exist, nonetheless, and they have intimate connections with certain mystical theological viewpoints. The area of compatibility between naturalism and theology is larger and more intriguing than people supposing naturalism must be anti-theological might assume. The shared territory opposes supernaturalism (in the sense of disembodied intentionality) and rejects supranaturalism (in the sense of ultimate reality as a divine person with awareness and purposes and powers to act in the world), and that is enough to make it religiously useless for some. By contrast, theologians supposing that God is not a personal being but rather the Ground of Being, *Esse*

Ipsum, God beyond God, *Nirguna Brahman*, or the *Dao* That Cannot Be Daoed immediately grasp the point: *there is harmony between such ground-of-being theologies and an anti-supernaturalistic, anti-supranaturalistic, spiritually potent form of naturalism.* Religious naturalism in this sense is an ancient view, with a profound presence in all of the great religious and philosophical traditions, albeit usually on the underside of traditions dominated by supernaturalistic and supranaturalistic ways of thinking.

Taking the second challenge (above: the need to evaluate large-scale systems of interpretation) with due seriousness entails that I accept certain limitations in this inquiry. In particular, I cannot mount a full defense of religious naturalism in my sense against its anti-religious naturalist detractors and its supernaturalistic religious critics. This task is taken up in relation to the human condition in *Science and Religious Anthropology* (Wildman 2009b), and in relation to the metaphysical systems themselves in a forthcoming work on science and ultimate reality. I do not leave the challenge of evaluating large-scale systems of interpretation entirely to those other books, however. From beginning to end, this volume presents a religious naturalist interpretation of RSEs in relation to alternative interpretative frameworks, anticipating criticisms and issuing challenges. The overall case for the superior plausibility of the religious naturalist interpretation depends on the whole book. Frankly, because this case rejects the supernaturalist and supranaturalist premises of many traditional theological interpretations of RSEs, it risks not achieving a fair hearing in that domain. Similarly, because the case rejects the anti-religious premises of some prominent naturalists, it risks being dismissed out of court there, too. For those willing to suspend these typical assumptions for the sake of argument, and (better) for the sake of exploring an alternative interpretative framework, I believe the case can be persuasive – welcomed for its plotting of a path through what formerly seemed to be an intellectual impasse, toward the instinctively attractive destination of an affirmative-yet-critical appraisal of RSEs.

An interpretation of RSEs developed in a religious–naturalist framework has some unusual but intriguing features. Important among them is that the interpretation can affirm the value of RSEs (in a host of surprising forms, within and beyond religious settings) even while exercising skepticism about the meanings people often attach to such experiences. In this sense, the inquiry presented in this book takes up a middle position between eager boosters and nasty detractors of RSEs, able to grant a significant amount of what each side cares most about while pushing back against less judicious aspects of their opposed interpretations.

Acknowledgements

This book first emerged as a series of lectures given at Boston University during the 2007–8 academic year. The lectures were organized by the Religious and Psychological Well-Being Project, an interdisciplinary collaboration funded by Metanexus Institute, through the Templeton Research Lectures for the Constructive Engagement of Science and Religion grant program. I am delighted to acknowledge this support from John Templeton Foundation, Metanexus Institute, and Bob Neville, Director of the Religious and Psychological Well-Being Project. I am also grateful to the members of the project, all of whom helped me refine the argument of this book: Linda Barnes, Nathaniel Barrett, Catherine Caldwell-Harris, David Eckel, Deb Kelemen, Brian McCorkle, Jon Roberts, Chris Schlauch, and George Stavros.

I was privileged on three occasions to be a teaching assistant for Huston Smith at the University of California, Berkeley, during graduate school. Because of the connection forged in those teaching experiences, Huston met weekly for almost three years with me and a couple of my graduate-school friends, including Kate McCarthy (now at Cal State Chico). I suspect Huston kept it up in part to convert us to his way of thinking, but he also seemed genuinely fascinated with our ways of thinking, including our reasonable yet stubborn refusal to buy into his perennialist worldview, which seemed so compelling to him. In the informal setting of those meetings, we talked about everything under the sun, including RSEs. It is to Huston's endless fascination with RSEs, and to the sheer force of his personality, that I owe the birth of my own intellectual interest in the subject. Moreover, the union of religious naturalism with ground-of-being theism and ultimately with apophatic mysticism, which is central to my intellectual profile as a theologian and also to the case presented in this book, derives in part from those formative conversations and Huston's influence.

Neuropsychologist Leslie Brothers (author of *Friday's Footprint*) was an early partner in my work on RSEs. Some years ago we jointly wrote a near-monograph-length paper setting forth a pragmatic theory of such experiences that drew as heavily on the semiotic theory of Charles Peirce as on social neuroscience and philosophical theology. Those early conversations were of great importance to me and I am grateful for Leslie's friendship and collaboration. More recently, Patrick McNamara has been a marvelous research partner on issues surrounding RSEs. It is fitting that his own book on *The Neuroscience of Religious Experience* appeared with Cambridge University Press in 2009; these two books reflect the complementarity of our work together in the Institute for the Biocultural Study of Religion.

This book is dedicated to Gay Lane, friend of many years, loyal companion through many joys and troubles, consistent supporter of my family, the occasion for my friendship with the inimitable Cowabunga-Dude Doug, and the person above all others who has made my adopted country feel like home. In her unique way, Gay represents many people for whom I would like this book to be especially meaningful: deeply curious, self-aware, morally inspiring, and blessed with spiritually profound experiences that do not fit the categories and naming conventions of traditional religions. Our manifold engagements with Ultimate Reality are more diverse than any religion will admit, more precious than their detractors pretend, more difficult to interpret than we realize, and more profound than we can express. That should encourage all of us.

A few sections of this book derive from previously published work, though there is only slender connection to the originals. I am glad to acknowledge the publishers of the following articles:

(With Leslie A. Brothers), "A Neuropsychological Semiotic Model of Religious Experiences," in Robert John Russell, *et al.*, eds., *Neurosciences and the Person: Scientific Perspectives on Divine Action* (Vatican City: Vatican Observatory; Berkeley, CA: Center for Theology and the Natural Sciences, 1999): 348–416.

"Consciousness Expanded," in B. V. Sreekantan and Sangeetha Menon, eds., *Consciousness and Genetics: A Discussion* (Bangalore, India: National Institute of Advanced Studies, 2002): 125–41.

(With Patrick McNamara), "Challenges Facing the Neurological Study of Religious Belief, Behavior and Experience," *Method and Theory in the Study of Religion* 20/3 (2008): 212–42.

(With Nathaniel F. Barrett), "Seeing Is Believing? How Reinterpreting the Direct Realism of Perception As Dynamic Engagement Alters the Justificatory Force of Religious Experience," *International Journal for Philosophy of Religion* 66/2 (2009): 71–86; published online December 17, 2008, www.springerlink.com/content/e7737tm607216745/fulltext.pdf.

Exploring a strange yet familiar landscape: a strategy for interpreting religious and spiritual experiences

INTRODUCTION

What is the point of studying religious and spiritual experiences (RSEs)? What can we hope to achieve intellectually and practically? These questions are deceptively simple, but compelling answers prove difficult to construct, suggesting that fascinating and important issues are at stake.

Some years ago in Montreal I had a private conversation with Dr. Andrew Newberg after he had delivered one of his fabulous stump speeches on the neurophysiology of RSEs. Well known for studying expert meditators using functional imaging of the brain, Newberg had colorful resources to draw on for his presentation, and it was entertaining as a result. The lecture was also pregnant with hints about the wider philosophical significance of the research. So when we met I asked him about the *point* of his study of meditation experiences. I noted that many in his audience that day were enthusiastic about his research and spoke as if he had produced evidence for the authenticity, cognitive reliability, and spiritual value of such experiences. I asked Newberg if he thought his data justified such a conclusion. He replied that he thought that the data justified neither that conclusion nor its opposite. Then he told me that when he makes the very same presentation to groups who tend to view RSEs in a negative light, they are equally enthusiastic and take his research to confirm the delusory and unhealthy character of such experiences.

When all was said and done, my question about the *point* of Newberg's neurological research into meditation experiences remained unanswered. Perhaps at that time this research was for him just a matter of satisfying curiosity in the way of much pure research, and he imagined no philosophical or moral or social or political significance beyond the considerable value of assembling facts (he has since developed a more positive theological viewpoint; see Newberg *et al.* 2001b). But this conversation left me with a puzzle that continues to bother me today. Why do intelligent people get excited in opposite ways about the neural embedding of RSEs? What do they think such research reveals about the truth or falsity of religious and spiritual beliefs, and about the value or disvalue of religious and spiritual behaviors? There seems to be much more popular excitement around such research than there is clear understanding of its significance.

Much the same applies to the social embedding of RSEs. Experts readily agree that social groups condition the way such experiences are felt and expressed, and that this embedding can magnify their political and economic effects in quite spectacular ways. For example, sociologist Max Weber argued convincingly that particular patterns of religious behaviors, beliefs, and experiences among Protestant Christians produced a distinctive form of economic practice that helped produce modern capitalism and thereby exercised a pervasive influence on Western civilization (Weber [1920] 1930). But what do we think such insights into the social embedding of RSEs reveal about the reliability or moral value of religious beliefs? Should the religious experiences and beliefs that proved vital to the emergence of capitalism be embraced because of their fruits or condemned? Why do people get excited in opposite ways about our growing knowledge of the sociality of RSEs?

The repeated drawing of opposite conclusions about the reliability and value of RSEs from the same data is a phenomenon deserving a name. I call it the *dongle phenomenon*. A dongle is a sealed hardware device that allows copy-protected software to run on your computer by means of a process that dongle distributors do not want you to understand. Basically, you know that a dongle is important but you have no idea why. This basic concept has penetrated our lives in a host of ways. For example, when an automobile mechanic has to repair a modern engine, he or she might point to something in the engine and say, "The car is not working right because that computer screen over there says this here dongle is broken." But the mechanic does not know any more about how the dongle works than we do. We all just know that it is important. That is the dongle phenomenon.

The neural and social embedding of RSEs is a premier instance of the dongle phenomenon. We know that these forms of embodiment are important but we do not really know why. Newberg's story about opposite reactions to the same talk makes the point perfectly. I want to know whether we can penetrate beneath the shallow enthusiasm and superficial skepticism that so many people bring to the discovery that the brain mediates RSEs, and to the equally important realization that social groups condition such experiences and mediate their effects. We probably can. But it is not easy. And here is why.

The neurology and sociality of RSEs inevitably refer to an extremely complicated network of possible linkages among the biological sciences, the medical sciences, the human sciences, and the humanities. Some authors even argue that quantum physics is vital for explaining RSEs, so we probably should add physics to that list. This network of linkages is so complicated that most people register only a fraction of the possible connections and implications. The possibilities they see first are typically those matching their background and experience, and thus confirming their preconceived notions about the value or disvalue of religious and spiritual behaviors, beliefs, and experiences. But one's first thought in this domain is often quite mistaken, and further study can thoroughly complicate those instinctive, preliminary convictions. We all know that the neurology and sociality of RSEs is important *somehow*, but a moment's thought shows that we may *actually* know less about this than we assume.

In this chapter, I present a framework for interpreting RSEs that can help untangle the maze of possible implications surrounding this topic. I shall explore different aspects of the framework in subsequent chapters. Throughout, I shall attempt to be clear about the values that guide my own research and thinking in this area so as to expose my interpretation to sustained scrutiny and constructive criticism, which is the best way to take responsibility for it and to improve it.

I just used the word "framework." The grid-like connotations of that word are potentially misleading. The territory of RSEs is wild and rambling, containing enormously more varied and colorful flora and fauna than most people realize. It reaches from near-death experiences to out-of-body experiences, from feelings of oceanic calm to dramatic conversions, from sudden bursts of unaccountable compassion to routine participation in religious rituals, and from centering meditation to the busy joy of shared meals within a religious community. It is a landscape that invites exploring and resists definitive classifications. So I propose a compass to guide that exploration. In fact, in honor of the complexity of the subject, I offer two compasses, each orienting explorers to a different dimension of the territory.

The first compass orients us to practical purposes in studying RSEs. Motivations matter in every domain of life. A compass of motivating concerns can help us be responsibly self-aware, appropriately suspicious, and steady in judgment. The second compass orients us to classic theoretical issues in the study of RSEs, each of which has a complicated history and lively contemporary manifestations. If we want a sound understanding of such experiences, we will have to work for it by penetrating these difficult issues.

As a final introductory remark, we need to clarify a key piece of terminology. My favorite phrase to encompass the territory we will be exploring is "RSEs." That is unwieldy but shortening it presents problems. If I abbreviate it to "spiritual experiences," I risk emphasizing individual states of consciousness at the expense of the corporate dimensions of experience. If I abbreviate it to "religious experiences" – perhaps recalling German philosopher-theologian Friedrich Schleiermacher's early usage – I risk failing to register the fact that many people who do not consider themselves religious have such experiences, a point with which Schleiermacher himself grappled as a young man (see Schleiermacher [1799] 1893). If I invent a new phrase I will just multiply confusion. So I shall use "RSEs" as often as possible, despite the awkwardness. I shall speak in the plural most of the time in recognition of the fabulous diversity of experiences under discussion. Though my focus is on experiences, I shall often use the phrase "behaviors, beliefs, and experiences" to indicate that experiences are inextricably entangled with behaviors and beliefs. Finally, I shall assume that RSEs have neurological and social embeddings that are subject to more or less rigorous scientific study. I do not believe that this assumption prejudices the discussion. In fact, I think it is possible to affirm all kinds of metaphysical worldviews and still accept that brains and groups play crucial roles in the expression and functions of RSEs.

MOTIVATING CONCERNS

RSEs have been the topic of extensive academic study from a host of disciplinary perspectives for well over 100 years (in addition to the works mentioned elsewhere in this book, see Ames 1910; Block 1992; Brinton 1996; Brown and Caetano 1992; Burhenn 1995; Callahan 2003; Campbell 1959, 1962, 1964, 1968; Currie *et al.* 1982; Donovan 1979; Eliade 1954, 1960, 1961; Fowler 1981; Frazer 1900; Griffith-Dickson 2000; Happel and Walter 1980; Hardwick 1996; Hood 1995; Hook 1961; Kapstein 2004; Kason 1997; Katz 1984, 1992, 2000; Kierkegaard [1843] 1983; Kokoszka 1992; Lévi-Strauss [1962] 1963; Main 1998; Masson 1980; Maxwell and Tschudin 1990; Meissner 1984; Moacanin 1986; Moehle 1983; Oxman *et al.* 1998; Pargament 1997; Pearson 2005; Rappaport 1979; Rizzuto 1979; Sharpe 1986; Spilka *et al.* 2003; Stark 1965; Taylor 2008; Tillich 1952; Tyler 1874;

Ullman 1989; Van der Leeuw [1933] 1964; Wildman 2002). The observer of these and other vast piles of books and articles from multiple cultural traditions cannot help but ask why people invest their valuable energy in this venture. What motivates them? And what do their motivations imply for their research?

The first compass tells us something about why we might be motivated to explore the landscape of RSEs. This compass will not capture the intricacy of each person's interests, of course, but most people can relate to at least one of the four motivating concerns I shall discuss. We do well to be aware of these possible dimensions of motivation. As we shall see, there is evidence that here, as in all human endeavors, guiding interests sometimes unduly influence interpretations.

Intellectual and spiritual curiosity

A non-religious scientist friend told me a few years ago about a spectacular personal experience that seemed loaded with religious and spiritual meanings. This intelligent and sensitive person was deeply moved and also confused by the experience and wanted to know what it meant and whether it could be studied in a way that would yield understanding that a scientist could appropriate with integrity. The aim of inquiry in this case was neither to explain the experience away nor to justify its apparent meaningfulness. And the emotional framing was neither desperate nor indifferent. My friend wanted to satisfy profound intellectual and spiritual curiosity.

Natural curiosity about a fascinating range of phenomena joined with a drive for authentic self-understanding is a motivating factor for many students of RSEs. Most scientists who engage in pure research for its own sake, even in the politically and emotionally charged area of religion, are deeply curious about why so many people report such experiences, some of which are quite strange. I should say that I am curious in this way. I engage topics such as RSEs because of their significance for a wider understanding of the human condition. Insofar as I am a philosopher, theologian, and ethicist, however, I am also interested in the relevance of such topics for satisfying my intellectual and spiritual curiosity about goodness, beauty, and truth, and about their ultimate source and meaning. Such philosophical and theological issues take those who pursue them far beyond the official borders of the natural and human sciences into the hinterlands of philosophy where descriptions fail and human cognitive limitations routinely trip up even the best-designed inquiries.

The types of curiosity driving students of RSEs do not always harmonize. Some of my science-for-the-sake-of-science friends feel irritated when someone like me introduces a philosophical agenda into this field of research, which they would prefer to pursue in a strictly empirical and descriptive way. They will be particularly worried when I talk out loud about the theological significance of RSEs. But my philosophical questions count just as much as their (and my) empirical questions, and if they feel uncomfortable then they really should broaden their intellectual horizons. To ask such philosophical questions is not immediately to fall prey to bias and superstition, as they fear. By the same token, people curious about the philosophical and theological significance of RSEs have to pay close attention to descriptive and empirical work lest they mistake the dark abyss of embarrassing ignorance into which they may be falling for profound insight. Curiosity gets us started, perhaps, but we get nowhere without discipline and expertise in a process of rigorous multidisciplinary cooperation.

Socio-political management

A second motivating concern is the need to manage the social and political effects of RSEs. The most famous American philosopher prior to the twentieth century was arguably Jonathan Edwards. A polymath, Edwards was also a Christian pastor at the time of the Great Awakening in New England. Much like the charismatic movement within American Christianity during the 1970s and 1980s, the Great Awakening produced spectacular experiences in the lives of Christians who were open to them. The experiences changed lives in a mostly healthy and pro-social way. But they also disrupted churches, including Edwards' church. His solution was to investigate and write a book about the issue. So in 1746 there appeared *The Religious Affections*, in which Edwards completely failed to express his subtle thoughts in ways that could have any effect on most of his target audience. Nevertheless, the book is remembered because of its determined attempt to distinguish truly gracious and authentic religious experiences from counterfeit or inauthentic ones. Edwards was particularly careful to emphasize the importance of loving behavior and to criticize as misleading the strength and fervor surrounding RSEs. Through his formidable sermons rather than through this book, Edwards exercised a salutary influence on the unfolding of the Great Awakenings.

This is an excellent example of studying RSEs in order to exercise social control. But it is by no means the only one. Political strategist Karl Rove studied the religious experiences of born-again Christians in the United States in order to appreciate how to leverage their voting tendencies for the benefit of the candidate he promoted. He did not study their born-again religious experiences like a psychologist or an anthropologist might, and he probably relied a great deal on intuition and his own experience. But he certainly learned how a politician could connect to those experiences and the moral and religious sentiments they engender. Researchers such as anthropologist Scott Atran, journalists Nasra Hassan and Hala Jaber, and psychologist Anne Speckhard have interviewed terrorists and their trainers in the Middle East and elsewhere in an attempt to understand how their RSEs, among other factors, lead them to make the choices they do, from forming political opinions to becoming suicide bombers (Atran 2003; Hassan 2001, 2004; Jaber 1997; Speckhard 2006; and the review in Schaeffer 2007). Presumably understanding this process could have a beneficial effect on interactions between Western and Islamic cultures.

Then there are the people who fervently believe, with a passion rivaling that of the most fervent religious fundamentalist, that religion is bad for you, bad for society, and bad for the global human future. For example, physicist Steven Weinberg said in a 1999 Washington D.C. speech, "Religion is an insult to human dignity. With or without it, you would have good people doing good things and evil people doing evil things. For good people to do evil things, that takes religion" (quoted in Dawkins 2006: 249). This seems to neglect the unprecedented violence of totalitarian regimes during the twentieth century, and also the positive behavioral transformations triggered by religious conversion and commitment, but Weinberg does have a point about the way people use religion to rationalize bad behavior.

According to biologist Richard Dawkins (2006), philosopher Daniel Dennett (2006), astronomer Victor Stenger (2007), writers Sam Harris (2006) and David Mills (2006), pundit Christopher Hitchens (2007), the UK's National Secular Society, the USA's Freedom from Religion Foundation, and numerous other individuals and organizations, we would be far better off without religion. These prophets of secular enlightenment long to make the sadly deluded religious people of the world wake up and see the truth. In a March 28, 2007 debate on the proposition "We'd be better off without religion" in London, Dawkins is reported to have said that "There are very good grounds to believe there is no actual truth in the claims of religion. I rather liken it to a child with a dummy in its mouth. I do not think it a very dignified or respect-worthy posture for an adult to go around sucking a dummy for comfort" (see the report in

Gledhill 2007). If Dawkins is right about that, then religion is an infant-ile attachment that produces comfort through misunderstanding. It really would be more grown-up to be rid of it.

Since it is not obvious how to rid the world of religion, this task requires quite a bit of thought. Unfortunately for the anti-religionist who longs for this cultural transformation, there are few successful models from which to learn. After all, the attempts of some Stalinists to kill religion off failed, and the USSR later collapsed under the overbearing weight of an inspir-ing but impractical socioeconomic and political vision. Some Marxists wanted to witness the withering away of religion as economic conditions gradually eliminated the deprivation that Karl Marx thought causes it (see Marx 2002; Marx and Engels [1846] 1970), but so far their longings have been in vain. Anyway, contemporary anti-religion evangelists are committed to democracy and non-violence. Being thus limited to con-sciousness raising and education, it is not surprising that they turn to the study of RSEs as a weapon in the war against religion.

For example, Dawkins describes religious and spiritual experience as the delusional result of the human brain's simulation software. "This is really all that needs to be said about personal 'experiences' of gods or other religious phenomena. If you've had such an experience, you may well find yourself believing firmly that it was real. But do not expect the rest of us to take your word for it, especially if we have the slightest familiarity with the brain and its powerful workings" (Dawkins 2006: 92). With a proper education, argue Harris and Hitchens, children can be liberated from religion. They can be taught that the brain occasionally throws off misleading experiences with huge emotional and existential significance, and thereby freed from the intrinsically persuasive effect of those experi-ences. These anti-religionists are equal opportunity haters of violence and superstition, whether it is authoritarian religion or absolutist politics. With John Lennon, they imagine a better world, "with no religion too." And the path toward that better world involves freeing ourselves from, among other things, the impression that our RSEs are as important as they seem to be.

Legitimation of group identity

Let us consider a third motivation that people bring to the study of RSEs. I shall relate three personal experiences and then ask what they have in common. First, several of my friends, disciples of the Dalai Lama, want me to practice meditation. They are confident that my experiences while meditating will demonstrate to me the transitory and ephemeral nature of reality, thereby freeing me from my attachment to the big and small concerns of life, and sparking within me a powerful form of compassion for all living creatures. *The experience will change my life and bring meaning and purpose that I never imagined possible.* Second, several of my New Age friends urge me to try any number of ways of connecting to the flowing energies just beneath the surface of ordinary life. Their Daoist-like worldview predicts that I will have powerful experiences of feeling centered, energized, and healthy to an unprecedented degree. *The experience will change my life and bring meaning and purpose that I never imagined possible.* Third, several of my evangelical Christian friends want me to experience the presence of the risen Jesus Christ as a living personal being, constantly communicating with me and being my companion in the trials and joys of this life, and my guide to the life beyond. All I have to do is confess my sins, welcome Jesus Christ into my life as my Lord and Savior, and love him and follow him with all my heart and soul and mind and strength. *The experience will change my life and bring meaning and purpose that I never imagined possible.*

What do these experiences have in common? Well, obviously, a number of people are trying to convert me to something, and evidently I come across as the sort of person who could profit from a conversion experience. But I want to draw your attention to something else, namely, the role that RSEs play in these conversion efforts. I am being asked in the first instance not to be a Buddhist or a New Ager or a supernaturalist evangelical Christian, but rather to undergo an *experience that will speak for itself.* My friends are confident in their beliefs because the RSEs they have had feel so compelling to them, and seem to confirm their beliefs so strongly. They believe that if I have these same experiences, then I will also believe as they do.

This illustrates the role that RSEs play in solidifying a person's religious commitment. But there is no surprise there. Most of us build our worldviews around the existentially potent experiences of bliss and trauma that we undergo in the course of our lives. RSEs are also the power source for the health and vitality of most religious movements. When diverse people reinforce each others' beliefs and encourage each other to adopt similar interpretations of potent experiences, their individual commitment to the group's doctrines and goals soars. They become like-minded: they know what they believe, feel confident about how to behave, and have ingroup companions with whom they can share some of the deepest parts of themselves, parts that outgroup people can never understand.

For me to have powerful experiences in Tibetan Buddhist meditation confirms the almost scientific predictions of Buddhist doctrine and
thus helps to legitimate Buddhist religious identity. If I am healed and
strengthened by resting with a crystal over my sixth chakra, then I may
become convinced of the wondrous spiritual depths of the natural world,
thereby confirming the New Age worldview and contributing to the
piece-by-piece legitimation of the loose-knit social identity of that spiritual movement. If I viscerally feel the presence of Jesus Christ with me,
I will confirm in my own experience the truth of Christian claims about
God and the world, and thus participate in the person-by-person legitimation of that movement's identity.

RSEs play a powerful role in nurturing religious movements. So it is
no surprise that some people study RSEs specifically in order to protect
and strengthen the identity of a religious or spiritual group to which they
are already thoroughly committed, and that others conduct such studies to put in place information that they hope will impact those religious
self-interpretations. The Dalai Lama encourages the neurological study of
meditating monks in part for this reason, and in part as an artful way to
spread enlightenment; he is impressively open about his motivation (see
Dalai Lama 2003). Some people study paranormal phenomena because they
seek scientific confirmation of experiences that have been extremely meaningful to them or because they feel worried about people being deluded
by their strange experiences (for a representative sampling of historical,
philosophical, and research studies see Griffin 1997; Haynes 1982; Persinger
1994b; Randi 1982; and the work of the Society for Psychical Research,
the Parapsychological Association, the Academy of Parapsychology and
Medicine, the Academy of Religion and Psychical Research, and the
Stanford Research Institute). Some people study glossolalia, or speaking in
tongues, either because they long for scientific confirmation of what they
most dearly believe about that phenomenon – namely, that it is a genuine
language and not comforting regressive babbling in a socially acceptable
context – or in order to put in place basic information that allows others to
formulate a sound interpretation of their experiences (see linguistic studies
such as Bryant and O'Connell 1971; Goodman 1972; Samarin 1972; and the
survey in Mills 1986; psychological studies such as Kildahl 1972; and neurological studies such as Persinger 1994c and Newberg *et al.* 2006). And some
people are powerfully motivated to study RSEs in order to show that they
are delusions, thereby confirming their deeply held anti-supernaturalist and
anti-religious worldview (see Booth *et al.* 2005; Persinger 1983, 1987, 2002,
2005; St.-Pierre and Persinger 2006).

The particular studies I have mentioned may be properly designed and interpreted. But because of the presence of these sorts of motivation, there is reason for caution when approaching the study of RSEs. Articulating the identity of a religious group, explaining and justifying truth claims made by a religious group, protecting a religious group from misunderstanding or distorted representation, and attacking religion as delusion are all valuable activities from certain points of view. But the danger of bias is real, and we do well to ask about the motivations that researchers bring to their studies. It is a case of *caveat emptor*, or buyer beware, because the sellers of ideas and agendas may not be fully conscious of how their special interests can distort the interpretation of research findings and become special pleading on behalf of religious or anti-religious doctrine.

Unfortunately, we can rarely be certain about a researcher's motivations in this area. Few people are as honorably open as the Dalai Lama about their reasons for supporting the study of RSEs. So we have to focus carefully on the quality of studies, knowing that in this area there is a special danger of unconscious distortion of data and biased interpretation.

Personal transformation and spiritual adventure

The final motivating concern I shall mention is the quest for personal transformation. I must confess to having cautious respect for people who explore RSEs because they want to break bad habits and forge good new habits through religious disciplines, achieve enlightenment through meditation, recover mental and physical health for themselves and others through shamanic interventions, or cleanse the doors of perception with entheogens so as to see the world as it most truly is. These people are the high adventurers in the realm of RSEs and I have been honored to know a number of them.

They make me aware that I take refuge in the precise evidential requirements of the sciences and the disciplined interpretative practices of the humanities, making micro-moves and trying to build expert consensus. Meanwhile, these bold explorers of the territory of RSEs blow right past my scholarly caution with a wink and a nod and just see what is out there. As much as I do not want to be like them, I cannot help admiring their boldness.

I recall once standing in front of a window high up in a San Francisco skyscraper during a birthday celebration. As I took in the sight of that beautiful city, an old man in ill health, an acquaintance more than a friend, walked over to stand beside me and admire the view. He then told me a remarkable story of a near-death experience that he had recently undergone after a cardiac arrest, and how it had transformed him from a bitter man fearful of death to a person ready to face his demise with dignity and confidence. Whether or not this man's reaction was warranted, his near-death experience did in fact change his life. Yet this experience was completely *unsought*, which is typically the case for near-death experiences. The thrill-seekers of RSEs want such experiences for themselves. If near-death experiences are too inconvenient to seek out deliberately, then they will go for whatever they can get. It is the awesome power and compelling beauty of such experiences that inspires adventurers to seek them actively and cultivate them deliberately.

There has to be something wonderful about meditating in the context of a monastic community, because such experts in the terrain of altered states of consciousness renounce a lot of other wonderful life activities that the rest of us embrace with joy. And something other than a spiritually empty high brings religious experimenters with mind-altering substances back again and again to what some of them call their sacrament, which might be LSD or a hallucinogenic mushroom or something else. These people know a lot about altered states of consciousness and their spiritual effects from direct experience. They learn to control the powerful emotions and interpret the vivid imagery that can accompany such experiences. Gifted shamans might be overwhelmed by psychotic states of mind at first but, gradually and with practice, they learn how to control the disruptive and disturbing experiences that afflict or bless them, and turn them to the benefit of others in their community. The saints and bodhisattvas did not become great in the art of compassion by accident; they cultivated their chosen religious goal with the same determination, discipline, and desire that drives greatness in all forms of life, from business to sports.

Nothing I have said about these great explorers of the realm of RSEs implies that they are correct in the way they interpret those experiences. In fact, I think that philosophers reflecting at a distance may be better at evaluating truth claims and assessing interpretations than those who go through those experiences personally. First-hand experience might be existentially compelling but potent experiences are not self-explanatory. Those who go through such experiences often fail to detect the cultural and personal assumptions that they bring to their interpretations. Moreover – and this is especially important – the human brain seems capable of producing confidence in more than one way. Usually we instinctively evaluate new experiences and beliefs by matching them against the whole sweep of existing knowledge. But a sufficiently powerful experience can override that global matching process and produce extreme confidence without the normal checking and evaluation (see Wildman and Brothers 1999). Because of this second possibility, we cannot take at face value the enthusiastic certainty demonstrated by the bold adventurers in this realm.

Nevertheless, these adventurers are the definitive experts in the qualities and effects of such experiences, and also in how to master them and bend them to specific religious and spiritual and behavioral goals. They possess invaluable information, as a result, and it would be foolish for a philosophical interpreter of RSEs to exclude their testimony just because they do things that make cautious philosophers feel uncomfortable. Unfortunately, this happens from time to time, and the philosophical interpretations are impoverished as a result.

For example, some philosophers insist that it is impossible to allow for cultural and contextual factors in mystical experience (see Katz 1978; Proudfoot 1985). Their arguments are persuasive as far as they go. But they neglect or marginalize the reports of experts in meditation to the effect that, with time and practice, it is in fact possible to gain insight into the constructed character of the meanings we attach to such experiences. These philosophers speak as if their own more prosaic experience were normative and thereby eliminate an experiential possibility that people with more experience insist can be realized. Yet it is also easy to appreciate the core concern of these philosophers. Just as they say, it is vital to be mindful of the role context plays in generating interpretations of RSEs. To put the point bluntly, most people undergoing such experiences are blissfully unaware of the role contextual factors play in generating their interpretations and beliefs. An experience of a presence is obviously Jesus to some, but obviously the Virgin Mary to others; it might be Krishna in South Asia, or perhaps an angel or a demon, or perhaps a disembodied spirit or a dead relative – all depending on cultural and social conditioning. Philosophers are obliged to point out this problem, especially when other interpreters naively take self-reported interpretations of RSEs as transparent and self-interpreting.

Nevertheless, philosophical caution should apply in both directions. We should not take self-reports at face value but neither should we rush to assert what is and is not possible in the realm of controlled experimentation with altered states of consciousness, particularly when our own more limited experience functions as the standard for judgment.

THEORETICAL ISSUES

With this we come to our second compass, which identifies four classic theoretical issues. RSEs influence what people believe, how they behave, whom they vote for, what they are prepared to invest energy in, and what they feel driven to resist morally. They bring great satisfaction and peace of mind, but they can also disturb and disorient. It is because of the pervasive existential and social importance of RSEs that so many vital theoretical questions have arisen about them.

As mentioned above, a bewildering array of disciplines impacts the important theoretical issues to which the second compass orients us. Each disciplinary contribution represents a kind of tactical move in the exploration of the landscape of religious behaviors, beliefs, and experiences. Some describe phenomena, some link levels of description, some detect causality, some discriminate effects, some integrate information into coherent interpretations, and some evaluate value and truth. Our framework for interpretation should help us to register the diverse data and theories that are relevant to each of these classic theoretical issues, to ensure that interpretations integrate multiple levels of information, to resist mono-disciplinary simplifications, and to accept that even experts may have to learn new perspectives and approaches. Nothing less can produce a truly satisfying interpretation of RSEs.

Psycho-social and evolutionary origins

The first theoretical issue concerns the psychological, social, and evolutionary origins of RSEs. Let us start with the roles that social context and psychological formation play in producing the particular content and quality of such experiences. We know that cultural context is an important influence on people's RSEs. For example, Hindus do not have experiences of the Virgin Mary and Christians do not have experiences of Krishna. We know that family context matters a great deal. For example, Muslim and Christian families growing up in predominantly Hindu communities tend to produce children whose religiousness matches that of their families. And we know that a community's interpretation of historical circumstances matters. For example, if secular Jews in the United States become religiously involved in a religion other than Judaism, they are more likely to become Buddhists than Christians. The history of Jewish–Christian relations appears to be the key factor in this tendency.

There is no shortage of theories that link psychological dynamics with religion. Sigmund Freud personally produced several such theories in books such as *Totem and Taboo* ([1913] 1918), *The Future of an Illusion* ([1927] 1928), and *Moses and Monotheism* (1939), with further pregnant hints in *Beyond the Pleasure Principle* ([1920] 1922) and *Civilization and Its Discontents* (1930). Other thinkers before and after him speculated along similar lines. The basic thought here is that human beings have built-in impulses and desires that are powerful, often conflicting or frustrated, and almost always operating below the level of conscious understanding and control. These structural dynamics produce all kinds of behavioral and cognitive consequences, many of which are emotionally colored by anxiety and neediness. This creates readiness for experiences that ease anxiety and meet emotional needs, regardless of how plausible or implausible the beliefs associated with such comforting experiences may be. It also creates room for social groups that vest ritualized bonding processes with ultimate significance, and thereby power to comfort pain and relieve anxiety.

Similar theories link social dynamics with religion. A foundational figure here is sociologist Émile Durkheim (see Durkheim [1912] 1915). His insights were drawn from tribal religions but have proved relevant to interpreting the roles of religion in other cultural contexts. The key insight here is that human beings are a social species living in chaotic circumstances. Nature is sometimes chaotic, but social life is often chaotic. Just as we need technology and agriculture to tame nature, so we need rules to tame social chaos. But what rules could possibly induce unruly humans to comply? Any rules backed by overwhelming punitive force tend to provoke rebellion, so this approach is unstable. Durkheim noticed that religion facilitates *willing* compliance with rules, which is a far superior arrangement. Religion achieves this feat by vesting the core moral principles of a society with ultimate significance, weaving the rules into a compelling narrative that helps people simultaneously to make sense out of their lives and to tame social chaos. To express it in theistic terms, religion exercises social control by writing human rules on the vast cosmos with divine ink. This cosmologization of rules inspires willing compliance partly through fear of divine punishment and constant awareness of divine scrutiny, and partly because RSEs under these circumstances yield reassuring orientation in chaotic life circumstances.

These psycho-social interpretations give theoretical depth to critiques of RSEs that skeptics have pressed since ancient times, and continue to press today. In short, people have RSEs because they need to have them. According to this critique, RSEs are for weak and anxious and needy people, the gullible folk who are easy to manipulate and control. Yet a careful philosopher is quick to point out that these psycho-social interpretations do not *entail* this critique. Here is a pro-religious interpretation that makes sense of the same body of theory and data. Freud and Durkheim and their successors furnish a serviceable account of human beings as anxious social creatures, and more or less correctly identify some of the roles that religion plays in human life. But this merely marks out the playing field within which human beings explore whatever intimations of ultimate meaning that they experience.

Now let us turn to the evolutionary dimensions of this first intellectual issue. Evolutionary biology leads us to step back and ask how we developed the capacities for RSEs. Are they adaptations that help us survive and reproduce, or are they side-effects of a big-brain cognitive system? The field of evolutionary psychology, which has sprung up at the junction of social psychology, cognitive psychology, and evolutionary theory, has a lot to say about this (for an introduction, see Barkow *et al.* 1992). I, too, will have a lot to say about it in subsequent chapters. For now I wish to note an often overlooked fact, namely, that evolutionary psychology has not yet found a way decisively to answer the question about the significance of RSEs.

Let us suppose that our capacities for RSEs are adaptations. That is, these capacities evolved specifically because having RSEs helped people in the long Pleistocene era of human evolution survive and reproduce. We might imagine that this guarantees the delusory character of RSEs. The thinking in this case is that the adapted character of such experiences rules out the possibility that they are essentially spontaneous and recurring experiences of sensing actual spiritual realities that lie beyond the regular senses. Yet we might also argue that adaptation guarantees the reliability of RSEs. The thinking in this case is that adaptation makes RSEs rather like sensory experiences such as sight and hearing, which are generally reliable.

Well, which is it? Does the adaptation hypothesis support the anti-religious skeptic or the pro-religious devotee? I think compelling evidence to resolve this question does not yet exist. So it is worrying that some experts eagerly jump on one bandwagon and speak as if there is no compelling alternative.

Now let us suppose that the most important types of RSEs *are not adaptations*. That is, biological capacities for RSEs did not evolve because such experiences were adaptive, but for other reasons entirely. The big-brain cognitive system was selected for its ability to detect patterns, make decisions, gather food, find mates, cooperate, evoke trust, detect freeloaders, and stay safe. RSEs are a mere side-effect of a system adapted for other functions, just as a train engine throws off noise even though its primary purpose is locomotion. How should we regard RSEs in this case?

As in the adaptation case, given the state of evidence at this point, I think this question can be argued both ways. On the one hand, most things of cultural value – dance recitals in elementary school, fabulous cooking, artful carving of stone, no-hitters in baseball – are side-effects of biological capacities that evolved for other purposes. Why should RSEs be any different? On the other hand, we have no reason to trust the cognitive content of RSEs if they are unselected side-effects of a big-brain cognitive system. And that suggests that they could easily be misleading. The bottom line is that we need more evidence and better experiments to settle these evolutionary questions, if they can be settled at all.

Some religious people feel driven to reject these psycho-social and evolutionary accounts of human life in order to protect religion. I can see how some people might feel threatened by such accounts, particularly if they are attached to perfect assurance commensurate with belief in supernatural powers that transcend the messiness of human life. The modern evolutionary view of human nature can seem to taint that perfect assurance. But I think that rejecting these theories out of hand amounts to a transparently self-protective denial of the obvious – and an unnecessary denial as well (see Wildman 2009b). I am drawn to the world of Freud and Durkheim and evolutionary psychology. We come to life in this world, marked by our evolutionary history and heavily influenced by impulses we do not fully understand and by contexts we cannot fully control. And it is in these circumstances that we strive to discover meaning and purpose in our lives; to build creative cultures and secure societies; and to realize the good, the true, and the beautiful. These are religious and spiritual activities, and we work out our salvation, our liberation, and our enlightenment as we pursue them.

Social and personal functions

The second point on our compass of theoretical issues concerns the *effects* of RSEs. They have social, historic, economic, and political consequences. Nobody living in the USA, Afghanistan, or Iraq after September 11, 2001 doubts that. They have behavioral, emotional, and existential functions, from character transformation to moral orientation. They have consequences for mental and physical health, both positive and negative, a formerly controversial claim that becomes increasingly intelligible as the psychosomatic aspects of human life are better understood (see Wiskeski and Anderson 2009). The leading questions for researchers in this area are two. First, what precisely are these functional effects of RSEs? Second, precisely how are these effects mediated through brains, bodies, and groups?

Regarding this first question, it is vital to get our facts straight. Religious and spiritual behaviors, beliefs, and experiences are important because of their effects, if for no other reason. So we need to know what those effects are. It is easier to detect the effects of some things than others. Behaviors, whether or not they are religious or spiritual in nature, are particularly convenient to study; the link between behavior and consequence is often obvious. Beliefs and experiences are much trickier. This is doubly so in the case of religious and spiritual beliefs and experiences.

One reason for the difficulty is the involvement of the brain, which synthesizes numerous influences into every decision and action, many beneath the level of consciousness and in ways that are difficult to observe. This familiar fact of mental life means that researchers cannot easily take subjective self-reports about the effects of RSEs at face value.

Another reason for the difficulty is that we cannot easily experiment on people's RSEs. To explain why this matters, consider a hypothetical medical study testing the theory that Vegemite speeds recovery from stroke. We get the idea for such a study perhaps from another study in which we notice a surprising correlation between Vegemite consumption and rapid recovery from stroke, but now we want a carefully controlled study to test this apparent connection. So we recruit stroke patients and randomly assign them to two groups who receive different treatment. The test group receives the regular regimen of treatment plus a daily cracker spread with Vegemite. The control group receives the regular regimen of treatment plus a daily cracker spread with a placebo – something harmless that looks and tastes like Vegemite. Just to be safe, we do not tell anyone involved with the patients which crackers have Vegemite and which do not. If the two groups are large enough then natural variations in the population should be about the same in both, and the only variable factor is the Vegemite-cracker treatment. If there is a correlation between the test group and a particular health outcome relative to the control group, we can be fairly confident that Vegemite is the reason why. Then we can notify the Surgeon General that one Vegemite cracker a day keeps the doctor away.

That is standard procedure in medical studies. But how are we supposed to do this with behaviors, beliefs, and experiences? The reason the controversy over the health effects of smoking took so long to resolve is precisely that we cannot randomly assign people to a test group of smokers and a control group of non-smokers. We can *observe* smokers versus non-smokers but they will not be *random* groups. That will make it difficult to be sure that smoking causes the health differences between the two groups; there may be a more fundamental cause that leads people to smoke cigarettes and also gives them higher rates of emphysema, lung cancer, and heart disease.

The very same problem applies to the effects of *religious and spiritual* behaviors, beliefs, and experiences. Consider the often alleged health effects of religion, for example. We cannot get random groups of people who are religious and non-religious. We *can* design a study that discovers a *correlation* between, say, attendance at religious services and longevity. In fact, George Comstock, a well-known epidemiologist from Johns Hopkins University, conducted just such a study in 1963, several years later reporting a significant relationship between participation in religious services and longevity (see Comstock and Partridge 1972). But later it occurred to Comstock that the reason he found a correlation is that many people who are sick cannot attend religious services. So Comstock duly reported this in a later paper: illness may in fact have been a confounder, the cause of *both* low attendance at religious services *and* death (see Comstock and Tonascia 1977).

Richard Sloan, a notable critic of religion and medicine studies, laments that Comstock's first study is often cited but the second study is almost completely neglected (see Sloan 1999: 665, 2006: ch. 6). Sloan believes that fact says something about people's motivations when they start looking for the health effects of religious behaviors, beliefs, and experiences, and I think he is correct. We do need to be cautious in this area. There is no substitute for careful study design. The ultimate research effort in this area, as with smoking, is not more cross-sectional studies but a longitudinal study over many decades that measures as many factors relevant to health outcomes as possible, along with religious and spiritual behaviors, beliefs, and experiences. That still will not produce the confidence of a randomized, double-blind, controlled study, but it is the best we can do when groups are self-selecting.

Regarding the second question, we would like to understand the mechanisms that mediate the effects of RSEs. Quite apart from satisfying curiosity, understanding these mediating mechanisms has great practical value. For example, if RSEs do in fact have positive health effects, and we discover the neural mechanisms that mediate these effects, then we are in a position to understand more clearly how to improve health. Similarly, to understand the way the social embedding of RSEs mediates effects gives policy planners new insights and opportunities.

It is especially important at this point to remember the complexity of religion and spirituality. Many studies purporting to detect a functional effect of religious and spiritual behaviors, beliefs, and experiences conceive of religiousness in extremely broad ways. For example, there is some evidence that attendance at religious services extends life despite the problems with the Comstock study mentioned above. Let us suppose that medical experts achieve consensus on this point. What are health policy experts supposed to do with this? "Attendance at religious services," like many other categories used in these studies, is quite vague. If it is the social relationships associated with such attendance that matters, then the health-care recommendations would be very different than if it were the worship and prayer dimensions of attendance that make the difference (for an assessment of the practical consequences of such research, see Sloan *et al.* 2000). The complexity of religion makes practical recommendations difficult, but we must grapple with that difficulty. Ultimately, we need to combine data about correlational studies with understanding of the neural and social mechanisms that mediate the effects of religious and spiritual behaviors, beliefs, and experiences. Unfortunately, that ideal still hovers on the horizon of contemporary scientific abilities.

Cognitive status

The third theoretical issue concerns epistemological questions. Are RSEs cognitively informative or illusory? Can they serve as supportive evidence for theological claims? Can they resolve age-old disputes between supernaturalistic and naturalistic views of reality? In short, are they modes of reliable knowledge or not? I will be devoting an entire chapter to this subject but I do want to make one preliminary remark about this emotionally charged issue.

Many religious people rely on inspiration from RSEs to guide their behavior and moral choices. Typically they do not have the luxury of treating the cognitive content of RSEs as a fiction while still counting on it for strength and comfort. A few people might be able to pull off such an existential juggling act but it requires an array of fine distinctions that do not mean much to most. Thus, it can be extremely disturbing for them to wonder whether they unconsciously attach to their experiences whatever cognitive content they need them to have – and this is doubly upsetting when they are accustomed to relying on RSEs for reassurance that their beliefs are true. It is no wonder that many people are deeply sensitive to the assertion that their precious and useful RSEs are delusions.

This "religion is delusion" viewpoint gives characteristically modern voice to an ancient criticism of religion as superstition and wish fulfillment. Contemporary forms of this criticism are more than mere skepticism, which typically leads to an agnosticism that might actually be respectful and reverent. Rather, they are full-blown attacks on the epistemological and moral value of RSEs, and of religion itself (Dawkins 2006; Dennett 2006; Harris 2006; Hitchens 2007; Mills 2006; Stenger 2007). In religious circles there has been a strong counterattack, defending religion and the reliability of RSEs, building on the older and quieter work of a few key intellectuals such as Richard Swinburne (1979) and William Alston (1991). But let us consider the attacks.

Sam Harris writes the following lines in his *Letter to a Christian Nation*, addressing conservative Christians who are supernaturalists and biblical literalists. "There is no question that it is possible for people to have profoundly transformative experiences. And there is no question that it is possible for them to misinterpret those experiences, and to further delude themselves about the nature of reality." How does Harris know this? Because "billions of other human beings, in every time and place, have had similar experiences [to blissful prayer] – but they had them while thinking about Krishna, or Allah, or the Buddha, while making art or music, or while contemplating the beauty of nature" (2006: 89).

Many thoughtful people can appreciate Harris' point, and the similar points made by Dawkins and other writers who attack the cognitive reliability of RSEs. Yet they also believe that these experiences are meaningful and valuable. So they are left with a problem: how do they affirm the meaning and value of RSEs if the cognitive content of those experiences is the result of an uncritical acceptance of overactive pattern-making capacities of the brain's remarkable simulation software? I will argue in another chapter that there is a resolution to this dilemma. Here I will say just this. Seen in the right light, the unreliability of cognitive interpretations of RSEs is beautiful. It creates an opening for intellectual and spiritual illumination. RSEs are self-deconstructing. They draw our attention to the emptiness of experience and to the spiritual significance of that emptiness. But such illumination is more compatible with some views of the world and of ultimate reality than with others. In particular, the more determinate and person-like the picture of ultimacy one has, the more one might expect unambiguous communication and straightforward interpretation, and the more disturbing the failure of that expectation proves to be. My point for now is simply to notice the dilemma's existentially portentous character.

Though the rhetoric of recent anti-religious writers is occasionally insultingly dismissive of religious and spiritual people, as we have seen, they are generally compassionate human beings and often quite reasonable. So they do not fail to notice the awkward existential problem that their arguments pose for religious and spiritual believers who rely on their experiences for reassurance and guidance. Dawkins has been quite straightforward about this. He makes the fair point that we should expect people who might be upset by anti-religious arguments to take them in their stride, with courage and dignity, and simply adjust, the way we all do when we encounter valid new information. He believes that this expectation conveys a high regard for the emotional strength and intelligence of his fellow human beings.

I think Dawkins' recommendation is sensible. As alarming as some of the awkward information about the cognitive reliability of RSEs may seem at first, there is a way to accommodate it within a worldview that is simultaneously empirically adequate and spiritually compelling. And the key to this accommodation is to stress not the cognitive reliability of RSEs but rather their function as one means of engagement with the depth and mystery of reality, in the same way that all of our experiences have this potential to varying degrees.

Ultimate spiritual meaning

The final point on the compass of theoretical issues represents a direction that scientists rarely take, at least in public. But it is an important issue for many religious people because it concerns the ultimate spiritual significance of RSEs. Can such experiences lead to salvation, liberation, or enlightenment, as many claim? Can they bring authentic hope for a future life after death or do they merely comfort and inspire us – and perhaps delude us with false comfort – while we endeavor to make the most of the present? This is now clearly a philosophical and theological issue, and perhaps one that is immune to any direct impact from the scientific study of religion. So let us enter the sometimes strange but always intriguing territory of theology and philosophy and try to make sense of these questions about the ultimate significance of RSEs.

Let us admit from the outset that many people do not acknowledge the meaningfulness of religious goals such as salvation, liberation, and enlightenment. Let us further note that even theologians who take one or more of these religious goals seriously conceive the issue very differently. Consider that theologians who are supernaturalists (i.e. accepting disembodied intentionality) and supranaturalists (i.e. conceiving ultimate reality as a personal being with awareness and purposes and powers to act) imagine an ontological arrangement of beings and powers, of relations and transactions that can make literal sense of salvation and liberation narratives in a way that is alien to naturalist philosophical theologians. For their part, religious naturalists (who reject both supernaturalism and supranaturalism) take seriously concepts of salvation or enlightenment but regard world pictures of heavens and hells, angels and demons under the supervision of a personal divine being as improperly anthropomorphic projections of human experience onto a universe that actually is not scaled to human interests and concerns.

Naturalists and super/supranaturalists have co-existed within every religious and philosophical tradition throughout the long history of human theological musing. Super/supranaturalists have been in the large majority in each tradition and they are currently as much in the majority as they ever have been. What is different about our era is that, in addition to religious–naturalist theological opponents, there is a group of anti-religious intellectuals who also defend naturalist worldviews and believe with varying degrees of militancy that, to use Hitchens' phrase, "religion spoils everything" (Hitchens 2007). There have always been atheists and skeptics, but never have they had at their disposal a worldview as robust as the one that scientific inquiry, global communication, modern medicine, historical knowledge, and democratic political organization has brought to birth. The medieval village atheist's view of the world was clearly parasitic upon the worldview that he or she rejected, but that is no longer so. In fact, Dennett has adopted the name "bright" from the so-called "Brights Movement" to designate his spiritual identity, specifically in order to distance himself from the parasitic connotations of the word "atheist" (see Dennett 2006: 21).

Admittedly these are three very broad and diverse groupings. Super/supranaturalist Christians, for example, include both biblical literalists and moderates who take the Bible seriously but not literally. Anti-religious naturalists range from the religiously hostile to those who think religion serves useful social and existential functions. And religious naturalists, among whom I count myself, vary from philosophically minded Buddhists (such as Nāgārjuna) who never used the concept of God, to philosophically minded theists (such as Aristotle) who gave what amounts to a naturalistic interpretation of the concept of God. Nevertheless, these three groups offer a serviceable map for my current purpose, which is to draw a double contrast with the views to either side of my religious–naturalist perspective.

On the one side, within the pro-religion camp, one major difference between super/supranaturalists and religious naturalists in all traditions is that the former have traditionally relied in part on the cognitive content of RSEs to support their worldview. To that extent, super/supranaturalists have a lot at stake in the contemporary investigation of the cognitive reliability of RSEs discussed above. They will try to claim cognitive reliability even while explaining away the apparent fact that people interpret qualitatively similar experiences in quite opposed ways. Alternatively, they will reduce their reliance on the evidential force of religious experience and emphasize instead the supernatural authorization of sacred texts such as the Bible, the Qur'an, and the Vedas, or else the supernatural establishment and maintenance of sacred communities such as the Catholic Church or the Buddhist Sangha. Following the German theologian Ernst Troeltsch, I have argued elsewhere that neither strategy is successful and that both involve special pleading on behalf of a favored religious or spiritual tradition (see Wildman 1998: 83–85). Such special pleading is more than implausible; it is undignified and dangerous.

Meanwhile, religious naturalists do not need to rely on the cognitive content of RSEs in order to authorize a supernatural worldview, or for any other purpose, so they can live more easily with any finding about cognitive reliability. Naturalists are also fully committed to the neural embodiment and social embedding of RSEs so there are no surprises lying in wait for them. But there can be surprises for supernaturalists who are committed to a supernatural soul and who struggle to articulate the body–soul connection forced upon them by the neural embodiment and social embedding of RSEs. In light of these considerations, a religious naturalist approach to interpreting the ultimate meaning of RSEs offers significant advantages.

On the other side, though religious naturalists share some common ground with the worldview of anti-religious scientists such as Dawkins, Stenger, Weinberg (2001), and Sagan (1996), there is a potent disagreement over the value of preserving religious communities, and often a subordinate disagreement over the value of RSEs.

Anti-religious naturalists have been forced by their critics to be quite explicit about what they are attacking. For example, Dawkins, Dennett, and Harris are going after super/supranaturalist religion and the moderate religion that gives it cover; they specifically exempt religious people who reject the idea of God as a personal being (supranaturalism), which includes religious naturalists. But they have another critique for anti-super/supranaturalist religious people. Dawkins complains that religious naturalists in the theistic camp are disingenuous, using "God" in a way that does not conform to its most common usage. I am sure many supranatural theists would agree with Dawkins at this point. But why should religious naturalists surrender the word "God," which has always been contested, simply turning it over to personalist, supranaturalist theists because Dawkins says they should? Surely it is a word worth fighting for. Of course, when trying to dismantle human religion, it is difficult to have much sympathy for religious naturalists who want to defend the value of religious quests by means of maintaining continuity with traditional religious communities, religious language and symbols, religious rituals and practices, and RSEs.

To Dawkins and his anti-religious co-conspirators, therefore, the religious naturalist is complicit in protecting an intellectual and moral disaster. To the religious naturalist, however, Dawkins and company are oversimplifying. At some point, they arbitrarily stop asking good and important questions. If we need to work hard to be good scientists, if we need to cultivate skill sets for art and literature, if we need to labor in defense of valuable institutions, then why should we not invest energy in the pursuit of spiritual quests? Cannot spiritual quests be pursued more and less expertly? And ought not the accrued wisdom of religious and spiritual traditions be relevant for the guidance of such quests, even if we also criticize those traditions? The anti-religious naturalists speak as if the spiritual quest were an unimportant or trivial matter that, contrary to every other great human adventure, requires no institutional support or traditional guidance. The religious naturalist demurs.

CONCLUSION

I conclude this chapter with a preliminary appeal on behalf of the value of RSEs despite the dangers that co-arise with this value, and also with strategic remarks about the unfolding argument.

RSEs have a vital place within the grand adventure of human life. The spiritual quests of humanity have been among the most passionate and prized pursuits in every culture and era, and that continues to be true today. The wisdom encoded in traditions is an essential resource for those quests, as are the institutions, rituals, symbols, and ideas that those traditions accumulate and sustain. There is no reason why scientific knowledge cannot also produce a kind of wisdom to help guide spiritual quests and criticize longstanding wisdom traditions. Even if RSEs do not reliably yield cognitive information that can be translated into doctrinal propositions – and at this point I have made no judgment on that question – they perform an invaluable function by engaging people with the ultimate mysteries to which they are drawn. Every part of human life and every aspect of human embodiment play roles in the seeker's quest to cultivate spiritual excellence. This necessarily involves imperfect institutions, such as religions. It involves flawed mentors and ambiguous efforts at character transformation. It involves mistaken metaphysics and odd ontology. And it involves experiences that engage us deeply without necessarily reliably informing us about great spiritual truths. Nonetheless, the entire messy process is a valuable journey through an awesome environment of existential meanings and social possibilities. RSEs are among the most captivating features of the landscape to be explored along the way.

Unfortunately, RSEs are not only beautiful and valuable, but also potentially dangerous. People's failure to understand the gap between beliefs that potent experiences seem to make self-evidently true and beliefs that are rationally well supported is a problem of terrible proportions in human history. Enough people have to understand RSEs in some depth in order to keep such enthusiastic experience-driven convictions in check. Wisdom traditions and discernment practices encode a great deal of common-sense guidance for managing such enthusiasm. When this bulwark of common sense fails, however, religion becomes the friend of irrationality and violence thanks to the power of religion to rationalize and lend cosmic significance to convictions that are central to the identity of a group and to the meaning of an individual life.

One measure of the danger of RSEs is that such experiences make a wide range of beliefs, including possibly beliefs that legitimate violence, internally incorrigible within the groups that hold them, despite the fact that they are externally corrigible to an extreme degree. That is, the self-righteousness and irrationality of religiously rationalized violence is difficult to see from within the social world that promotes it yet painfully obvious from the outside. Nothing expresses the tragedy of RSEs more acutely or compactly than the phenomenon of conversion at the point of a broadsword or a scimitar, when it is wielded by a human being who acts out of absolute conviction, with heart full of bizarrely distorted compassion for the supposedly lost soul under threat of death, and with a visceral feeling of divine confirmation and command.

If we are to come to terms with both the value and danger of RSEs, it cannot be by rejecting them outright in the name of overcoming religiously rationalized violence, for this is both to demand the biologically and socially impossible, and also to refuse to drink life-giving water from the wells of our most treasured experiences. It would be akin to banning happiness or grief. Nor can we come to terms with this terrible ambiguity by imposing on everyone else one of the many internally incorrigible belief worlds inspired and supported by RSEs, while ignoring the particularity and external corrigibility of that universalized perspective. Rather, we must patiently build a sound understanding of the nature and functions of RSEs at every level of relevance, from their evolutionary origins and their neural expressions to their existential meanings and social effects. Then we must make this knowledge available to others. This requires education that helps political and religious leaders make wise policy decisions. It also requires finding appropriately supportive ways to help religious and non-religious people with no special training gain a sound understanding of the value and potential danger of their own RSEs.

My concern here is with the first phase of this project: knowledge-based understanding of RSEs. As the survey in this chapter has indicated, this is a complicated project requiring input from numerous disciplines. The next chapter takes up a particularly hopeful line of scientific inquiry into religious experiences: the brain sciences, from cognitive neuropsychology to neural imaging research. The hope is that the brain sciences in league with evolutionary theory can produce insights into RSEs, eventually including cognitive and neural models, which help to isolate core features and dynamic processes amid the intricate particularities of the cultural expression, existential significance, and bodily and social effects of RSEs. There is as yet no comprehensive cognitive model or neurological theory of RSEs, only a few partial insights. But the hope that neurology and evolutionary biology can help produce robust interpretations with cross-cultural relevance is genuine, the rate of advance rapid, and the prospects of success good.

After the discussion of spirituality and the brain in Chapter 2, the plan is to map the territory of RSEs in such a way as to illuminate the sheer diversity of experiences with religious and spiritual significance, and thereby to resist reductionist simplifications of the domain of such experiences. I take up this task in Chapter 3. Along the way I consider several subclasses of RSEs, some of which have received extensive attention, and some of which are under-studied. Distinctive types of RSEs are amenable to specific research approaches and have concrete relevance for particular interpretative questions. For example, some mystical experiences lend themselves both to neurological scanning techniques, because of their reproducibility, and to philosophical questions about whether there is a common core to all of the world's religions in the form of shared fundamental ontology and truth claims. My particular interest in Chapter 5 is to evaluate the cognitive reliability of RSEs and in Chapter 6 to assess the social power of such experiences. To address those questions, I have found it more helpful to seek out another class of RSEs, one that is as neurologically universal as possible within the human species, and thus as evolutionarily well established as possible, and then to investigate that class of experiences in more detail.

To that end, Chapter 3 proposes that intensity – understood neurologically as intensifications of sense experience that trigger richly interconnected activation, and phenomenologically as spiritually meaningful and emotionally spectacular experiences – identifies this useful class of RSEs. Chapter 3 maps intense experiences in relation to other classes of RSEs. The way this map locates intense experiences impacts the emerging interpretation of RSEs by showing that the neurologically most universal and fundamental generative sources of existentially potent human meanings – the intense experiences – are relevant far beyond the borders of what most people are prepared to call religious. This alerts us to the spiritual potency of many domains of human life, thereby "sanctifying" those domains as spiritually potent and potentially valuable even if they lie beyond the limits of explicitly religious groups and experiences. This in turn suggests that the precisely delimited but capacious and varied class of intense experiences may represent a more efficient means of accurately understanding the nature, functions, and value of RSEs than the culturally variable and group-dependent domain of so-called religious experiences, or specialized sub-domains such as mystical experiences.

Chapter 4 develops this hypothesis about intense experiences and investigates their phenomenological characteristics. The aim is to forge links between the neurological, phenomenological, existential, and social dimensions of RSEs, thereby preparing for subsequent discussions of epistemological reliability and social potency. It is the domain of intense experiences within the wider territory of RSEs to which the analogy with neurologically fundamental and evolutionarily stabilized perceptual experience applies most closely. Thus, it is there if anywhere that we should look for evidence of well-tested capacities for dynamic engagement that are capable of registering religious and spiritual realities in the depths of nature and experience. Intensity – again, in the specific sense of an intensification of sensory experience that triggers broad and deep awareness and connects us with the valuational depths of reality – underlies the powerful instinct for the sacred – for the powerful and the valuable, for the good and the true and the beautiful, for the unspeakable and the sublime – that draws human beings along paths of dynamic engagement that we call spiritual quests.

Chapter 5 explores the epistemological relevance of intense experiences with this guiding suggestion about the compelling lure of intense experiences in mind, but also keenly aware of the fact that RSEs appear capable of generating consensus around beliefs only in the contexts of groups. In teasing apart these two fundamental phenomena of human life – the belief-inducing power of RSEs and the group dependence of consensus around beliefs – I shall argue that we find little basis for regarding RSEs as a reliable evidential basis for religious beliefs. But I shall also conclude that there is considerable reason to treat such experiences as types of causal engagement with existentially vital aspects of reality, about which we creatively construct beliefs guided by the traditions and cultures of which we are parts. Within the domain of RSEs in general, however, the intense experiences – when interpreted with appropriate caution, in full awareness of the factors conditioning experience-based belief formation, and in a suitable ontological framework – furnish the most reliable basis for accurate beliefs about religious and spiritual realities. The cognitive content of those most reliable beliefs is, however, not as elaborate or specific as the beliefs of any particular tradition of religious practice and commitment. What William James called "overbeliefs" – sustained in relatively like-minded communities – are the norm for religious traditions.

Chapter 6 takes up the question of the social embedding and effects of RSEs. This question is profoundly reframed by the foregoing chapters, which lay down a basis both for affirming the multidimensional value of RSEs and for criticizing their cognitive consequences and social effects. The argument is that the social power of RSEs is best grasped in the context of an evolutionary understanding of the brain-group nexus, which is the intricate social interlinking of individual human brains. The evolution of the brain-group nexus invites interpretation in terms of a dynamical system with regimes of stability and characteristic transition phenomena. RSEs manifest social power both in maintaining stability and in destabilizing existing social arrangements for the sake of realizing newly imagined forms of life, which those experiences can help to inspire. I deploy this framework to analyze the role of RSEs in the exercise of social power and the application of moral judgments.

Chapter 7 raises the specter of RSEs in the future. In particular, it focuses on how the human future might change if this bivalent affirmative yet critical understanding of RSEs were more broadly and deeply absorbed. It also speculates as to the price we pay if we fail to become more aware of both the values and liabilities of RSEs. And it seeks to evaluate the emerging possibilities of more refined control over the generation and effects of RSEs.

Finally, Chapter 8 weaves the strands of the argument together into a concluding interpretation, both summarizing the book and consolidating the case for an affirmative yet critical, religious–naturalist understanding of the nature, functions, and value of RSEs.

CHAPTER 2

Spirituality and the brain: a revolutionary scientific approach to religious and spiritual experiences

INTRODUCTION

The fact that the brain mediates RSEs is an unwelcome discovery for some religious people, particularly if they sense that the materiality of the brain somehow taints the spiritual perfection of such experiences. Others feel sure that the neural embodiment of RSEs should yield evidence that the neurosciences confirm their religious beliefs. For yet others, both religious and anti-religious, neural mediation is exciting because it opens up lines of inquiry into the causal conditions and functions of religious behavior, belief, and experience that formerly seemed non-existent. I count myself in this last, religiously mixed group of intellectuals. We support the neurological study of RSEs not because of any expectation that such research by itself can settle questions about the truth or falsity of religious beliefs, or about the value and liabilities of RSEs, but because of the potential of the neurosciences to illumine the functions and causal conditions of RSEs.

While this book presumes that the human brain mediates RSEs, it is important not to take this completely for granted. Exhaustive neural mediation is a minority view in the history of thought and across cultures at the current time, despite its widespread acceptance among Western philosophers. We need to ask about the reasons to believe the hypothesis that RSEs are exhaustively neurally embodied. What is the philosophical significance of this idea? And precisely how can we mount fruitful research into the neural expression of RSEs? These are the questions to be examined in this chapter. We begin with an orienting survey of the history of thinking about spirituality and the brain, followed by a discussion of the mind–body problem as it takes shape in the modern period. We shall then turn to the real promise of the neurosciences in this area: not the evaluation of religious truth claims but the generation of cognitive models and eventually neural models of RSEs, with the corresponding expansion of our understanding of their causes and effects. There are many problems facing such inquiries but researchers are making creative advances every year.

Unavoidable intuitions and contestable inferences

Curiosity about the brains of human beings and other animals is thousands of years old. It is not difficult to see why. Though the brain is enclosed in a hard protective shell, human beings are unlucky, violent, or stupid sufficiently often that we have had ample opportunity to see what happens when we damage skulls. Hit someone with a club and their state of consciousness may change. Fall out of a tree and what is inside your skull may come outside. Get in a hunting accident with a spear through your head and, if you survive, you may find your behavior so altered that you cannot help wondering what is going on in there. Then there are headaches and dizziness, and also the senses of hearing, sight, taste, and smell, all of which seem more or less obviously located inside the head. The same is true of speaking, which is so closely related to thinking and feeling. Clearly something is going on inside those skulls.

Preserved human skulls show evidence of head surgery and perhaps brain surgery dating back at least 10,000 years. Called "trepanation" or "trephination," this surgery involves removing a piece of skull, presumably to release fluid pressure within or to remove bone fragments after injury (for a survey, see Arnot *et al.* 2003). While some of these surgeries appear to be extremely precise, others seem to be amateurish, leading to speculation that trephination was used both by medical experts as a treatment for injury and by surgically inexpert shamans as a technique to heal emotional or spiritual disturbances. The practice was culturally widespread, reaching across Asia from Europe to Russia, and across oceans from the Americas to northern Africa to the Pacific islands. This distribution pattern suggests that the common experiences described above reliably produced similar intuitions about the brain and associated technologies of healing.

The earliest written evidence about the brain's role in human life is an Egyptian papyrus from 1700 BCE, which is thought to be a copy of an original document from about 3000 BCE. It was translated by James Henry Breasted (see Breasted 1991). Named the Edwin Smith papyrus after the man who purchased it in Egypt, it consists of a series of generalized case studies covering bodily injuries, including head injuries, and prescribes treatments and assesses likelihood of recovery. The discussions of head injuries clearly link brain trauma to motor disruption. Yet mummification at about the same time typically involved removing the brain, supposedly on the assumption that the heart rather than the brain was the seat of intelligence.

The coexistence of multiple medical traditions surrounding the brain is not surprising, in Egypt or elsewhere, because interpretation of the organ's role is not straightforward. In China and Mesopotamia, writers left evidence of understanding that the brain was linked to human behavior and health, evidence almost as old as that from Egypt. About 1400 BCE, South Asian Ayurvedic medical records located intelligence and identity in the brain. By the fifth century BCE, some Greek medical traditions identified the brain as the seat of intelligence and sensation; the Greek physician Hippocrates (460–379 BCE) even wrote of epilepsy as a brain disturbance. But in all of these cultures, competing traditions located the seat of intelligence elsewhere than in the brain.

It seems that recognition of the human brain's importance for health and behavior developed early and consistently across cultures. But identifying the brain as the seat of what is most distinctively human is a more complex inference, less clearly supported by common-sense experience. As a result, the source of human reasoning and emotion, morality and spirituality, has been a contested subject. In ancient Greece, for example, while everyone believed that mentality was not a purely physical phenomenon, Plato (428/7–348/7 BCE) followed Hippocrates in linking the brain to the intellect but his student, the astute observational scientist Aristotle (384–322 BCE), situated mental processes and sensations in the heart and regarded the brain primarily as a kind of radiator for cooling the blood. Aristotle conjectured that the relatively large human brain helped human beings achieve greater cooling and thus superior control over "hot-blooded" emotions than other animals with relatively smaller brain-to-body-size ratio. This conflict would continue for millennia, and in some circles continues even today.

The difficulty of inferring a role for the brain in human mental and spiritual life is understandable. The ethereal quality of thought and spirit contrasts sharply with the material character of meat and metabolism. The brain, being clearly a material object, seems to have closer affinities to the bodily aspects of life than to the mental and spiritual aspects. Yet the role of the head seemed central to what was distinctively human. The Greek physician Galen (128–200 CE) found a way to hold all of these intuitions together with knowledge built from his extensive dissections and surgeries. He linked intelligence to the head, but to the brain ventricles rather than brain tissues. Ventricles are fluid-filled spaces in the brain, which apparently suggested ethereality, whereas brain tissues suggested materiality. He assigned the harder tissues of the brain such as the cerebellum to the control of bodily motion and the softer tissues of the cortex to the processing of sensations.

Galen's hypothesis held sway among medical professionals in the West until the Renaissance. At that point, the anatomy of the brain rapidly became more detailed, and many past mistakes of interpretation were corrected. But the conflict over the link between brain and mentality became even sharper. The more studies of the structure and function of the brain illumined its material causality, the less suitable it seemed for a role as the seat of the distinctive qualities of human mind and spirit. René Descartes (1596–1650) famously proposed that the human body was a material machine controlled by an immaterial soul (see Descartes [1649] 2003). That left him with the problem of explaining the influence between the two. Descartes argued that the tiny pineal gland, which he mistakenly believed was unique to humans, must be the connecting point. But this simply shifts the problem to explaining how the soul influences the pineal gland, which has struck many subsequent thinkers as a sure sign that Descartes was thinking in the wrong way about the brain (see Damasio 1994).

Descartes thereby gave birth to the peculiarly sharp modern form of the mind–brain problem. Increasing knowledge of the natural world in his time catalyzed the problem of miracles, transforming them from exceptional events with religious significance to blunt violations of natural law. In a similar way, knowledge of the brain sharpened the mind–body problem, in two ways at once. On the one hand, it made it virtually impossible to conceive a causal connection between an immaterial soul and a material brain, which has been a problem for dualist theories of mind ever since. On the other hand, it made mentality seem more sharply opposed to materiality than ever, which has posed an insuperable challenge to materialist theories of mind (see Chalmers 1995, 1996; Levine 1983).

The modern mind–body problem

The numerous philosophical attempts to solve the mind–body problem since this hardening of categories in the early modern period collectively resemble a kind of agonized intellectual writhing (in addition to works discussed below, important representative classics include Dennett 1991; Jaynes 1976; Penrose 1994; Varela *et al.* 1991). The philosophical descend-ants of Descartes' dualism are in the unappetizing but unavoidable situation of lacking a robust scientific research program that can either support or contradict their metaphysical hypothesis. Their strongest sup-port would come from the failure of their materialist opposition, but that just leaves dualists standing around waiting. Meanwhile, far too many materialists incoherently posture at being able to solve the mind–body problem simply by studying the brain more and more extensively.

For example, Patricia Smith Churchland and Paul Churchland defend an eliminativist form of materialism (see Churchland and Churchland 1998; Patricia Churchland 1986; Paul Churchland 1988, 2007). They stipu-late that there is no such thing as mentality, *eliminating* it by arguing that all is *material* and that common-sense beliefs in the immaterial aspects of thought and feeling are merely delusions – thus *eliminative materialism*. They then content themselves with redescribing human experiences in terms of brain processes, as if those experiences possess none of the phe-nomenological properties that we feel in our own consciousness. While the Churchlands intend this as a virtuous and valiant attempt to free human beings from the delusory grip of folk psychology, few interpreters have followed their rejection of first-person, subjective features of mental experience (so-called qualia). Most experts continue to believe that qualia are ontologically informative, even though folk psychology appears to be clearly mistaken in some respects.

A less extreme materialist viewpoint is epiphenomenalism, which admits that mental events occur but denies that they have any causal relevance in human life (see the classic example of Huxley 1874, and the review in Caston 1997). On this view, mentality is a meaningless side-effect of the material causality of life – a *phenomenon* that rides upon (Greek: *epi*) causally effective processes without itself being causally rele-vant, like steam from a kettle. We may believe that our thoughts have causal effects but, on this view, our thoughts are nothing more than reports on a causal process that mind can never interrupt or influence. Epiphenomenalists have the same ontological explanation problem as most other materialists – that is, saying what the stuff of thought is – but they can afford to ignore the problem because solving it has no import-ance for understanding intelligence, emotion, morality, or spirituality.

The eliminativist type of materialism gives great comfort to its dual-ist enemy by implausibly denying mentality. Likewise, dualists find the epiphenomenalist type of materialism easy to attack because the evidence of our experience that mentality matters in human behavior is compelling. But not all materialists are so convenient for dualists to handle. The dominant viewpoint in the philosophy of mind is an emergence doctrine whereby matter joined with intricate organization produces the various mental properties of complex systems. Emergentism is a philosophical program with close links to the sciences, because every new discovery about complex systems such as the brain further elaborates the emergentist model. But the emergentist position is famously vague on ontological questions. David Chalmers has pointed this out forcefully, correctly saying that the essential qualitative distinction between mind and matter cannot be bridged by emergence alone, no matter how correct emergence may be on its own terms (see Chalmers 1995, 1996). Thus, the mind–body problem in our time calls for a philosophically rooted ontological solution to complement a science-based account of the causal mechanisms by which the emergent properties of complex systems arise.

Most researchers studying the human brain do not concern themselves with philosophical worries about the mind–brain problem. Rather, they focus on gathering evidence about the neural embedding of human behaviors, beliefs, and experiences. This is understandable, because there is an overwhelming amount of work to do and philosophical issues can certainly afford to take a back seat to actual working understandings of the brain for a while. Among philosophers who do concern themselves with both the brain sciences and philosophical worries about the mind–brain problem, there is a rough strategic consensus about how to approach the ontological dimensions of the issue. The preferred strategy is neither eliminative materialism nor epiphenomenalism, on the one side, nor dualism or immaterialist idealism, on the other side, but rather one or another variation of what I shall call di-polar monism.

The core hypothesis of di-polar monism is that there is one kind of basic stuff and it involves both mental and material aspects. One of its most famous and influential representatives was William James, whose radical empiricism naturally led him to hold together all phenomena under a unified description (see James [1909] 1996, [1912] 2003). In contemporary philosophy of mind, however, "di-polar monism" is little more than a guideline. It expresses a double conviction that philosophical proposals about the mind–body problem (i) should remain tightly correlated with the neurosciences, and (ii) should make sense of the special qualities of both material reality and conscious experience, including their mutual causal interaction. This general guideline permits many detailed strategies, from the dual-aspect monism of William James and Thomas Nagel (1974, 1986) to the anomalous monism of Donald Davidson (1970) and the biological naturalism of John Searle (1992, 2004). I, too, affirm this broad di-polar strategy, though in a way that draws on the semiotic theory of Charles Peirce (1931–35, 1955, 1958) and Robert Corrington (1992, 1994, 1996, 1997, 2000). I shall not take up the details here, but I will advance a case for di-polar monism in general terms below.

From epistemology to ontology

Within the circumscribed philosophical culture of analytical philosophy, the debates in this area become extremely intricate, but they hover around trying to specify necessary and sufficient conditions for an adequate resolution of the mind–body problem. A debate about rules and strategies is, however, not the same as developing a working ontological model. How do we know a theory of the brain-mind could ever meet these necessary and sufficient conditions for adequacy? On this question, analytical philosophy of mind has been characteristically modest and retiring. In metaphysically more adventurous traditions of philosophy, such as American pragmatic naturalism, philosophers have boldly developed elaborate metaphysical systems to test whether di-polar monism can really account for our experience of both material and mental reality.

For example, Alfred North Whitehead presented a novel theory of causation that explained how the entanglement of the mental and physical poles of reality could produce the ordinary experiences with which we are so familiar (Whitehead 1978). Both Peirce (1931–35, 1955, 1958) and James ([1909] 1996, [1912] 2003) developed less elaborate metaphysical theories that satisfy the general conditions of the di-polar monist theory. Without such ontological elaborations it is difficult to tell whether anyone could ever really implement the epistemological stipulations of the philosophy of mind in a workable theory of human experience.

Testing ontological hypotheses about the brain-mind by means of elaborate metaphysical theories strikes some ivory-tower intellectuals as futile because there seems to be no basis for correcting and improving such philosophical theories, and they fear that the result will be confusion and obscurity. I am not convinced that such fears are well founded. Be that as it may, avoiding this challenge creates its own kind of confusion and obscurity. Even if we can never definitively confirm a particular metaphysical system, we can still hypothetically deploy such systems to evaluate the coherence of ontological resolutions of the mind–brain problem.

In relation to the interpretation of RSEs, metaphysical theories have special importance because they set limits on what interpretations can be plausible. Is there a supernatural realm or not? Are there supernatural beings with which human beings can communicate? Is the world of experience fundamentally illusory? Is the soul exclusively embodied in the brain so that the dissolution of neural organization destroys the soul as well? Are there other realms of reality into which people can travel and from which they can gain information? Is transmigration true? Are there flows of power that we can tap for the purposes of wisdom, healing, and social control? Do religious practices such as petitionary prayer change merely the attitude and actions of those who pray or also the wider world? The metaphysical framework for interpreting RSEs directly impacts such questions, which are pressing issues for ordinary people and for the religious and anti-religious communities which they revere and serve, or ridicule and shun, as the case may be.

In relation to every kind of human experience, therefore – and *especially* in relation to RSEs – we are obliged to pay attention to competing ontological theories of the mind-brain as well as neurological theories of the mental processes that give rise to experience. The most frustrating aspect of this obligation is that most of the major classical ontological theories produced within human cultures can be reframed so as to survive in the face of our contemporary knowledge about the neural embedding of RSEs. Body–soul dualism can survive – we can say that brain damage destroys the soul (the physicalist and di-polar views), or else that it destroys the antenna-like means by which the indestructible soul connects causally to the body (the dualist view). Shamanic travel through other-worldly realms can survive – experiences of such journeys may be partial misunderstandings of unusual brain phenomena that may have value anyway (the physicalist and di-polar views) or the mind's best way of comprehending the supra-physical soul's actual journey (the shamanic view). Even demon possession survives – who really knows how putative demons would interact with human bodies and brains?

This suggests that philosophical neutrality is the average impact of neurology on ontological questions in the history of religions; that is, we can defend any ontological viewpoint no matter what the neurological facts. But philosophical neutrality is roundly rejected by many neurologists and writers who follow the neurosciences. Most operate within a naturalistic framework (whether materialist or di-polar) because that is what most effectively keeps them looking for causal processes that are tractable for neurological study. And because this framework is compelling on a daily basis, it understandably tends to dominate their ontological imaginations. But investigators of brain correlates for RSEs cannot allow the functional naturalism of scientific work to become a full-blown naturalistic ontology without due consideration. And the "consideration due" turns out to be extremely complex and not everyone is expert at keeping track of the relevant details. This is how some popular books slip so quickly from "RSEs are realized in the brain" to "a naturalistic ontology is correct and supernaturalistic religious belief is delusion" or some other over-crisp but half-baked inference. This hasty reasoning must be resisted for the sake of a responsible interpretation of RSEs – and I say this as a thinker who actually does defend a naturalistic ontology and di-polar monist resolution of the mind–brain problem.

Lest I suggest that I am espousing the philosophical neutrality of neurology, however, let me clarify. In fact, I also reject the philosophical neutrality of neurology to ontological questions in the area of religion and spirituality. I do not believe that traction between neurology and philosophy can occur at the coarse level of proofs and refutations, however, the way some contemporary popular and semi-popular writers do. Rather, traction occurs at the subtle level of cumulative weight of empirical evidence joined with the plausibility of integrative interpretation. So the pressing problem becomes precisely how the neurological study of RSEs can produce the kinds of traction necessary for resolving ontological and practical questions. Assessments of this kind require the patience and perspective of the philosopher.

An argument in passing for a naturalistic ontology

To illustrate, I sketch my reasons for thinking that a di-polar monist form of naturalistic ontology achieves greater overall coherence with neurology than a dualistic ontology when it comes to interpreting RSEs. I shall do this in two stages and briefly, but I shall return to the theme of naturalism in later chapters.

The first stage is a criterion for discriminating basically adequate from inadequate ontological views. This narrows the field of competing hypotheses by eliminating weaker candidates. I think the most fundamental constraining evidence on philosophical resolutions of the mind–brain problem is *bi-directional causation between mental and physical events*. That is, mental events have physical bodily effects, and physical bodily events have mental effects. To accept this rules out both eliminative materialism and epiphenomenalism. But di-polar forms of monism, including an ontologically elaborated emergence theory, survive. So do forms of dualism in which mental events and physical events have their own governing laws but somehow interact. The intricate and public physicality of the brain also makes ontological idealism a deeply perplexing position, unless it is reframed as di-polar monism, so I include the viable versions of idealism under that heading (see, for example, Velmans 2000, whose "reflexive monism" does something like this).

Di-polar theories perpetually struggle to explain how the mental and physical can be aspects of the same stuff, even with emergence in the picture. Dualist theories constantly struggle to explain how the mental and the physical can interact. But every other theory has much more severe problems. Specifically, alternatives either do not register the phenomenological qualities of material or mental reality, or else they fail to account for mind–brain interaction. By contrast, both the di-polar monism and dualism theories clearly recognize the mental and the material – as distinguishable poles of a unitary ontological stuff or as distinct ontological substances, respectively – and attempt to explain causal interaction. Thus, these theories have the potential to make sense of how consciousness, meanings, emotions, and spirituality are expressed in the brain in a way that alternatives do not. In what follows, therefore, I shall keep the dualist theories and the di-polar monist versions of emergent physicalism in the forefront and relegate the rest. In particular, strictly mono-polar forms of materialism do not pass the filter of this first stage; they simply lack the right conceptual equipment to get the explanatory job done.

The second stage argues that di-polar monism (considered generally as a class of views) fares better than dualism (also considered generally as a class of views) in the face of our knowledge of the neural embedding of religious and spiritual behaviors, beliefs, and experiences. Note that neuroscientist Mario Beauregard's argument for dualism against materialism strangely does not even consider plausible forms of naturalism, such as di-polar monism, let alone other metaphysical accounts of the mind–brain problem (see Beauregard 2007; Beauregard and O'Leary 2007). This is a case of comparing a shiny new Ferrari with a beat-up old Volkswagen and declaring the Ferrari the "best car" while pretending that there are no other cars to enter into the comparison. Beauregard's argument, therefore, certainly does not clinch the case for dualism. I have pointed out already that mind–body dualism is not obviously wrong, because the body can be an antenna for a supra-physical mind or an immaterial soul rather than just the embodiment of mind and soul. So the argument against dualism will be a delicate matter of interpretation rather than a knock-down proof.

Let us dub the hypothesis that the brain exhaustively mediates the mind the *neural mediation hypothesis.* This thesis does not imply that the di-polar monists are right and the dualists wrong, but only that *the mind does nothing we can detect that is not exhaustively mediated by and expressed in the brain.* Clearly, di-polar monists *require* the neural mediation hypothesis to be correct, while dualists can live with or without it. Now, suppose that the neural mediation hypothesis fails in just one respect. In that case, the di-polar monist hypothesis fails decisively, putting the dualists in a fabulously strong position. Alternatively, and much more likely, suppose that the neural mediation hypothesis is never refuted and that the current trend of empirical support for it continues unabated into the indefinite future. In that case, we can predict that the philosophical dispute between dualists and di-polar monists would continue also. But the dualist position would become increasingly vulnerable to the criticism that it makes unparsimonious assumptions about immaterial souls, assumptions that do no useful explanatory work. While di-polar monists can steam ahead aided by a strong scientific research program that elaborates their position, dualists would be confined to face-saving moves designed to protect their ontological convictions at all costs.

This contrast illustrates the meaning of a plausible versus an implausible ontology. It takes a while for the difference to show itself, but it has happened over and over again in the history of thought, slowly filling the graveyard of implausible philosophical interpretations with mostly forgotten inhabitants. In this sense, and only in this sense, traction between neurology and ontology exists, and this traction can be effective in supporting one view over and against another in a drawn-out process of evaluation.

EVIDENCE FOR THE NEURAL MEDIATION HYPOTHESIS

In the philosophical history just sketched, by far the most dramatic development is the relatively recent discovery that the brain mediates mind, including RSEs. This has firmed up into what I am calling the neural mediation hypothesis – again, that the mind does nothing we can detect that is not exhaustively mediated by and expressed in the brain. There is a lot at stake here. In addition to the philosophical considerations just discussed, there are practical implications.

For example, suppose it becomes possible to produce RSEs on demand, simply by popping a pill to stimulate the relevant neural networks – this would put us in the strange position of being able to produce spiritual intoxication when it suits us. Then the case for the naturalness of RSEs becomes almost irresistible, and religious references to supernatural entities that have hitherto been thought by many to cause RSEs would eventually seem superfluous. I suspect that this is in fact where the gradual buildup of correlational and neurochemical data is taking us. This raises difficult ethical questions – a topic that I shall address in Chapter 7 on the future of RSEs. Less controversially, clinicians may find neurological knowledge of RSEs useful for helping religious patients better access their under-utilized religious coping strategies. Neurological knowledge invites pharmacological or therapeutic interventions to help patients with religiously tinged psychopathologies such as persecution delusions or obsessive moral scruples to rein in their unhealthy compulsions. And some evidence suggests that the use of religious coping strategies may improve health outcomes for some people (there is a large and complex literature on this issue, in fact).

In short, the consolidation of the neural mediation hypothesis paves the way for studies of the functions of religious behaviors, beliefs, and experiences, and opens the door to technologies of manipulation and control, in both good and bad senses. For both philosophical and practical reasons, therefore, the neural mediation hypothesis is important for interpreting the significance of RSEs. But what exactly is the evidence that the brain exhaustively mediates RSEs? I shall present six lines of evidence for the neural mediation hypothesis.

Basic framework evidence

First and foremost, neuroscience has produced a compelling theoretical framework, backed by countless observations and experiments. This framework implies that every aspect of mind is mediated by the brain. As small as the brain is, its internal structure is staggeringly complex. Where Aristotle once saw only a cooling device for the blood, modern neuroscience has detected intricate networks of electrical currents using chemical signals, supported by an incredibly robust and flexible biochemical system of neurons, synapses, neurotransmitters, and support systems. The information capacity of the brain is unimaginably large, its processing power enormous, and its flexibility prodigious. The numbers are so huge that we cannot meaningfully imagine them (see the compilation of textbook statistics in Chudler 2007). There are about 100 billion neurons in the human brain, about 3,000 billion glial cells, and 150,000 billion synapses. The neuron growth rate in utero is about 4,000 per second and the neuron death rate in adults about 1 per second. The length of myelinated fibers in the brain is about 170,000 kilometers. If it once seemed impossible to imagine that complex human behaviors and experiences could be expressed through the brain, it no longer does. The brain in any species, and unquestionably in human beings, is – for want of more eloquence – amazing.

Moreover, RSEs overlap in large measure with other experiences whose expression in the brain is well understood. For example, many RSEs prominently involve emotions. Everything that neuroscientists know about the neurology of emotions is thus implicated in the neurology of RSEs. Similarly, RSEs involve memory, belief, evaluation, inquiry, sense perception, sociality, behavior, movement, and everything else we do as human beings. Despite many outstanding problems, neuroscientists know an enormous amount about these topics in general terms, and thus also about those aspects of RSEs. These general theoretical considerations constitute overwhelmingly strong evidence in support of the neural mediation hypothesis.

Functional neuroimaging evidence

Second, neuroscientists have studied certain RSEs using functional neuroimaging techniques such as fMRI, PET, SPECT, MEG, EEG, and qEEG. The functional magnetic resonance imaging (fMRI) technique tracks not electrical activity in the brain but oxygen usage a couple of seconds after increased electrical activity. The key to this technology is the fact that oxygenated hemoglobin in blood has a different response to a magnetic field from deoxygenated hemoglobin, and a magnetic resonance machine can be tuned to detect this difference. The positron emission tomography (PET) technique uses instruments to detect radioactive substances as they decay. The key here is to attach radioactive tags to chemicals that are vital to the brain's metabolism, such as oxygen or glucose, and then inject them into the experimental subject's bloodstream. The single photon emission computed tomography (SPECT) technique also uses radioactive tags injected into the bloodstream but these tags attach to the places where they are used in the brain within about one minute of injection and form a stable snapshot of activity at that time. Where PET scans are limited to short events, SPECT scans can be taken well after the time of injection, which is convenient for some kinds of studies. How long the scan can be delayed depends on the half life of the radio-isotope tag. The magnetoencephalography (MEG) technique measures not the brain's use of metabolic products but the brain's actual electrical activity, combining that with structural information from MRI scans. Moving charges create magnetic fields, and this is true of the ions that chemically transmit electrical signals through neurons. If enough neurons are involved in producing a current, if the current is moving in roughly the same direction in those neurons, and if the resulting magnetic field extends outside the head – admittedly that is a lot of "ifs" – then that magnetic field can be measured and localized using extremely sensitive detectors. Electroencephalography (EEG) measures electrical changes on the scalp, and quantitative electroencephalography (qEEG) uses computer software to produce localization and connectivity information from multichannel EEG data.

All of these methods have their advantages and disadvantages. The fMRI technique's resolution is about a tenth of an inch, which is slightly better than PET and about three times more precise than SPECT techniques. The MEG technique is more precise still. The MEG temporal resolution is about 1ms, which is similar to that of an EEG and invasive measurement of electrical activity during brain surgery (IEEG). The spatial resolution of MEG is about 1 mm, which is finer than fMRI, but even more than EEG the MEG is currently limited to the kinds of surface neural activity that produce detectable magnetic fields outside the head. The fMRI approach has become the preferred method for brain mapping, but it is important to keep in mind that current fMRI scans cannot easily detect some parts of the brain, such as the anterior temporal lobe, which is probably important in high-level social activities and thus is relevant to RSEs. The qEEG technique is relatively new and looks promising for gaining both high temporal resolution and sound information about localization and connectivity. All of these approaches, including radioactive imaging, have important applications in various branches of neuromedicine.

Functional imaging of the brain during RSEs is not easy to arrange, and few types of experiences are suitable for studying in this way. After all, very few meditators can drop into a particular conscious state on demand, and it is impossible with current technology to measure the functional neural effects of a faith-healing ritual in anything like a natural way. Nevertheless, a number of excellent imaging studies in this area clearly demonstrate that RSEs have neural correlates.

For example, Richard Davidson's famous Laboratory for Affective Neuroscience at the University of Wisconsin-Madison has studied the effects of meditation on Tibetan Buddhist monks (see Davidson and Harrington 2001). Davidson's functional MRI studies have discovered that regions containing circuits associated with attention are activated in these patients for vast lengths of time compared to novice meditators. Nothing surprising there, obviously, but the point is that the subjective experience of preternatural concentration actually has a brain correlate, thus confirming the neural mediation hypothesis.

Mario Beauregard's neurological research at the University of Montreal has included fMRI studies of Carmelite nuns recalling intense experiences of deep prayer. The results show richly diverse activation of numerous brain areas rather than a uniquely important "God spot" in the brain (Beauregard and O'Leary 2007; Beauregard and Paquette 2006). Andrew Newberg of the University of Pennsylvania has conducted fMRI studies on Christians practicing glossolalia, or speaking in tongues (Newberg *et al.* 2006). Here, too, there are distinctive neural correlates for this experience. Newberg has also studied expert meditators using fMRI and SPECT equipment with results that both confirm Davidson's results about increased attention activity but also indicate a small reduction in metabolic activity in areas containing circuits associated with spatial orientation and localization (Newberg *et al.* 1997; Newberg *et al.* 2001a, 2001b; Newberg and Iverson 2003). Though this effect is very small, Newberg conjectures that this might correspond to the subjective reports of meditators who say that they lose the feeling of bodily boundaries and merge with their environment.

While these studies vary in robustness and also in the degree of controversy surrounding them, the main point is that there is a consistent pattern of support for the neural mediation hypothesis. That support strengthens with every new study.

Electrical activity evidence

Third, neuroscientists have used the EEG to measure the brain's electrical characteristics during RSEs. EEG scans have refined temporal resolution but (until the qEEG technique arrived) poor spatial resolution, so they are better at detecting frequencies of oscillating signals than at localizing those signals. The analysis of EEG recordings has given rise to names for characteristic electrical activity such as alpha, beta, gamma, delta, and theta rhythms, as well as the misleading popular terminology of "brain waves."

Neuroscientist Michael Persinger of Laurentian University has used EEG equipment to study the response of temporal-lobe epileptics to religious stimuli and also to study the temporal-lobe expressions of religious experiences (Persinger 1987, 1994a). The functional imaging studies mentioned above used EEG techniques in addition to fMRI and SPECT methods, detecting distinctive electrical patterns corresponding to the RSEs their subjects were undergoing. In fact, EEG has long been used in the study of meditation experiences, because many meditators can produce an increase in electrical signaling in the theta range (4–7 Hz), which the EEG can detect. Neuroscientist James Austin of the University of Colorado produced evidence that meditation practice sometimes takes advantage of neuroplasticity to produce long-term structural changes in the brain, partly on the basis of EEG evidence (see Austin 1998), though the long-term studies needed to confirm this are only now underway. Herbert Benson coined the phrase "relaxation response" to sum up the numerous bodily effects of some types of meditation with distinctive EEG signals (Benson 1975, 1996). Once again, there is ample evidence from such studies in support of the neural mediation hypothesis.

Localized lesion evidence

Fourth, neuroscientists have studied particular RSEs by observing people suffering from neurological conditions or brain lesions. For example, Patrick McNamara of Boston University, whose work we will revisit later, has studied the RSEs of people with Parkinson's disease (McNamara and Durso 2006; McNamara *et al.* 2003; McNamara *et al.* 2006). The fact that they undergo changes in their RSEs relative to pre-morbid measures shows that the circuits affected by Parkinson's disease are also implicated in the neural expression of RSEs.

Studies of temporal-lobe epileptics dating back several decades to the work of neuroscientists David Bear and Norman Geschwind have noted hyperreligiosity in some temporal-lobe epileptics, suggesting that the temporal lobes have a role to play in RSEs (Bear 1979; Bear and Fedio 1977; Bear *et al.* 1982; Geschwind 1979, 1983). More recently, neuroscientist Vilayanur Ramachandran studied such patients, showing that their condition produces strong emotional responses not just to arbitrary stimuli but specifically to religious stimuli (see Ramachandran 1997; Ramachandran and Blakeslee 1998). Once again, these studies offer strong support for the neural mediation hypothesis.

Neurochemical and genetic evidence

Fifth, neuroscientists have studied particular RSEs at the neurochemical and genetic levels. McNamara's research just mentioned links RSEs to the neurotransmitter dopamine because it is the dopamine-related circuits of the frontal lobe that are impaired in Parkinson's disease. Rick Strassman at the University of New Mexico, building on Hungarian psychiatrist Stephen Szára's work from the 1950s, injected subjects with externally synthesized dimethyltryptamine (DMT) to assess its role in brain functions (see Strassman 1996, 2001; Szára 1989). DMT is a serotonin-like psychoactive chemical naturally secreted in small amounts by the pineal gland at the base of the brain – yes, the same pineal gland that so fascinated Descartes. Strassman's subjects went through hallucinogenic RSEs, frequently including feelings of presences and something like near-death experiences. Though Strassman's interpretation of these results was extremely speculative, the point for our purposes is that this particular brain chemical appears to be correlated with some kinds of RSEs.

Heritability of a tendency to religiousness has been confirmed in some rigorous studies. For example, Laura Koenig and Thomas Bouchard's work in the Minnesota Twin Studies program showed that authority, conservatism, and religiousness tend to be jointly heritable to a significant degree (see Koenig and Bouchard 2006). Dean Hamer of the US National Cancer Institute went one step lower to the genetic level. He found a correlation between people who scored relatively high on a psychological test for the personality trait of self-transcendence and a variant form of the so-called VMAT2 gene (see Hamer 2004). The correlation was very weak and the study has not been replicated, but Hamer's work at least illustrates the possibilities for genetic study of RSEs that are starting to open up as the richness of data increases.

Direct experimental evidence

Sixth and finally, occasionally neuroscientists have even gained insight into the neural correlates of RSEs by means of direct brain stimulation during neurosurgery or indirect brain stimulation by means of magnetic fields. A number of neurosurgeons have reported that direct stimulation of a patient awake during brain surgery can produce RSEs; for example, stimulating some places in the parietal lobe supposedly sometimes produces a religiously tinged out-of-body experience. Persinger has used extra-cranial magnetic stimulation of the temporal lobes in an attempt to induce religious experiences, guided by his neurological model of those temporal-lobe epileptics who experience religiously potent hallucinations (see Persinger and Healey 2002). He reports that 80 percent of his subjects experience a sense of a presence with them, and some describe this as a religious experience. He even tried this on famous anti-religionist Richard Dawkins, but nothing happened so they concluded that Dawkins must be in the 20 percent who are immune to this effect. A second laboratory failed to reproduce Persinger's results (see Granqvist *et al.* 2005), triggering a controversy over experimental design (see Granqvist 2005; Persinger and Koren 2005). That has not stopped the marketing of Persinger-inspired helmets for home-based cultivation of spiritual experiences. There is even a published study comparing two such products, the Shakti and the Koren helmet (Tsang *et al.* 2004).

These six classes of evidence are representative of published studies and ongoing research on neural correlations of RSEs (see the authoritative survey in McNamara 2009). Collectively, they constitute overwhelming evidence in support of the neural mediation hypothesis – that is (in application to our target subject), RSEs are exhaustively expressed in and through the brain. In fact, this thesis is so well supported at this point that, if skeptics were to say that RSEs were not exhaustively mediated by the brain, the burden of proof would definitely be on them to explain what they could possibly mean. It follows that any philosophical interpretation of RSEs must be scrupulously consistent with the neural mediation hypothesis, and that is a non-trivial constraint.

PROBLEMS FACING THE NEUROSCIENCE OF RELIGIOUS AND SPIRITUAL EXPERIENCES

Many scholars have offered interpretations of the importance of the neurosciences for understanding RSEs (as a representative sampling, see Andresen 2001; Ashbrook 1984; Ashbrook and Albright 1997; Holmes 1993; McKinney 1994; Porush 1993; Teske 1996). But this wealth of research rarely includes direct neurological studies of RSEs. In fact, the most surprising aspect of neurological research into RSEs is that there is so little of it compared with research in other areas of neurology. Neuroscientist Richard Davidson, mentioned above, said in 2007 that scientifically rigorous publications on meditation neuroimaging number no more than twenty (see Redwood 2007). Meanwhile, there are thousands of neurological studies on vision and hearing. This is partly because of social realities. Neurologists are generally not taken seriously if they study religion, unless they have already made their reputation in another area, as Davidson has. The same used to be true of sex research within the field of psychology. In both cases, colleagues are most comfortable trusting research results when they are confident that the researcher in question will not fall prey to special interests, and apparently most people assume that everyone is vulnerable to failures of impartiality around sex and religion.

The deepest reason for the scarcity of such research is conceptual. To explain this, I shall discuss five perplexing methodological challenges facing the neurological study of RSEs. I shall call them (roughly in order of increasing difficulty) the complexity, modularity, reporting, evolution, and semantic problems. After saying a word about each, I shall describe how cutting-edge methods promise to ameliorate these problems to some degree and open up RSEs, along with their causes and effects, to cognitive and neural modeling (see Wildman and McNamara 2008 for greater detail).

The complexity problem

The diversity and complexity of religious and spiritual behaviors, beliefs, and experiences implicates virtually every aspect of brain function. That makes religiousness and spirituality awkward objects for neurological study. Unsurprisingly, investigators often focus on a single paradigmatic religious practice, belief, or experience. But this simplification strategy generates its own problems.

For example, conclusions drawn from functional imaging of meditators (such as Azari *et al.* 2001; Beauregard and O'Leary 2007; Beauregard and Paquette 2006; d'Aquili and Newberg 1993, 1998; Davidson and Harrington 2001; Newberg and Iverson 2003; Newberg *et al.* 1997, 2001a, 2001b, 2006) cannot safely be generalized to the entire suite of religious and spiritual phenomena. Such research is necessary and valuable but it is almost irrelevant to the full range of religious and spiritual behaviors, beliefs, and experiences in ordinary, untrained people, including even those who meditate or pray regularly but are not experts. Again, the study of religiousness in a subgroup of temporal-lobe epileptics establishes a link between one particular brain region and hyperreligiosity associated with interictal personality disorder (Bear 1979; Bear and Fedio 1977; Bear *et al.* 1982; Dewhurst and Beard 1970; Geschwind 1979, 1983). But this link says little about these phenomena in other populations, or about other RSEs.

In short, most existing neurological research says less than everyone would like about the whole range of religious and spiritual behaviors, beliefs, and experiences. Researchers need to overcome the tendency to exaggerate claims about the religious relevance of a particular neurological finding, because many people fall prey to sensationalized reports. Interpreters should avoid treating religious and spiritual behaviors, beliefs, and experiences as if they had a uniquely identifiable essence. And they should definitely avoid suggesting that this fictitious essence is somehow captured in the latest neurological discovery.

The modularity problem

The modular theory of brain organization and function (Fodor 1983; but see qualifications of his earlier view in Fodor 2000) asserts that the brain consists of interconnected modules, each with a distinctive function. Modularity plays a crucial role in theories of brain evolution because it allows for the possibility that, say, the vision module and the reasoning module might have been exposed to selection pressures relatively independently and simultaneously. The modularity thesis is also needed for brain localization studies because it links brain anatomy with brain function in a way that partially compensates for the coarseness of lesion-correlation techniques and existing imaging technologies.

Unfortunately, the modularity hypothesis does not always serve us well. There is slender basis for assigning an interesting phenomenological feature of an experience to one function in one brain region. The classic example of such hasty associations is talk of a God part of the brain (Alper 2001; and see the discussion in Ramachandran and Blakeslee 1998) – as if all religious people are interested in God, and as if the neural embedding of the vast variety of RSEs can be localized in a single brain region. Neither premise is remotely sound.

Equally importantly, the modular theory of the brain itself is seriously flawed. There is neurological structure and specialization of function, to be sure; functional imaging clearly establishes that for focused, isolable activities. But there are also overlaps of different functions in any given region, and all functions operate within an overarching integrating process of global electrochemical signaling. The neural representation of a state of consciousness with any degree of cognitive or behavioral richness is extraordinarily complex, so we need to approach functional imaging studies of RSEs that presuppose the modular theory of brain organization with appropriate caution.

The reporting problem

A far-reaching challenge that has thwarted rapid advance in the neurological study of RSEs is the inevitable reliance on subjective reporting. Many battles over this have already been fought in the methodological literature of consciousness studies, with behaviorists resisting introspection and subjective reporting (Skinner 1974; Watson 1913; Watson and McDougall 1929), and phenomenologists of various stripes eventually reasserting the value of such modes of data collection (see Kukla 1983; Lieberman 1979; Pekala 1991; Revonsuo 2006).

The problem is not so much the possibility of deliberate deception by subjects; this can be minimized through careful experimental design. Rather, there is the problem that subjective reports are unlikely to reflect accurately all of the factors relevant to a state of consciousness, particularly when research turns on subtle details such as the order of conscious processing. There is the problem of interference, whereby the experimental subject's report materially alters the state of consciousness under study. The problem of selection bias occurs when the experimental subject unintentionally emphasizes particular aspects of a state of consciousness in order to answer a question framed in a particular way or to please the questioner. There is the problem that intense conversion experiences can distort a subject's impressions of why they hold the beliefs they do. There is the problem that people can describe phenomenologically or neurologically similar experiences in quite different ways. The energy problem arises when subjects mention aspects of experience that are easy to describe and suppress aspects that require a large investment of energy and skill to explain. Moreover, experimental attempts to abstract particular states of consciousness from their natural contexts might effectively destroy some of their salient features. For example, remembering is not the same as directly experiencing, both because of its second-order character, and because of the selective processing involved in memory recording.

No wonder the behaviorists were so opposed to relying on subjective reports of states of consciousness. But perhaps there are ways of making use of subjective reports despite the difficulties involved.

The evolution problem

Evolutionary psychology and cognitive science have jointly sponsored some of the most notable and controversial interpretations of RSEs in recent years (for example, see Atran 2002, 2004; Boyer 2001; Dawkins

2006; Dennett 2006). The promise of the evolutionary framework for understanding the emergence of human brain functions, including those associated with RSEs, is superficially obvious. Knowing how humans developed the neural capacities for varied religious and spiritual phenomena is supposed to help us understand, predict, regulate, and evaluate such phenomena. This is correct, as far as it goes. But the evolutionary interpretation of RSEs is filled with uncertainty and conflict. There are at least two reasons for this.

First, researchers need to be able to assume that similar reports correspond to similar underlying neural processes (see the reporting and semantic problems). But it seems quite possible that individuals may offer similar reports of experiences that are neurologically quite different, and quite different reports of neurologically similar experiences. Indeed, this is likely given neural plasticity, cultural conditioning, and individual variations. A great deal of work is required to support the assumption of species-wide neural mechanisms for producing a suite of RSEs, and it is not always clear how to get such work done.

Second, researchers want to identify the functions of RSEs. That crucially depends on interpreting them in evolutionary terms because the evolutionary framework shows which experiential capacities are adaptive in which settings, which are side-effects of adapted traits, how changing environments might make maladaptive some functions that spring from traits that were adaptive in another context, and so on. This understanding is vital for assessing the negative and positive value of RSEs, but it is difficult to achieve because it involves knowledge of past eras that we cannot inspect but can only imagine.

These two reasons for conflict within the evolutionary interpretation of RSEs show both that the evolutionary framework is crucial and that it is difficult adequately to construct.

The semantic problem

Access to the contents of consciousness is, at least initially, at the semantic level of concepts and meanings. Yet the neural embedding of RSEs is at the level of brain regions, neurotransmitter functions, and specific neurological processes. What is the relationship between the semantic level of reporting and the neural level of brain functions?

This vast problem is well known because it is so obvious. Yet its intractability constitutes a systematic weakness in this area of neurological study. Researchers have to contend with individual differences in neural-semantic network mapping, with neural plasticity and the effects of training, and with the possibility of multiple neural realizations of phenomenologically similar conscious states within a single person. More than anywhere, this is where a breakthrough is needed in the neurological study of consciousness in general, and of RSEs in particular.

CREATIVE RESPONSES

Advancing on the complexity and reporting challenges

There is no silver-bullet solution to these five methodological challenges, but there is no shortage of creative responses, from both psychology of religion and the cognitive neurosciences.

Consider the plethora of tests and measures related to religious belief, behavior, and experience. For example, a significant portion of the 124 instruments in Hill and Hood's collection of *Measures of Religiosity* (1999) are at least indirectly relevant to RSEs. A few focus specifically on RSEs, especially the Christian Experience Inventory (Alter 1999), the Religious Experience Questionnaire (Edwards 1999), the Religious Experience Episodes Measure (Hood and Rosegrant 1999), the Word–Spirit Orientation Scale (Hsieh 1999), the Index of Core Spiritual Experiences (Kris *et al.* 1999), the Mysticism Scale (Hood 1999), and the Nearness to God Scale (Gorsuch and Smith 1999). A number of other instruments have been created more recently to study RSEs. And some instruments not devised specifically to study RSEs have proved valuable as well, such as the Peak Experiences Scale (Mathes *et al.* 1982). There has been an average increase in sophistication in these measurement devices as researchers gradually became aware of and subsequently tried to overcome simplistic assumptions about RSEs deriving from theistic and usually Christian religious and theological frameworks. Two instruments illustrate the advances that empirical psychology of religion can make on some of the methodological challenges described above. Both have appeared since the Hill and Hood collection was published in 1999.

The Fetzer Institute and National Institute on Aging collaborated to produce a multidimensional measure of religiousness and spirituality (Fetzer 1999), building on and correcting many earlier attempts at multidimensional religiosity scales (see Hill and Hood 1999: 269–342). This achievement represented a major advance in relation to the *complexity problem* by acknowledging that religiousness, and also RSEs, cannot be fitted into a single, simple model; rather, models need to be flexible enough to comprehend simultaneously a number of diverse dimensions. The twelve dimensions highlighted in the Fetzer instrument are daily spiritual experiences, meaning, values, beliefs, forgiveness, private religious practices, religious and spiritual coping, religious support, religious and spiritual history, commitment, organizational religiousness, and religious preference. This list of dimensions by itself serves as a sharp reminder of the diversity and complexity of RSEs, as well as the prima facie unlikelihood that every kind of RSE could possibly have a unique and universal neural signature. The Fetzer instrument became important almost immediately because of the correction to existing habits within the field that it represents.

A similarly important advance, in this case especially on the reporting problem, appears in the work of Xinzhong Yao and Paul Badham of the Religious Experience Research Centre, Lampeter, part of the Sir Alister Hardy Trust. The survey instrument used in their study of religiousness among the Han Chinese was properly adapted to the Chinese setting. It emphasized RSEs in several modes, such as experiences of power, changes in life understandings and life ways, dreams, mysterious feelings, mysterious events, and mergers of the individual with the universe. Such categories are crucial in the Chinese setting but do not usually appear in Western instruments, which are typically theistic in orientation. This intelligent and flexible instrument is now inspiring the comparison of RSEs across cultures (see Yao and Badham 2007).

The key to the success of cross-cultural inquiries that directly confront the reporting problem is intimated in Yao and Badham's work, and also in the Hardy Institute's typology of RSEs (Hardy 1979) on which they partially rely: we require categories that are as free of ideological and cultural bias as possible. This is not a simple goal. We can move toward it by avoiding categories that are obviously culturally or theologically laden, as was common in the early study of mystical experiences – and indeed remains common thanks to the fact that many instruments employed to study RSEs unselfconsciously refer to God or presume a particular idea of God (say, a personal being) as normative. Rather, we should look for categorizations that are as neurologically basic as we can construct. This involves focusing on culturally universal features such as sensory elements, basic cognitions, triggering factors, relational elements, dreams, and universal aspects of sociality – relatively stable features that are evolutionarily ancient and extremely widespread in the human species.

These two examples show how the *complexity* and *reporting* problems are proving tractable within the psychology of religion. Despite difficulties in moving from translation to interpretation, there is promise here of advancing on questions such as what kinds of RSEs occur across cultures, with what frequency, and under what descriptions. In relation to the other three methodological challenges – the modularity, evolution, and semantic problems – approaches from the psychology of religion are less immediately effective. But other forces are at work on these fronts.

Advancing on the modularity, evolution, and semantic challenges

The increasing sophistication of neurological scanning studies is a mixed blessing for addressing the *modularity* problem. While such studies are forced to presuppose a strongly modular model of the brain, they are increasingly interpreted in relation to expanding knowledge of neurotransmitter systems and with the aid of cognitive and neural modeling techniques. Unfortunately, cognitive modeling and neural modeling has barely begun for RSEs, so research remains very much in thrall to the modularity paradigm. Neurological research in numerous more specific brain systems – from vision to language, and from movement to dreaming – shows the way forward: use neural correlates to produce testable cognitive models and eventually specific neural models.

Numerous disciplines are making advances on the *evolution* problem. One fruitful approach involves comparing brains across species, especially human and other hominid species, and then correlating information about brain shape and size with what primate studies and paleoanthropology reveal about the behavior of other species. For example, when paleoanthropologists discover that Neanderthals apparently buried their dead with provisions and tools, they naturally assume that at least some Neanderthal brains were complex enough to support existential questions about the meaning of death, and in particular to imagine the continuation of life into another realm where provisions and tools might be needed. From the shape of Neanderthal skulls relative to their evolutionary ancestors who seem not to have intentionally buried their dead or supplied them with provisions, neurologists can draw inferences about the parts of the brain that appear to have evolved in such a way as to make this kind of Neanderthal behavior possible. And from dating these grave sites – undisputed instances date to 100,000 years ago, with more questionable examples from 300,000 years ago (see Klein 2002; Lieberman 1991) – paleoanthropologists can estimate when these neurological capacities might have arrived. This approach calls for an extraordinarily complicated process of aligning data from numerous disciplines and the generation of hypotheses that can be corrected by the incomplete data that exist.

Another approach to the evolution problem in relation to RSEs involves correlating theories from anthropology and evolutionary psychology about human religious behavior. Yet another involves correlating theories of language evolution with theories about the relationship between language and religion. It is also possible to unite game-theoretic models of costly signaling and reciprocity with theories of the evolution of cognition to explain how RSEs may have increased fitness under certain cultural circumstances. In short, the array of approaches is as large as the challenge is daunting (for an overview, see McNamara 2006a, 2006b, 2006c; I will return to this subject in Chapter 6).

The *semantic* problem appears to be the most intractable of the five challenges. There is a vast chasm between knowledge of experiences and meanings and knowledge of their neural representations. But the situation is not hopeless. In fact, the semantic problem is not appreciably more difficult in the case of RSEs than in the case of any other sort of human experience. Most neuroscience research with living subjects has to grapple with the linkage between the semantic network of reports of states of consciousness and the neural network of brain systems. The scale of the challenge is reasonably clear and the methods for making progress are fairly well understood. The key is the generation and testing of cognitive and neural models.

Advance in neural modeling is fastest when the neural systems under study do not require subject reports, as in autonomic nervous system processes that humans share with many animals. It is next most convenient when the neural systems can be abstracted from the fact that we find out about subjects' experiences through what they say. This happens in the case of sensory experience, where subject reports are used to gather information about what is heard or smelled or seen or felt or tasted, but those reports are not included in the modeled neural processes. Significantly more challenging is emotion research, where the actual content of reports of emotions felt is central to the research. In this case, however, researchers can often check the validity of reports with reference to subject behavior because emotion and behavior are often closely linked. The most difficult situation is when subject reports contain conceptually and emotionally loaded interpretations of complex experiences, which is the case in RSEs. This multiplies the number of factors that might condition such reports to the point where cognitive and neural modeling becomes extremely and possibly overwhelmingly complex. Let us consider this challenge in more detail.

A semantic network has meanings for nodes and relations between meanings for network links. Each meaning node in the semantic network corresponds to a particular activation pattern – understood as a short-term process – in the neural network. Each link between nodes in the semantic network corresponds to a causal relationship between activation patterns in the neural network. Mapping the semantic network gives access to relevant functional properties of the neural network, even if the details of the neural network's physical structure remain out of reach. Thus, narrative information about an experience is separated from neural correlate information by at least two steps. (1) Narratives are substructures within the semantic network, drawing in memory, emotion, and conceptual resources already established, as well as creativity and artistry in expression. (2) The semantic network has the systemic relationship to the neural network just described. But this is exactly what we should expect. Any simple association of a specific brain location with a semantically loaded feature of RSEs such as a narrative would not make sense. RSEs are at least as likely to be associated with high-level properties of the semantic network (say, approximation to scale-free network geometry) as with the presence of particular nodes in the semantic network (say, the node for "God"). After all, geometric network properties are universal in the human species, whereas the particular nodes in any given brain's semantic network are highly dependent on culture and experience.

Cognitive and neural models of RSEs simply have to manage this multilayered complexity. They will do so typically by breaking the problem down into component pieces, as when a single neural correlate is discovered for a particular kind of religious experience. When enough relevant components exist, researchers can put the pieces together into a testable cognitive model that helps to bridge the chasm between the semantic and neural networks. From there, it may be possible to produce neural models of particular types of RSEs that approach the sophistication of existing neural models for other brain capabilities. Research is currently far from the goal of working cognitive and neural models of even one kind of religious experience, let alone RSEs in general.

The most elaborate attempt at a cognitive model of a subset of RSEs is that of neurophysiologist Andrew Newberg, drawing on the fundamental ideas about myth and ritual developed by psychiatrist Eugene d'Aquili (see d'Aquili 1972, 1975, 1978, 1983, 1993; d'Aquili and Laughlin 1979; d'Aquili and Newberg 1993, 1999, 2000; Newberg and d'Aquili 1994, 2000; Newberg and Iversen 2003; Newberg *et al.* 1997, 2001a, 2001b, 2006). Newberg's work is popularly known for the theory mentioned above about a proposed neural correlate for the experience of merging with the surrounding world reported by some meditators (see Newberg *et al.* 2001b: 1–10). But the long-term importance of his research is related to the cognitive and neural model for RSEs deriving from such merger experiences, a model that he proposed with d'Aquili and has since elaborated (see Newberg 2006, 2009).

There are experiences of meditation in which the customarily sharp sense of self gradually becomes less and less distinct, as a feeling of unity with all of being steadily arises. While it lasts, such an experience is existentially potent and ontologically compelling, producing new behaviors and unshakable beliefs in a world of unity and power beneath the surface of the world of ordinary experience. Experience of this supposed other world produces confidence that it has resources to help us manage our lives in ordinary life. Newberg believes such experiences occur not only through intentional meditation practices but also through corporate ritual practices and even through solitary experiences of focused attention. His moving example of the latter is the desperate deer hunter who is so focused on finding food for his family and friends and so hungry and anxious that he accidentally produces the conditions for such an experience in the course of the hunt, feeling the presence of the Great Stag and believing that it leads him to what he needs (see Newberg *et al.* 2001b, 134–38). Newberg links up the neural capacity for this sort of experience, which he thinks derives evolutionarily from the co-opting of sexual arousal circuitry, with the social significance of such experiences, which includes calming and reassuring people and giving them a feeling that they can control their dangerous environment through marshalling powers from the world beyond. In this way, amazingly enough, Newberg extends his theory about a neural correlate for one apparently exceptional meditation experience into a full-blown theory of religion. And the key is a cognitive-neural model that links up the neural production of a particular experience with the diverse ways such an experience might be expressed in particular cultural settings.

While it is vital to remember that religious and spiritual experience is enormously more complex and varied than Newberg's model of it suggests, it is also important to appreciate the example he sets. It is by developing cognitive and neural models in this way, hopefully drawing on a richer base of neural correlation data, that we advance on the semantic problem and gain the deepest insights into the causes and effects of RSEs. Producing these models is the basic breakthrough needed to place the neurological study of RSEs on the same rigorous and systematic footing that the neurological study of many other human brain capacities enjoys.

Quantitative signatures of extended states of consciousness

In recent work, neuroscientist Patrick McNamara and I have developed an approach to the neurological study of RSEs that addresses all five of the methodological challenges in a distinctive way. Our ultimate aim is to produce cognitive and neural models of at least some kinds of RSEs – models capable of guiding future neurological research and shedding light on both the production and effects of RSEs. I shall devote the balance of this chapter to explaining our approach and how it represents a modest advance on the five challenges I have described.

If we wanted to produce frequency statistics for a variety of RSEs – an important question whose answer should eventually yield constraints on cognitive and neural modeling efforts – we would use the Yao and Badham instrument discussed above, or something more detailed that picks up on more of Hardy's typology of RSEs. If we were focused on the functional meaning and value of RSEs, particularly in relation to their health effects – again, an important issue eventually capable of constraining cognitive and neural modeling of RSEs – we would use the Fetzer instrument discussed above, or a modified version that takes account of other effects of RSEs such as economic practices, political preferences, and interpersonal relationships, not just health effects.

Neither these instruments nor other existing methods are well suited to producing cognitive and neural models of RSEs with the requisite complexity, even if they prove useful for identifying constraints on such a model once it exists. While it is premature to produce full-blown cognitive models, let alone neural models, of RSEs, it is possible to prepare for that task by identifying the basic cognitive and neural component processes in RSEs – surely there are many more of these than Newberg deploys in his model. The complexity and diversity of these experiences arguably calls for a rather complex array of component cognitive and neural processes, organized in quite different ways depending on the type of experience in question. How should we handle this?

It would be ideal to identify such core features as exist within the diversity of RSEs, and concentrate on discovering the component cognitive and neural processes of those core features. This would require guarding against over-generalization, because the full diversity of RSEs may have no core features, but only family-resemblance relationships.

Indeed, virtually all attempts to identify the "core" of RSEs – Newberg's model is one but there are others with less neurological specificity – have dramatically narrowed the full range of RSEs without due notice, which has resulted in the neglect of everyday religious experiences as well as some uncommon experiences. This danger notwithstanding, significant subclasses of RSEs may prove to have core features that are susceptible to analysis in terms of component neurological processes. I suspect that one such class is the intense RSEs, which will be discussed extensively in later chapters.

The tools needed to identify a suite of component neurological processes for stocking cognitive and neural models of RSEs should use mid-level neurological features as basic categories – features that are as close as possible to basic neurological processes that play key roles in cognitive and neural modeling efforts while still remaining linked to phenomenological features of experience that surface in reports of RSEs. Existing component-based analytical tools for the study of RSEs do not meet this criterion. In fact, the analytical components in existing tools are relatively high level, as befits the rather different interests of the psychology of religion as compared with the neurosciences. That is, each high-level component involves a complex assembly of numerous neural processes, so the components prove to be more useful for psychological analysis of meanings and behaviors than for cognitive and neural modeling. For example, the twelve component categories of the Fetzer (1999) instrument – to recall: daily spiritual experiences, meaning, values, beliefs, forgiveness, private religious practices, religious and spiritual coping, religious support, religious and spiritual history, commitment, organizational religiousness, and religious preference – all appear to have neural realizations at a much higher level in the brain architecture than is ideal for the purposes of cognitive and neural modeling. Evidently, another approach is needed.

Our approach attempts to fill this need by quantifying the formal features of a large class of RSEs, as well as specific subclasses, using as analytical components a variety of phenomenological characteristics that are neurologically as basic and universal as possible, while still being relevant and intelligible to test subjects so that survey instruments remain applicable. Analyzing formal features of RSEs discloses which phenomenological components combine in which proportions to produce a particular type of experience. This constrains cognitive modeling efforts, because cognitive models must explain how the cognitive system produces each particular experience with its specific structural features.

Cognitive models that could be built from or constrained by such basic phenomenological components are mid-level beasts. Their components are closer to neural structures than most psychological categories but they are not as close to neural structures as the component elements used in standard neural models. But this middle level is the right place to exert effort at the present time. Once we identify the components for cognitive models, we can learn how to translate both upwards to more familiar high-level psychological categories, and downwards to neural processes as relevant neural correlates become available.

We proceed with test subjects as follows. We ask test subjects to recall a religious or spiritual experience as well as experiences that serve as a baseline for comparison. Using questionnaire tools, we analyze the reported experiences into elementary phenomenological components, measuring the relative strength of each component. This yields a multidimensional *quantitative signature*, where each dimension corresponds to what appears to be a species-wide capacity of human beings. When we compare quantitative signatures for different kinds of RSEs and different kinds of baseline experiences in a single person, the quantitative signatures often display clear variations. Going further, we also notice consistent patterns of variation across individuals, thereby producing individual-transcending quantitative signatures for particular states of consciousness. We call one of these a *general quantitative signature* (GQS). To imagine examples we have not tested, deep grief may produce more or less the same GQS for most people who experience it, and the same might be true of ironic enjoyment, peaceful prayer, high stress, or loyalty under pressure. A GQS is meaningful when the variances in at least some dimensions of the underlying data set are relatively small, suggesting that people experience the phenomenological properties of the experience in question in similar ways. In general, some components of the multidimensional GQS will have tight variances, and the averages for those components will be particularly salient, whereas other components will have loose variances, and their means will be relatively uninformative about the qualities of the underlying experience.

What tools can help us produce useful GQS data? The right class of instruments for our purposes is retrospective phenomenological analysis instruments – that is, surveys that ask participants to recall an experience and answer questions about their state of mind at the time of that experience. Subject answers enable a quantitative breakdown of the reported experience into the right kind of relatively low-level analytical components. There are other ways of quantifying RSEs; for example, linguistic analysis of narratives produces a higher-level description of the content of RSEs. But retrospective phenomenological analysis instruments are particularly apt for our purposes because they furnish access to basic phenomenological properties of experiences that should correspond to (roughly) mid-level neurological processes – at least at a significantly lower level than familiar psychological instruments, and at a level low enough to permit basic cognitive modeling, even if not yet sufficiently low-level to permit neural modeling. We are currently developing a retrospective phenomenological analysis instrument that focuses specifically on the phenomenological features and underlying neurological processes that are most relevant for understanding the formal structure, the causes, and the effects of RSEs. In the meantime, we have found existing retrospective phenomenological analysis instruments quite serviceable for generating preliminary GQS data for RSEs.

Why use the gentle approach of a retrospective instrument, prompting for memories, when more intrusive methods are available? After all, it is possible to induce some types of experience using sensory deprivation techniques, virtual reality environments, and pharmacological methods. All of these approaches give the experimenter more control over the type of experience that the participant undergoes, but the price can be high. The more vigorous the attempt to induce a religious or spiritual experience, the more artificial the experience will be and the more morally questionable the experiment. We do not want accidentally to convert or traumatize someone during an experiment. There is a lot to be said for the ecological validity of memories of actual experiences with genuine existential significance for those who have them, especially because it is the way experiences are remembered that most closely expresses their ongoing existential importance and behavioral effects.

The retrospective phenomenological analysis instrument we have used in pilot studies is the Phenomenology of Consciousness Inventory (PCI), which was developed by Ron Pekala and his associates (see Pekala 1991). The PCI has been used for many consciousness-related studies, including hypnotic susceptibility, out-of-body experiences, eating disorders, shamanic states, drumming, creativity, phobias, depression, anti-social feelings, kleptomania, epilepsy, and meditation (see Angelini *et al.* 1999; Forbes and Pekala 1993; Grant 2004; Hand *et al.* 1995; Huang *et al.* 2000; Hutchinson-Phillips *et al.* 2005; Johanson *et al.* 2008; Kumar and Pekala 1988, 1989; Kumar *et al.* 1996a, 1996b; Maitz and Pekala 1991; Manmiller *et al.* 2005; Maurer *et al.* 1997; McCloskey *et al.* 1999; Pekala 1995a, 1995b, 2002; Pekala and Forbes 1997; Pekala and Kumar 1984, 1987, 1988, 1989;

Pekala and Nagler 1989; Pekala and Steinberg 1986; Pekala *et al.* 1989, 2006; Rock *et al.* 2008; Spinhoven *et al.* 1993; Szabó 1993; Vanderlinden 1995; Varga 2001; Venkatesh 1997).

The PCI gives a quantitative profile of the contents and qualities of personal consciousness along twenty-six measures, grouped into twelve major dimensions. The twelve major dimensions are positive affect, negative affect, altered experience, imagery, attention, self-awareness, altered state of awareness, internal dialogue, rationality, volitional control, memory, and arousal. Again, note that these categories are mid-level: they are significantly lower in cognitive and neurological complexity than those in the Fetzer (1999) instrument, but not yet ideally close to distinct neural processes; and note that each is still meaningful to test subjects. Thus, this tool meets the basic criterion discussed above. In graphical terms, a quantitative signature produced using the PCI is a bar graph with twelve (or twenty-six) vertical bars extending from a baseline of zero up to a maximum. A quantitative signature can also be depicted in a radar graph, with each dimension along a radius having zero at the center and the maximum at the outer edge. A GQS is an average of such quantitative signatures and has the same geometric features.

The question, of course, is whether a distinctive GQS emerges when the PCI or another retrospective analysis instrument is applied to RSEs. In a pilot study with thirty-nine volunteers using the PCI, McNamara and I discovered that religious experiences do indeed have a distinctive GQS regardless of other modalities of the experience (Wildman and McNamara 2010). Our study participants rated religious experiences as significantly more meaningful than a control group of ordinary experiences, with stronger altered states of awareness, increased inwardness of attention, higher amounts of imagery, more internal dialogue, and lower levels of volitional control. Religious experiences also registered higher in negative affect and lower in positive affect than ordinary experiences, though on the whole they still tended to be welcome and emotionally enjoyable experiences. Other dimensions did not vary significantly from baseline measures.

This is useful information for developing and testing cognitive models of RSEs, and far more useful for this purpose than the higher-level instruments typically used in the study of RSEs. We also found that the GQS for RSEs varied significantly for demographic variables such as sex and handedness. Given that a lot is known about the neurocognition of sex and handedness, these sorts of links to RSEs are assets when approaching cognitive and neural modeling tasks. Furthermore, we discovered that certain subclasses of RSEs display significantly different GQS data, from which it follows that this approach has the capacity to handle at least some of the diversity of RSEs.

Alarmingly, when an expert scorer of RSE narratives produced GQS data for comparison with the GQS data from our subjects, we discovered that a lot of salient information about the phenomenological qualities of RSEs drops out when people narrate them. This calls into question the adequacy of narrative-based approaches to analyzing the phenomenological properties of RSEs, which has been the dominant approach within the phenomenology of religion in the past. The GQS approach is far superior for this purpose, though narrative analysis is still indispensable if approached with due caution and in full awareness of its limitations.

Of course, some RSEs may not produce a distinctive GQS. In such a case, we are led to ponder whether we are asking the right questions for detecting a GQS, or whether there is no individual-transcending neural basis for a GQS in that instance. Hopefully, a tool better adapted to the study of RSEs than the PCI will prove sensitive enough to avoid this situation.

The practical importance of general quantitative signatures

The GQS is a powerful tool for the study of RSEs. What can we do with it? Also, what can we do with the cognitive models that might be built from its component analytical categories? In what follows, I illustrate how the GQS approach helps to advance on each of the five challenges facing the neurological study of RSEs discussed above.

First, in relation to the *complexity* problem, as we have seen, it is extremely difficult to register the full range of RSEs and the exquisitely personal and contextual features of religious behavior and belief. Despite their usefulness for many purposes, vague categories such as spirituality, religiosity, and self-transcendence often fail to register the salient features of RSEs. Multidimensional scales for measuring religiosity such as the Fetzer (1999) instrument help with this problem to some degree, but not in a way that casts much light specifically on RSEs. By contrast, the GQS technique is of little use for religiosity in general and well suited to generating stable discriminations among specific subtypes of RSEs.

To appreciate this contrast, consider that most multidimensional scales of religiosity, which are the best tools for registering the complexity of religious behaviors, beliefs, and experiences, include a dimension for religious experience (for example, in addition to Fetzer 1999, see Boan

1999; Cornwall *et al.* 1999; DeJong *et al.* 1999; Faulkner and DeJong 1999; Glock and Stark 1999; King and Hunt 1999; Lenski 1999; Rohrbaugh and Jessor 1999). But none of these scales is capable of discriminating a variety of types of religious experience, and most simply seek to measure the strength of the one type of most interest to the survey designer. Even scales designed specifically for studying RSEs (discussed above), quite apart from often being culturally limited, do not have the internal structure necessary to discriminate types of RSEs. The Yao and Badham (2007) survey is better placed in this regard, allowing the discrimination of six broad types of RSEs.

The GQS approach is subtle by comparison with such blunt instruments. It asks how each phenomenological component (such as the amount and vividness of imagery) varies among people and experiences. In this way, it is possible to use the GQS approach to compare systems of descriptive categories, locating overlaps and redundancies, and giving the key descriptive elements robust definitions in terms of GQS data that may be able to survive translation across cultures. The result, which is still a long way off, should be the holy grail of a reliable and neurocognitively linked toolbox for describing and discriminating RSEs. The GQS approach can do this much better than approaches using higher-level analytical components.

Second, the GQS approach can indirectly help address the *modularity* problem, in two ways. On the one hand, GQS data can help to locate neural correlates for specific aspects and types of RSEs. In our pilot studies, for example, we discovered that patients with Parkinson's disease have a different GQS for religious experiences from our healthy control group, with significantly decreased meaningfulness, physical arousal, and internal dialogue, and significantly greater volitional control. The sample size is too small to draw firm conclusions but the data certainly suggest that the dopamine system of the frontal lobes has a powerful impact on the dimensions of consciousness that figure most strongly in generic religious experiences. Identifying such neural correlates properly complicates the perception of the roles of brain regions and neurotransmitter systems. On the other hand, the GQS approach generates the analytical categories that are the raw material for and primary constraints on cognitive models. These mid-level cognitive models in turn should yield increasingly detailed neural models of RSEs at some point in the future, which ultimately is the most effective way to manage the modularity problem.

Third, the GQS approach directly addresses the *reporting* problem in a distinctive way that complements the advances made in these directions by the research tools described above. Because it is so difficult to tell whether two people are having the same type of experience, we now have a proliferation of categorizations and analyses of RSEs – the resulting phenomenological jungle is the theme of the next chapter. At this point, we do not have an effective way of combining these many categorizations into a standard set of descriptive categories for describing RSEs. The use of GQS data can change this, eventually. A reasonable conjecture is that a persistent GQS reflects distinctive activation patterns in the brain's neural network that correspond to recognizably similar narratives constructed within the semantic network. Only cognitive modeling and eventually neural modeling of RSEs can confirm this, but it is a hypotheses possessing considerable initial plausibility.

Understood in this way, the GQS approach can penetrate to some degree beneath the vagaries of subjective reports to identify types of RSEs based on quantitative signatures, and to some extent independently of a subject's own way of naming such experiences, which our research indicates is more reliable in some dimensions of experience than in others. We have yet to test this across languages but our pilot studies have involved testing across fundamental worldview and cultural differences among subjects living in the United States. The results lend weight to the hypothesis that GQS data can detect similarity of experiences at the phenomenological component level, despite differences in description and naming. Thus, this approach promises to complement existing cross-cultural approaches such as that of Yao and Badham (2007).

Fourth, the GQS approach helps with the *evolution* problem. This happens first and foremost by generating cognitive and neural models that cast light on the species-wide neurological features of the human brain that are relevant to RSEs. These models make reference to brain processes whose evolutionary development is already understood, and the study of RSEs is able to capitalize on this existing work.

It is also possible to use GQS data to test opposed hypotheses about the evolutionary origins of RSEs. Consider the relation between what people are willing to call religious and what they are willing to call subjectivity intense (note that this has something to do with the specifically delineated theme of intensity to be discussed in later chapters but is not precisely the same concept). On the one hand, we might suspect that (i) qualitatively intense experiences are evolutionarily fundamental, and so conjecture that the GQS for intensity should appear in quantitative measures of intense experiences of all kinds, whether or not they are RSEs, and (ii) any specifically religiousness-related GQS will be subordinate to the intensity GQS. On the other hand, we might suspect that religiousness is evolutionary fundamental, and so conjecture that (i) the GQS for one or more types of religiousness will be dominant, and (ii) the intensity GQS subordinate. If one of these conjectures turns out to be correct and the other mistaken, this would have important implications for interpreting RSEs in an evolutionary framework. In fact, our pilot studies returned a mixed result on this question, which appears to rule out both of the simple hypotheses sketched above and points to a more complicated story about the evolution of RSEs. In this way, we see GQS data functioning as a constraint on evolutionary theorizing.

Finally, the GQS approach advances on the difficult *semantic* problem, albeit in a modest way, by clarifying the relevant components of cognitive models, and thereby ultimately helping to construct neural models of RSEs. It may never be fully possible to translate between the semantic meanings and the neural expressions of human mental life. But any advance in this direction promises a great payoff. To express it coarsely, whereas ideas affect the brain via the semantic network, ingested substances and diseases and medicines and Shakti devices know nothing of ideas and affect the brain through the neural network. Because every cognitive experience involves both neurons and meanings, every cognitive experience is potentially vulnerable to modification, stimulation, and inhibition by means of *both* the neural and the semantic networks. We advance our understanding when GQS techniques help us conclude that the dopamine system in the frontal lobes is important not for RSEs, *unqualified*, but specifically for expressing certain aspects of RSEs, particularly meaningfulness, physical arousal, internal dialogue, and volitional control – and these are features of narratives built from the resources in the semantic network. This is a modest but genuine advance on the semantic problem. The GQS approach has the potential to increase precision in this way across the whole sweep of the neurological study of RSEs.

CONCLUSION

This tour of spirituality and the brain leads to at least the following four conclusions. First, the neural mediation hypothesis appears to be extremely well supported. Second, new methods such as generalized quantitative signatures are vital for stabilizing descriptive categories, for linking neurons and meanings, for generating cognitive models, and thus for moving research into RSEs forward. Third, nothing in this type of research can produce knock-down arguments capable of bluntly eliminating dualist or di-polar monist or any other ontological theories of RSEs, so long as they are consistent with the neural mediation hypothesis. Yet, fourth, an accumulation of correlational data can have a significant long-term impact on philosophical disputes by making di-polar monist interpretations progressively more compelling while reducing the dualist philosophical program to face-saving maneuvers aimed at defending an ontological postulate that does no explanatory work.

Collectively, these points express a very different conclusion from that of the noisy anti-religion writers of our era who seem so confident that the neurology of RSEs proves that religious beliefs are delusions. It is also a challenging conclusion for those religious and spiritual people and groups whose working world pictures depend on supernatural beings and disembodied souls. I have stressed that both groups can hold their ground more or less indefinitely, with the aid of locally nurtured plausibility structures. But their viewpoints become increasingly implausible with each gain in understanding of, and control over, the neural expression of RSEs, and with each step towards a richer appreciation of the value and functions of RSEs.

Finally, we should note that the neurology of RSEs is beginning to live up to its long-term promise. Psychology of religion surveys of the Yao and Badham (2007) type are helping to stabilize discourse about these experiences across cultural and religious differences. The generalized quantitative signature method promises to organize the currently untamed jungle of phenomenological categories that are used to describe these experiences and to distinguish them more decisively from one another, and also to make cognitive modeling of RSEs more tractable. And both survey-based and scanning-based neurological studies are beginning to illumine the host of complex mechanisms that are involved in producing the peculiarly potent characteristics of certain RSEs. It remains to be seen how far this effort can go toward the ultimate goal of a robust neurological theory of RSEs, or indeed toward a compelling theory of religious phenomena as a whole. But there is no question any longer that this is more than a whimsical dream. The contemporary neurological sciences are drawing us, ready or not, into a new era in the understanding of RSEs.

CHAPTER 3

A smorgasbord of dangers and delights: the phenomenology of religious and spiritual experiences

INTRODUCTION

Religious behaviors, beliefs, and experiences are astonishingly diverse – far more varied than most people realize. Some of these phenomena are exciting, life-changing events; some are mundane, everyday happenings; some are devastating and terrifying; some co-occur with psychologically anomalous experiences; some are profoundly threatening to mental stability and the fabric of social life. The best way to think about the whole range of religious behaviors, beliefs, and experiences without trivializing them or improperly taming their wildness is to find out about their diversity, the conditions that affect their expression, their functions in individual lives, and their social effects. After we know something about all this, we should repeatedly remind ourselves of it because we are apt to constrict our view to that with which we ourselves are personally most familiar, or that which our favorite theory of RSEs can most easily accommodate.

Beyond simply knowing about and remembering the diversity and range of RSEs, it is also vital that our descriptive tools are well crafted to avoid accidentally nurturing a distorted interpretation of the nature, functions, and value of RSEs. This imposes a burden on the phenomenologist, the expert in richly describing phenomena. This burden is best shouldered by means of evidence-based arguments on behalf of the categories, distinctions, and multidisciplinary insights that the descriptions employ.

In describing some of the diversity of RSEs in this chapter, however, I shall not attempt to be exhaustive or even-handed. In fact, I shall pay special attention to a particular class of RSEs which I call "intense experiences." I will identify these experiences in the first instance in terms of their phenomenological characteristics, as simultaneously spiritually potent and emotionally spectacular kinds of experiences that seem to engage people with their ultimate concerns. Though the class of intense experiences is internally diverse, and familiar under many names to students of RSEs, they are close to the potent heart of RSEs and important for understanding the functions and effects of religion and spirituality in human lives and groups. I shall eventually argue (in the next chapter, and somewhat conjecturally) that intense experiences appear to be the product of an evolutionarily and neurologically distinctive suite of capacities for intensity, in a special sense involving an intensification of ordinary experience that triggers richly interconnected neural activation; and thus that this capacity is virtually species-wide, and certainly cross-culturally universal, persisting within and beneath the exquisitely particular influences of local contexts and personal circumstances.

The class of intense experiences is well suited – better suited than mystical experiences or meditation experiences, which have been more extensively studied but are less relevant to everyday RSEs – to the complicated task of evaluating the value and cognitive reliability, the nature and functions of RSEs. This is the subclass of RSEs, in other words, for which the strategic plan of this book calls. I aim to produce a serviceable description of the class of intense experiences that locates them in relation to neighboring types of experiences, especially so as to avoid ambiguous usage and oversimplification of the domain of RSEs. I shall then discuss the class of intense experiences in more detail in the next chapter.

MAPPING THE TERRAIN OF RELIGIOUS AND SPIRITUAL EXPERIENCES

Map is not territory

To recall a famous title of Jonathan Z. Smith's, a map is not the same as the territory it represents (see Smith 1993). If we get confused between the two, we may not be able to make sense of territory that we come across. I have had this problem when orienteering, obsessively consulting my mistaken map for guidance, wasting precious minutes when I really should evaluate the map by paying more attention to my surroundings. The map might be useful on the scale of hills and valleys and the basic geometry of paths but at the level of details all maps are misleading to various degrees. And most maps are distorted at the larger scales, as well – for instance, representing a curved surface as a flat one for convenience. Even most spinning-globe maps represent the earth as a sphere, where in fact the earth is really an oblate spheroid, flattened slightly at the poles as a result of axial rotation.

In relation to RSEs, we need to recognize that here, too, maps can be useful, but that we must guard against confusing map with territory. The problem with famous phenomenological maps of RSEs is that we get attached to them and do not allow the phenomena we are considering to speak to us directly, and if necessary freshly. The people who originally produced those phenomenologies and categorizations typically did not make the mistake of confusing map with territory. They had some understanding of the limits of their categories and definitions. But others sometimes so appreciate the orientation a good map brings to the complicated territory of RSEs that they rely on it too heavily. In this way, the categories and definitions of treasured phenomenologies take on a life of their own, structuring imaginations in ways that would worry the original inventors.

For example, in his famous *Varieties of Religious Experiences*, the psychologist-philosopher William James offers a definition of religion as "the feelings, acts, and experiences of [individuals] in their solitude, so far as they apprehend themselves to stand in relation to whatever they may consider to be divine" (James 1902: 31). This definition has been repeated over and over as if it expressed James' view of religion. But in context James is completely clear that he is adopting an arbitrarily narrow definition for the sake of delimiting the subject matter of his lectures, and that he has no intention of furnishing a comprehensive definition of religion – just as well, too, because this definition is woefully inadequate in relation to the social dimensions of religion. While James did not confuse map with territory in this instance, many of his readers have done so, and have also made it seem as if he himself did. And they did this partly because they so appreciate James' typically insightful characterization of the part of religion on which he focused.

The same fate has befallen Rudolf Otto's *The Idea of the Holy* (Otto [1917] 1925). Otto has repeatedly been taken to be talking about religion in general with code phrases such as *mysterium tremendum* and *fascination* (12–41). Yet he is utterly clear that these key ideas refer only to the irrational, non-doctrinal, non-social aspects of religion. In fact, Otto is deeply interested in how the mystery and fascination elements of religious experience relate to the more public and rational aspects. But he does not allow the two to coalesce into an undifferentiated muddle, and would be alarmed that some of his interpreters have done so.

It is not just definitions of religion that are haunted by the spectral failure to distinguish map from territory. In *Varieties*, James develops distinctions – often since repeated – between the melancholic sick-soul and the optimistic healthy-soul, and between the once-born and the twice-born individual. James, with his typical empirical sensitivities, thoroughly disrupts these categories by admitting marginal and mixed cases, but this fact is difficult to discern from reading some works that cite and reuse these distinctions. Similarly, W. T. Stace's (1960) distinction between introvertive and extrovertive types of mysticism and R. C. Zaehner's (1957) distinction between theistic mysticism and monistic nature mysticism have been treated far too crisply by some readers. In these cases, Stace and Zaehner themselves may have taken their distinctions too seriously and too unempirically, to some degree inviting the wooden readings they occasionally received.

The same can be said of Huston Smith's (1992) *Forgotten Truth*. His map of mystical experiences provides a much-needed correction to Zaehner in the form of an empirically more adequate fourfold distinction of mystical personality types (also see Smith 2000). These four types correspond to four ontological levels of reality: that of the terrestrial mystic who engages the depths of nature, the intermediate mystic who engages angels and demons and discarnate entities, the celestial mystic oriented to relationship with a personal deity, and the infinite mystic oriented to sublime union with the ineffable God beyond God. But Smith's map has its own abstraction problems. If he could show that his hierarchical ontology was correct, then he would have a first-rate argument for his phenomenology of mystical personality types. But there are many other ontological proposals in the varied worlds of religion that do not fit the pattern, and many RSEs are not registered in the fourfold typology of spiritual personality types.

Stace, Zaehner, Smith, and others have produced genuinely useful maps that draw our attention to some salient features of RSEs. But each map is also problematic when the relevant data are considered in sufficient detail, especially because the maps are loaded with theological and philosophical assumptions that are considerably more dubious than the describable elements of the experiences themselves. Such maps tend to ignore or marginalize uncooperative data in order to stay true to their guiding conceptual principles, which are typically theologically derived. In this way, unfortunately, such theologically and philosophically inspired maps also risk distorting even what they do illumine. It does little good to establish a compelling superstructure of philosophical and theological interpretation of ultimate reality and human interaction with ultimacy when the underlying conceptual foundation is plagued with cracks. And cracks there are. The biggest crack of all amounts to a gaping chasm into which the entire edifice of philosophical and theological interpretation threatens to plunge: the salient aspects of people's RSEs are often not their ontological aspects but their personal and existential aspects. Even if Smith or Zaehner were right about their ontologies, therefore, their ontologically driven phenomenologies of mystical experiences will often fail to describe the existentially and socially salient aspects of those experiences.

Connecting description and interpretation

For these reasons, I consider the philosophically and theologically oriented distinctions that have attracted so much attention in the study of RSEs finally to be of quite limited use. The most serviceable maps of the territory of RSEs are laid out according to the phenomenological qualities of the reports of RSEs that have been gathered in the hundred years since careful empirical study of these phenomena was first attempted in the West. And these phenomenologically driven maps are most robust when the features that underlie key distinctions are traced back to human neurology, developmental psychology, evolutionary theory, and the existential and social functions of RSEs.

To be concrete about this, consider the marvelous descriptive work on RSEs carried out by Oxford zoologist Sir Alister Hardy and his successors. In founding the Religious Experience Research Unit at Oxford's Manchester College in 1969, he intended to focus attention on the empirical study of RSEs. He reported on the first eight years of that work in his *The Spiritual Nature of Man* (1979). In that book, Hardy summarized his analysis of over 3,000 reports of RSEs. For each report, he noted the phenomenological properties of the experience described by his subject. As the data set grew, he was able to group those properties into categories pertaining to biologically basic features of the human organism. This enabled him to collect the first important frequency data about RSEs, though the data are based on the experiences that volunteers chose to share, so in fact are of relatively little value for understanding the frequency of RSEs in the wider population.

Hardy noticed that "sensory or quasi-sensory" features were common in the reports he received of experiences that people were willing to call religious. He further noticed that these sensory features came in about twenty-two different variations, and that these could be clustered under visual, auditory, touch, smell, and extra-sensory headings. This is a phenomenological distinction that is rooted in human physiology and thus seems particularly sturdy in the sense that it is relatively independent of culturally specific interpretations of the experiences in question. The fact that the categorization reflects characteristics basic to human physiology means that the frequency numbers predict the *relative* likelihood that human beings are likely to undergo experiences of each kind. The *absolute* likelihood of such experiences would depend on systematic survey data using a random population rather than volunteers; this is the approach used by Yao and Badham (2007).

Other categories in Hardy's classification system relate to higher-level cognitive or behavioral features of human life. He found four types of behavioral changes related to belief in superhuman powers, twenty-two types of cognitive and affective elements, fourteen aspects relating to the way the experiences developed over time (grouped into three subtypes), five types of constructive or destructive dynamic patterns, just one type of dream experience, twenty-two types of trigger including two related to drugs, and three types of consequences of the experiences. This list has been elaborated further since Hardy's time, but in all cases the basis for classification is directly related to biologically basic kinds of behavior, sensation, and cognition. It is thus likely that the classification can win a significant degree of consensus across diverse historical eras and cultural settings. But Hardy was sharply aware of the need to test this likelihood in actual cross-cultural experimentation (1979: 141–42), as was James in pondering the cross-cultural generality and stability of his own study in *Varieties* (James 1902: Postscript).

Having in hand empirically adequate descriptions of RSEs stabilizes speculative attempts at philosophical and theological interpretation. James set the first important example of this approach, and Hardy the second. Like them, I think that omitting philosophical and theological interpretation is irresponsible. Also like them, I think that rushing to philosophical and theological interpretation without a firm empirical basis causes more problems than it is worth. It is like trampling through the prodigiously varied flora of a rainforest in search of the three or four flowers you are totally convinced must be there somewhere. It is better to pause, look around, and take in what there is. But at some point we have to return to integrative theological and philosophical interpretation in order to make sense of the whole, and also to exercise public responsibility for our work.

The integrative interpretations offered by James and Hardy were modest. We may think of them as being on the empirically robust and theologically cautious end of a spectrum of interpretations of RSEs that reaches all the way to the theologically ambitious and empirically awkward offerings of Zaehner and Smith, as well as others such as Aldous Huxley (1945) and Robert Forman (1990, 1999). Strangely enough, despite the many diverse details that he adumbrated in his classification scheme, the thrust of Hardy's theological conclusions is more or less in line with that of James at the end of *Varieties*. Hardy himself wonders whether this might have been due to having so thoroughly absorbed James' earlier work (1979: 131). Using the gendered language of his time, despite having twice as many women as men participate in his research, Hardy summarizes his interpretative conclusion as follows:

It seems to me that the main characteristics of a man's RSEs are shown in his feelings for a transcendent reality which frequently manifest themselves in early childhood; a feeling that "Something Other" than the self can actually be sensed; a desire to personalize this presence into a deity and to have a private I–Thou relationship with it, communicating through prayer. (1979: 131)

Some degree of psychological nuance is evident in this interpretative summary. For example, Hardy speaks of "feelings" and "desires" rather than taking for granted that his theological categories are self-evidently confirmed as real by the experiences he is analyzing. But he determines his theological categories by looking for the most common elements in his reports and then linking those elements into a narrative framework that he personally finds compelling. In other words, Hardy should be concluding that his interpretation expresses a plausible reconstruction of *one common trajectory* in the way these experiences become religiously important to people who are subject to particular socio-cultural and religious conditioning.

Because of this shortcoming, Hardy's interpretation does not even achieve the generality and robustness of James' interpretation from seventy-seven years earlier. James used higher-level and more existentially loaded distinctions than Hardy did, which might normally lead us to expect that James would fall prey to ontological or theological assumptions hidden (or not so hidden) within those distinctions. But in fact James resists this to a commendable degree. He infers from his data certain core beliefs that characterize the religious life in the specific sense in which he is investigating it, which was discussed above. They are:

1. That the visible world is part of a more spiritual universe from which it draws its chief significance;
2. That union of harmonious relation with that higher universe is our true end;

3. That prayer or inner communion with the spirit thereof – be that spirit "God" or "law" – is a process wherein work is really done, and spiritual energy flows in and produces effects, psychological or material, within the phenomenal world. (James 1902: 485)

James goes on to add the following psychological characteristics of religion in his distinctive sense of the word:

1. A new zest which adds itself like a gift to life, and takes the form either of lyrical enchantment or of appeal to earnestness and heroism.
2. An assurance of safety and a temper of peace, and, in relation to others, a preponderance of loving affections. (James 1902: 485–6)

While still an interpretation that averages and consolidates the rich data he had at his disposal, we can tell from our very different position that James framed this interpretation in a way that is surprisingly open to the non-theistic religions of the world, with which he admitted he was not intimately familiar. It is James' ability to sift through so many reports and come up with a robust general interpretation that explains why his book has been so treasured. And it is Hardy's patient approach to description and classification that has made the Hardy Centre's work so well known in the study of RSEs.

With those two virtues in mind, I adopt here a quite particular approach to mapping the territory of RSEs, one driven by phenomenological research such as that of Hardy, by empirical psychology research such as that of James and many others since then, and by neurological research that is starting to flower in recent years. Its leading categories are mid-level, which is to say somewhere between Hardy and James, and its leading distinctions have both empirical and existential rationales. When the map is sketched, and its defects appreciated, I will entertain integrative philosophical and theological interpretations, as well as evolutionary interpretations of the origins of the classes of experiences discriminated in the map. In so proceeding, I believe the interpretation is both more culturally general and less theologically specific than James' or Hardy's interpretations, and nowhere near as theologically aggressive as interpretations such as those of Zaehner or Smith.

The practical point of integrating description and interpretation

I argued in Chapter 1 that keeping track of the motivations of people writing in the area of RSEs is important. My motivation here is threefold.

I am curious, of course. And I am often concerned by uncritical interpretations of RSEs whose enthusiasm in either positive or negative directions produces socially undesirable effects. But I am also in search of an
intellectually compelling interpretation of RSEs capable of helping the
many people who are confused by such experiences. These three motivating factors of inquiry, criticism, and practical humanism are present
throughout.

We can almost taste a world in which religious quests harmonize with
our worldly aspirations and adventures, in which we naturally see our
biology and sociality and spirituality as inalienably related, and in which
we can accept the strangeness of others as reflecting an unexplored part of
our own potential, or at least the potential of our species. We can almost
taste it, as I say, but it is tragically far from being a living reality. Perhaps
the human condition is such that we can never realize anything even
remotely like this, though I am not describing an ideal Shangri-La so
much as a shift in global consciousness. In fact, I think education and
understanding can produce great strides in a healthy direction, especially
when it comes to helping people come to terms with RSEs, which are typically the most potent conviction-producing and action-inspiring experiences of their lives.

The kind of integrated understanding I envisage helps people regulate
or make use of such experiences, turning them to socially beneficial ends,
decreasing fanatical violence and other dangerous behavior, and increasing social harmony and understanding of differences. And how do we
start in such a commendable direction? We begin by learning about these
experiences, their existential meanings and their practical effects.

BASIC DISTINCTIONS IN THE MAP

Vivid experiences, religious experiences, spiritual experiences

I shall use "vivid experiences" to refer to the relatively unusual, typically colorful states of consciousness that are either of enormous religious
or spiritual significance, or else are very strange and of deeply uncertain
meaning. Vivid experiences are far more diverse than any one person's
individual or professional experience might lead one to suppose. Mystics
think first of mystical experiences, New Age enthusiasts of shamanic
journeys or psi-related phenomena, traditional religious people of corporate worship or ritual experiences, and nature lovers of feelings of peace
and awe while hiking alongside a still mountain lake. Psychologists might

first think of psychosis or conversion experiences, anthropologists of painful or strange rituals and the associated states of consciousness, and theologians of the formative experiences that generate confident religious beliefs.

There is no comprehensive phenomenology of the full range of such vivid experiences. Rather, there are many partial phenomenologies directed by the interest and attention of the researcher, including those I have already mentioned, and many others besides (see Twiss and Conser 1992 for a review of key writings in the phenomenology of sacred experience). I have my own interests, as I have explained, and my own ideas about what counts as intellectually compelling and practically useful in a phenomenological presentation of RSEs. Here I attempt to coordinate what I have learned from existing phenomenologies and categorizations with what I have discovered in my own research to produce a richer account of vivid experiences.

It is important first to distinguish vivid experiences from "religious" experiences. Involvement in religious groups is associated with a host of experiences from the spectacular to the mundane, from the individual to the corporate, and from supportive to disruptive of ordinary social processes. Thus, some religious experiences are vivid and some are not. Any attempt to capture the diversity of religious experiences in a definition seems futile. Defining religion is itself a famously difficult task – indeed, after so many hundreds of attempts, perhaps a humorously hopeless one. The diversity of experiences associated with religious involvement is at least as complex. For my purposes, the way to proceed is to capitalize on the vagueness of the word "religion" and simply use "religious experiences" to refer to the experiences people have by virtue of being religious or being involved in religious groups. This does no more than distinguish religious experiences from non-religious experiences, of course, but at least it establishes a modicum of resistance to oversimplifying treatments of religion.

Just as some religious experiences are vivid and some are not, so some vivid experiences are routinely associated with being religious, with religious involvement, or with religious practices, while others are not. Thus, the relation between religious and vivid experiences is one of significant overlap, with vivid experiences probably being more diverse but less common than religious experiences and neither being a subset of the other (see Figure 3.1). The "religious experience" category is one of convenience, matching the vague way in which the word "religion" itself is used, as I have said. The vivid experience category is demarcated with reference to

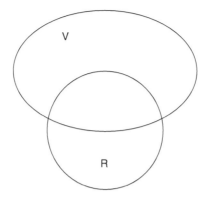

Figure 3.1. Overlap between vivid [V] and religious [R] experiences.

both significance and strangeness, which draws our attention to the borderline between the normal or mundane, and everything else. This borderline is set by our physiology in interaction with our environment, which allows certain habits to form, including expectations for what is normal, unproblematic, and deserving of no special attention. Vivid experiences encompass both this borderline and everything beyond, whether or not it has religious significance.

Vivid experiences are constituted by two major overlapping classes of experiences: anomalous experiences and ultimacy experiences. These are the strange experiences and the significant experiences just mentioned. The domain of the strange – "anomalous experiences" – and the domain of the significant – "ultimacy experiences" – require detailed explanation, and I will come to that presently. The strange and significant overlap significantly, but they are not identical. There are many reports of RSEs that are pregnant with significance and yet contain no hint of strangeness, in the sense of involving extreme outliers on the range of possible human experiences. Likewise, there are strange experiences that remain bizarre, inassimilable in their strangeness, and never take on even the promise of deeper significance. The overlapping relationships among ultimacy, anomalous, and religious experiences are sketched in Figure 3.2.

Note that the diagram does not express anything about either the frequency or the importance of the three classes of overlapping experiences. Importance would depend on varied interests. And if we were to select sizes so as to take into account what we learn from Hardy and subsequent research about the relative frequency of these experiences, I suspect we would end up with something like Figure 3.3. Religious experiences that are

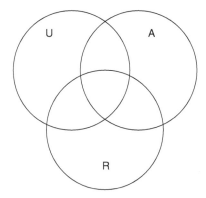

Figure 3.2. Relations between religious [R] experiences and the two overlapping classes of vivid experiences: anomalous experiences [A] and ultimacy experiences [U].

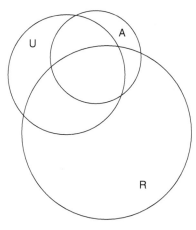

Figure 3.3. Relations between religious [R] experiences and the two overlapping classes of vivid experiences: anomalous experiences [A] and ultimacy experiences [U]. The sizes of the six regions in this diagram indicate the relative frequency of the various types of experiences.

strangely anomalous and yet not ultimately significant seem to constitute a relatively small class, whereas the non-anomalous religious experiences that have some ultimate importance for people is a relatively large class. Unfortunately, frequency data for most of the classes of experience I am focusing on do not exist, or else must be inferred inductively from gathered reports in the way Hardy did, with all the accompanying problems. Hopefully future research will eventually fill this gap in our knowledge.

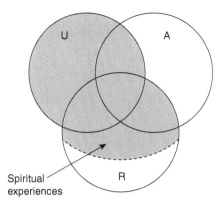

Figure 3.4. Locating spiritual experiences (shaded area), as including all of ultimacy experiences [U] and a usage-dependent portion of religious experiences [R] that are not already also ultimate experiences.

I shall not pay attention to frequency data in what follows, and the other diagrams I present express only relationships of inclusion and overlap.

The category of "spiritual" experiences, like "religious" experiences, is a term of art, used differently in different settings. Sometimes "spiritual" is used to describe the aesthetic, moral, or circumstantial experiences that seem pregnant with existential and ontological significance and yet more or less obviously not related to organized religion, and thus do not seem religious to many people, as in "spiritual but not religious." But religious people also use "spiritual" to refer to dimensions of what they also naturally call religious experiences. I think the distinction within the class of vivid experiences between the significance of ultimacy experience and the strangeness of anomalous experiences is helpful for getting at what people want to accomplish by speaking of "spiritual" experiences. The entire range of significant experiences is a part of what is meant – that is, the ultimacy experiences – as well as a rather large chunk but definitely not all of the domain of religious experiences (see Figure 3.4).

RSEs, therefore, comprise the union of ultimacy and religious experiences, which encompasses religious-but-not-spiritual, spiritual-but-not-religious, and both-spiritual-and-religious experiences. This is a relatively stable category, because the culturally and contextually variable borderline between religious-but-not-spiritual and spiritual experiences is included within RSEs.

Other types of experience lying within the vivid domain (the union of ultimacy and anomalous experiences) have received phenomenological attention, and I discuss below three such classes that overlap with the religious domain. First, though, I describe the two major classes of vivid experiences: the significant realm of ultimacy experiences and the strange domain of anomalous experiences.

Anomalous experiences

The term "anomalous experiences" refers to experiences that apparently violate the operations of the world as these are understood in normal life. The word "abnormal" has unwarranted negative connotations but in a quite literal sense we can classify anomalous experiences as abnormal precisely because they are unlike what we normally experience and expect. This says nothing about the normalcy or mental health of those who undergo such experiences. This usage of "normal" arises chiefly from the habit-establishing linkages between physiology and environment, already mentioned.

Though anomalous experiences are diverse, psychologists have studied many types (see George 1995). Cardeña *et al.* (2000) offer survey articles on a number of types of anomalous experiences, including hallucination, synesthesia, lucid dreaming, out-of-body experiences, alien abduction, anomalous healing, past-life, near-death, psi-related, and mystical experiences. Other anomalous experiences include mental phenomena associated with drug-induced altered states, psychiatric disorders, extreme circumstances, ecstatic states, group frenzy, snake-handling, fire-walking, possession, as well as more marginally anomalous experiences such as dramatic self-deception, uncanny insight, and spectacular creativity. There are also anomalous experiences associated with severe brain trauma, such as fits of rage, and with severe emotional trauma, such as amnesia or the self-protective fictitious reassembly of fragmented memories.

The investigation of anomalous experiences is in its early days. Neurological studies have been conducted in some of these cases but not to any great extent, partly because subjects are not always easy to locate, and partly because most anomalous experiences do not lend themselves to convenient study. Experiences linked to brain trauma have received a great deal of attention in the neuropsychological literature because they help establish correlations between brain regions and functions. Only in the last couple of decades have careful investigations disclosed the devious magician-like techniques associated with some anomalous experiences, such as psychic healing and cold reading (see Randi 1982; Shermer 2002; and the investigative reports discussed in *Skeptical Inquirer* magazine).

Survey data on the frequency and effects of such experiences have barely begun to be collected, though there are considerable frequency data on the incidence of psychiatric conditions, some of which involve predictable patterns of anomalous experiences. Thus, it is difficult to draw stable conclusions about the causes and dynamics of anomalous experiences. Several generalized comments are possible, however.

First, anomalous experiences usually feel out of the control of those who have them. Even when they are sought, which is sometimes the case with out-of-body or lucid dreaming experiences and usually the case with drug-induced and hypnotic states, typically the experiences themselves feel beyond the conscious control of the subject.

Second, despite the first point, the study of anomalous experiences shows that some of them are reliably reproducible under the right conditions. For example, bright and fast-changing lights, loud and rhythmic music, a dynamic central personality, and an intensely supportive social atmosphere are recurring factors in cult conversions, group frenzy, anomalous healing experiences, and dramatic self-deception. Certain neurological conditions may be relevant, also, making a person more likely to experience a whole range of anomalous experiences. For example, people with schizophrenia tend to be vulnerable to individually varying triggering circumstances, which more or less reliably produce psychotic events.

Third, anomalous experiences are emotionally and cognitively potent. They often produce powerful convictions in those who have them, convictions about the nature of reality, about the significance of events, about what future actions to take, and about what one's life priorities should be. These convictions are strong because the experiences that inspire and confirm them are emotionally potent. As mentioned in Chapter 1, neuropsychologist Leslie Brothers and I have conjectured that a swamping mechanism succeeds in activating brain processes that we usually rely on for concluding correctness and persuasiveness, but does so without forcing new experiences through the usual global semantic matching process (Wildman and Brothers 1999). In this way, powerful anomalous experiences can cause people to attach unwavering conviction to beliefs that most people reject as completely implausible.

Fourth, anomalous experiences often have little to do with religion and spirituality. Of course, they do sometimes occur in the context of religious involvement – indeed, some religious groups make unconscious or deliberate use of environmental factors that render people more likely to have anomalous experiences. They also commonly occur in non-religious contexts and are felt to have great spiritual significance. A common situation is the occurrence of anomalous experiences outside the context of religious involvement, followed by the construction of an idiosyncratic spirituality, inspired by the cognitive and emotional impact of the experience, and by a search for like-minded people with whom the experience can be shared safely, people who will understand easily and deeply. But plenty of anomalous experiences, whether shocking, terrifying, or enjoyable, have no religious or spiritual significance; they are just odd.

These impressionistic remarks indicate the importance of further research in this area. Anomalous experiences are more common than many people who have not experienced them might estimate. Their impact on personal self-understanding and worldview, and indeed on the origins of religious movements, is easily underestimated, accordingly. They are vital factors in any attempt to understand how people come by their convictions and why they make the decisions they do. They are a colorful part of the experiential fabric of human life and a crucial component in the formation of religious and spiritual beliefs and behaviors. But their existential meaning is most apparent when they overlap with ultimacy experiences, to which we turn next.

Ultimacy experiences

If anomalous experiences are defined by objective strangeness, ultimacy experiences are defined by subjective judgments of ultimate significance. These are experiences that a person feels are of vital importance for his or her life. They bring orientation and coping power, inspire great acts of courage and devotion, underlie key life decisions, and heavily influence social affiliation. They overlap with anomalous experiences, but anomalous experiences can occur without the subjective judgment of ultimate importance, and ultimacy experiences can occur in recognizably normal fashion, so the overlap is significant without being total.

The term "ultimacy experiences" is controversial because it involves the theologically loaded word "ultimacy." But its use here does not require an elaborate theology. Many people describe experiences that have a kind of ultimate importance for them, and say that these experiences engage them with what they take to be ultimate realities. We do not need to settle the question of the value of such convictions and experiences, nor the reality of their putative objects, to affirm the importance of ultimacy experiences for any adequate description of RSEs. While calling these experiences "God experiences" or "experiences of the Buddha mind" would dramatically narrow their scope in culturally parochial ways, using the vague term "ultimacy" properly acknowledges their diversity. Some involve ultimate subjective importance, some engagement with an ultimate reality, and some both at once. The suitability of the terms "ultimate" and "ultimacy" for the tasks to which I put them here is one of the results of the Cross-Cultural Comparative Religious Ideas Project (see Neville 2001, vol. 11).

When the parsing of experience begins from subjective judgments of ultimate significance rather than objective judgments of strangeness (as in anomalous experiences), very different distinctions emerge. Most prominent is the need for a contrast between short-term and long-term ultimacy experiences. Almost all anomalous experiences are short-term neurological events. But experiences possessing the subjective quality of ultimate importance are both long-term and short-term in character. The obvious phenomenological difference between discrete states and extended experiences is directly attributable to neurology: short-term states are tied to discrete brain episodes whereas extended experiences usually require a rich social context to sustain them. It is discrete ultimacy experiences that overlap most significantly with the anomalous experiences just reviewed. Both types have recurring characteristics.

Extended ultimacy experiences arise in two ways, as "dynamic, socially embedded processes of orientation and control in relation to the cosmos, the social world, and one's self" (Wildman and Brothers 1999: 359); and as "gradual and chronic experiences of personal change or self-transcendence, such as Confucian self-cultivation, Christian sanctification, and possibly also character changes having little explicit connection with religious symbols and practices" (361). These are social and transformative ultimacy experiences, respectively. The four common elements that recur in both types of extended ultimacy experiences are: (1) existential potency, (2) social embedding, (3) transformation of behavior and personality, and (4) transformation of beliefs (362–65).

Many extended ultimacy experiences serve simultaneously as social experiences of orientation and as provocations to transformation. Orientation ultimacy experiences are vital for the stability of human social life. The embedding of ultimate ethical and religious commitments in social patterns (see Berger 1967; Berger and Luckmann 1966; Durkheim [1912] 1915) is a process that achieves coherence and conviction for individuals only when supported by orientation ultimacy experiences. For example, most people would not enforce moral rules that they did not feel convinced were good and wise. People also need to change, to break free from oppressive social constraints, and to transcend their culturally limited imaginations. Whether sought or not, transformation ultimacy experiences facilitate such change.

Both the orientation and transformation types of extended ultimacy experiences have the same recurring characteristics in different relative weightings. Both types are existentially potent. They are embedded in a social context to various degrees, which is particularly important in the case of orientation ultimacy experiences. They also involve the transformation of behavior, personality, and beliefs, in different ways; whereas transformation ultimacy experiences obviously require change, orientation ultimacy experiences more subtly require changes that serve to fit individuals comfortably into the regularities of a social environment, minimizing unwanted cognitive dissonance.

Discrete ultimacy experiences have very different characteristics, which is to be expected given their association with short-term brain states. They involve the following five recurring elements (Wildman and Brothers 1999: 358–59): (1) sensory alterations, including perceptions that are incongruous with the current environmental situation; (2) self alterations, including out-of-body experiences, loss of the sense of the individual self, union of the self with an entity such as God or the Infinite, or the self as profoundly threatened by judgment or annihilation in the presence of a being of enormous power; (3) presences, including non-physical beings, either benign or evil, such as angels or demons, and being invaded, inhabited, or controlled by such beings; (4) cognitions, including sudden illumination, increased awareness, a sense of unreality, sense of sin or weakness, assurance of salvation or healing, and powerful convictions; (5) emotions, including feelings of ecstasy, awe, dread, guilt, safety, tranquility, or utter darkness and despair.

Discrete experiences often occur at the beginning of a process of personal transformation and then sometimes recur periodically within that process; this is one way in which discrete and extended ultimacy experiences are related. Some discrete ultimate experiences have been studied neurologically. Prominent examples are Persinger's (1987) study of the subset of discrete ultimacy experience that he calls "God Experiences," Newberg's (2006) study of glossolalia or speaking in tongues, and Beauregard's (2007), Newberg's (Newberg *et al.* 2001a), and Davidson's (2001) parallel studies of meditation and prayer experiences. Such studies help to identify the neural correlates of particular types of discrete ultimacy experiences.

In summary, the neurologically driven distinction between discrete and extended ultimacy experiences defines two subclasses of interpenetrating phenomena that have very different evolutionary origins, biochemical conditions, behavioral effects, and existential significance. It is a distinction that is very much needed, therefore, even if all of its connections to other experiences are not immediately obvious.

I suspect that almost everyone has ultimacy experiences of one sort or another even when they never get close to any anomalous experience – and this is so regardless of how they would deploy the inevitably slippery categories of the religious and the spiritual. This makes them important in an evolutionary theory of human experience. An evolutionary interpretation of human experience could perhaps set aside many anomalous experiences as bizarre side-effects with no cognitive or existential value – though this remains an open question – but *ultimacy experiences have to be placed front and center in any evolutionary account because of their potent functional effects on self-understanding and behavior.* That is, human beings may well have been subject to selection pressures based on their ability to undergo ultimacy experiences. Of course, merely imagining this settles nothing about what is currently an extraordinarily complicated issue in the evolutionary study of religion. But unless the distinction between anomalous and ultimacy experiences is scrupulously respected, the arguments over the evolutionary origins of RSEs can never achieve clarity over precisely what is to be explained.

The link between ultimacy and anomalous experiences

A sound understanding of vivid experiences (the union of ultimacy and anomalous experiences) is constantly threatened by the reduction of ultimacy experiences to anomalous experiences or vice versa. For example, some dismiss particular ultimacy experiences of great existential moment by associating them with psychosis or emotional instability. Some people, perhaps in the grip of psychotic states, claim that their anomalous experiences are existentially important and cognitively reliable, merely on the basis of their compelling qualities and without regard to cognitive content or context. These reductive approaches trivialize the complexity of human experience and lead to the underestimation of the ambiguous significance of vivid experiences for healthy human beings.

To understand how these domains of experience fit together naturally, consider McNamara's (2009) novel neurocognitive explanation of ultimacy experiences. This account purports to be of religious experiences in general but in fact is limited to the domain of meaningful RSEs, here called ultimacy experiences, with implications for other vivid experiences.

He uses a theory of self to present a compelling answer to the all-important question concerning ultimacy experiences, namely, "What is the 'meaningfulness' of an experience?"

For McNamara, an experience is meaningful in the ultimate way characteristic of some RSEs when it promotes decentering of a current self-construct. In the cognitive process of decentering, the current self suspends control over attention and behavioral goals while searching semantic memory for a self-concept that better addresses the needs of the individual. Semantic memory hosts possibility spaces with alternative models for the self, often influenced by religious rituals and narratives that make ancestors or moral exemplars, saints, or bodhisattvas relevant to the individual's life. Once an alternative model of the self is located – a selection process often governed by training and repetition – narratives help to integrate it into a modified self-construct, thereby redirecting attention and altering behavioral goals in a direction more consistent with the new self-construct. This is the creation of new meaning in action. The neurological elements of the process of decentering are compelling, drawing on the pronounced overlap between brain regions important in self-constructs and brain regions important in many types of RSEs.

McNamara points out that the decentering process is hazardous. Any one of the steps can unfold atypically, leading to what he calls "aberrant" phenomena, such as fanatical obsession or negative spirit possession. Presumably sometimes this human capacity for decentering even operates independently of the self-reconstruction process that defines the meaningfulness of experiences. Here we arrive at a plausible neurocognitive explanation for the domain of vivid experiences. The cognitive mechanism of decentering unfolds in a variety of ways. Some decentering processes go nowhere in terms of integrated self-reconstruction and thus are not particularly meaningful; these are the anomalous-but-not-ultimacy experiences. Some decentering processes produce ultimately meaningful experiences in the way described; these are the ultimacy experiences. When the qualities of the experience are unusual (unfamiliar, unexpected), the experiences lie in the overlap between ultimacy and anomalous experiences. When the qualities of the experience are usual (familiar and perhaps highly ritualized and deliberately cultivated), the experiences lie in the ultimacy-but-not-anomalous domain.

We have here an intriguing picture of the human being: an organism with an evolved capacity to reconstruct integrated self-concepts in order to take advantage of the adaptive benefits of sophisticated executive functioning that such dynamism confers. To make this possible, the organism's dynamically integrated self has to be capable of being decentered, of being taken offline, so that alternative self-concepts can become relevant to behavior. A suite of experiential possibilities promotes such decentering, with attendant side-effects that seem maladaptive, persisting alongside adaptive forms of the dynamic adjustment of the self-construct. This makes sense of the domain of vivid experiences, and of the contrast and overlap between ultimacy and anomalous experiences. It also helps to explain why the domain of RSEs extends well beyond ultimacy experiences: religion is complex enough that other neurocognitive processes are also relevant to religious beliefs, behaviors, and experiences.

It is inevitable that the decentering explanation is insufficient to explain all aspects of neurocognition within the domain of ultimacy experiences; the phenomenology of ultimacy experiences sketched above entails this. Nevertheless, the decentering process lies close to the heart of ultimacy experiences. The dynamic adjustment of self-constructs is one of the main ways in which we create meaning.

EXPLORING SHARED TERRITORY IN MORE DETAIL

Having mapped out religious, spiritual, anomalous, and ultimacy experiences, and discussed the relations among them, let us press more deeply into the territory they share. This is the intriguing and extensive region of intersection among the strangeness of anomalous experiences, the significance of ultimacy experiences, and the conventionally identified domain of RSEs. A number of distinguishable types of experience arise within and around this intersection. Of these, meditation, intense, and mystical experiences are especially notable.

Meditation experiences

The area of vivid human experiences enjoying the most extensive phenomenological, physiological, and neurological study has been and continues to be meditation experiences. This is not surprising. Many meditation experiences are reproducible, making them convenient to study; they have many welcome practical effects, making their study therapeutically useful; and they are of enormous importance within a large number of religious traditions, increasing the number of researchers with a natural motivation to study them. Meditation experiences are also useful as tools for studying consciousness; South Asian and Buddhist traditions, particularly, include vastly elaborated distinctions of states of consciousness achieved in meditation.

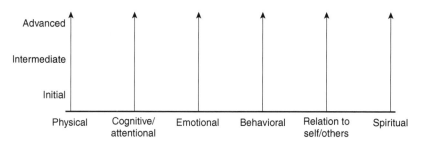

Figure 3.5. Schema for Kristeller's multimodal developmental model of meditation effects (particular effects would appear at different places on the grid).

An impressively comprehensive survey of meditation effects from within the field of experimental psychology is that of psychologist Jean Kristeller (2004, 2007), who has developed a multimodal developmental model to organize the relevant data. Kristeller distinguishes six domains of meditation effects: attentional-cognitive, physical, emotional, behavioral, relation to self/others, and spiritual. For all of these types, she distinguishes between effects achieved early in the practice of meditation, those that require moderate meditation expertise, and those that tend to appear only in advanced practitioners. Together, the "modal" and the "developmental" axes constitute a two-dimensional grid upon which can be placed a host of recognized meditation effects (these effects are not shown in Figure 3.5, but only the grid-like schema; see Kristeller 2007: 398).

Apart from its intrinsic interest, Kristeller's model has significant value for clinical psychological and medical intervention. If impulse control or awareness of behavior patterns is a problem for a client, for example, then a clinical recommendation of meditation may be appropriate because increased impulse control and heightened awareness of behaviors are effects under the "behavioral" category that can be expected quite early in the process of developing meditation skills. But pain control is a physical effect of meditation that requires considerably more meditation experience, so it may not be appropriate as a therapeutic intervention with patients who have no existing meditation experience.

Research into the therapeutic effectiveness of meditation began in the West during the 1970s in response to claims made on behalf of Maharishi Mahesh Yogi's technique of Transcendental Meditation, which dates back to 1958. Early research on meditation was first typically ignored and subsequently often attacked within mainstream medicine for methodological problems and bias. I think the criticisms were generally well earned, but this is a difficult area of study and it took time to refine techniques. While controversy still swirls around such research, especially when supported by the special interests of the Transcendental Meditation movement, studies these days are often much better designed, cover many kinds of practices, and demonstrate strong correlations between certain types of meditation practice and specific types of effects.

One of the simplest meditation methods is the so-called relaxation response described by Harvard physician Herbert Benson (1975). Benson was introduced to meditation research by one of his students, a practitioner of Transcendental Meditation. Benson drilled down to the physiological roots of the meditation practices he found out about and concluded that the most medically salient aspect of them all was the relaxation response. Benson's approach has the advantage of not necessarily being religious, which has made studying it less controversial within the medical community, though its presumption of powerful mind–body linkages still proves problematic for some (see Benson 1996). The publication of *The Harvard Medical School Guide to Lowering Your Blood Pressure* shows that there is now a broad (though not uncontested) consensus that Benson has established his claim that there is a relaxation response and that it can reduce stress and thus help mitigate the problems associated with stress-related illnesses (see Casey and Benson 2005; see also Wisneski and Anderson 2009).

Not everyone reacts the same way to meditation practices. Some people engaging in the tantra meditation techniques of Vajrayāna Buddhism, which often involve intensive visualization, report terrifying and personality-disintegrating experiences, a psychological possibility that Western meditation teachers have learned to monitor as carefully as their Asian counterparts do. Moreover, others seem immune to at least some of the reported effects of meditation. Such considerations are particularly important if meditation is to be conceived as a means of therapeutic intervention. The therapeutic dimensions of meditation also need to be more closely integrated with existing work on the physiology of meditation (see Fischer 1971 and a host of work since that time) and new work on the neurophysiology of meditation (mentioned above).

The fact that meditation regularly produces recognizable experiences is important. This reproducibility underlies the interpretation of meditation as a technology of self-cultivation and, in turn, the formation of communities devoted to meditation practice in religious and medical traditions throughout the world. An evolutionary interpretation of vivid experiences must take account of this fact; any pattern in human capacities that is widespread in the species requires an evolutionary explanation. Direct

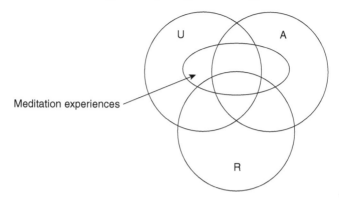

Figure 3.6. Relationships among meditation experiences, religious experiences [R], and vivid experiences, where the latter class is constituted by ultimacy [U] and anomalous [A] experiences.

selection effects may or may not be involved, but evolutionary stabilization is still in evidence, and that is a significant element of what needs to be explained.

This suggests that meditation experiences might be well suited to serve as the class of evolutionarily stabilized, neurologically basic experiential capacities that we are seeking as a way to press deeper into the evolutionary origins and existential importance of RSEs. But there are two problems with this. On the one hand, meditation experiences encompass many different experiential and neurological capacities. This means that this class of experiences is not ideally simple. On the other hand, and more importantly, meditation experiences cover a relatively narrow range of the human population, since most people do not explore them. We would prefer experiences that are more universal within the human species.

Figure 3.6 indicates where meditation experiences fit within the proposed map of RSEs. They may or may not be religious in nature but they are routinely both strange and significant, which means that they are centered on the intersection between anomalous and ultimacy experiences.

Intense experiences

Ultimacy experiences are important for people's existential self-interpretation and orientation in the world, and are defined precisely in order to register those characteristics. It is of special interest for understanding

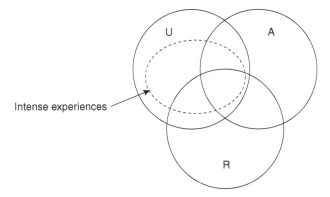

Figure 3.7. Relationships among intense experiences, religious experiences [R], and vivid experiences, where the latter class is constituted by ultimacy [U] and anomalous [A] experiences.

human spiritual formation, therefore, that a couple of subclasses exist within the class of ultimacy experiences: intense experiences (see Figure 3.7) and, within them, mystical experiences (discussed below).

"Intense experiences" is admittedly a name capable of multiple construals. But there is a genuinely important distinction to be drawn here for which no name is currently in wide usage, and thus the name I select will have to serve for now under the weight of the definition that I assign to it. The awkwardness of the name derives partly from the fact that the adjective "intense" suggests merely *high activation*, and in this narrow sense intensity appears to have nothing in particular to do with the realm of existentially significant human experiences. For example, the summer light in outback Australia can be blindingly intense in a way that would register clearly on a functional imaging scan of the brain but seems to have nothing to do with existential significance, except indirectly as a source of metaphors for describing overwhelming experiences. Yet there is another sense of intensity that, in popular usage, expresses *intense existential significance*, and it is this meaning that I am relying on when I make the domain of intense experiences a large subset of ultimacy experiences – sometimes anomalous and sometimes not, sometimes religious and sometimes not, but always spiritual and always related to matters of ultimate existential concern.

In the next chapter, I shall take up the question of whether there is a neurological basis for intense experiences, answering that there probably is a neurological basis that unites intense experiences into a class with about the same cohesion as the class of intense experiences possesses by virtue of its phenomenological characteristics. Specifically, in terms of McNamara's neurocognitive model of decentering discussed above, intense experiences trigger decentering and facilitate self-reconstruction with great force. If future research bears out conjectures about a neurological basis for intense experiences, then we will have the beginnings of an argument that the neural capacity for intense experiences arrives early in the evolutionary history of modern humans, probably about 50,000 years ago, and thus that intense experiences are vital component features of RSEs from the outset. This has quite striking implications for philosophical and theological interpretation, including making everything in reality potentially spiritually significant, and not merely those things so deemed by the authority and conventions of religious groups. But the implications of the neurological correlations are secondary at this point because the same conclusions can be drawn, albeit with less force, from the phenomenological description itself.

It is worth reflecting on the qualitative features of intense experiences prior to a more detailed examination in the next chapter. The combination of strength of feeling and interconnectedness of ideas, memories, and emotions that characterizes intense experiences is what makes them important and leverages significant personal and social effects. To have a moment of such intense love that one feels irrevocably bonded to people and places outside one's own familiar world is to be launched into new possibilities for behavior, new visions for social life, and new values. To be flooded with sharp awareness of a pattern of meaning in one's life history forges resolve to face what lies ahead and sparks confidence in one's life calling. To be struck down with the terrible realization that one is utterly dependent on processes beyond one's control is to experience grace and gratitude, if it does not collapse the psyche completely.

Concepts from information theory can yield a kind of theoretical quantification of intensity. Picture a two-dimensional grid for plotting states of consciousness, with strength of feeling and vividness of awareness increasing upwards in the vertical direction, and breadth of interconnectedness of feelings and thoughts increasing rightwards in the horizontal direction. The information content of a state of consciousness is related to its position on this grid, with high-information states toward the upper right of the grid. That is the domain of intense experiences: they are exceptionally information-rich experiences that are generative of new insights, new behavior patterns, and new values.

A similar analogy can be constructed from semiotic theory, in the version of Charles Peirce. In such a semiotics, the basic units of meaning are signs and the basic causal activity is interpretation that amounts to sign transformations (see Wildman and Brothers 1999). This semiotics incorporates capacities for interpretation at a more basic level than physicalist ontologies, yet without (what I take to be) the metaphysical liabilities of the closely related philosophies of organism in Alfred North Whitehead (1978) and those he influenced. In terms of the distinction drawn in Chapter 2, this is a di-polar ontology where the basic stuff is signs and sign transformations, with these things having both mental and material poles. In this framework, reality is a flux of semiosis, with signs standing for other signs and the patterns of sign transformation marking the causal connections that underlie both physical causation and relations of significance that are detectable by organisms with sufficiently complex nervous systems. The density of sign transformations serves in such a scheme as a qualitative indicator for intensity of feeling, much as richness of information does the same in the information-theory framework. When sign transformations are especially dense and especially widely distributed, as they are at certain memorable moments for conscious beings, reality is richly registered in intensity of feeling and awareness. Thus, intensity increases with the density and breadth of distribution of sign transformation.

Such abstract approaches to intensity may not seem worth the trouble to the scientist because they are not directly testable. Yet both information theory and semiotic theory offer heuristics for articulating more specific, testable hypotheses. They offer ways to express what can be said about that which inevitably escapes the net of systematic theory. And they furnish serious answers to the charge of arbitrariness and excessive ambiguity laid against the concept of intensity.

Intense experiences answering to approximately this description have been of enormous interest to scholars of religion because they seem to be one of the generative power sources for religious convictions and behaviors. Social needs, economic conditions, evolutionary instincts, and neurological processes unrelated to intensity also play their roles, as the sociology of religion, the sociobiological accounts of the origins of ethical and religious systems, and the neurocognitive study of religion have shown. But even the most unconscious social process has some manifestation in the experience of individuals; people buy into a social framework because it makes existential sense to them. Because of this, theories of the social origins of religious beliefs and practices have a reciprocal relationship with theories of the intense experiences that religious people often make reference to when explaining why they believe what they believe and do what they do. Each helps to explain the functions and significance of the other.

This portrayal of the social and existential importance of intensely significant experiences invites an interpretation of human beings as a species whose members' subjective lives and social behaviors are conditioned by the irregular occurrence of these intense experiences in a variety of ways.

- Intense experiences feel important to, and command the attention of, almost every person who has them.
- Intense experiences occur unpredictably and with wide variations in frequency in the population.
- Most people have intense experiences, though they are not necessarily comfortable calling them religious experiences and may be in tension with their understanding of religion.
- Intense experiences are extremely diverse in kind even though the intensity of these diverse experiences is recognizably similar.
- Intense experiences often provoke religious interest, belief, and activity.
- Intense experiences often supply justification for religious interest, belief, and activity.
- Intense experiences often serve as touchstones for a person's self-interpretation.
- Intense experiences can provoke cognitive dissonance and so can be avoided, feared, and marginalized in a person's self-interpretation.
- Intense experiences occur to people on a spectrum of mental health, from the desperately ill to the optimally healthy.
- Intense experiences range along a spectrum of affect, from the pleasant and important to the terrifying and repellant.
- Intense experiences lie along a spectrum of intention, from occurring spontaneously to being intentionally cultivated.
- Wisdom traditions include techniques for refining the ability to have intense experiences more often and more potently, with a view to increasing the felt-sense of the meaningfulness of life.
- People sometimes ingest chemicals to induce intense experiences, both within and outside existing wisdom traditions.
- The recurrence of certain intense experiences strengthens subjective appraisals of their importance and meaningfulness.
- Intense experiences that are recurrent, intelligible, and desirable within a group can consolidate that group's identity.

- The intense experiences of non-religious people are sometimes difficult to assimilate for the lack of any conceptual framework or social context for making sense of them.

Treating the full diversity of intense experiences as a single class is unusual. Many students of intense experiences, under whatever name, have analyzed a particular subclass of them as thoroughly as possible. This is the approach both of scientific studies of neurological disorders that sometimes produce distinctive intense experiences, such as temporal-lobe epilepsy (see Bear 1979; Bear *et al.* 1982; Fenton 1981; Mesulam 1981; Mungas 1982; Ramachandran and Blakeslee 1998; Schachter 2006; Tucker *et al.* 1987), and of psychological studies of certain types of intense anomalous experiences (see Cardeña *et al.* 2000). "Drill-down" approaches of this sort are particularly relevant to the health and well-being of people suffering from unwanted but emotionally and behaviorally intrusive experiences. Other students of intense experiences focus on one subtype of intense experience as representative of RSEs as a whole – this risky approach has been followed both by neuroscientists inspired by a spectacular neural correlate for one type of intense experience (Beauregard and O'Leary 2007; Newberg *et al.* 2001b; Persinger 1987) and also by a wide variety of psychologists and philosophers who latch onto mystical or sublime experiences, rhythmic-affective or hypnotic-dissociative experiences, as somehow the generative core of RSEs in general.

By contrast with these focused approaches, I aim to furnish a more comprehensive description of the class of intense experiences as a whole, in accordance with the argumentative strategy of this book. For that purpose, when I return to intense experiences in the next chapter, I will deploy the phenomenologist's toolbox to identify the significance and value of intense experiences as well as the phenomenological elements that vary among types of intense experiences and afford them their special qualities. I will also discuss the possible neurological underpinnings of intense experiences as a group, rather than a particular subgroup of them. The capacity for intense experiences is virtually species-wide, after all, so attempting to treat the entire class all at once has special value for understanding RSEs in general.

Mystical experiences

Another subclass of ultimacy experiences is also a subclass of intense experiences: mystical experiences. In fact, mystical experiences lie at the

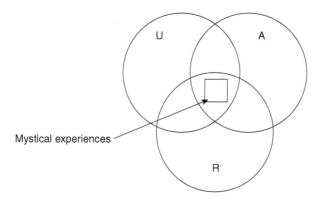

Figure 3.8. Relationships among mystical experiences, religious experiences [R], and vivid experiences, where the latter class is constituted by ultimacy [U] and anomalous [A] experiences. Mystical experiences lie at the triple intersection of religious, ultimacy, and anomalous experiences.

triple intersection of ultimacy, anomalous, and religious experiences; they are intense experiences that are also anomalous and religiously potent. Figure 3.8 displays the location of mystical experiences on the working map.

Mystical experiences have been the most studied of all ultimacy experiences. They have also benefited from cross-cultural study more than any other RSEs, thanks to extensive literary traditions of mystical writings. The diversity of experience evident in mystics' self-reports has provoked many distinctions that are supposed to do explanatory work and to furnish theological interpretations – we need only recall those of Stace (1960), Zaehner (1957), and Smith (1992) mentioned above to get a sense for these ventures. The interpretations typically mute some of this diversity or force details to fit the conceptual scheme, perhaps because the ruling theological construal of mysticism is narrower than the data, or perhaps in order to make the models of mysticism theologically more coherent. In fact, however, mystical experiences both display repeating patterns, at one level, and defy those patterns, at another level. To detect the patterns, it is necessary to abstract from the historical, environmental, nutritional, social, cultural, linguistic, and theological features of the operative context. But the mystical ideas at this abstracted level are not experiences, and probably can never be experienced in a psychologically compelling way. The power of mysticism appears only when the contextual details, from diet to weather, are kept fully in the interpretative picture. And at this level of detail, the high-level abstractions of theorists of mysticism seem rather beside the point.

But there is no particular problem here. We abstract for some purposes and keep details in the picture for other purposes. We do this routinely and with positive effects. The scientist will use an abstract point mass to represent the earth in a calculation of its trajectory around the sun, but will not hesitate to drop that way of thinking when it comes to driving home that evening. We notice the blue in all parts of a painting in an effort to picture the painter's palette, and we are glad to lose track of the blue when we see the whole. Both analytical abstraction and synthetic sensitivity to intricate wholes are vital cognitive skills that human beings make practical use of every day. In the same way, we can profit from both intricate appreciations of mystical experience and from abstract analyses of patterns in experience. It would be short-sighted and destructive to the understanding of mystical experience to neglect either one of these two levels of analysis.

Perhaps the most widespread distinction in use among theorists of mysticism is the essentially theological contrast between kataphatic and apophatic mysticism. Kataphatic mysticism is characterized by concrete imagery and a focus on a personal I–Thou relationship with the mystical object, while apophatic mysticism involves a refusal of attachment to imagery and construes ultimate union as absorption rather than intimate relationship. This distinction is closely related to the distinction between exoteric and esoteric forms of thought. Exoteric thought involves external, public ideas and connotes the egalitarian possibilities of comprehension, discussion, and verification. Esoteric thought focuses on inner conscious states and connotes secret or hidden wisdom that is powerfully trans-formative, the reception of which must be carefully prepared. Esoteric thought lines up with apophatic mysticism because of the transpersonal and ultimately incomprehensible quality of the highest reality beyond ordinary experience, whereas exoteric thought joins with kataphatic mysticism and refuses such ideas as a kind of evasive nonsense that forsakes the actual concreteness of relationship with the divine in the name of some diffuse abstraction.

This rubric of kataphatic-exoteric versus apophatic-esoteric is a classic example of an abstraction that seems to hold good in the analysis of mystical texts and experiences across eras and cultures and traditions. Yet it is difficult to determine with any confidence at the level of contextualized details whether the experiences of mystics divide as neatly as this distinction suggests, because the hermeneutical issues involved in interpreting mystics' self-reports are complex. I think it is likely that most mystics tend to understand themselves in one framework or the other, that temperamental differences produce this basic preference, and that in practice most mystics move through vast worlds of complex symbolization and deconstruction of attachment to symbolic expressions. At the level of actual mystical practice, therefore, the kataphatic-exoteric versus apophatic-esoteric rubric is more of a distraction than an aid to understanding. It is more interesting to diagnose intricate methods of symbol usage and how they impact conceptual and behavioral change. In short, both levels of interpretation are useful and illuminating, and neither alone is sufficient for an adequate interpretation of mystical experience.

The most infamous debate over mysticism is directly related to the issue of analytical abstraction versus contextual appreciation, and has extended through most of the twentieth century. It concerns what can be inferred about mystical experience and reality itself based on apparent similarities and differences between mystics' self-reports across the chasms of culture and era. Constructivists hold that local contexts are the leading factor in mystics' accounts of their experiences, to the point that stable generalizations are extremely difficult to make, and thus theological conclusions about the realities underlying mystical experiences virtually impossible to draw (see Bagger 1999; Katz 1978; Proudfoot 1985). Opposed are those who defend the viability of abstract analysis of theologically meaningful patterns (such as Huxley 1945; Smith 1992) that reliably disclose the nature of reality.

This latter view has been defended vigorously in recent years by those who claim that a so-called "pure consciousness event" can be detected recurring in mystics' self-reports (see Forman 1990, 1999), and that this forms the basis for reliable theological inferences about ontological realities underlying mystical experiences. At times, this debate seems to be conducted in the murky realm of unverifiable, untestable hypotheses, which is doubtless why it has persisted for so long. In our time, I suggest, the most productive questions about mysticism are the empirically tractable ones, such as the discovery of neural correlates for reliably reproducible mystical states of consciousness, and the elaboration of similarities and differences among mystical self-reports at all levels of generality.

Most people do not have mystical experiences. Those who do tend to seek them out. The fact that such experiences are cultivated even while being so difficult to achieve is thought-provoking and leads directly to questions about the value for people of such unusual experiences. Why go to such extraordinary lengths for mystical experiences? There appear to be

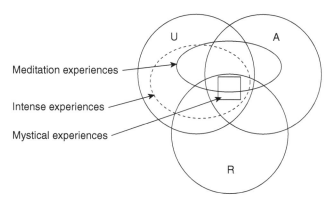

Figure 3.9. Relationships among all types of experiences discussed: religious [R] experiences, vivid experiences (constituted by ultimacy [U] and anomalous [A] experiences), meditation experiences, and two subclasses of ultimacy experiences: intense experiences and mystical experiences. RSEs are the union of the ultimacy and religious experiences.

three answers: the experiences feel stunning, they produce desirable practical effects, and they inspire compelling beliefs about reality. At least, that is how mystics seem to view matters. These are compelling enough reasons for some to pursue mystical experiences, perhaps, but evaluation of the associated epistemological claims to truth and the moral claims to beneficial effects needs to be carried on using means in addition to the positive self-assessments of mystics.

Precisely because of the narrow segment of the population that has significant mystical and meditation experiences, these classes of experience are not as well suited as intense experiences to serve as a doorway into a broadly based understanding of RSEs. Thus, it is with intense experiences that I will be particularly concerned in succeeding chapters.

CONCLUSION

The description of vivid experiences and their relationships with the experiences that people are willing to call religious or spiritual is now as full as space allows. Combining all of the types of experience mentioned to this point, the diagram illustrating relations of membership and overlap among classes is now as shown in Figure 3.9.

The distinctions and relations that the map expresses are based on tangible experiential, descriptive, or neurological rationales, as I have explained. The least sharply defined region is religious experiences because that designation is allowed here to follow the contours of ordinary usage, which are highly varied and inconsistent; but the vagueness is harmless because the important distinctions arise elsewhere in the map. Thus, the map is relatively neutral theologically and philosophically, as well as relatively non-specific with regard to the wide range of religious and spiritual practices and traditions, past and present. Its major disadvantage is that it focuses on elaborating vivid experiences (i.e. the union of ultimacy and anomalous experiences), whereas a great deal of religious experience is not vivid, involving neither significant matters of ultimate concern nor strange anomalous events. I have not elaborated the non-vivid parts of religious experience – the Seder meals, the coffee hours after worship, the efforts to educate and learn, the familiar rituals, the ordinary attempts to apply religious convictions to decision-making, and the everyday structuring of moral and spiritual imagination under the weight of religious symbols. But these aspects of religious experience could be elaborated, and indeed I will take up some of them in a later chapter on the social embedding of RSEs. So the focus on vivid experiences is not harmful as long as we know what it emphasizes and what it marginalizes.

This map of the diverse territory of vivid experiences and RSEs suggests a conclusion about prosaic lives. Some people claim humdrum experiential histories but I suspect that this is meant merely to exclude mystical or other anomalous experiences, and perhaps the more unusual discrete ultimacy experiences. Many other experiences count as spiritually significant in a vivid way so as to qualify as ultimacy experiences, and few people indeed are entirely bereft of vivid experiences so construed. Within tolerable limits of precision, therefore, and in anticipation of better survey data to confirm this, it is safe to conjecture that vivid experiences are normal and common, while the truly prosaic life is exceptionally rare and, correspondingly, difficult to comprehend. This perspective should affect what counts as relevant and plausible in an evolutionary interpretation of vivid experiences.

For the purposes of the larger strategy of this book, the most important conclusion to be drawn from this chapter concerns the status and role of intense experiences. My hypothesis is that the capacity for intensity in this special "depth of significance and breadth of awareness" sense is a species-wide characteristic, present in almost all individuals, rooted in evolutionarily stabilized neural capacities, profoundly modified in activation and expression by cultural context yet recognizable to the careful observer beneath the more prominent cultural and circumstantial variations, and detectable with properly tuned psychometric instruments. I shall appraise the evidence for this hypothesis in the next chapter.

Finally, I make the strategic observation that mapping the territory of vivid and religious experiences has had an important payoff for the wider argument. It has identified a suite of distinctions that can enhance appreciation of the complexity of the territory of RSEs and increase precision in talking about such experiences. Using this descriptive map, for example, intense experiences will not be confused with religious experiences, however understood in a given context, or with anomalous experiences or ultimacy experiences, or with meditation or mystical experiences. But awareness of the variety of RSEs, including those that are not intense experiences, is kept sharp at the same time.

CHAPTER 4

Gateway to ultimacy: the importance of intense experiences

INTRODUCTION

In the previous chapter I introduced intense experiences and located them in a phenomenological map of RSEs as a subset of ultimacy experiences. I begin in this introduction by stating the *intensity hypothesis* – a suite of interconnected phenomenological, neurological, evolutionary, philosophical, and theological claims – and will devote this chapter to expounding and supporting it.

Definition

Intense experiences involve strong and broad neural activation, corresponding to existential potency and wide awareness, involving both strength of feeling and interconnectedness of ideas, memories, and emotions in such a way as to engage a person with ultimate existential and spiritual concerns and leverage significant personal change and social effects. This is intensity not in the neurologist's narrow sense of strong activation only, but in the common usage that expresses amazement at meaningfulness. Intense experiences are particularly useful for my purposes because *their distinctive characteristics open a pathway to a species-wide understanding of the nature, functions, and value of RSEs*, an understanding that encompasses their evolutionary origins, their cognitive structure, their emotional texture, their neurological embedding, their bodily and social effects, and their existential and cultural importance.

Affiliation with other terms

Intensity is not the only factor that matters for RSEs, by any means. My own research has made that quite clear, both in phenomenological and neurological terms. Under a variety of names, however, the experiential characteristics I am collecting under the banner of "intensity" have been central in the phenomenology of religion, construed as the beating heart of many diverse and powerful RSEs, as well as potent aesthetic experiences and transformative experiences of creativity that have no recognizable religious connection but here are called spiritual. Indeed, students of the phenomenology of religion will immediately recognize the affiliations. Schleiermacher's absolute dependence, Otto's *mysterium tremendum et fascinans*, Maslow's peak experiences, Forman's pure consciousness events, and Newberg's experiences of absolute unitary being are subclasses of intense experiences. The same is true of many of the experiences more generically designated liminal, profound, numinous, extreme, transcendental, traumatic, sublime, *samādhi, vipaśyanā, ānanda*, nondual consciousness, wide awareness, flow, and so on. These affiliations show the internal diversity of intense experiences and also indicate how these variously named experiences might have shared features focusing on meaningfulness – which is why the map situates them within ultimacy experiences.

Similarities and differences

It is important to be as precise as possible about how the internally diverse class of intense experiences sustains shared features. Intense experiences display a distinctive family resemblance. The two most widely shared features in the family are cognitive and emotional potency that focuses attention; and rich interconnection of ideas, memories, and emotions that weaves normally separated parts of life into a single field of meaning. These features catalyze existential and spiritual potency and qualify intense experiences as a species of ultimacy experiences. Other features are widespread but not universal within the class of intense experiences. These include alterations in experience, including its bodily, perceptual, and time-sense aspects; changes in meaning and awareness; shifts in the direction of attention away from the surrounding mundane world and toward one's internal life and states of mind; large amounts of vivid imagery; significant feelings of fear and sadness, joy and love; and a decrease in both rational processing ability and control over one's own volitional powers. The diversity of intense experiences derives from these variable features, while their unity derives especially from the strength of activation and breadth of interconnection features.

Universality and social importance

The capacity for intense experiences in this depth-and-breadth sense appears to be virtually species-wide, regardless of their intricately personal and culturally specific manifestations in many kinds of RSEs. Anthropologists appear to have found no human group lacking this capacity, which is deeply, and perhaps characteristically, human. Also, intense experiences are probably the principal experiential driving force behind human spirituality in most of its forms, whether designated religious or not. Religion as a social reality arises mainly on the back of evolutionary pressures having to do with the regulation of human sociality for the sake of cooperation and stable social life, but the neurological capacity for depth-and-breadth intensity is vital in making religion existentially important and functional as a social reality. These two reasonable ideas jointly imply that intense experiences have special significance for the analysis of RSEs across cultural boundaries and over individual differences.

Neurological expression

Presumably existential potency and wide awareness requires pronounced neural activation in some processes as well as interconnection of neural activation sufficient to account for the rich linking up of ideas and feelings and memories without sacrificing focus of attention. Jared Diamond (1991) conjectured that neural capacities something like the depth-and-breadth activation I am describing require brain connectivity that was not present in other species and probably not in humans prior to 50,000 years ago, after which this capacity became one of the distinctive markers of modern humans. Diamond calls this era the "Great Leap Forward" on account of the vast effect on culture that this increase in neural complexity permitted. The capacity for depth-and-breadth intensity probably originates in this same era and thus is joined at the root to the cultural and technological creativity of the human species. It is difficult to investigate this, obviously. But contemporary neurological studies do show promise of generating cognitive and neural models of complex experiences such as RSEs, so at some point it may become possible to link up intense experiences, as well as RSEs more generally, to theories about the evolution of the human brain.

Philosophical and theological significance

Intense experiences often involve an intensification of ordinary sense perception that, conjoined with judicious interpretation, permits (without guaranteeing) cognitively reliable perception of, and imaginative engagement with, the valuational depths of nature. This is a large and important claim, controversial outside of (and even within some) theological circles, but actually quite modest in the form it receives here, because there is no guarantee of cognitive reliability but merely the assertion of a possibility. Thus, the analysis of intense experiences promises a way to evaluate both the reliability of religious cognitions and the value of religious behaviors.

Collectively, this mixture of empirical claims, theoretical interpretations, and descriptive elements constitutes the "intensity hypothesis." Each claim is complex and needs careful discussion. I begin with a phenomenology of intensity in an attempt to isolate the fundamental subclasses of intense experiences that make them religiously and spiritually meaningful, and that recur in varied combinations in every instance. Toward the end of the chapter I take up the question of the evolution of the neurological capacity for intense experiences. I defer discussion of the possibility of cognitive reliability until the next chapter.

From the outset it is important to be quite frank about the tentative nature of the intensity hypothesis. It is early days in the marriage of the neurosciences, evolutionary psychology, and the scientific study of religion, and it is unclear how happy or fruitful the union will be. A great deal of imaginative and challenging research is required to assess fully the variety of claims advanced in the intensity hypothesis. This is made more difficult by the challenges of studying the evolutionary stabilization and cultural universality of domains of experience that are subject to the degree of cultural and individual variation that intense experiences, and indeed RSEs, are. The personal specificity and context-dependent manifestations of intense experiences are necessary conditions for their existentially gripping character. But this flexible expression also makes assessing hypotheses about the evolutionary stabilization and cultural universality of the capacity for intensity a particularly challenging task.

There would be value in the argument of this book even if the intensity hypothesis were mistaken in its neurological or evolutionary conjectures, so long as the phenomenological insights were sound. The argument could still show the impotence of theories of the nature, functions, and value of RSEs articulated in isolation from evolutionary and neurological accounts of their origins and functions. It could still show that claims on behalf of the cognitive reliability of RSEs tend to overreach. It could still demonstrate the fabulous diversity of RSEs, thereby offering resistance to oversimplified accounts. It could still trace the phenomenological characteristics of RSEs, as well as their functional effects in individuals and social groups. And it could still discern the ways in which RSEs are valuable. But the evidence in favor of every aspect of the intensity hypothesis is persuasive, to various degrees, and this evidence is strengthening as research into RSEs expands its reach.

This chapter begins with phenomenology and ends with neurology. In the first section I discuss the three impulses or pressures that distinguish the core phenomenological components of intense experiences, here called "faces" of intensity. In the second section I present the five faces, which I dub depth, horizon, scale, complexity, and mystery. Subsequently, I compare these results with those of related efforts, discuss my terminology, and indicate how one might produce a theologically more systematic interpretation of intense experiences on the basis of these results. Finally, I discuss the evolution and neurology of intense experiences.

IMMEDIATE RESPONSES TO INTENSE EXPERIENCES

The method I employ in what immediately follows is a version of first-person phenomenological analysis merged with philosophical reflection. The aim is to draw salient generalizations about intense human experiences from particular instances of them.

The pressure to silence

One mid-November morning some years ago, I made my first visit to the Vietnam War Memorial in Washington DC. The design was unsettling, with the path plunging into the ground before arcing through and back up and out again. The mass of names, a veritable horde of them, swarmed around me as I slowly paced this gash in the earth. A young man traced a name on the wall. A few children were playing a short distance away. I could hear cries of "Catch it!" and teasing and laughter as I walked.

Though it was not part of my experience, I thought of the controversy surrounding the Vietnam War. I had heard stories of people losing life-long friends, ministers being run out of churches, and parents alienated from their own children, all because of their different perspectives on the war. I had seen films of crowds surrounding returning US soldiers, some shouting "Baby-killer!" and a few protesters even spitting on the fortunate who survived. I had read about the difficulty that returning soldiers had in reintegrating themselves into the fabric of society, and the high psychic cost of the war both for veterans and for the nation as a whole.

I pondered the sense of humiliation that burdened and perhaps still burdens some in the United States about the war. For some this humiliation was about not being able to stop communism from spreading in Vietnam. For others it was about the "police" role the US and its allies played in deciding what should happen in Southeast Asia. For still others it was about losing a war to which the armies allied with the North Vietnamese were so committed that their human losses alone were probably an order of magnitude greater than those of the armies allied with the South Vietnamese. For yet others it was about the undignified way in which public debate about the war was conducted across the USA, the shameful way that courageous American soldiers were treated, and the political short-sightedness of anti-war sentiment.

I thought of my country of origin, Australia, going to war on its Southeast Asian neighbor as an act of loyalty to its gargantuan cross-Pacific ally. The confusion about the war in Australia was complicated by other factors. Australians were one step further removed from the war than the US public, for whom the spread of communism was a more prominent issue, one more clearly worth fighting about. Yet Australia bordered Southeast Asia and had to concern itself with regional developments, and the US Navy and Marines had come to the rescue during the Second World War as Japanese troops headed south towards New Guinea and Australia. A country with memories of the rank incompetence of British commanders causing the pointless deaths of thousands on the shores of Turkey in the First World War, however, is always anxious when serving the interests of an ally even when it has interests of its own at stake.

I thought of Vietnam. I had never been there and had not then seen the shocking figures on Vietnamese casualties of the war, but I knew about defoliants, the horrific fate of some small villages, and the resentment toward the interfering West. I knew about Vietnam's reputation as a paradise and how the war dramatically changed the landscape, at least for a while. I thought about the grief over lost children affecting many more families in Vietnam than in the United States and its allies combined, rumbling through the generations as such unrelenting sorrow does.

These thoughts drifted through me as I walked the path. They were registered wordlessly, as feelings rather than as a series of thoughts. This wordlessness was the only way to let the furiously diverse perspectives on the war coexist in my imagination. I was silent for a long time afterwards. Just as I did not speak for more than a day after seeing the film *Gallipoli*, a retelling of some of the most tragic events of the Great War remembered ever after in Australia and New Zealand on Anzac Day (April 22), so I stayed silent for the rest of the day as I wandered about Washington. This silence was no ritual act of respect to the fallen; at least it was not primarily that. Mostly it was an attempt to allow the enormity of the events space to breathe in my imagination, a space that words would close off as soon as they began to intrude, which they would all too soon.

This pressure to silence was strong, then, and welcome. It is almost always welcome. It has the dimensions of home and the colors of winter. It is the full silence of thick, windless snowfall. It is fire-in-the-hearth relief from the harsh, time-bound linearity of language. It is an anti-social withdrawal from inane chattering, which in that state grates on my nerves and includes almost everything spoken or written. It is restful, then, but tinged both with a patient grief that anticipates the inevitability of silence broken and with a slightly desperate vigilance. When in such moods, my re-entry is unpredictable. It might be a smile and a courteous, simple reply to a child's question. Or it might be a selfishly savage attempt to defend my silent habitation, which is of course instantly destroyed by so harsh a move. These days, I try to smile.

Looking back on that emotional journey through the War Memorial and rethinking remembered currents of the stream of my consciousness at that time, I am impressed by an abiding conviction, namely, that a rational piecing together of these perspectives on the Vietnam War would be in bad taste. Floating along the silent flow of the river of feelings and ignoring the paddling option of thinking things out now seems to have been absolutely necessary for the significance of that experience to have had a chance of sinking in, of transforming me, of being honored in me.

The intensity of things sometimes conjures the pressure to silence. Rushing upwards from the unfathomable depth of our experiences, the pressure to silence engulfs us, we who are blessed with such a facility for language that we are used to being able to say almost anything to the point of being cavalier, unknowing victims of linguistic hubris. The shock of the pressure to silence is partly surprise at the sudden unmasking of language as a sinister adjunct to a subtle social habit of papering over the painful intensity of things. This habit lulls us into a flatly comfortable world defined by predictability and colored merely by aspirations for relatively harmless, well-controlled excursions into the terrible and the blissful and other extremities.

The pressure to silence is also about the need to acknowledge the failure of something. This might be the failure of language to capture that which we wish to express, but this risks misdescribing the situation as having chiefly to do with expressibility. It is perhaps more centrally the failure of the will to express. Whenever making the effort to speak the intensity of our experience strikes us as futile, as a distraction from action, as imprudent or immodest, as distasteful or dangerous, we are liable to be pressed to silence. Poets might dare to speak under such circumstances, but poetry is all the more dangerous for its hazardous aspirations, its winking disruption of the blanket of calm warmth that language wraps around our societies. All of these considerations are independent of the question of whether we can express everything we can think, with or without the aid of specialized languages and expert discourse communities to maintain them. From this it follows that the pressure to silence is not one thing in every instance, but rather is complex and shaped by context. Unsurprisingly, then, it is also constrained by the intensity that evokes it.

The pressure to speak

Feeling the pressure to silence and yielding to it in situations like the one I have described is my way, and I know that it is not the only way. I vividly recall a car trip back to Krakow after visiting Auschwitz and Birkenau, a far more overwhelming experience about which I dare not speak at all, and a very different sort of pressure to silence from the one I felt at the Vietnam War Memorial. That return journey was filled with the agonized and highly intellectual verbal processing of a friend as he struggled to come to terms with what he had seen. I was suffocating for want of silence even as my friend yielded to another pressure, familiar to me only in more mundane situations, to talk it out and to think it through. Though I suspect that my friend was as desperate for comfort and understanding as I was, the ways we responded to the existential crush and went about getting what we needed were quite different. We human beings are such diverse creatures! One seeks to defer to the intense through silence, while another bends the full power of intellect to a similar goal. In fact, both the pressure to speak and the pressure to silence are familiar to most people, and it is probably a blend of circumstances and personal style that determines which is activated.

There is a strange relationship between the pressure to silence and the pressure to speak. To see this, consider the familiar paradox that mystical writers of the apophatic sort have to embrace. Whereas their self-appointed task is to describe an object of experience that drives the mind away from familiar categories and words and toward something like undifferentiated unity or perfect emptiness, the medium available to them for expressing the idea of such experiences and for maintaining traditions of such expression is verbal. The paradox is obvious in the stating but prodigiously subtle in the outworking. The stresses induced in language by the end that apophatic mystical writers force it to serve are extreme. The great exponents of such writing have been similarly extreme in the creative production of techniques for getting the point across without vitiating the infinitely delicate final goal. Some scholars have analyzed these techniques at the level of syntax and grammar (see, for example, Knepper 2005; Sells 1994). There are also techniques at the level of symbol systems, such as balancing mechanisms (see Wildman, 1999) and conceptual trajectories (see, for example, Wildman 2001), and techniques depending on the historical play of symbolic transformations (see, for example, Neville 1996; Pelikan 1996, 1999).

The question to be asked in light of these phenomena is this: why do apophatic mystics bother to speak at all? Why not allow the pressure to silence free rein and just stop talking about such matters? Some do embrace silence in just this way; some members of silent religious orders are one example and another might be those Sufis who cultivate disciplined, joking, story-telling evasions of talk about ultimate matters. Mystical writers do not choose these paths, however. They experience a pressure to speak that is powerful enough to compete with the pressure to silence that their writings describe. Note that this has nothing to do with the *via negativa* or the *via positiva*, both of which are ways of speaking that represent themselves as paths toward deep visions of God and ultimately toward differently modulated silences. It has to do with the motivation of mystical writers. Most apophatic mystical writers manage to intensify the paradox of their bothering-to-speak-at-all by speaking mostly of the pressure to silence and saying relatively little about the pressure to speak. Yet it is the pressure to speak of the pressure to silence and that which provokes it that drives them into the position of intense creativity and makes their writings so memorable.

What, then, is this pressure to speak? By way of contrast, consider that there is a generalized habit among human beings of speaking, for diverse purposes and with effects of varying value. This is a biologically basic side-effect of a triple correlation: the development of vocal-tract physiology, the spontaneous creation of systems of language, and the evolution of the neural capacity for symbolic reference and other requirements of language. The pressure to speak as I mean it here refers not to this more or less unrestricted urge, however interesting it is – and it is fascinating – but to something every bit as distinctive and complex as the pressure to silence. The pressure to speak derives from this basic capacity for language as a specialized response to extraordinarily intense conditions.

My friend in the car trip away from Auschwitz and Birkenau felt one form of this pressure to speak; the poet experiences another; the prophet is driven by another; and the scholarly inquirer is subject, as I am here, to yet another. Each develops special techniques as subtle as those of mystical writers for speaking about that which, when felt most intensely, is difficult or impossible to capture in words and can even defeat the desire to speak. The poets play with language and become the high adventurers of trope. The inquirers create specialized discourses and cultivate traditions of knowledge. The prophets battle beneath the interminable wet blanket of oppressive social convention with masterful rhetoric. The worshippers speak and sing in ritualized ways whose expressive and transformative power finally turns more on blessed repetition than on cognitive content. These specific forms of the pressure to speak are distinguishable from the generalized urge to speak by context. Just as things show up as differently intense in different contexts, so human beings experience pressures to respond, in silence or by speaking, to that intensity.

The pressure to move

Distinguishing the pressure to speak from the pressure to silence seems to demand that we distinguish between the pressure to move and the pressure to stillness. Indeed, there is a point to this. I will collapse this sensible distinction and speak inclusively of the pressure to move, however, because there is no extended tradition of thought demanding recognition of the pressure to stillness (except in connection with meditation practices, which is not the focus here) as there is with the pressure to silence. This difference in intellectual heritage may reflect the linguistic distinctiveness of our species, so that the cessation of speech is more notable than cessation of movement, which we share with an enormous number of other animal species. Besides, we comprehend stillness as a kind of movement, so the possibility of no-motion is registered in what follows.

The neural hardwiring for movement refined in the evolutionary process is our inheritance: our central nervous system has everything from distributed processing that provokes the withdrawal from danger without having to waste time in centralized cognitive processing, to a flight response that triggers such cognitive confusion that the direction of our movement is as unknown to us as it is unpredictable to a dangerous foe. Our species has an enormous range of instinctive movements from means of locomotion to facial expressions. We have formidable dexterity that, combined with cognitive abilities, allows us to compensate for relative weaknesses in the strength and agility departments with tools and culture by means of which we can organize ourselves to penetrate and usually dominate most of our planetary home's diverse ecosystems. Our movement is geared to emotional states almost as much as to perception and cognition. We feel through moving and move in response to feeling in an incredibly fine-tuned feedback process. Without it we could never master the perpetual tumbling that is walking, nor learn to balance well enough to move in any other way, nor figure out how to compensate for our endlessly moving sense organs so as to stabilize perception.

Our brains develop in the early years on the basis of a complex hardwired connectivity of feedback processes among perception, emotion, and movement toward a prodigiously subtle set of finely adjusted neural connections. The resulting system makes all of our movements possible, from the subconscious rhythm of breathing and other autonomic bodily processes to the masterful elegance of the dancer or the breathtaking power of the sportsman. Indeed, the very aesthetic criteria by which we assess beauty, economy, and elegance of movement themselves derive from this same conjoining of hardwiring and learning that makes us able to move and to recognize movement in others. Nothing makes this clearer than the mirror neurons that cause our brains to react to the perception of moving human beings in the same way our own brains would fire if we ourselves were moving, save that other neural processes necessary for activating movement do not occur. We appreciate the movements of others literally by experiencing them to some degree in our own minds. This is how we judge beauty of movement as well as estimate the motivations and intentions associated with movements we see.

It is no wonder, then, that we have characteristic impulses to move when we undergo intense experiences. Of course, speech is a special kind of movement and the pressure to silence and the pressure to speak have been described. Beyond this, however, the pressure to move is extremely powerful. It is a visceral reaction to intensity that manifests itself in an enormous variety of ways, from sitting quietly and alert to the furious movement of limbs and torso in wild dancing, from the violent physical outburst to the joyous sprint, from cowering in terror to rocking a crying baby back to contentment. All of these physical movements are modulated by cognitive considerations. For example, prudence may determine that one's anger be expressed in a white-hot stare rather than bodily assault, and a cultured environment may determine that a subtle hand movement enters a bid at an auction even though such a movement would not be noticed elsewhere. One group may interpret falling down in a religious act of worship in a most positive light, whereas another group might read such movement as a medical emergency.

The diverse range and contextual variations of movement make correlations with intense experiences difficult to discern and even more difficult to explain. In the final analysis, the plausibility of associations between core features of intense experiences and various movements depends on identifying underlying primitive neural structures while controlling the effects of cognitive considerations related to personal style and social context. Little research has been done on this topic, whether in terms of surveys justifying associations of intense experiences with particular movements or in terms of the neural entanglements of emotion and movement. I think something can still be said, however, and I also think something ought to be said, if only to raise awareness of the importance of associations between feeling and movement that play a vital role in intense experiences.

FIVE CORE FEATURES OF INTENSE EXPERIENCES

Building a phenomenological toolbox

Philosophers and theologians, psychologists and poets with a special concern for intense meaningfulness of RSEs have long used metaphors to express the way certain experiences feel existentially significant for those who have them. Key metaphors of this type are depth, mystery, and horizon (used, for example, by Tillich 1951, 1957, 1963; and Rahner 1987, both influenced by Heidegger [1927] 1962). In each case, these terms draw interpreters of intense experiences beyond the bounds of the recognizably and officially religious toward the wonders and perils of the whole of life. These metaphors have thus become sensitive phenomenological tools for describing intense experiences in such a way as to open up the realm of spirituality to many people who consider themselves non-religious and even cultivate a degree of antipathy toward organized religion.

Interestingly, the toolbox of phenomenological categories for describing intense experiences is incomplete, or at least the tools are scattered and need to be collected together. For example, attending to the spiritual insights of scientists in their work invites the introduction of another phenomenologically tuned metaphor, complexity. And the metaphor of scale enables us to distinguish the familiar mystical experience of oceanic calm from the experience of depth. The aim of the discussion below is to manifest some of the key qualitative characteristics of intense experiences, and to relate these to the modulation of combinations of the five phenomenological categories, the faces of intensity: depth, horizon, scale, complexity, and mystery.

The intensity of experience may provoke behavioral consequences, but it has several immediate effects: the pressure to silence, the pressure to speak, and the pressure to move. These pressures arise in a variety of ways because the five faces of intensity – the component power sources of depth, horizon, scale, complexity, and mystery – can combine in different ways. I shall describe intensity by building a descriptive and conceptual bridge between the immediate effects or pressures of intensity and these component five power sources for intensity.

The result of this description could be given a grid-like expression in a diagram. On one axis would be ranged the five faces of intensity, while on another axis would be categories with reference to which the five are distinguished from one another. These categories would have three subgroups: the more definitive features of intensity (the three pressures), more generic expressions of intensity (emotion, action, sociality, ritual, and spirituality), and more specific cognitive-emotional features (attention, memory, rationality, and volitional control). Each of the resulting spaces in the diagram would be filled with descriptive material that, taken together, would compel the reader to ponder the claim that five faces of intensity are distinguishable in a convincing way. An actual diagram would mislead by suggesting unattainable clarity and comprehensiveness. I do intend to make an argument for a stable fivefold distinction, however, and the reader might keep this undrawn diagram in mind as the discussion unfolds.

It is important to ask about the stability of this phenomenology of intense experiences across cultures, eras, personalities, and mental capacities. That I cannot formally test here, but my exposure to the core texts and motifs of world religious traditions has guided the description and will continue to correct it (see the volumes of the Cross-Cultural

Comparative Religious Ideas Project, Neville 2001, which helps to inform my judgments in this regard).

Depth

First, depth is registered in feelings of intense fear, joy, or bliss. Associated mental states typically have no direct object. The primary activity invited is that of surrender, with consciousness of being at the mercy of something that may or may not be worthy of trust, but which is trusted nonetheless, inevitably. This is the import of Yahweh placing Moses in the cleft of the rock for his protection, David dancing in the temple, and Shiva dancing in destruction across the face of the earth. In such situations, our ultimate environment shows up as deadly and yet gracious, though there is absolutely no rational cause to believe that grace can be counted on in the situation. Thus, surrender is the natural response. This is the founding experience of grace in religious life, regardless of the doctrinal framework furnished for it. Attempts to understand are irrelevant in this state.

No social structures are associated with the recurrence of these kinds of feelings, but in small communities the achievement of this awareness is prized and rewarded with admiration and respect. Liturgy registers the reality of this experience of depth in praise, whether verbally or musically, and more especially in adoration, where the particular cognitive content of what is said or sung fades, allowing something akin to a blissful trance state to predominate. Repetition of songs and mantras as well as rhythmic techniques can help relativize cognitive content on the way to such states of consciousness.

The pressure to silence associated with the experience of depth is that of surrender to fear and bliss, which involves the prohibition of pretenses to control such as language typically connotes. The pressure to speak associated with the experience of depth is that of playful babbling, incoherent singing, glossolalia, screaming, and mumbling – the forms of speaking that deconstruct the illusion of control associated with the cognitive grasp of language. The pressure to move is especially interesting here: the experience of depth seems to be the consistent inspiration for solo dancing and trance dancing.

Horizon

Second, horizon is registered in feelings associated with recognizing difference, such as fascination, alienation, fear, disgust, or hate. The experience of horizon can be aggressively internalized as failure to recognize oneself or a part of one's body, with the associated sense of panic or violation. It can also be spectacularly externalized into powerful senses of presence, which may be hostile or benign. The mental states in which horizon is realized always have objects and thus are intentional states, but the objects may be either diffuse or specific. The primary activity associated with horizon is engagement, which can cover everything from defending and fighting to dialoguing and flirting. Understanding this response involves interpretation, comparison, and dialogue.

Politics is the institutional sphere in which the recurrence of this experience in human life is most directly registered, and the typical social form that presupposes it is the group that represents special interests. There are legitimation processes associated with any group's perpetuation and function; the legitimation processes of special-interest groups are essentially ideological and self-protective. Liturgy responds to the prevalence of this human experience with confession, intercession, and supplication. Consciousness of ourselves and our own pain and interests and concerns is centralized in such liturgical acts, but they also engage us with the Other as essential to our own well-being.

The pressure to silence associated with the experience of horizon is that of fearful and fascinated recognition of difference, a pregnant silence in which words are necessary, yet all words are premature. When engagement demands the breaking of the dangerous silence, the pressure to speak takes the form of the language of politics, words that serve the end of surviving and thriving: diplomacy, prophecy, negotiation, rhetoric, and persuasion. These special kinds of verbal dance are akin to the pressure to move evoked in experiences of horizon as dancing: flirtatious dancing, body-grinding dancing, teasing dancing, the ballroom tango, and the candlelit balcony waltz of lovers.

Scale

Third, scale is registered fundamentally in feelings of awe, which can involve oceanic calm or the anxiety of agoraphobia, vastness, or emptiness, and which leads out into feelings of benevolence, compassion, wideness of heart, or loss of self. The panoramic appreciation of the nature mystic is typically dominated by scale; the natural world becomes vast and all-encompassing, abundantly fertile and creative, from the very large to the very small, and from the very far to the very near. The feeling of emptiness is correlated with this feeling of vastness, because, as the appreciation of the vastness of reality widens, the filtering of that reality through personal interests lessens, to the point that utterly succulent vivid awareness coincides with emptiness of self. The need to register the mutual determination of vastness and emptiness is the reason why this face of ultimacy is better called "scale" than either "vastness" or "emptiness," though "scale" is admittedly a bit obscure (but then "depth" and "horizon" would also seem obscure were they not stabilized by extant habits of discourse). While intense experiences of scale are sometimes terrifying and can skittle psychic stability, they can also induce peacefulness, equanimity, and wideness of heart. It is just as the Buddha taught: the realization of vastness/emptiness evinces compassion, for the reason that everything is related in an all-encompassing vista, so that my interests are viscerally experienced as merged with those of every being everywhere. The mental states associated with experiences of scale are typically objectless, as with experiences of depth. But experiences of scale are distinguishable from experiences of depth both because of the feelings involved and because the basic urge is not to surrender (as in depth) but to behold, an essentially selfless reaction. As with experiences of depth, attempts to understand experiences of scale are irrelevant because they interfere with beholding.

No social institutions exist in specific recognition of the prevalence of experiences of scale; both they and experiences of depth are essentially deconstructive impulses within human social life, unmasking self-protection and mocking clever legitimation strategies. Liturgy responds to the presence of experiences of scale in human life with songs of grandeur, with heart-stoppingly glorious architecture, with awe-inspiring language.

The pressure to silence in this case prohibits words in the name of making us small so that the universe can expand in our imaginations, consuming us. The pressure to speak shows itself as unselfconscious, rippling laughter on the way to speaking "Om," when it is the word that comprehends all and evokes all. Yielding to the pressure to move in this case leads to dancing alone among trees, dancing alone under the stars, running in trains of hand-holding friends streaming like wind gusts across grassy hills, or else sitting quietly in the open-bodied lotus position.

Complexity

Fourth, complexity is registered in feelings of confusion, disorientation, irritation, surprise, and wonder. A mental state in which complexity is dominant has an object. The object might swarm around us, as the world does for the airplane pilot in twisting freefall. Or else the complexity of this object might be newly noticed, provoking "oohs" and "aahs" and stimulating curiosity. The primary activities associated with experiences of complexity have to do with the satisfaction of curiosity, the relief of confusion, and the solving of problems, all of which lead to serious attempts to control and understand that which irritates or provokes curiosity. Understanding in this case involves inquiry and associated activities of model building, experimenting, testing, and exploring. Liturgy addresses the prevalence of experiences of complexity with the reading and exposition of sacred texts, with educational and inspirational public speaking, and with moments of pastoral care.

There are many social institutions whose reason for existence depends upon the recurrence of experiences of complexity, from educational and research institutions with explicit missions to understand, to family and community institutions implicitly devoted to controlling the problematic environment of human life. These institutions protect and provide resources for solving theoretical and practical problems; for comforting the confused, orienting the lost, and soothing the irritated; and for giving free rein to wonder and curiosity. It is here that human beings are at their creative best, transforming overwhelming confusion into social arrangements that steady the spinning world and inventing technologies that control and alter the environment for human life.

This describes the pressure to speak, but the pressure to silence hovers nearby. We are driven to respectful silence by wonder: the cell under a microscope, Jupiter's moons through a telescope, a finely tuned ecosystem, or the proof of Pythagoras' theorem of right-angled triangles. We are compressed into silence by the suffocating confusion of complex problems: the production and fair distribution of food on planet earth, the endlessly rebellious teenager, the inner workings of our own minds, or the way long chains of amino acids consistently fold into the same-shaped protein. In no sphere of intense experiences does the pressure to silence yield so quickly to the pressure to speak. But the pressure to silence hovers beneath and at the boundaries of human confusion and our prodigious efforts to solve problems. The pressure to move is as powerful as the pressure to speak in this case, and gives rise to making, molding, and crafting; poking, prodding, and exploring; looking under, around, and through; weighing, testing, and measuring; finding out, finding more, finding *it*; researching, recording, rethinking, and retracing steps. The whirlwind of movement spins as fast as the words flow.

Mystery

Fifth, mystery is registered in feelings of ignorance and incomprehension. Whereas the experience of complexity yields to curiosity through positioning the object as a tractable problem, the experience of mystery involves being stopped in one's tracks. The object in this case always seems diffuse, beyond our control, and cognitively impenetrable. This is so whether or not the object really can, with right effort and skillful means, be specified, controlled, or understood. The primary activity associated with mystery is reverence, which involves recognizing that the mystery must be set apart and made holy. Attachment to mystery is common, which leads to rationalizing its incomprehensibility by distinguishing between secular and sacred, creating rules that protect the sacred and defend it from incursions of the curious, and delineating ritual space and time within which the mystery can be savored with proper reverence.

Religious institutions are the social forms that most directly recognize the recurrence of experiences of mystery in human life. Ritual, sacrament, vestment, and symbol are the lifeblood of the liturgical recognition of mystery. Hierarchy and authority are the concomitants of institutionalizing commitment to the defense of mystery. Hierarchical authority can be used to suppress and resist incursions of the curious by framing them as lacking the requisite appreciation and respect for the mystery and carelessly trampling on that which deserves reverence. Reverence is enormously captivating. At the heart of institutionalized religion lies not merely Nietzsche's priest, cruelly sucking the life out of the weak and dependent, but also people captivated by mystery, at times perhaps obsessive like the desperate lover, but revering that which is more valuable to them as mysterious than as comprehended. And though many former mysteries have proved to be tractable to inquiry in recent centuries, the primal mystery of our existence remains, undergirding all life and evincing reverence from all who sense it.

The pressure to silence in this case is the silence of reverence. Whereas the silent wonder of complexity yields quickly to the chatter of inquiry, the silence of reverence is difficult to interrupt for lack of any motivation to do so. The pressure to speak in this case is driven by the needs of sacrament and liturgy, authority and legitimation. The pressure to move in this case is the power source for ritual, for the raising of the hands just so, for the pouring of the milk just so, for the delicately tuned timbre and inflection of voice, the simple but elegant economy of movement, the impeccably careless casting of rose petals.

THE FACES, FUNCTIONS, AND COGNITIVE VALUE
OF INTENSE EXPERIENCES

Comparison with extant phenomenologies of intense experiences

The approach to intense experiences taken here comprehends a number of other attempts to articulate core components of intense experiences. For example, as mentioned in passing above, intense experiences are prominent in what psychologist Abraham Maslow called peak experiences, though not necessarily with the connotations of ineffability or ecstasy or transcendence that Maslow gave them, nor are they necessarily joyful or exciting, or even affectively positive (see Maslow 1964, and also Maslow 1970, 1971). Intensity is also prominent in experiences of flow, as described by Hungarian psychologist Mihály Csikszentmihályi (see Csikszentmihályi 1990), in what German philosopher Rudolf Otto called experiences of the numinous (see Otto [1917] 1925), in what has been called sublime experiences since ancient times in the West and later in Romantic poetry and aesthetics (see especially Burke 1757 and Schopenhauer [1819] 1977), in experiences of bliss or *ānanda* in South Asia (see especially Yogananda 1954, 2004), in experiences of vivid awareness and florid sensory perception, in certain potent dream states, and even in experiences of terror and horror.

Many philosophers and theologians have attempted to evaluate the epistemological and moral significance of RSEs by drawing inferences about the causes of intense experiences. These approaches often include a descriptive component that is deployed prior to drawing theological conclusions, and it is worth considering how these descriptive efforts relate to the one presented here. I have made a representative selection of a large group of thinkers who have done this, but the group is rich enough to illustrate the point that the five faces of intensity create the possibility of understanding these existing efforts as partial perspectives on the wider class of intense experiences. These partial perspectives are adequate for the particular aims of each thinker, but actually capable of generalization, with associated benefits in understanding.

First, Friedrich Schleiermacher ([1820–21] 1928) contended that a "feeling of absolute dependence" pervaded thought and action in the sense of being a condition for their possibility. Schleiermacher's controversial way of speaking about dependence as a feeling may express the need for a distinction between feeling as a real metaphysical relation of dependence, on the one hand, and feeling as a way of detecting this metaphysical relation, on the other. In terms of the analysis of intense experiences given here, Schleiermacher's dependence is most closely related to depth and horizon. When we are aware of our pervasive dependence, we are at the mercy of something wondrous by which we are fascinated and to which we might be inclined to surrender, which is the depth form of intensity. We are simultaneously vividly aware of that on which we are dependent as utterly other, which is the horizon form of intensity.

Second, Rudolf Otto's phenomenology of the irrational dimensions of religious experience leads to its analysis as encounter with the holy (see Otto [1917] 1925). This holy corresponds in the current scheme to a blending of the depth, scale, and mystery forms of intense experience.

Third, Paul Tillich's investment in depth psychology and Neoplatonism led to his use of such images as depth, ground, and abyss to describe the ultimate that is disclosed in human existence (see Tillich 1951). Human beings are anxious, alienated, and in need of the courage to be. In Tillich's case, therefore, we hear the accent on the depth and horizon forms of intense experience.

Fourth, Karl Rahner (1978) offers a beautiful analysis of human freedom, whereby the moment of choice is disclosed to be an infinitely graced presentation of the depths of being, inviting the movement toward the horizon of future possibilities. These are the elements of depth and horizon melded together, much as in Tillich. Yet our ignorance of the source of this grace, the formal impossibility of grasping or controlling it, is strongly emphasized in Rahner, thereby drawing in the mystery form of intense experience.

Fifth, Gordon Kaufman (1993) emphasizes the fact that human beings are biohistorical creatures, evoking or provoking awareness of an unendingly complex dependence on a biological web of being and an endless entanglement with the historical constraints on and possibilities of human existence. Here we see in particular the scale and complexity forms of intense experience woven together in a scientifically sensitized portrayal of human nature. Despite the title, *In Face of Mystery*, Kaufman's interest in the mystery face of intense experiences is not especially pronounced; his is the silence of wonder that yields to inquiry rather than the silence of reverence that yields to protection of mystery.

Sixth, recent neurological studies of religious experience have the potential to illumine a phenomenological description of intense experiences. For example, Newberg proposes a correlation between the reduction of brain signaling to a specific brain area (what he and Eugene d'Aquili call the "orientation association area" that determines where the self is in relation to its environment) and subjective reports by Tibetan monks of experiences in which the boundaries of self merge with the environment and the world is perceived as vastly interconnected, as suddenly free of filtering through the ordinary categories of language, and as productive of benevolence and compassion (see d'Aquili and Newberg 1999; Newberg *et al.* 2001b). This is an instance of an intense experience of scale. Similarly, Persinger's investigations of the temporal-lobe correlates of mysterious experiences of presences refers to what here is comprehended as an intense experience in the mode of horizon (see Persinger 1983, 1987, 1994a, 1994b; Persinger and Healey 2002).

Finally, recall the short-term and long-term ultimacy experiences discussed in the previous chapter (Wildman and Brothers 1999). Short-term episodes involve sensory alterations, self-alterations, sense of presences, compelling cognitions, and powerful emotions; while long-term experiences involve existential potency, social embedding, transformation of behavior, transformation of personality, and transformation of beliefs. This neuropsychological categorization – particularly of short-term episodes, which are directly relevant to intense experiences – harmonizes with the five faces of intensity because each element of the neuropsychological description of short-term ultimacy experiences can be intense in differently modulated ways. For example, compelling cognitions are intense, but they may be differently intense depending on the content of the cognitions and their existential importance to those who have them; they may be cognitions about the vast ocean depths (probably intensity dominated by scale), about the intricacy of cellular machinery (probably intensity dominated by complexity), or about an unnerving encounter with a stranger (probably intensity dominated by horizon).

Assessing the personal and social effects of intense experiences

Intense experiences provoke varied responses in those that have them, with both personal and social effects. This is where McNamara's (2009) neurocognitive account of decentering (discussed above) is particularly valuable: it helps to explain how intense experiences produce changes in behavior and self-understanding. These effects can be both positive and negative to varying degrees, and sometimes both at once in different respects. Of course, assessing positive versus negative effects is a delicate matter involving culturally formed criteria and group commitments that determine or at least influence the values that figure in such assessments.

I shall discuss a range of effects of intense experiences in what follows by means of a case study.

Suppose a man has a terrifying intense experience. He describes it as an encounter with a demon who means to harm him and those he loves. This is an intense experience dominated by the element of horizon, possibly with a subordinate degree of the depth element. As an intense experience, it is also an ultimacy experience, and in this case one that involves four of the five elements of short-term ultimacy experiences: sensory alterations, sense of presences, compelling cognitions, and powerful emotions (self-alterations are less evident; see the previous chapter's discussion of Wildman and Brothers 1999). This person experiences a degree of terror that makes him anxious and vigilant. Having formerly thought of demons and other discarnate entities as superstitions, he is now utterly confident of their reality. The experience also spurs commitment to a suitably minded group that employs ritual practices in an attempt to control malevolent discarnate entities through cultivating loyal relationships with more benevolent and protective discarnate entities – in this case, revered and powerful ancestors. He hears of another group that solicits angels rather than ancestors for protection from demonic powers, but entreating help from ancestors feels more powerful to him because his ancestors have a special interest in his health and happiness and that of his family. His participation in his group's ritual experiences is a long-term commitment that involves four of the five characteristic features of extended ultimacy experiences: existential potency, social embedding, transformation of behavior, and transformation of beliefs – with transformation of personality being the least prominent feature.

When considering this case study, the impartial outsider naturally asks whether the beliefs about discarnate entities are true, whether the psychic vigilance flowing from the encounter experience is healthy, whether protection-seeking ritual practices are efficacious, whether ancestor-focused rituals are in fact superior to angel-focused rituals, whether a group identity built around this swirl of beliefs is worthy of any degree of personal commitment, whether the existence of such groups is good for society, and whether there are any subtle long-term effects on mental and physical health of embracing this worldview and the associated group practices. Moreover, those who are not impartial and those who are insiders may have their own assessment questions. For example, someone whose own worldview affirms the reality of discarnate entities may still question the validity of ritual processes that attempt to solicit protective favors from some of these beings in order to control others. And wise folk in the same group as the man in the case study might judge that the trauma of the original encounter experience has produced in this particular person a degree of psychic vigilance that has crossed fully over into personally destructive paranoia, interfering with healthy functioning in daily life.

This array of assessment questions points both to a wide range of possible effects of intense experiences and a variety of loci of evaluation. I will discuss the former in the framework furnished by the latter. The three loci of evaluation are intra-group discernment, inter-competitor comparison, and external assessment; each is suited to evaluating certain effects.

Within a like-minded group, discernment practices are typically employed to assess the way people respond to intense experiences, especially experiences that the group recognizes and cultivates. In this case, common-sense understandings of physical and mental health are present and operative through the accumulated wisdom of the "old heads" and "powerful personalities" in the group. The failure of intra-group discernment within groups of young people that lack or exclude older or more experienced people is one of the factors triggering cult-like beliefs and behaviors, sometimes to the point of violence or self-destruction. This shows that intra-group discernment can be effective in regulating the effects of intense experiences even when an outsider would judge that the group's worldview is mistaken and its practices useless. In other words, people can move toward emotional and spiritual maturity within groups that hold mistaken beliefs and practice futile rituals.

Inter-competitor comparison occurs between fundamentally similar and therefore competitive groups – say, groups recommending alternative ritual ways of leveraging supernatural resources for protection against malevolent discarnate entities. Between such groups, relatively compatible comparative measures of efficacy typically emerge, which allow people to rationalize their commitment to one group's outlook in the presence of clear alternatives. In this case, there are competitive groups that appeal for help either to ancestors or to angels, and each is typically suspicious of the other. Each group occasionally refers to the other in such a way as to imply that their own group is superior because their members access more powerful supernatural resources and thereby win greater peace of mind. These comparative measures are virtually never deployed fairly or impartially or even publicly. After all, their purpose is not to help people decide which group to join but to rationalize existing group commitment and to mitigate the cognitive dissonance induced by awareness that a close competitor exists. It is socially inevitable that inter-competitor comparisons should exist, and almost inevitable that they are deployed to serve chiefly the interests of group identity and personal comfort. Their interpretation of the effects of intense experiences is virtually worthless.

Between fundamentally different groups – say, science-oriented health practitioners and researchers, on the one hand, and devotees of rituals for enjoining ancestors for protection from malevolent demons, on the other hand – relatively incompatible criteria operate to assess the truth of group beliefs and the value of group practices. Though evaluation will run in both directions, naturally, the pertinent direction for my purposes is the outside group's evaluation of a group whose existence depends to a significant extent on the occurrence and effects of particular sorts of intense experiences. When the evaluating outsiders are not biased in principle against the claims of the group of devotees, and the criteria and methods of external evaluation are subject to scrutiny and adjustment as necessary, it is often possible to generate significant consensus among differently minded experts about the value of the intense experiences in question, at least in certain respects – and this gives these effects public standing and credibility. Those in the evaluated group may or may not concur, depending on the evaluation. Which effects of intense experiences can external evaluation handle effectively?

The mental and physical health effects of a few kinds of intense experiences, particularly as they occur in the context of religious groups, have proved amenable to public scientific evaluation. For example, there is a large, albeit controversial literature around the health effects of meditation practices, which are sometimes religious and sometimes not. But the effects of meditation practices are not necessarily the same as the effects of individual intense experiences in meditation; it is quite difficult to disentangle the two. It follows that asking about the health effects of an individual experience is normally not a meaningful question. There are exceptions: a single traumatic intense experience can have devastating consequences for mental health, and some traumatic experiences lead to suicide. More positively, a single near-death experience can dramatically alter health-relevant convictions and behaviors, virtually overnight. Generally speaking, however, the health effects of individual intense experiences are extremely difficult to assess.

One of the most obvious effects of intense experiences is new beliefs. The intensity of some experiences can produce potent cognitions that are seared into a person's belief structure where they function with a confidence that massively outstrips any and all available evidence, long after the formative intense experience itself. This reflects the intensity-triggered swamping of global semantic matching processes that ordinarily dictate whether a candidate for a belief should be accepted or rejected, and with what degree of confidence (mentioned in earlier chapters; see Wildman and Brothers 1999). This is why a well-meaning advisor may find it virtually impossible to talk someone out of a course of action to which he or she is strongly committed on the basis of intense experiences, no matter how unwise it seems to the advisor and to those who have not been through those experiences.

When an entire group prizes a particular type of intense experience – speaking in tongues or handling snakes, fire-walking or faith-healing, risky mission work or public protests, extreme sports or encounters with malevolent discarnate entities as in our case study – an initiate having that experience for the first time can feel a special bond with the group, temporarily unshakable in its strength, and capable of producing life-altering decisions that baffle outsiders. In such situations, would-be advisors from outside the group are typically deemed pitiful souls who lack the requisite spiritual wisdom and experience to possess an authoritative opinion; this interpretative framework helps to rationalize the group's identity while marginalizing competing authorities.

There are some exceptions to this stalemate scenario. Consider glossolalia, which usually involves intense experiences of various degrees, though typically tongues-speaking remains under the volitional control of the one who does it. This phenomenon has a rich cross-cultural presence, so it is difficult to generalize about the reasons for its appearance offered in local narratives. In the Christian context, the appearance of glossolalia in sacred scriptures helps to produce a cross-cultural consensus, so that people who speak in tongues refer to glossolalia explicitly as a gift of the Holy Spirit – an intimate personalized gift that enables the believer to communicate with God "in sighs too deep for words." Christians who experience glossolalia also usually believe that their "language" is a genuine language, either a living or dead human language or an angelic language. Most of these beliefs lie beyond the reach of any evaluation. But the claim that gift of glossolalia is a genuine language is subject to assessment. The bottom line here, as mentioned in an earlier chapter, is that the independent phonetic components of glossolalia are too few and too repetitively employed for it to be any genuine human language (see linguistic studies such as Bryant and O'Connell 1971; Goodman 1972; Samarin 1972; and the survey in Mills 1986). This does not rule out the claim of an angelic language, but it does entail that any such angelic language would have to be far more primitive and underdeveloped than any human language. Naturally these conclusions of objective linguistic analysis carry little weight among most people who speak in tongues. But this does show that some aspects of beliefs triggered by an intense experience can be evaluated in a public, rational way. Most beliefs produced by intense experiences appear to be beyond the reach of public, scientific evaluation, and require the subtle reasoning of philosophers who can work competently across disciplines and religious traditions.

The effects of intense experiences can be immediate and can also accumulate. So the shock (perhaps of other-awareness) of an intense experience, when repeated and ritualized, can accumulate into a new lifestyle, as in our case study. The affective unpleasantness of an intense experience can induce immediate avoidance, and when repeated can accumulate into aversive and paranoid personality structures. The wonder of an intense experience can trigger curiosity, and several such experiences can induce extended investigations. The cognitive elements of a single intense experience can produce new beliefs, and repetition and socially aided conceptual framing can lead to the construction of worldviews with relative coherence, including legitimation of social support and rationalization of exceptions. The potent aesthetic elements of an intense experience – say, a compelling experience of flow – can accumulate into inspiring motivations for self-cultivation, with the aim of increasing virtuosity in one or another realm of appreciation or performance.

The phenomenon of virtuosity is particularly valuable for appreciating the cumulative effects of intense experiences that may not arise in religious contexts. Consider a musical, dramatic, or sports performance, an act of meditation, or an interpersonal encounter in which the performer experiences such identification with the task that they lose all traces of self-consciousness and feel in complete unity with the art form, whatever that might involve in a given case. Such flow experiences produce an unguarded spontaneity of behavior that is the hallmark of virtuosity, explicitly thematized particularly in Confucian cultural settings and prized in all cultural contexts. By contrast with the unexpected and unwanted demonic encounter in our case study, above, virtuosity is a highly cultivated form of intensity that often involves most or all of the five component elements simultaneously. Such experiences are possible only through rigorous training and focused self-discipline. But one of the motivations for the rigors of such training is the experience of flow itself, which is an intrinsically rewarding experience that induces budding experts to return again and again to their sphere of expertise. Intense experiences of this kind, considered both singly as flow experiences and cumulatively as virtuosity, appear to be fundamental aspects of human potential that are deeply spiritual without having any specifically religious aspects.

This draws our attention to another dimension of variation within the domain of intense experiences: degree of virtuosity. The degree of virtuosity varies from reflexive spontaneity (where one is caught off guard and has no control), through cultivation in disciplines and practices (where one gains control), to a sophisticated spontaneity (where control is so great that exceptional fluency and creativity become possible). All five component elements of intensity can appear in intense experiences with all three degrees of virtuosity. For example, the element of horizon in experiences of encounter and confrontation at the lowest level of virtuosity produces the shock and surprise of unexpected horror or bliss. At the middle level, the experiences are routinized, ritualized, and the objects of disciplined reflection, so that they can be produced more reliably and their emotional effects better controlled. At the highest level of virtuosity, the same experience of horror or bliss occurs without shock or confusion, is taken in stride as a manifestation of the otherness of reality, and disciplined awareness causes this otherness to be experienced as a wondrous aspect of the self. For another example, the element of complexity in intense experiences transforms with increasing virtuosity from simple wonder and awe at the lowest level, through a middle level in which those feelings are structured and complemented by disciplined study and sound knowledge, to an ever-present awareness that is both emotionally potent and profoundly and accurately knowledgeable at the highest level of virtuosity.

From intense experiences to intensity

I now broach questions of terminology and metaphysics. I begin with the rationale for using the adjective "intense" to qualify "experiences." I then ponder the possibility of using the nominalized "intensity" to refer not only to the quality of depth-and-breadth intense experiences but also to the Whence of intense experiences – that is, that to which intense experiences are in some sense a reaction, which they express in more or less colorful and existentially vital ways.

First, then, consider names. The quality of intense experiences could have been called profundity or richness, perhaps, though these terms have their problems. The main liability of the term "profundity," beyond its semantic proximity to the already reserved word "depth," is that it misleadingly suggests an intellectual state by means of its familiar association with ideas. The main problem with "richness" is its invocation of balanced harmony and evaluation, with the corresponding diminution both of the element of immediacy suggested by "intensity" and of the possibility of a distinct lack of balance in the way the five component elements appear in intense experiences. In fact, alongside experiences of harmony, I have tried to describe those moments when we human beings feel most vividly alive, whether in terror or wonder, or most open to and aware of the environment of our lives, whether constructively or destructively. To use a spatial analogy, such experiences involve a combination of the vertical dimension of vivid awareness – the intensity of feeling vividly alive – and the horizontal dimension of openhearted connection – the intensity of relationship with other living beings and even with the cosmos itself in some sense. These dimensions occur with varying weightings in the five component elements of intensity. Depth, for example, is most strongly associated with the vertical dimension, whereas horizon is most strongly associated with the horizontal dimension. Scale is a mixture of both, as are complexity and mystery in distinctive ways.

Multifaceted experiences featuring many of the five faces of depth-and-breadth intensity can be intense even when they are limited in either the vertical or the horizontal dimensions. For example, the ecstasy of obsessive fulfillment, as when lovers feel the need for nothing besides each other, involves openheartedness that is genuine but tightly constrained, being limited in scope to each other and focused by obsessive attachment; the vertical dimension is the most evident. Similarly, great servants of humanity in their ordinary activities are compassionately open to the needs of others to an extent that would collapse lesser souls, yet intensity of feeling (the vertical dimension) is limited in the everyday exercise of compassion. "Intensity" seems to register both dimensions at once about as well as any English word does.

Second, can we safely extend the reference of "intensity" from a name for the general quality of intense experiences, which we have freely admitted are diverse, to a name for that to which intense experiences are ultimately a response? That is, can the characterization of intense experiences as environmentally conditioned, as a response to *something*, justify using the name "intensity" for that environmental *something*? This is a procedural question of great interest to philosophers and theologians who might want to construct atop the foundational phenomenological analysis offered here a superstructure in the form of comprehensive theories of intense experiences that will illumine questions of their causation and their moral and epistemic significance.

To put the promise and the problem of this possibility in a pointed way: if there are stable patterns of inference from intense experiences to the nature of intensity, then we have discovered something important about reality, something of enormous interest to students of religion and philosophy. Indeed, a theory of intensity might be forthcoming that would have the proportions of a theological account of ultimate reality. Rather than sneaking this possibility into the imagination by means of surreptitious usage of the word "intensity" it is wise to reflect on the overtones of this way of speaking, to flush the hidden metaphysical controversy into the open, and to inquire explicitly about the feasibility of the associated inference.

Ordinary people routinely draw inferences about the moral and metaphysical nature of reality on the basis of their intense experiences, particularly those approved of within a group to which they belong. A few philosophers have defended this common-sense procedure by shifting the debate from experience to perception, by arguing that ordinary perception is just as epistemically dubious as extraordinary perception, and then by proposing to allow the corporate wisdom of socially located discernment procedures to do for extraordinary perception what trial and error in everyday life does for ordinary perception (we will take this up in the next chapter; see Swinburne 1979 and especially Alston 1991). Other philosophers have attacked the defenders of common-sense inference from intense experiences by urging recognition of contextual and epistemic complexities, much as always has been done within the traditions of the hermeneutics of suspicion. Yet other critics have urged that ordinary perception is far more reliable than extraordinary perception because the former is subject to more robust fidelity conditions (such as survival of the perceiving organism) than the latter, even when it benefits from the most sophisticated discernment practices operative within a socio-linguistic community (see especially Bagger 1999).

If the skeptics (such as Bagger) are correct, the sort of inference constructive metaphysicians seek to make from intense experiences to the nature of intensity is always invalid. If common-sense reliabilists (such as Alston) are correct, then the constructive metaphysicians have an embarrassment of riches, with allegedly robust chains of inference leading to bluntly contradictory conclusions about the nature of ultimate reality. (Alston [1991] tries to deal with the problem of religious pluralism, but I think his effort on this front does not rise above the well intentioned.) My own view is that both sides are extreme. The question about the feasibility of inference from intense experiences to the nature of intensity can and should be framed in empirical terms. That is, the possibility of this sort of inference can be neither established nor rejected definitively in advance, so one needs to try and see. When we try and see, we learn quite a lot.

For example, we learn that inferences from intense experiences produce a high degree of metaphysical conflict. Thus, we need to treat such inference with great caution, attending to the contextual specifications of the vague categories used to express the inferences in question. Yet when inference is properly sensitive to considerations of vagueness and context, it has proved possible to achieve sensitive interpretations of religious ideas that do not provoke the specter of unlimited metaphysical conflict. This was the burden and also the achievement of the Cross-Cultural Comparative Religious Ideas Project (Neville 2001). So what would happen if a similarly sensitive form of inference were attempted from the cognitive content of intense experiences rather than from traditionally established religious ideas?

I will take up this subject in more detail in the next chapter but I shall anticipate here slightly. I think that we should expect partial success in gaining insight into the Whence of intense experiences. The limiting factors are significant, and call to mind some of the challenges facing the neurological study of RSEs discussed in Chapter 2: (i) the irresolvable vagueness of terms used in self-descriptions of intense experiences, (ii) the lack of stable correlations between neural states and self-reports by which vague categories might be stabilized, and (iii) our poor understanding of the large role played by social context in conditioning self-reports of intense experiences.

From one point of view, the problem is our limited understanding of the ways intense experiences are like and unlike sense perception. The value of likening intense experiences to sense perception (as Alston and Bagger both well understand from their opposed points of view) is that our understanding of how sense perception produces reliable knowledge claims is then made relevant for making sense of knowledge claims arising from intense experiences. This analogy, if it holds up in the right respects, ameliorates all three of the limiting factors above. But the hard truth seems to be that intense experiences are only partly like perception; they are far more entangled with emotion and embodied responses than sense perception is, and seem to have a different type of presentational immediacy, or way of making manifest their objects – and thus the limiting factors listed above appear to be genuinely difficult to remove.

I shall argue in the next chapter that sense perception is not understood correctly in the mainstream of this debate. Sense perception is better understood as a form of dynamic environmental engagement, much as intense experiences are a form of dynamic environmental engagement. This rules out the presentational immediacy that Alston relies on to establish the cognitive reliability of religious experiences, but it does not contradict his direct realism. It also rules out the sharp contrast between sense experience and intense religious experiences that Bagger relies on to buttress his skeptical outlook. Positively, a proper understanding of both sense experience and intense experience as dynamic forms of engagement opens up complex but promising lines of inference from intense experiences to their ultimate environmental Whence. What could this mean in practice?

I think that these lines of inference can be stabilized to the point that we could produce a vague characterology of Intensity, thought of as that to which intense experiences are a response and that which is perceived in and through intense experiences. This hazy vision of the nature of intensity in the reality we engage would not immediately connect with particular traditions of wisdom about ultimate reality, primarily because it would be generated within the socio-linguistic community of a certain sort of phenomenological philosophy and expressed using the technically vague language of that community. But translation ought to be possible, at least so as to allow this characterology of Intensity to constrain any theological account of ultimate reality, even if it could not decide among the best of the alternatives. And that would be a valuable outcome. It would not be enough for Alston, because it would offer little support for his preferred form of personal theism, and no less support for atheistic Buddhist *śūnyatā* (emptiness) accounts of ultimate reality than for any kind of theistic accounts. It would be too much for Bagger, because it asserts some degree of informational reliability in intense experiences, even though this reliability merely constrains without determining theological accounts of ultimate realities. But that is always the way with extreme views.

Most importantly for the strategic argument of this book, my contention is that these lines of inference are virtually impossible to stabilize for RSEs in general. *They can be stabilized for intense experiences*, however, because intense experiences are forms of dynamic engagement with an environment – somewhat like sense perception. Moreover, if the neurological and evolutionary elements of the intensity hypothesis are sound, then the component capacities for intense experiences are neurologically fundamental in modern humans, and thus enjoy cross-cultural universality. This adds to their value for assessing the cognitive reliability of RSEs. I shall take up cognitive reliability in detail in the next chapter. I turn now to the final task of this chapter, which is to give an evolutionary and neurological framework for the foregoing phenomenological account of intense experiences.

EVOLUTION AND THE NEUROLOGY OF INTENSE EXPERIENCES

I consider here first the shared features of intense experiences, and subsequently the features that drive their diversity.

Evolution and the neurology of the shared features of intensity

As discussed in Chapter 3, McNamara's (2009) neurocognitive model of decentering helps to explain certain features of intense experiences, such as their existential vibrancy, their relationship to meaning construction, and their production of changes in behavior and self-understanding. It also helps to explain their evolutionary importance: they facilitate the dynamic construction of an executive self, which is a generally adaptive feature of human beings. This articulates the neurocognition and evolutionary stabilization of some central features of the class of intense experiences, though it does not immediately settle the question of whether the associated capacities were selected for their adaptive benefits or arose as side-effects of some other selective process.

The phenomenological analysis shows that decentering and affiliated construction of meaning are not the only neurologically intelligible feature of intense experiences. The depth-and-breadth quality of intense experiences is important, too, and it also makes neurological sense. An intensely meaningful experience typically causes us to see connections of significance among disparate aspects of our lives, which are often co-present in our thoughts and emotions during that experience. Neural activation must be widespread enough to call to mind a host of ideas and memories and feelings all at once, strong enough to leave a lasting impression of meaningful connection among elements of that intense state of mind, and complex enough to produce the almost aphasic inexpressibility of the densely interconnected quality of such experiences. Beauregard's (2007) report of neuroimaging and EEG experiments on nuns recalling subjectively intense religious prayer experiences supports the claim of widespread and strong neural activation corresponding to subjective states of intense meaningfulness. In fact, breadth of activation was one of the most notable features of the states of consciousness that Beauregard studied.

Interestingly, most neuroimaging studies have focused on meditation experiences that involve intense focus of attention and aim to eliminate complexity of thought or anything else that distracts from utterly single-minded concentration. How does this fit with the characterization of intense experiences as involving strong and broad activation? To begin with, we should recall (from Chapter 3) that some meditation states simply are not intense experiences in the depth-and-breadth sense. Others may be, however, despite appearances. Consider any of the widely publicized fMRI images from meditation states: they do not look as if they are describing intense and widespread neural activation (for example, Newberg *et al.* 2001b: 4). But all fMRI images reflect decisions made about thresholds. A researcher wanting to stress a particular point about a scan, such as the activation of frontal regions associated with attention, will set thresholds so as to maximize contrast between the area of interest and other areas. This is perfectly valid, but the typical result is that many areas will appear inactive even when there can be significant activity occurring. If Beauregard's EEG scans are any indication, it is possible to achieve high levels of focused concentration in the very same state that involves broad activation of neural networks.

The case for the evolutionary stabilization of highly meaningful depth-and-breadth intense experiences can go a step beyond McNamara's case (above) about the adaptiveness of a dynamically adjusted executive self. It is easy to appreciate how an organism's survival is aided by the embodied capacity to register an enormous amount of diverse information simultaneously, to be instantly aware of multiple meanings and possibilities for interpretation latent within that information, and still to be able to synthesize the whole into effective action plans. If the awareness of some information is not present (i.e. if observational skills are weak), or if appreciation of possible meanings is not present (i.e. if inferential and interpretative skills are weak), then the organism is in danger of missing something crucial and selecting action plans that are unfavorable for survival. Similarly, in the context of communicative environments and sexual reproduction, it is not difficult to imagine that greater levels of observation and awareness make a potential mate on average more sensitive and intelligent, and thus more attractive as a companion and as a partner in the evolutionarily crucial adventure of rearing offspring.

Such selection pressures are well-understood components of standard evolutionary explanations for the emergence of perception and intelligence. But the implications of this for understanding intense experiences are not appreciated as widely as they might be. Intense experiences are prodigiously efficient information-processing and meaning-making neurocognitive operations. They do not require slow narration or piece-by-piece assimilation; in fact, they operate so efficiently that they produce a kind of aphasic wordlessness, as noted above. The adaptive advantage conferred by the ability to make meaning out of a wealth of information simultaneously present to awareness is obvious. The capacity for intense experiences may well be directly selected, in light of this adaptiveness. Even if it is not, however, it is at the very least a side-effect of the evolution of the cognitive skills of perception, inference, interpretation, and information-guided decision-making. In either the adaptation or side-effect version of the evolutionary history of intensity, the mundane awareness of meanings sufficient to guide safe and smart behavior can take on particularly intense forms. The resulting intense experiences presumably will have a more cognitively overwhelming and existentially loaded impact.

The case for evolutionary stabilization is strengthened by the fact that the capacity for intensity appears consistently across cultures. Though poststructuralists resist acknowledging it, the structural universals discovered to date in human cultures do seem to reflect evolutionarily stabilized cognitive capacities in response to recurring problems that human groups had to solve. All known cultures have kinship structures, ritualized responses to death, economic exchange practices, complex mate-selection processes, and a variety of other characteristics – in each case, a combination of cognitive capacities matched to recurring challenges in social environments. These structurally universal challenges are addressed quite differently in different cultures, however. The associated problems must be solved, but there are many ways to explore the space of possible solutions. The prodigious processing power of meaningful depth-and-breadth perceptual experiences is the species-wide response to the structurally universal challenges of survival in complex natural and social environments. Intense experiences are directly implicated in this cognitive-emotional capacity, and they receive culturally variable expression and social framing as befits the diversity of religious behaviors, beliefs, and experiences.

Direct study of intense experiences across cultures, while rare, has occurred. The perennial philosophy's advocates (including Aldous Huxley 1945, Fritjof Schuon [1948] 1953, and Huston Smith 1992) are not merely speculating when they say that there is a common core of mystical experience, awareness, and belief across the world's religions. They are reporting on the experience of those who have lived in more than one religion, including themselves – Smith has spent significant numbers of years in each of the world's major religions. Even if this shared core is not relevant to the highly contextualized and specifically textured experience of most religious people in a given tradition, the phenomenological testimony of the perennialists adds significant weight to their claim that the capacity for intense experiences is culturally widespread.

Robert Forman's close encounters with religious adepts of many traditions have led him to uphold the perennialists' claim of a cross-culturally common core in relation to two experiences: a "pure consciousness event" and a "dualistic mystical state" (Forman 1990, 1999). Both appear to be intense experiences. Forman's evidence is weakest when studying texts from eras where allowing for context is extremely difficult, and strongest when relying on face-to-face connections with religious adepts; after all, in personal encounters, questions and answers can produce cross-checking of interpretations. Again, this does not secure the cross-cultural universality or the evolutionary stabilization of intense experiences beyond question, but it does add to the evidence in support of the evolutionary stabilization of the capacity for depth-and-breadth intensity.

Evolution and the neurology of the diverse features of intensity

In addition to its shared features, the class of intense experiences has built-in diversity, including the five faces of intensity described above. What can be said about the neurocognition and evolution of intense experiences at this level? If the intensity hypothesis is correct in its neuro-logical and evolutionary aspects – that is, if the capacity for depth-and-breadth intensity is evolutionarily stabilized and thus a virtually universal feature of human brains – then we would expect the recurring structural components of intense experiences to have neural correlates that make sense in evolutionary perspective. Specifically, do the capacities for depth, horizon, scale, complexity, and mystery have neurological roots as distinctive as their phenomenological characteristics? Can the broad diversity of intense experiences be traced back to an array of fundamental neural processes that combine with various strengths and in various ways to produce that diversity?

Little is known about the neurology of the phenomenologically distin-guishable components of intense experiences, because they have not been studied directly. We can draw useful inferences about the neurocognition of the five faces of intensity from related lines of research, to some extent, but basically we are reduced to imagining how future research might proceed. Several guidelines are relevant to research in this area.

First, though intense experiences are a subset of RSEs, they are rather often spiritual but not religious, as these words are used. Thus, to inquire into intense experiences is to ask about a *part* of the territory of religious experiences but not the whole, and also about territory beyond the religious as most people use the word. Nevertheless, there is significant overlap between intense experiences and religious experiences, so what we learn about one should have an impact on what we know about the other. It follows that we can expect to gain neurocognitive insights into intense experiences from both religious experiences and non-religious ultimacy experiences, so long as these insights pertain to the overlapping territory between the two. For instance, researchers could seek to apply to the components of intense experiences both what has been discovered about the neurocognition of explicitly religious intense experiences such as *vipassanā* or insight meditation, which seems highly relevant to the depth and horizon faces of intensity, and what has been discovered about the neurology of non-religious intense experiences such as some forms of flow, which seem pertinent to the depth and complexity faces of intensity. At the very least, existing neurocognitive models of specific types of intense experiences should constrain models of the components of intense experiences.

Second, neurological models that demonstrate independence of the five faces of intensity should be a goal of future research. It would also be important to investigate neurologically the claim that all five faces are present to various degrees in, and jointly account for, all or most of the full variety of intense experiences. The detailed phenomenological profile of intense experiences that emerged from my research with McNamara (discussed in Chapter 2) can help here. Experiences that subjects describe as highly intense appear centrally to involve alterations of experience and awareness, inwardness of attention, a lot of imagery, affective complexity, and a lowering of rationality and volitional control. This is the case whether or not the experiences in question are recognizably religious to the person undergoing them. Generally, when intense experiences are also religious, internal dialogue becomes a strong factor, affect shifts slightly more toward the negative (on average), imagery further strengthens in amount, and rationality and volitional control further decline.

This is the average phenomenological profile for intense experiences as an entire class. What happens when we apply the same approach to sets of intense experiences distinguished by which of the five faces are dominant? In recent (as yet unpublished) pilot work, McNamara and I generated evidence for the independence of two of the five faces of intensity, namely, the depth and horizon dimensions. We grouped a set of narratives rated as subjectively intense by participants according to which of the five faces of intensity was most prominent in them. The result was two subgroups large enough for analysis, one (consisting of thirteen cases) in which depth was most prominent and the other (consisting of thirty cases) in which horizon was most prominent. Analysis of the two groups showed a clear difference between "predominantly depth" experiences and "predominantly horizon" experiences. Specifically, intense experiences dominated by the depth dimension produce higher levels of absorption and internal directedness of attention than intense experiences dominated by the horizon dimension. Moreover, depth experiences turn out to involve less rationality and volitional control, and are more difficult to remember clearly than horizon experiences. This is what we expect for depth experiences: they direct attention inward to the mysterious, wondrous, and awe-filled aspects of life, which defy complete comprehension, are difficult to recall clearly, and invite surrender. Meanwhile, horizon experiences direct attention outwards to encounters with other people and to events that we can rationally analyze and remember more easily.

These results indicate that at least two of the faces of intensity have stable, intelligible, and publicly detectable phenomenological signatures that depend on cognitive-emotional features such as attention, memory, rationality, and volitional control. This suggests that the five faces of intensity are worthy of careful study in the same terms. Moreover, the fact that something is known about the neurocognition of attention, memory, rationality, and volitional control, as well as about other phenomenologically distinctive aspects of intense experiences, promises an eventual answer to the question about the neurological realization of the fives faces of intensity.

Third, future research into the neurology of the five faces of intensity should seek a plausible theory of their evolutionary origins linked to a testable theory of their neurocognitive workings. This theoretical exercise depends on meaningful traction between the neurosciences and evolutionary psychology, which is a difficult requirement given the current state of development of these scientific ventures. The difficulties all center on the fact that we do not have experimental access to human beings in the evolutionary past. Despite the difficulties, progress appears to be within the reach of several experimental techniques and theoretical approaches.

For example, priming experiments can establish the causal role of aspects of experience, and thereby furnish a basis for testing the independence and scope of multiple entangled causal factors in more complex experiences – just what is required to make sense of the five faces of intensity. In such priming experiments, behaviors or contents of consciousness are measured in groups of participants who receive contrasting prompts – subtly delivered so that the participant is not aware of the purpose of the experiment. Some prompts cue the target factor being assessed while others cue control factors. The output states of consciousness or behaviors often manifest significantly different qualities based on the prime received. This allows testing of causal hypotheses, which in turn helps to identify more and less fundamental components in cognitive and neural models. Priming experiments have been crucial for disclosing the evolved mechanisms that underlie the cognitive aspects of religiosity (see, for example, among other studies, Epley *et al.* 2008; Norenzayan and Hansen 2006). There is every reason to believe that priming techniques using primes related to the five faces of intensity should help to trace out the causal linkage of component factors in the production of intense experiences.

More speculatively, while reconstructions of evolutionary history do not count as direct evidence for evolutionary origins, they can test the coherence of evolutionary hypotheses. For example, the capacity for mystery appears to be rooted in the experience of ignorance, which carries with it a kind of terror of the unknown other, to which we then readily impute the *mana* of taboo. This is a socially potent configuration of feelings and beliefs with the potential to produce divisions between sacred and not-sacred and structures of protection around the sacred. But the root experience seems basic to human life. The capacity for scale appears rooted in the breakdown of perception and imagination in face of vast spaces and great chasms, from the ocean's depths to the desert's vastness, from the bright blue sky to the inky blackness of the night. The thought-stopping power of vastness is existentially loaded because we understand ourselves in relation to that which dwarfs us, beggars our puny imaginations, and breaks our powers of perception.

The phenomenological articulation of the five structural elements of depth-and-breadth intensity, and how they figure in ordinary human impulses and behaviors, points the way to the speculative reconstruction of their emergence in human cognitive evolution. In all cases, there is a kind of failure of cognition involved, built atop prodigious powers of perception and understanding. The liminal space between practical perception and cognition, on the one hand, and its inevitable breakdown at the margins of human experience, on the other hand, is the habitation of the five faces of depth-and-breadth intensity. This liminal location is crucial for making intense experiences existentially potent and cognitively meaningful; indeed, it may be a crucial trigger for McNamara's decentering process (above). Without intense experiences, we would know nothing of the borders of life where the familiar gives way to the terrifying-yet-captivating, and where the controlled gives way to the chaotic-yet-mesmerizing. Depth, horizon, scale, complexity, and mystery are the doorways not into a world beyond the familiar one, but into the unfamiliar but ever-present liminality of that familiar world.

CONCLUSION

The capacity for depth-and-breadth intensity appears to have recurring structural features, stable neurological underpinnings, characteristic behavioral and social manifestations, and intelligible evolutionary origins. It springs from primal experiences of liminality that are common to human beings in every context and era. We handle and articulate the experiences in culturally and historically variable ways. Yet intensity and its five faces – depth, horizon, scale, complexity, and mystery – are likely to prove every bit as much structural universals as are means of economic exchange and kinship structures. More research is needed finally to confirm this.

I shall proceed from this point by taking as provisionally established the intensity hypothesis. That is, I shall assume that the phenomenologically distinguishable features of intense experiences, in the sense of experiences involving strength of activation and richness of interconnection, are evolutionarily stabilized and thus cross-culturally universal. This means that the suite of cognitive and emotional capacities in human brains that are needed to express the variety of intense experiences is present in more or less similar ways in almost all human beings, and that this species-wide suite of neural capacities derives from shared ancestral challenges and experiences that varied cultures addressed in creatively different ways. No doubt this hypothesis will have to be refined in the future. But the hypothesis is sufficiently well supported to build upon it arguments about the value and functions of RSEs.

What is the significance of the intensity hypothesis? I shall restate my answer to this question in different terms. Consider the following dilemma. On the one hand, religious experiences are too diverse and too complex to have common neurological features. The meditating monk and the soup-ladling shelter worker, the worn-out priest and the young father venerating his ancestors, may have experiences with a rich set of phenomenological features in common, but it seems unlikely. The academic study of religion has generated a widespread consensus on this point: it is destructively reductionistic and intellectually vacuous to minimize the diversity of RSEs by treating them as a single class with core features. On the other hand, we gain little for understanding human nature and the social and individual effects of RSEs if we focus on each experience individually. Such understanding demands generalization and the analysis of species-wide patterns.

This dilemma calls for a third way between the reductionisms evident at the universalistic and individualistic extremes. Accordingly, I have sought to define the largest possible subset of RSEs whose member experiences do have closely related phenomenological features and whose enabling neural capacities are evolutionarily stabilized across the human species. This is the class of intense experiences. Though studying this class does not come close to capturing the full diversity of RSEs, it does register many of the experiences that are pivotal for producing religious beliefs and behaviors. Therefore, granting the intensity hypothesis, its species-wide relevance makes it ideally suited to serve as the basis for analyzing the cognitive reliability of RSEs (Chapter 5) and the social importance of RSEs (Chapter 6). We will not forget RSEs in their full richness. But a great deal is gained when we explicitly address a subset of RSEs without pretending that the subset is in fact the whole set, and when the subset we study yields species-wide insights into RSEs.

Can you trust your instincts? The cognitive reliability of religious and spiritual experiences

INTRODUCTION

Most people rely on their experiences to authorize their beliefs, including their religious and anti-religious beliefs. In fact, such reliance is so instinctive and pervasive that we are apt to take it for granted, and thereby likely to underestimate the degree to which existentially loaded and socially potent experiences inspire the fundamental beliefs and ways of thinking that orient our lives and guide our behavior. The question under discussion in this chapter is whether we can trust our RSE-based instincts. What reasons exist to accept or reject the beliefs to which the cognitive elements of RSEs give rise? In an era where many people are familiar with phenomena such as self-deception and brain washing, group-think and the manipulation of beliefs and behaviors by the mass media, the question of the cognitive reliability of RSEs is an especially pressing one. Unsurprisingly, many philosophers of religion in recent decades have attempted to evaluate the cognitive value of RSEs.

Previous chapters complicate the reliability question in precisely the right way. In particular, most of the short-circuited answers have already been rejected, leaving us with a less tractable but also more relevant puzzle. I begin here with a discussion of some possible answers to the question of the cognitive reliability of RSEs. I then take up what I think is the most promising line of analysis, namely, to regard some kinds of RSEs as types of perception. This approach enjoys wide support in recent philosophy of religion, but it requires careful evaluation because the senses in which the perception approach is illuminating do not always match the senses in which it is taken to support claims about the cognitive reliability of RSEs. I shall then furnish a more adequate interpretation of the religious-experience-as-perception approach in terms of an ecological-semiotic theory of engagement. In this ecological-semiotic framework, the question of the reliability of RSEs has contours that properly match the possibilities and problems we actually encounter in making religious sense of the environment of human life. This is the right theoretical framework within which to interpret the cognitive content of these experiences and to assess its reliability.

Along the way, we shall see how important it is that the argument of the previous two chapters allowed us to isolate a class of RSEs – the intense experiences – that are both evolutionarily stabilized across the human species and vitally important for handling our existential situation and negotiating our social worlds. Evolutionary stabilization makes the class of intense experiences a key resource for evaluating cognitive reliability in light of religious and cultural diversity.

DEEPENING THE RELIABILITY QUESTION

The question of the reliability of the cognitive elements of RSEs has been debated since ancient times in every philosophical tradition. From then until now, a series of standard answers has been produced repeatedly in recognizably similar forms across virtually every wisdom tradition that has made permanent records of thought on the subject. The debate continues because these standard answers are widely and perpetually felt to be inadequate, and also because each new generation is forced to ask the question anew, such is its importance for orienting existence, guiding decisions, and organizing society. In posing the question again here, a useful guide to what counts as a better answer gives an appreciation of what is wrong with the standard answers.

Religious cognitions

The reliability question seems more or less clear, at least in a preliminary way. It centrally concerns beliefs that are induced or influenced by RSEs. The reliability question asks whether those beliefs tend to be true. To the extent that RSEs tend to produce true beliefs, we judge the experiences to be cognitively reliable. To the extent that those experiences tend to produce false beliefs, we think of the experiences as cognitively unreliable.

This formulation of the reliability question is acceptable as far as it goes, but it does not go far enough. Four considerations demand a more flexible interpretation. First, the distinction between true and false in a world of symbolic discourse is often far from clear; in fact, it requires a theory of symbolic truth that lies beyond the scope of this project (but

see Neville 1996 for a sophisticated version of the sort of theory needed).
I will identify the joints in the argument where this becomes important.
Second, the focus on belief is unduly narrow. It is also appropriate to ask
about how other aspects of human cognition – such as perception and
memory, reasoning and imagination – are more or less successful insofar
as they are induced or influenced by RSEs. Third, aspects of human life
traditionally regarded as non-cognitive – such as emotions and behaviors,
mental stability and physical health – can also be induced or influenced
by RSEs and are subject to judgments of success. In this case, the reliability of these experiences is assessed with reference to their tendency to
produce goodness or beauty in individual actions and cultural products,
and optimal function in mind and body. Fourth, the norms invoked here
that govern success – goodness, beauty, truth, health, and optimal function – are fabulously controverted ideas and are themselves in need of an
account specifically in relation to the effects of RSEs. That lies beyond the
scope of this book, but we will have to remain alert to the way we deploy
such norms.

These considerations show that the reliability question is only superficially clear. To avoid oversimplification, we shall have to accommodate as
many layers of complexity as possible. I have stated that theories of norms
for judgment and theories of symbolism lie beyond the scope of this
book, but I attempt to comprehend as many of the elements of the reliability question as possible. The ecological-semiotic approach presented
below supports analyzing reliability in terms of both cognitive and non-
cognitive aspects of human life with equal facility and ultimately with no
sharp distinction between the cognitive and non-cognitive. To keep the
treatment manageable, however, the focus of this chapter is cognitive reliability, understood as encompassing all cognitive operations that are subject to judgments of greater and lesser success. Beliefs are front and center,
but the overall theme is religious cognitions insofar as they are induced or
influenced by RSEs.

It would be convenient to have a compact phrase that elegantly
expresses the idea of "religious cognitions insofar as they are induced or
influenced by RSEs" because we will refer to this idea frequently in what
follows. While an obscure acronym might serve, I shall simply use the
phrase "religious cognitions" with the understanding that we will be considering religious cognitions insofar as they are induced or influenced by
RSEs, and not in other respects. In fact, this shorthand is not particularly
misleading, and there is something to be gained by a brief discussion of
this point.

There are several sources of and influences on religious cognitions, including rational reflection and habitual absorption, so RSEs are certainly not the only salient factors in forming religious beliefs. Understood broadly, however, RSEs encompass experiences that are both vivid and non-vivid (and thus not ultimacy experiences), in the technical sense employed in Chapter 3. Thus, forging beliefs and frameworks for interpretation through the ritualized absorption of worldviews even in the absence of any vivid experiences is an instance of religious cognitions being induced or influenced by RSEs. For many religious intellectuals, moreover, rational reflection on religious matters is a religious act that properly belongs in the broad class of RSEs, and they are often quite explicit about this. In the context of Christian thought, for example, St. Augustine is treasured for using the phrase *fides quaerens intellectum* (faith seeking understanding) to express this point. St. Anselm is revered for explicitly framing his theology in these terms, to the point that, following Augustine's example in the *Confessions*, Anselm wrote his *Proslogion* in the form of prayerful address to God.

In light of these considerations, it appears that there is a rather small difference between religious cognitions in the most general sense and *religious cognitions specifically insofar as they are induced or influenced by RSEs*. This is a measure of the extent to which RSEs play vital roles in the formation of religious and spiritual beliefs. Thus, it is reasonable to use "religious cognitions" as shorthand for the longer phrase.

Extreme answers to the reliability question

Three standard answers to the question of cognitive reliability of RSEs are extreme and relatively easy to dismiss. Several further answers depend on distinctions that organize the conceptual messiness surrounding the reliability question. We shall begin with the extreme answers.

First, it is sometimes argued that RSEs have no significant cognitive element and thus that the question of their cognitive reliability does not, or should not, arise. This is famously evident in the logical positivists' treatment of religion (see, for example, Ayer [1936] 1946). To the extent that RSEs produce cognitions that are even capable of being expressed as statements of belief, those statements are not meaningful propositions because a falsifiable interpretation of their propositional content cannot be formulated. There being no propositional content associated with RSEs, there is nothing cognitive about them.

Extreme arguments such as this capture more attention than assent. In this case, the logical positivist program failed to make good on its own conceptual foundations because the meaningfulness criterion is not meaningful according to its own standards. Moreover, religious cognitions include structures of imagination and ways of reasoning, not just putative beliefs, so the contracted focus of this intensely skeptical position leaves too much out to be relevant. Finally, it is more or less obvious that RSEs influence belief formation and that the resulting beliefs can be more or less accurate; this is the "king has no clothes on" response to the pretensions of those who would deny that RSEs have any cognitive elements.

Second, a relatively common religious point of view is that religious cognitions are straightforwardly reliable. Like plain-sense literal readings of sacred religious texts, religious traditions sometimes give rise to plain-sense interpretations of the cognitive content of RSEs. In such approaches, a religious experience of, say, God communicating with a believer reliably produces true beliefs that God exists, that God communicates, and that God has intentions, thoughts, feelings, and whatever other characteristics are manifested in the communication. How does this work psychologically? A pattern of religious involvement in a social group equips an individual with a worldview-scaled web of beliefs and imaginative structures that are highly functional for that individual in the context of that religious group. Such cognitive frameworks serve as relatively sound guides to life, so external criticisms of implausibility or incoherence have little impact on the believer's confidence; they are internally incorrigible despite their external corrigibility (see the discussion of internal versus external corrigibility in Körner 1974). The RSEs appear reliable because they only ever reinforce the emergent web of cognitions that they induce and influence. Minor crises of incoherence usually provoke agile adjustments that serve only to show how powerful the cognitive framework is, and correspondingly how reliable the RSEs that give rise to it are.

The problem here is painfully obvious. The gap between internal incorrigibility and external corrigibility is in many cases a vast chasm of incomprehension. The "plain-sense" reading of the cognitive content of RSEs requires a dramatic narrowing of information flow to prevent framework-threatening ideas from having their natural consciousness-raising effect. To resume the earlier example, the religious person who believes God is a communicative being because of formative religious experiences must somehow remain unaware of, or else delegitimate or demonize, the vast numbers of non-theistic religious people, as well as the many theists who do not think of God in these terms. The internal incorrigibility of the cognitive structures induced and influenced by RSEs is more fragile than it appears to be at first and thus more dependent on participation in an information-constricting community that constantly reinforces the putative match between experience and cognitive content. Such communities often have positive aspects, particularly in helping people order their lives effectively and sustaining powerful moral visions with salutary effects on society. In respect of the way they constrict the natural flow of relevant information, however, such communities mask the complexities that surround judgments of reliability of religious cognitions.

A third extreme view holds that religious cognitions are irreparably deceptive. Proponents of this view, such as Richard Dawkins (2006), allow that religious experiences have cognitive content, unlike the logical positivists, but assert that there is no rational reason to believe that RSEs reliably produce accurate perceptions, true beliefs, sound judgment, or responsible behavior. On the contrary, he believes that rational consideration of the evidence points in the opposite direction and so argues that psychological health and indeed the security of the human future demands a wholehearted attack on religion. Presumably this would involve re-education whereby people prone to RSEs would learn to treat any associated cognitive content as a kind of entertaining fiction with no moral or rational importance.

I have discussed this view in earlier chapters and will not repeat the rational and empirical reasons to reject it that I have already mentioned. But I will pause to add a new reason to reject it, namely, that it seems to express a timid approach to life that exchanges the blessed rage and volatile color of vivid experiences for the white-knuckled grip and blanched-face visage of desperate control. The vivid experiences I have discussed are very common in human life. While they can be disturbing, and they can also produce dangerously fanatical beliefs and behaviors, it seems to be a case of massive overkill to rule all of them out, and non-vivid RSEs along with them, as entirely unproductive of accurate cognitions. It is better to look and see with a looser grip and a genuine appreciation for the colorful and even bizarre aspects of human life.

Non-extreme but inadequate answers to the reliability question

Once these three extreme views are eliminated, the reliability question is located, as with all interesting philosophical questions, in the messy mental mid-lands where epistemological judgments are perpetually difficult and ontological inferences even more so. In this territory, interpreting the cognitive import of RSEs requires exquisite judgment. The associated wisdom is always hard won in human life because it requires groups to achieve discerning consensus, wisdom traditions to guide those discerning groups, and the cultivation of intellectual and moral insight at every level of individual and social life. In recognition of this, four other answers to the reliability question have repeatedly surfaced in the world's religious traditions. Each grapples with the complexities involved by drawing a distinction that is supposed to help explain why some religious cognitions are accurate while others are not, reflecting the centrality of discernment in those traditions. The distinctions pertain to types of experiences, types of people, types of interpretation, and types of behavioral effects.

The first distinction stipulates that some types of experience reliably produce accurate religious cognitions, including true religious beliefs, while other types of experience do not. The principle discriminating factor in this case is typically the causal context of the experience. RSEs occurring within and governed by an established wisdom tradition are usually taken to be reliable, at least by insiders, whereas others are not. Again, RSEs referred to within, and authorized by, a sacred text are taken to be reliable by those who accept the authority of that text while others are not. The bluntest deployment of this distinction focuses on supernatural causes of experience, saying for instance that some experiences are divinely caused while others have demonic origins. This difference in putative causal origins supposedly impacts both the truth of beliefs (those with evil causal origins may be seductively deceptive) and the value of other cognitions (those with evil causal origins may produce bad behavior). These context-based discriminations are deployed in widely varying ways, and often result in implicit or explicit attacks by ingroups on outgroups on the grounds that outgroups that foster RSEs lack the ingroup's markers of reliability, and in the opposite direction on the grounds that ingroups improperly control the spontaneity of spiritual realities. Unfortunately, this social loading is so pervasive in the implementation of such judgments of reliability that any epistemological value they may possess is swamped by the role these judgments and declarations play in legitimating and authorizing ingroup identities and persecuting outgroups.

A second approach distinguishes between types of people who can experience reliable religious cognitions and types who cannot. The principle discriminating factor in this case is typically the cognitive apparatus of the person undergoing the experience. For example, some people may be further along in a supposed samsaric cycle of lives and thus objectively capable of experiences that others cannot achieve because of their relative spiritual immaturity. Again, some supposedly saintly people may be blessed with innate spiritual gifts for RSEs while others have no such aptitudes. And some people may have brains that make for more unreliable forms of RSEs, perhaps making them vulnerable to private hallucinations, bizarre beliefs, and erratic behavior. To the extent that this distinction is not reducible to the "effects" consideration discussed below, its indebtedness to ontological frameworks makes it difficult to deploy in public discussion of the cognitive reliability of RSEs. For example, we cannot expect ourselves to settle debates over the reality of supposed transmigration or of alleged spiritual personality types before taking up the reliability question.

A third approach asserts a distinction between types of interpretation of the cognitive content of RSEs. The principle discriminating factor in this case is typically related to richness of experience and degree of awareness of the ways that the cognitive content of RSEs both line up with and develop at cross-purposes to the rest of our knowledge about reality. This is a far more promising approach, in my view. For example, it furnishes a basis for recognizing that some people may be more spiritually mature interpreters of religious and spiritual experience than others without having to invoke ontologically complicated and controversial explanatory concepts such as samsaric cycles or spiritual personality types. This approach also accommodates the important fact that the discernment processes cultivated in some groups promote far greater judiciousness than those present but barely operative in others; there is a rich literature on discernment practices in religious groups that addresses this dimension of difference in interpretative skills.

This approach also harmonizes with the obvious fact that human beings can learn and improve their judgment. At one point in their lives they may take a profound religious experience to mean that God wants them to kill abortion clinic workers or become a suicide bomber on behalf of an overridingly valuable cause. If they survive these dangerous adventures in interpreting religious cognitions, they may later come to conclude that these beliefs derived from their profound religious experiences were somehow mistaken or distorted, perhaps because they did not have in place checks on enthusiastic interpretation that they since implemented. In other words, learning improved their interpretative skills. This also serves to show that interpretation-based criteria for the cognitive reliability of RSEs cannot really answer the reliability question in general or absolute terms. Such criteria work best to point people in the direction of *more effective* interpretation. This does not settle the question of whether *truly accurate* interpretation is ever possible.

A final approach proposes a pragmatic distinction based on the effects of religious cognitions. On this view, RSEs are cognitively reliable to the extent that they inspire religious cognitions (beliefs, imaginative symbols, acts of reasoning) with good, true, and beautiful outcomes. For example, someone may experience such a flood of compassion in meditation (this is the founding experience) that they become convinced that reality is ultimately pervaded with compassion (this is the cognition) and subsequently give themselves in compassion to family, friends, neighbors, enemies, and strangers as a religious act of harmonizing themselves with the way they believe ultimate reality to be (this is the effect). This approach expresses an unimpeachable criterion for the cognitive value of RSEs, one that is emphasized in virtually all of the world's sacred religious texts and traditions, as well as in the common-sense judgments of ordinary life. But it is far from being a sufficient condition for cognitive reliability. The fact of religious pluralism is sufficient to show this. Religious traditions produce numerous people with an unusually strong commitment to compassionate behaviors, but these people are diverse in the extreme with regard to their religious beliefs and their worldview-level motivations for these behaviors. In other words, pragmatic criteria may be more useful for detecting cognitively unreliable RSEs than for isolating those that are reliable.

Criteria for a better approach to cognitive reliability

I have argued that the three extreme answers to the question about the cognitive reliability of RSEs are mistaken and that the four moderate answers are at best only partially useful because they fail to take fully into account the relevant complexities. Some of these answers may prove satisfying in religious or anti-religious communities whose identity depends on a definitive account of the cognitive reliability of RSEs, positively or negatively. But a wider perspective quickly manifests their evidential and conceptual defects.

Why are people willing to satisfy themselves with these short-circuited answers to the question of the cognitive reliability of RSEs? The basic reason is that people *need* answers to the reliability question. In particular, they need those answers to *do important work* for them, either by heading off doubts about religious beliefs in order to consolidate confident action, or by ruling out RSEs as delusory and so not relevant to forming true beliefs about reality. Religious, spiritual, and metaphysical beliefs are among the most potent psycho-social forces in our lives. They have an enormous impact on how people behave, think, and feel about their lives, their communities, and the wider world. The Durkheimian tradition of sociology of religion suggests that they are key components in the rationalization and legitimation of social practices and authority structures. The Weberian tradition of sociology of religion shows that they can transform entire webs of economic practice. The Marxist tradition of sociology of religion laid bare some of the ways that psychic needs are tangled up with economic and social conditions, with religious beliefs and practices helping to smooth over the incoherencies that undermine the complex power transactions that govern the perpetually uneasy marriage of individual and group. It is to be expected, therefore, that anything playing directly into people's confidence about these powerful beliefs would become the focus of close analysis, edgy suspicion, and anxious defense.

Once we are aware that something important is at stake in the reliability question, and that plenty of people stand ready to embrace short-circuited answers to it, we are led to be as clear as we can about the kinds of considerations that ought to figure into a more satisfactory answer. On the basis of the discussion to this point, I suggest that the following six criteria are crucial.

First, the *Cognitive Immediacy Criterion*. We have to take proper account of the immediacy of RSEs. This immediacy seems epistemologically important, conferring on such experiences an impressive kind of definitiveness. The immediacy includes at least three distinct aspects: these experiences seem to be cognitively self-interpreting, ontologically self-evident, and epistemologically self-confirming. Their cognitively self-interpreting character derives from the experience of them seeming more or less straightforwardly cognitively determinate and intelligible, even when they are quite intense. That is, we usually know what they seem to be about, and only the most bizarrely vivid experiences present significant interpretation problems. Mostly they just show up already as meaning something particular, and there are no traces of the subject of the experience adding meaningful content to something more basic and raw. Their ontologically self-evident character derives from the fact that the experiences just show up as being about something real. The object of the experience (Allah, a bodhisattva, an angel) seems built into the experience itself in the sense that there is nothing in the experience that makes thinkable the ontological possibility that the experience could have been *of anything else*. Their epistemologically self-confirming character derives from the feeling of certainty that accompanies many such experiences, particularly intense ones. In fact, they often feel more definitively true than ordinary experiences, and demand allegiance in a way that ordinary experiences do not. These three features of many RSEs call for extreme caution but also must be taken with due seriousness.

Second, the *Conceptual Mediation Criterion*. We have to take proper account of the conceptually mediated quality of all RSEs. This mediation is difficult to detect even with careful introspective attention; the immediate features are more obvious. But experience and dialogue with others shows us that we experience in ways that reflect our culture and religious formation. For example, an angel would probably speak to me in English not Swahili; a theist is likely to experience God and a Buddhist a bodhisattva; and a Christian is more likely to be moved to an intense religious experience by a familiar ritual such as the Eucharist than an unfamiliar one, such as marching around a snakelike statue of Murgan, son of Śiva, Lord of the Serpents in certain Tamil contexts, to enhance fertility. This is not merely Kantian structuring of experience in terms of space and time and the categories of the understanding. This is specifically cultural and religious cognitive preconditioning. While such preconditioning does not guarantee that the cognitively self-interpreting, ontologically self-evident, and epistemologically self-confirming aspects of RSEs are delusory impressions, it does require that we evaluate that possibility with due seriousness.

Third, the *Epistemic Tradition Criterion*. We have to take account of the fact that the formation of beliefs is culturally and socially *traditioned*. We see things the way our group sees them, for good or ill; exploring the world appears to be inevitably a team sport. Traditions guide our best thoughts and bear forward insights that make our own adventures more efficient and more effective than they would otherwise be. The tradition criterion is closely related to the conceptual mediation criterion but needs to be distinguished because they are different levels of contextual conditioning. For example, conceptual mediation can refer to basic species-wide cognitive biases and evolutionarily formed tendencies to form particular types of beliefs (such as the tendency to interpret potential threats in terms of intentionality and agency). The role of traditions represents a comparatively high level of contextual specification, as when traditions of social interaction determine the polite way to greet other people.

Fourth, the *Rational Coherence Criterion*. We have to pay attention to rational coherence between the beliefs prompted by RSEs and those we arrive at through the most disciplined rational reflection. In an earlier chapter I pointed out that human beings appear to have several neurologically distinguishable ways of arriving at confident judgments of truth. Some of these subvert the ordinary global semantic matching processes on which rational judgment depends, probably through a kind of intense swamping process, while others do not. This is one of several bases for self-deception and cognitive error in human beings. The overwhelming feeling of cognitive accuracy makes people unready or unwilling to notice the fact that they are at that moment bypassing ordinary rational evaluation. But we must allow for the possibility of self-deception and error, as well as the limitations of our culturally and contextually specific cognitive frameworks of ideas and beliefs.

Fifth, the *Symbolism Criterion*. We must take account of the fact that the cognitive content of RSEs is richly symbolic. The religious and spiritual domain is no place for wooden interpretations of ideas and images, any more than the domain of dreams. In fact, religious traditions have routinely emphasized that univocal and literal interpretations of words and images purporting to describe our ultimate concerns leads directly into an intellectual and spiritual cul-de-sac. Anything that can properly function as an ultimate concern for us must somehow transcend us more or less definitively, which makes talking about it and imagining it genuinely difficult. As a result, all religious traditions promote indirect forms of speech, modesty of ideas, symbolic and imagistic forms of exploration, and non-cognitive modes of engagement. Of necessity the cognitive content of RSEs will participate in this symbolic character, and all the more so when the one undergoing the experience is imaginatively formed in a particular tradition of spiritual disciplines and religious beliefs. The symbolic character of cognitive content of RSEs is a crucial consideration in attempting to address the previous point about their coherence with beliefs that we arrive at through the disciplined rational reflection.

Sixth, and finally, the *Value Criterion*. We have to do justice to the value-laden quality of RSEs. Values pervade the cognitive content of these experiences as well as their emotional elements and behavioral effects. Valuation is particularly evident in the beliefs inspired and influenced by RSEs because such beliefs furnish norms governing moral judgment, social participation, personal self-assessment, and the disposition of one's most precious devotional energies and powers. Most people studying RSEs readily stress their value-laden quality, either with approval or disapproval. Despite this, the value-suffused character of RSEs sometimes appears only as a passing note in philosophical analyses of their cognitive reliability. More than this is needed: the way RSEs give birth to life-orienting values and reinforce those values even in the face of the greatest resistance is one of their existentially and socially most important aspects.

Honoring the cognitive immediacy criterion, the conceptual mediation criterion, the epistemic tradition criterion, rational coherence criterion, the symbolism criterion, and the value criterion helps us avoid pre-emptively closing off the reliability question. For instance, in doing justice to the immediacy of these experiences we are also careful to honor the rational coherence criterion, which means not taking putative cognitive content at face value. Similarly, in noticing that there are coherence problems in richly symbolic religious cognitions, we do not simply reject the value of all truth claims to which RSEs give rise. We avoid the short-circuited answers criticized above by honoring all of the criteria simultaneously and to the greatest extent possible.

THE PERCEPTION ANALOGY

I think the most compelling philosophical attempts to mount a case for the cognitive reliability of RSEs in recent decades have revolved around an analogy with sense perception. The basic instinct here is sound, namely, that the cognitive immediacy of RSEs seems remarkably similar to the cognitive immediacy of sense experience. We can do justice to the cognitive immediacy criterion by using sense perception as a guide to building a theoretical framework for evaluating the cognitive reliability of RSEs.

This perception approach has had many versions, from the so-called "spiritual senses" of mystical traditions (Cattoi and McDaniel in press; Gavrilyuk and Coakley in press) to the "spiritual capacities" of faculty psychologies (an interestingly modulated version of which appears in Hick 2004), and from the "religious a priori" approaches of Friedrich Schleiermacher ([1799] 1893, [1820–21] 1928), Rudolf Otto ([1917] 1925), and Paul Tillich (1951, 1957, 1963) to the dualist "divine-mind-to-human-soul direct communication" approach common in supranaturalist theologies. In contemporary philosophical forays into the reliability question, the perception approach has often been deployed as an answer to skeptics who say that the human cognitive apparatus is ill-equipped to form true beliefs on the basis of RSEs. This apologetic deployment of the perception analogy is straightforward: sense perception is generally reliable so, if religious experience is like perception in the relevant respects, religious perception will be similarly reliable. Indeed, we may be able to show that we have cause to *presume* that religious perception is reliable in the absence of contra-indicating evidence.

The attack I will mount on apologetic deployment of the perception analogy should not be mistaken for a wholesale rejection of the strategy of using sense perception to make sense of cognitive characteristics of RSEs. Indeed, I shall make extensive use of the connection between sense perception and religious perception as two instances of the same physiological-hermeneutical process of dynamically engaging reality in which both experiencing subject and experienced world appear. In the next section I shall describe an ecological-semiotic theory of engagement that makes sense of this claim. For now it is important to keep in mind that I intend to reframe the perception analogy, not completely abandon it.

Alston's classic statement

William Alston's *Perceiving God* (1991) is not the first apologetic deployment of the perception analogy aimed at defending the reliability of the cognitive elements of RSEs. Indeed, Richard Swinburne famously made use of the analogy in his argument for the existence of God (1979), and many others have explored the same theme in a variety of ways before and since Swinburne. But Alston's argument has become the classic expression of the apologetic deployment of the analogy because of its sophistication and detail. Swinburne and Alston have provoked a lot of philosophical discussion with their perception-based approach to the reliability question (representative examples include Barrett and Wildman 2010; Byrne 2000; Gale 1994a, 1994b).

At the heart of Alston's approach is an account of perceiving objects that he calls the "Theory of Appearing." One might reasonably expect a theory of perception, even just a *philosophical* account of the *concept* of perception, to be rather more complex than what Alston presents. But Alston simplifies matters by taking as basic and unanalyzable the idea that *an object of perception, X, appears to a subject, S, as so-and-so*. After that, the concept of perception amounts to nothing less and nothing more than a proposition of "breathtaking simplicity": "For S to perceive X is simply for X to appear to S as so-and-so" (Alston 1991: 55). This is Alston's way of registering the cognitive immediacy of RSEs. His concern is to evaluate whether experiential awareness of God helps to justify beliefs about God to which those experiences give rise (1).

Alston says that his Theory of Appearing involves direct realism because to perceive an object X on this account is for X to exist (55). Apologists for theism might get excited at this point because, though Alston explicitly states that he has no intention of offering a proof for the existence of God, he also acknowledges that his argument certainly would serve that end (3–4). But things turn out to be more complex than this suggests, in two ways. On the one hand, Alston allows that it is possible that an object X appears to a subject S in a way that differs from what X actually is. Strangely, he treats this as a minor qualification despite the fact that his direct realism serves as a potent premise for his subsequent argument (56). On the other hand, Alston accepts the possibility that the object S perceives is not after all the physical object that S believes it to be but rather a "vivid mental image"; this qualification is supposed to accommodate the phenomenon of hallucinations. Once again, strangely, Alston sets this aside as a negligible detail in his wider argument (56; see fn. 43). But it needs to be fully aired if we are to do justice to the conceptual mediation and symbolism criteria. We will return to both of these qualifications on the Theory of Appearing when we try to take full account of the symbolism criterion. For now, to be able to track Alston's argument, we have to grant that these two qualifications do not derail his direct realism.

Alston's Theory of Appearing carries a large part of the argumentative burden of the book by construing the idea of perception in such a way as to entail the reality of the object perceived, and by attaching self-interpreting cognitive content to perceptions that give rise to matching beliefs. He argues that this is what "perception" means in the case of sense perception, which is supposed to make us amenable to the next step of his argument. That is Alston's attempt to argue that the Theory of Appearing covers not only sense perception but also the experience that he calls "perceiving God" or "experiential awareness of God." For now, let us bracket the important question of whether Alston's Theory of Appearing properly describes the meaning of "perception" in experiences of sense perception. In fact I think this is almost but not quite right; a properly ecological theory of sense perception requires a slightly different analysis of the cognitive and ontological implications of perception from the one Alston furnishes, and those differences prove to be important for evaluating the reliability of religious cognitions. But let us press onwards.

Alston's next move is to ask how perception (in general; i.e. sense perception and also any other kind of perception) produces beliefs. He considers causal accounts of the linkage between perception and belief but settles on a more flexible doxastic-practice approach that owes a great deal to Ludwig Wittgenstein. "Doxastic" here simply means "belief forming," and "practices" are akin to the language games that Wittgenstein described as spontaneously arising within the life worlds of human groups. Thus a doxastic practice is a contextual way of assembling beliefs from the cognitive elements of perception. The advantage of Alston's doxastic approach is that it does better justice to what I have called the conceptual mediation criterion than the causal approaches that he considers. The disadvantage, as he fully recognizes, is that a doxastic-practices approach risks greater internalism in his account of the origins of religious belief than he really wants. That is, he does not want to explain merely why people in such-and-such a group hold a religious belief or merely why that belief seems true to them, which the doxastic-practices approach is particularly well suited for. Commendably, he also wants to furnish a basis for speaking of the ordinary public truth of the religious belief in question. Fortunately, the direct realism of the Theory of Appearing helps with that when the doxastic-practices approach does not have the power to establish a properly public basis for evaluating religious truth claims.

For doxastic practices to be relevant to debates about cognitive reliability, they have to meet a number of quite strict conditions. Alston passes by many temptations to make his case easier at this point and focuses on the sort of doxastic practice "that is socially established, that yields outputs that are free from massive internal and external contradiction, and that demonstrate a significant degree of self-support," where "self-support" means that the doxastic practice is internally coherent and consistent, and equipped with mechanisms for detecting inconsistency of its output (184). He argues that sense perception is a doxastic practice in this sense (ch. 4) and that "Christian mystical practice" (including the perception of God) is also a doxastic practice in this sense (ch. 5). This gives Alston a Theory of Appearing that covers both sense perception and the perception of God, and allows him to speak of truth of beliefs in the common-sense, public way. And he has a doxastic-practices account of the emergence of beliefs from perception that covers both sense perception and God perception. This is the theoretical framework within which Alston proposes to raise the question of cognitive reliability.

Alston rightly concludes that there is no way definitively to prove the reliability of perception, not even sense perception (ch. 3). This may appear to defeat his approach at first; after all, if we cannot give adequate reasons for the ordinary practice of basing beliefs on sense perception, then surely the case will be much worse for the same practice in relation to experiential awareness of God. But Alston has particular foes in mind, namely, those who argue that the sense-perception is reliable but God perception is not (102–3; see fn. 2). In relation to that argument, Alston's strategy is to put both sense perception and God perception on the same playing field, namely, the playing field in which no adequate reasons can be given for the games played out there. In all cases, he argues, the arguments aiming to show reliability are circular, if not otherwise flawed. That being the case, it would be irrational merely to dismiss out of hand claims about the reliability of God perception because they are unlike sense perception in certain respects.

In fact, Alston deliberately attempts to induce an epistemic crisis by arguing that all belief-forming practices – from sense perception to memory and from introspection to inductive and deductive reasoning – are subject to the same inevitably circular form of justification. After getting everyone panicked about circularity, and thus about the justification of all belief-forming cognitive practices, he plays the pragmatist's card, or perhaps it is merely a half-card: he points out that there is nothing wrong with circularity (ch. 4). All belief-forming practices operate by venturing beliefs on the presumption of reliability and subsequently evaluating results. I sympathize with the rhetorical strategy of inducing panic before explaining that panic is not necessary after all; it indicates the communication problems facing Alston as he tries to convey a partially pragmatist outlook to analytically minded and epistemically foundationalist philosophers of religion. Circularity is almost always vicious for most in his target audience, whereas it holds no terrors for the pragmatist, so long as resources exist to support correction of hypothetical beliefs (see Wildman 2010). Ironically, the pragmatist senses that this key aspect of pragmatism is underdeveloped in Alston's discussion, even though it is vital to the pragmatist's case for the reliability of perception.

According to Alston, therefore, we are not able to prove the reliability of any of our cognitive operations, from memory to reasoning, and from sense perception to God perception, without presupposing what we are trying to prove. But this is a desperate problem only for epistemic foundationalists. In fact, the rest of us can proceed rationally despite this simply by using our doxastic practices and, if necessary, correcting the mistakes that arise. More than this, Alston argues that "for any established doxastic practice it is rational to suppose that it is reliable, and hence rational to suppose that its doxastic outputs are prima facie justified" (183). This is not proving reliability, which is a much stronger result, and a result that is unnecessary for practical purposes. It is affirming the rationality of acting *as if* a doxastic practice is reliable. This key result applies to all doxastic practices that meet his criteria (mentioned above), including the doxastic practice associated with Christian mystical perception or God perception – the Christian variety of what Alston calls "religious perceptual doxastic practice." We are supposed to feel that this is sufficient because, after all, the doxastic practice associated with sense perception is no better off than this.

Key objections and Alston's replies

The final phase of Alston's argument consists in trying to deflect objections to the reliability of the doxastic practice associated with Christian mystical perception. These objections include the following (ch. 6):

- There are no significant checks on Christian mystical perception.
- Christian mystical perception does not yield contact with external reality.
- Christian mystical perception's putative God object does not exist.
- There is no non-circular reason to believe that Christian mystical perception is reliable.
- The reliability checking system of Christian mystical perception presupposes that Christian mystical perception is reliable.
- Christian mystical perception produces contradictory beliefs.
- Religious experience can be explained without presuming God's reality.

Alston identifies "certain recurrent fallacies that underlie many of these objections – epistemic imperialism and the double standard," both of which involve unflattering comparisons between God perception and sense perception. The double-standard fallacy condemns God perception on the basis of features that it shares with sense perception. The epistemic imperialism fallacy requires God perception to possess features of sense perception that do not properly belong to it (255). In this way, Alston believes he disposes of objections based on naturalistic explanations of religious experience, inconsistencies in the output of Christian mystical perception, and conflicts between Christian mystical perception and secular doxastic practices such as natural science, history, and naturalistic metaphysics.

Alston's replies to the objections he handles are well taken. Unfortunately, he considers these objections only individually and does not concern himself with the fact that a number of them reflect an alternative large-scale interpretation of RSEs to the one he defends. In the context of a sufficiently rich alternative interpretation of RSEs – say, a naturalistic interpretation – it can make good sense to demand that Christian mystical practice have features that are prominent in another type of doxastic practice, and to deem it unreliable because it lacks those features. But to evaluate such large-scale questions requires an approach that Alston does not explore.

The most difficult objection, as far as Alston is concerned, is the existence of multiple conflicting religious doxastic practices within the world religions (ch. 7). He points out that conflicting diversity within Christianity itself is even more problematic because the conflicting beliefs are more obviously about the same subject. Alston's commitment to the common-sense, public understanding of truth and reliability prevents him from collapsing his case back to the internalist "you believe your reliable truth and I'll believe mine" option. This communitarian response to religious pluralism expresses a kind of relativism that some other philosophers influenced by Wittgenstein have embraced (see, for example, Philips 1993), in relation to both intra-Christian diversity and inter-religious diversity; Alston believes it is needlessly skeptical.

In relation to inter-religious pluralism, Alston allows that the existence of uneliminated competing religious perceptual doxastic practices does reduce the maximal degree to which Christian mystical practice produces justification for Christian beliefs. But he argues that the reduction is not sufficient to vitiate the justifying power of the Christian religious perceptual doxastic practice, which he continues to speak of in the singular despite his awareness that there is more than one within Christianity. In other words, he continues to hold the rationality of Christian mystical practice – both "the rationality of engaging in it and the rationality of taking it to be sufficiently reliable to be a source of prima facie justification for the beliefs it engenders" (278). Part of the reason he continues to affirm this degree of rationality is that he believes Christian mystical practice produces behavioral fruits that help to support the associated beliefs. It is genuinely strange that he applies this consideration to Christianity alone and not to other religious beliefs; he appears at this point to have only partly absorbed the force of the critique from religious pluralism.

The need for a better theory of perception

I have pointed out several problems with Alston's argument as we have worked our way through it. Despite these shortcomings, I think that it does not take a large dose of generosity to recognize that the argument is very nearly sound. It certainly gets a great deal right. For instance, it takes seriously the cognitive immediacy criterion, thanks to the Theory of Appearing. It is equally deeply committed to the rational coherence criterion and the value criterion. And the emphasis on doxastic practices honors parts of the epistemic tradition criterion and at least some aspects of the conceptual mediation criterion. Meanwhile, other aspects of the epistemic tradition and conceptual mediation criteria are muted and the symbolism criterion is almost completely ignored.

We noted in passing that Alston should have taken more seriously his qualifications on the Theory of Appearing. Sense-perceptual illusions and hallucinations show that it is possible both that a perceptual object might not be what it seems and that the object of some perceptions might be merely a vivid mental image instead of the external object it appears to be. There may be value in cognitive errors of this sort, to be sure, but they are nonetheless reasons to think that sense perception is unreliable. Because of this, psychologists have gone to great efforts to chart the limits of the accuracy of sense perception, discovering the conditions under which we are likely to misperceive, and tying this in to the types of mistakes that human beings are likely to make in forming beliefs (see the catalogue of cognitive errors in Gilovich 1991 and the study of superstition in Vyse 1997). These data on sense-perceptual and cognitive errors have helped cognitive neuroscientists to track down some of the brain processes underlying sense perception, both when it produces accurate beliefs and when it does not. Evolutionary psychologists working on cognition have tried to identify the kinds of evolutionary pressures that produced the sensory apparatus that misfires in precisely these ways.

What emerges from this monumental effort is not a justification of the reliability of sense perception, *simpliciter*, but rather a precise understanding of the ways in which sense perception and other kinds of cognitive judgments work and do not work. The natural sciences have helped us determine the boundary within the territory of our cognitive capacities that divides the reliable and non-reliable regions, the reasons why there is a boundary, the way cognition works on both sides of that boundary, and the consequences for human life of there being both reliable and non-reliable domains. To work out an analogy with religious cognition properly requires something rather different from what Alston has furnished. The case of sense experience should predispose us to expect that religious cognition will have areas of reliable functioning and areas of non-reliable functioning. We ought to be searching out the boundary between the two domains, paying attention to both sides, and tracing out the consequences for religious beliefs and behaviors of there being two sides (see Wildman 2009a). Arguing solely for the reliability of religious cognition misconstrues the analogy. To adjust for this defect in Alston's approach is to do better justice to the conceptual mediation criterion.

We pondered whether the Theory of Appearing really describes the meaning of "perception" in sense perception. Alston's own qualifications suggest that he is oversimplifying, or perhaps over-idealizing, when he treats as unanalyzable the idea that to perceive means that an object of perception, X, appears to a subject, S, as so-and-so. Precisely because we are aware of the possibility of perceptual errors, the very idea of perception also includes the awareness of the possibility of subsequent correction. That is, the philosophical analysis of the meaning of perception should include a dynamic, interactive aspect, which Alston suppresses. It is possible to build this into the Theory of Appearing without destroying its special virtue of taking the cognitive immediacy criterion with great seriousness. Cognitive immediacy will then consist not of self-interpreting and self-authorizing cognitive content so much as thoroughly embodied, emotion-infused, and action-linked engagement with a complex environment. The cognitive quality of immediacy shifts from Alston's direct realism (in the link between cognitive content and world) to effectiveness of cognitions (perceptions, memories, beliefs, acts of reasoning) in helping us to navigate our complex environment successfully and creatively. This requires, in other words, not a Theory of Appearing but a Theory of Dynamic Engagement. To move to a Theory of Dynamic Engagement preserves immediacy while being more realistic about the way perception actually works for us, and what the word "perception" actually means for us.

We noted that Alston moves quickly from a causal to a doxastic account of the link between perception and belief formation. But these are two levels of description and ideally they should harmonize. That is, an account of perceptual-doxastic practices should be consistent with a matched causal account of the way we form beliefs based on experience. If we focus only on the doxastic level we risk failing to take proper account of the neurological and evolutionary conditioning of human cognitive activity, which is one of the problems in Alston's approach. By the same token, if we focus only on a causal account, we risk failing to take proper account of the way that cultural and religious traditions impact our cognitive activities. To keep both levels of theoretical description in the explanatory picture is another part of the meaning of doing justice to the conceptual mediation criterion.

We saw that Alston does not properly come to terms with the diversity of doxastic practices in either the intra-Christian setting or the inter-religious setting. In relation to the former, he does not take seriously enough that Christianity has numerous doxastic practices rooted in RSEs, not just one, and that these diverse practices yield sharply different religious beliefs. An obvious example is the difference between perceiving God as a divine person and perceiving God as Being Itself – doxastic practices of both types have coexisted within Christianity (not to mention other theistic religions) almost from the beginning. In relation to the latter, we noted that Alston does not allow the full severity of the problem of religious pluralism to arise. He does concern himself with the possibility of conflicting beliefs but allows the fact of positive behavioral benefits of those beliefs to accrue only to the benefit of Christianity. All of the major religions appear to have similar entitlement to claim every type of justification that Alston might want to divert to Christianity alone. In these areas the epistemic tradition criterion is not getting its proper due.

Finally, Alston's presentation is from beginning to end tone deaf to the music of symbolism. Were he more attuned to this, the problem of religious pluralism might become tractable, the understanding of a religious cognition would be transformed, the meaning of a religious perceptual practice would similarly shift, and the senses in which religious perception is unlike as well as like sense perception would be front and center. In particular, we can use the degree and type of symbolic reference in human cognitive activity to furnish a rough but usable characterization of the differences between sense perception and religious perception. Alston's refusal to allow this drives his rebuttal of criticisms of the cognitive reliability of RSEs (ch. 6); his "epistemic imperialism" and "double standard" replies depend on flattening out the salient differences between sense perception and religious perception. A proper appreciation of symbolism revives those differences and, with them, many of the criticisms of reliability that Alston rejects. Meanwhile, symbolic appreciation also makes possible different kinds of replies to those criticisms. Properly honoring the symbolism criterion demands far-reaching changes in Alston's account of the cognitive elements of RSEs.

By means of this series of criticisms I have indicated what needs to be done differently from Alston to frame the reliability question adequately. But it is important to recall that, despite the differences in approach, which accumulate to produce sharply contrasting frameworks for understanding the cognitive dimensions of RSEs, the proposal here is in the same family as Alston's. It treats RSEs as a kind of perceptual activity, it honors the cognitive immediacy criterion and stresses the rational coherence and epistemic tradition criteria just as Alston does. But this is a case of sensitive dependence on initial conditions: several small adjustments in the conceptual framework to refine support of the conceptual mediation, epistemic tradition, and symbolism criteria combine to yield a dramatically different outcome. In fact, unlike Alston's explicitly anti-naturalistic approach, which is necessary for his answer to the reliability question to be feasible, the framework I shall propose comprehends both supernaturalistic and anti-supernaturalistic ontologies, and also furnishes grounds to decide between these competing ontological frameworks. And it all begins with exchanging a Theory of Appearing for a Theory of Dynamic Engagement.

AN ECOLOGICAL-SEMIOTIC THEORY OF DYNAMIC ENGAGEMENT

Perception is not about things appearing to us out of nowhere or somewhere, after which we just need to decide whether perceptual objects are real or hallucinations. It is about dynamic engagement with an environment in which we learn to negotiate its physicality with our embodiment and to register its value structures with our aesthetic sensitivities. We know sense perception goes wrong from time to time, so we are always trying things out, on the lookout for errors, capitalizing on feedback from our exploratory efforts, and seeking the kind of ecological mastery that allows us to navigate our physical and social surroundings effortlessly and at times perhaps even stylishly.

Everything we know about the neurology of human cognition suggests that religious cognitions are forged in and through the same processes that produce ordinary sense-perceptual cognitions. On a supernaturalist cosmology, the ecological factors in RSEs are the media for cognitive content that derive ultimately from, or at least refer to, one or another supernatural being, such as a personal God or a bodhisattva. On a naturalist cosmology, the encounter with ultimacy occurs in the valuated depth structures of the ecology of perception itself. In either case, the ecology character of perception is the same and our various belief-forming (doxastic) practices differ simply by virtue of their different perceptual inputs and cognitive outputs.

In the final section of this chapter I shall argue that we are justified in rating the reliability of religious cognitions most highly in the presence of a naturalistic cosmology in which we engage ultimacy symbolically through referring to the valuated depth structures manifested in the ecology of perception. Thus, I shall speak of an ecological-semiotic theory of dynamic engagement, where "semiotic" refers to the necessarily symbolic modes of interpretation that we must deploy to cognize ultimacy. I shall also argue that the reliability argument quickly collapses when we give up any one of these three components: a naturalistic cosmology, an ecological-semiotic account of perception as dynamic engagement, or a symbolic account of religious cognitions. In the current section, I shall discuss these three components and describe how they fit together (for more detail, see Barrett and Wildman, 2009).

The ecology of perception

Most scientific ventures have their famous, well-funded mansions and their lesser-known, under-funded bungalows. In cognitive psychology and cognitive neuroscience, for several decades the research projects garnering the most attention and funding have been those that analyze human cognition using the model of the digital computer. On this view, the mind's cognitive operations are programs operating in the brain's hardware, or rather its wetware, and the programs for cognitive activities are portable in principle because they are logically distinguishable from any particular hardware implementation. This outlook gave birth to artificial intelligence (AI), in the strongest versions of which programmers attempted to model human cognitive operations by implementing programs in silicon-based hardware. While philosophically more modest forms of AI research continue apace, the strong AI program has widely been judged a failure. This is not surprising, because the human brain does not act like a digital computer and its programming appears not to be logically distinguishable from its embodied platform after all (see Searle 1984, 1992, 2004). Nevertheless, the digital computer continues to be the governing metaphor for human cognition, from perception to memory, and from reasoning to belief – a kind of afterglow effect from the heyday of strong-AI research.

In recent times, a more balanced view of human cognition has been reasserting itself with empirical credentials that are far more robust than those of research programs in thrall to the digital-computer metaphor. This more balanced view takes mathematical and computer modeling with complete seriousness. In place of cognitive programs that can logically be separated from their hardware platforms, however, this alternative view stresses the embodiment of human cognitive activities and the ecological setting for human cognition. This ecological form of cognitive psychology reclaims older insights about human cognition that fell out of favor after the arrival of digital-computer technology and combines them with a new-found empirical precision and neurological insight. This new approach has had a decisive impact on AI research and robotics because it shows how to think about the interaction between an entity (organism, robot) and its environment.

The root ideas of an ecological theory of perception are already present in the work of psychologist James Gibson (Gibson 1950 focuses on visual perception, Gibson 1966 on other senses, and Gibson 1979 contains a systematic presentation of his theory in its most developed form). He conceived perception as an exploratory and hypothetical system by which organisms interact with and manipulate the surrounding environment. The organism samples the environment for information about interactive possibilities, which Gibson intriguingly and aptly called "affordances." This means both that the environment is perceived according to the organism's interests and that the organism's possibilities for action within its environment are disclosed according to both the way the organism is prepared to interact and the way it actually behaves in its surroundings. If a hypothetical, exploratory move in relation to an object or circumstance yields no affordances – no way to manipulate it, no way to navigate it, no way to comprehend it, no way to appreciate it – then that interactive behavior is frustrated and the hypothesis it expresses may be abandoned in favor of an alternative. Experience and memory, as well as observational and interpretative skills, determine how efficient the production of workable hypotheses is. Smart mice learn the most useful way to behave and thereby "tame" their environment the most quickly; the role of the relevant kinds of intelligence is the same for human beings. Cooperation helps here, as the creative contributions of many communicating and mimicking organisms are more likely to unlock the environment's affordances.

The exploratory perceptual interaction within an environment is the means by which human beings perceive and act, and thus also the means by which they gain understanding of every kind. The encounter with a world that possesses an "affordance profile" reflects organism interests and social organization and also determines accuracy and fidelity of perception and understanding. To reach out for the handle on a photo-realistic painting of a door fails to yield an affordance that matches organism interest, and this in turn refines perception, modifies action, and rectifies understanding. And all of this can be as intensely emotional as it is thoroughly embodied. Our exploratory, hypothetical interactions with the ambient environment thus have the structure of a dynamic dialectic between perception and action, a dialectic with bodily form and emotional texture.

Gibson battled against several alternative accounts of perception during his lifetime, and each battle had profound philosophical implications for him. Early in his career, he fought against the strong behaviorist program according to which the only properly scientific subject matter for psychology is publicly observable behavior. Behaviorists of this and even some other less extreme kinds saw no reason to speak about the human mind (or animal minds), intentions and decisions, interests and desires, or even perceptions and ideas. But Gibson's experimental work had convinced him that visual perception, at the very least, was incomprehensible within the framework of behaviorist psychology. Some of the tools necessary for an adequate explanation of organism–environment interaction had been banished from the behaviorist's toolkit, strictly understood: interests, emotions, desires, expectations, plans; imagining, trying, failing, succeeding, modifying; and determination, irritation, frustration, resolution, satisfaction. Of course, from a certain point of view, Gibson's own approach owed a lot to the behaviorist program, particularly in that he, too, stressed organism–environment interaction in his account of perception. But his account of that interaction referred to minds with interests and emotions as well as external stimuli and organism responses.

Later in his career, Gibson took on the information-processing view of perception proposed by the so-called cognitivist program in psychology – one of the fields deeply influenced by the digital-computer analogy mentioned above. According to this view, perception was an information-processing mechanism that could be modeled with computer programs capable of processing information from the equivalent of sensory inputs (cameras, pressure sensors, and the like) to produce valid inferences about how to act. The problem here is that a computer model of perception could not capture the infinitely variable quality of the environmental context, let alone the complex behaviors that rely on perception. If the behaviorists neglected the necessary role of internal states of mind, then the information-processing cognitivists and artificial-intelligence researchers neglected the thoroughgoing embodiment of human minds in a dynamic environment. The brain's environment constitutes an intensely intricate ecology of relations (see Dreyfus 1992 and Dreyfus and Dreyfus 1986, who draw on Martin Heidegger's account in *Being and Time* [(1927) 1962] of human beings as thrown – as always, already embodied and embedded in a prodigiously complex and dynamic environment). Here, too, Gibson's approach owes something to the cognitivist program he fought against. He was targeting not so much the idea of information processing, to which his analysis of perception lends itself, nor the idea of computer modeling, but rather the relatively environment-independent way information processing was conceived in his day.

Gibson also battled the cognitive psychologists who urged that perception was strictly indirect – that is, that we perceive not the world itself directly but rather only internal cognitive representations of the world. Immanuel Kant argued for the inaccessibility of things in themselves to direct rational inspection because of the way that knowledge is always necessarily mediated spatially, temporally, and by the categories of the understanding. The indirect theory of perception in psychology drew support from this influential account of mediated knowledge, and also from the accounts of Sigmund Freud and others of unconscious psychic processes that subtly impact perception and understanding. Gibson's direct theory of perception insisted that organisms perceived aspects of the environment directly, and not merely mental representations of the environment, just as the environment impacts organisms directly, and not by means of mental representations. Direct perception is the dynamic dialectic between perception and action that lies at the root of all understanding; this is doing justice to the cognitive immediacy criterion.

As with his other philosophically loaded battles, time has made the gap between the Gibsonian dialectical version of direct perception and the theory of indirect perception smaller than it once seemed. Nothing about Gibson's direct theory of perception entails that we would have uncomplicated access to understanding of the world, or that we should be able to generate consensus in the cognitive realm just by concentrating hard on what we perceive, either of which would be contrary to experience. Rather, organism interests determine what aspects of the environment are sampled for affordances to manipulation or navigation or appreciation. That means that things show up for sensing organisms as tentatively categorized, but also as capable of resisting hypothetical explorations. There is, therefore, a *causal basis* for the generation and mutation of categorical schemes, and this basis is the dynamic organism–environment interaction itself. This is not a theory of direct perception in the sense of Alston's Theory of Appearance, therefore, but neither does it bear out Kant's strict prohibition of knowledge of things in themselves. The dichotomy between direct and indirect theories of perception is far from sharp in an ecological account of the dynamic perception–action relation operating between interested organism and ambient environment. And the contrast between the causal and doxastic levels of explanation for the formation of beliefs similarly becomes helpfully and properly blurred in the ecological framework.

Despite these considerable virtues, this ecological conceptuality has not taken the field of perception and action psychology as a whole by storm, such is the lingering power of the digital-computer metaphor (see Good 2007). But the ecological viewpoint is gaining ground overall. In fact, a number of cognitive psychologists have been trying to foment a revolution whose purpose is to reclaim cognition for this more balanced ecological viewpoint (see Núñez and Freeman 1999). The general perspective of embodied perception and an appreciation for the mutual constraints between action and perception is a dominant theme of contemporary perception psychology, albeit in less metaphysically modulated terminology than either Gibson or ecological psychology as a whole is inclined to use. In fact, the Gibsonian history of this view, its earlier history in the psychology of William James and the early American pragmatists, and its later history in contemporary pragmatist philosophers (see Frisina 2002, for example) is often unknown by working cognitive psychologists, such is the degree to which its fundamental outlook has been absorbed. The ecological framework has also become central in cognitive psychology and the neurological study of perception. In AI research, it serves as the new guide for robotic modeling; think of a robotic vacuum cleaner navigating its unpredictable environment. Moreover, ecological psychology has had a vital impact on artifact design, software interface design, architecture, and other fields that focus on design or usability. There are important lines of critique to contend with, but these apply at a more detailed level than the general points relied on here. In all, the ecological theory of perception–action has proved to be an empirically robust corrective to more abstracted and less embodied theories of perception and action.

The ecology of value

Scientific work operates at many levels simultaneously, but often clumsily, so that one level does not appreciate another. The predictable result is complaints of reductionism. Thus, ecological psychologists from Gibson onwards decry behaviorists for reducing cognition to input–output analyses of behavior while treating mind as a black box that is irrelevant for understanding cognition. Ecological psychologists also decry cognitivists for selling out to the strong-AI program and reducing everything to information processing that is logically independent of embodiment and environment. But ecological psychologists are vulnerable to their own form of information-processing reductionism, namely, that they too rarely pay attention to the way that value is encountered in the environment and appreciated in the sensing organism. Experts working on aesthetics or the emergence of moral or religious beliefs will naturally complain that the ecological framework should properly account for the emergence of value in human affairs and in the environment with which human beings interact. And, indeed, the ecological theory of perception at its best supports this.

Theories of perception focused on value tend to be highly philosophical in character, and they certainly are rarer than they should be (for a premier instance, see Neville 1981). But it turns out that the ecological framework is amenable to value categories and well suited to giving an account of the encounter with, the appreciation of, and the arising of beliefs about values of every kind, from aesthetic to moral to religious. To gain some appreciation of how this works, consider a simple example.

I have a friend who loves cars. Let's call him Erol. Erol reads magazines about cars, likes to study cars, takes his car purchases very seriously, and loves to care for his cars. He still installs his tires with white walls facing out, though he has to fight his mechanic to do that because it is unfashionable. A few years ago, Chrysler introduced a retro-styled wagon called the PT Cruiser. It immediately captured Erol's attention. When Erol saw the PT Cruiser, he had feelings that I did not have, and he perceived lines and shapes in a different way from me. I have not asked him about this, but I imagine that he readily imagined himself driving around in the roomy little car, happily waving at other PT Cruiser owners, feeling content and at home within something like a blast-from-the-past community of like-minded souls that nobody else understood. That is, the PT Cruiser shows up for him not merely as an object that can be climbed into and driven, but also as host a of special meanings that can impact his life in ways that go well beyond the fact that it is a means of transportation. The car's affordance profile in Erol's perceptual ecology is not merely about door handles and steering wheels, engine controls and the positioning of mirrors, but also about shapes and feelings and old memories and the evolving of a personal identity. Erol's love of cars and the associated training of his imagination is a key factor in opening up this particular world of value-laden affordances because he has spent a long time studying lines and grilles and thereby has cultivated a sophisticated taste for design novelty and interest. His personal history plays a role, too, as it equips him with certain longings that the PT Cruiser unexpectedly satisfies. All this is a part of his perceptual encounter with the vehicle.

Perception is not just about deciding what is real and what is imagined. And it is not just about successfully navigating a world of objects, as it is in the simplest version of ecological psychology's model of perception. It is also about a dialectic of values encountered in the environment and values imposed on the environment that is every bit as important in human life as the perception–action dialectic.

It is a mistake to imagine these two levels of ecological exploration as utterly distinct. Our exploration of an unknown physical object is guided by past experience and current interests, as well as the object's geometry and features. The combination is what produces affordances. As we study and feel our way around the object it is as much our emotions and our values as anything else that determine how we explore and what will show up for us as we do so. For example, we feel frustrated and give up, or we are intrigued and remain mystified. Or it does not occur to us to smash the object on the ground because it seems somehow impolite to do that. I recall trying out for a job in a supermarket as a wiry young teenager. There were about a dozen kids at the interview. At one point we were shown a very large cubic box about four feet on each side with a rope around it and then asked to lift it from the top part of the rope. I was first up and had nobody to mimic. So everyone studied me as I tried to find the trick – the affordance that comported with my value-driven expect-ations that people should avoid attempting to pick up large and awkward objects while off balance, particularly if they worked in a supermarket that has to be on the alert for work-related injuries. So I poked around for a minute until the interviewer told me to just grab the thing and lift it. Unfortunately for me, the test was intended to evaluate the ability to lift a large and awkward object while off balance as a sign of strength, not to evaluate how to avoid having to do that as a sign of safety-mindedness. Well, nobody needs a philosopher working in a supermarket. Our aware-ness of value is an essential component in navigating even the physical environment.

In some situations, perception seems all about values and very little about navigating a physical environment. For example, people familiar with the social conventions and purpose of an art museum know that an oil painting in a frame on the wall should not be touched out of respect for the painting and for the sake of its safety and preservation. Rather, it should be observed and appreciated from a distance. The physical challenges thus negotiated, hopefully without any docent reprimands, everything subsequently about the act of perception relates to aesthetic appreciation. This is very much a dynamic and dialectical process, as in the example of Erol's perceptual encounter with the PT Cruiser. There are values encountered in the painting and values brought to the appreci-ation of the painting. Traditions play a role in structuring and manifest-ing those values both in the perceived object and the perceiving subject.

In all such encounters, but especially in those where aesthetic sophistication is present, the dance of values is enormously complex and rewarding, with powerful emotional colorings. These might trigger strong impulses toward bodily movement, such as dancing or weeping, but those normally would be suppressed out of deference to social norms governing museum behavior.

The ecology of semiosis

The ambient environment is physically complex and laden with values, which is to say that it is ready to be perceived this way by perceiving organisms possessing appropriate cognitive faculties, interests, preparation, and opportunities. Some of these values are so complex and dense with significance that we cannot easily describe them. Fortunately, we can express meanings and values indirectly, stimulating the imaginations of others in directed ways toward a shared appreciation of that which we perceive. This reflects the root meaning of "symbol" – it is a directed throwing (βάλλω) of meanings together with (συν) one another so as to stimulate imaginations toward shared understanding.

Even when we cannot name or describe without misleading, we can still create shared understanding of the values that we engage as we live in our complex environments. Erol may not be able to say quite what it is about the PT Cruiser that just makes him feel so happy, but he can sweep his hand along the curves of the car's profile and grin broadly to indicate something indirectly. Or he can show a photograph of the cars he used to drive as a younger man. Expressing the values engaged in a museum encounter with an excellent oil painting is made easier with the technical languages of art history and art criticism. But even in the absence of such specialized languages we can use analogies and metaphors to describe how we respond to the painting and what it is we see in it.

Our entanglement in symbolism is not merely a kind of cognitive last resort, an expression of the failure of imagination and intelligence that should be eliminated by carefully translating indirect and non-literal forms of discourse into direct and literal ways of speaking. This kind of literal translation is rarely within our grasp. This is true even in beholding a painting or the curve of a car. But the role of symbols in religious perception is even more central than in these examples of complex aesthetic encounters. Religious objects are, at least sometimes, beyond expression in a more or less definitive way. Symbolic discourse is unavoidable in such cases. Preparing to perceive religious objects requires symbolism, forming beliefs based on religious perceptions requires symbolism, expressing those beliefs requires symbolism, and forging shared understanding through language and practices requires symbolism.

Semiotic theory, or the theory of signs, analyzes the way we wield symbols to navigate the exquisitely complex world of super-abundant meanings. I have already said that this is not the place to develop or even present such a theory, either in general or specifically in relation to RSEs (again, see Neville 1996 for the most fine-grained application of semiotic theory to religion). I shall confine myself here to noting that symbolic modes of understanding and communication are not optional frills on the sturdy dress of perception. Their necessity for navigating the meanings of many life situations, both non-religious and religious, means that symbolic modes of understanding are deeply embedded in all of our cognitive operations, including perception (Lakoff and Johnson 1980, 1999 take up this theme in great detail). Our cognitive neural processing manifests this at many levels. For example, the cortex uses categorizations that allow one thing to stand for others. In the process of cognitive and specifically perceptual integration, information-rich pathways are simplified and represented using these categorizations. We know this just from introspection, to some degree, but the functional architecture of the brain expresses it also.

The way we interact with our ambient environment in perception is thus already imbued with symbolic forms of thought, from categorical representations to root metaphors that govern and guide our understanding. These symbolic-cognitive resources are essential for making sense of a world that otherwise remains a perpetual mystery to us, and a dangerous one at that. Symbolic-cognitive resources are particularly important for engaging the subtler aspects of reality that may not be registered in the experience of cognitively simpler organisms. We are, as Terrence Deacon so aptly expressed it, the symbolic species (Deacon 1997).

From epistemology to ontology: the emergence of self and world

This understanding of perception satisfies the immediacy criterion but not in Alston's way, in that it does not necessarily imply direct realism in his sense. In fact, a phenomenologically sensitive account of the emergence of self and world from the symbolically and conceptually mediated interaction of organism and environment problematizes the claim of direct realism. To complete this presentation of an ecological-semiotic theory of dynamic engagement, we need to consider the move from epistemology to ontology that is so important for assessing the reliability of any human cognitive activity.

The ecological psychology of cognition that I have been presenting is unusually faithful to the actual elements of our experiences of learning, navigating, understanding, acting, and appreciating. Once we can get some distance on our ordinary ways of thinking about what is real and try to cleave to our basic experiences, we quickly notice that our impression of the real is a socially cooperative endeavor built on the perception–action dialectic in engagement with an ambient environment that opens up to our understanding only in the respects in which we are prepared to engage it. Where direct realism takes for granted from the outset a sharp border between perceiving subject and perceived object, the more empirically scrupulous way to proceed is to pay attention to the way this borderline emerges from our experience and remains to some degree hazy.

To the extent that I attempt to discern the subject–object border in relation to the experience of unsuccessfully navigating that part of the ambient environment that is responsible for my stubbing my toe, I can speak with some confidence of a sharp distinction between I, the subject feeling pain, and the rock-like object that appears not to be suffering even a little bit. The more we attend to the value dimensions of our experience, however, the more blurred the subject–object borderline becomes. What is a mere scrawling of chalk to one person can be an extraordinarily beautiful equation from quantum chemistry to another, and what is a solid, opaque rocky mass to the person who accidentally kicks it is to the quantum chemist a mostly empty configuration of matter–energy whose interacting components are described by that chalk equation. The boundary is even more blurred in personal relationships, where our projections govern much of our behavior regardless of the degree to which more careful attention would force the correction of those projected representations of other people.

The classic Western philosophical debate over primary and secondary qualities addresses this issue exactly, trying to distinguish between the qualities we encounter in the environment and the qualities we impose on it. But this debate only scratches the surface of the issue, because it has tended to be somewhat neglectful of the value dimensions of our experience in the ambient environment that we sense and navigate and appreciate. We cannot resolve the subject–object boundary in the most relevant respects by focusing merely on the difference between objective shape and texture that we encounter, on the one hand, and subjective color that we contribute, on the other. We need also to account for the processes of interpretation that work through the fusing of horizons, which involves the blurring of subject–object borderlines in the value domain (for example, see Desmond 1995, 2001, 2008; Frisina 2002; Gadamer 1975).

It is possible for direct realism in Alston's sense to reassert itself, of course. We can always say that the world is what it is and we are what we are, that our cognitive interactions with the world are imperfect and shot through with errors small and large, and that as we learn we discover that direct realism was correct after all. But this is only compelling in relation to the sheer physicality of subject–object distinctions, when they apply. In fact, as we learn about value-laden dimensions of reality, we discover precisely the opposite of what direct realism suggests we should. That is, we learn that what is most important to us, such as love and social harmony, spiritual fulfillment and intimate relationships, calls for all kinds of mergers of self and other that positively require hazy lines between subject and object. This is not mere metaphorical speech, except to the direct realist and the value-averse materialist. It is simply taking with complete seriousness and proper empirical-mindedness our experiences of navigating the axiological dimensions of reality.

The distinction between subject and object is an experiential phenomenon for which we need a sophisticated cognitive apparatus. Presumably animals have this capacity to a significant degree. But collapsing the distinction between subject and object in the name of exploring our value-laden ambient environment and creatively forging new experiential possibilities requires even more cognitive sophistication. Only human beings, as far as we know at this point, have cognitive powers sufficient for that task. This calls to mind McNamara's (2009) decentering process discussed in earlier chapters: the dynamic construction of an executive self requires relaxing the vigilant maintenance of the current self in order to register and engage environmental importance in new and more fruitful ways.

Now, how does this impact the all-important journey from epistemology to ontology? In the dynamic engagement model of perception, the basic posture is that we form beliefs tentatively and act on them experimentally, as though reaching our hand into a dark corner to discover what is there. This is all very exhausting and anxiety-producing. Fortunately, habits of experience simplify our engagement with the world and equip us with a host of working beliefs about that world that serve us quite well. When they do not serve us well, as happens often enough, we make adjustments. In this way, the ontological landscape of our experience emerges from the mist of sense experience. We adjust our hypothetical cognitive map of that landscape as needed – easily and without even noticing the subtle adjustments, or with great difficulty and emotional resistance, depending on how disruptive the change is to our typically comfortable and efficient engagement.

Many parts of that cognitive map of ontological realities are universally shared; these are the bits we tend to call physical reality, though they also include the basic problems that all human cultures have had to solve. Other parts are culturally specific, as we discover when we travel; this is particularly true of values governing social interactions. Still other parts are specific to religious outlook, as we discover when we encounter those whose religious beliefs differ from our own; this is particularly applicable to the ontology of non-physical realms and value realms. And yet other parts of our working ontological maps are even more idiosyncratic, some perhaps completely private. In general, the more value-laden the object of our engagement, the more symbolic our mode of registering it, the more group-specific the belief that expresses it, and the more likely it is to matter existentially to us. The journey from religious perceptions to cognitive representations of ontology typically is made within the high-value end of this spectrum of variation.

THE RELIABILITY OF RELIGIOUS PERCEPTUAL ENGAGEMENT

We have done enough conceptual work now to return to the cognitive reliability of RSEs. As Alston discovered during his many years of reflecting on the issue, we can answer most securely aspects of the reliability question pertaining to the degree to which we are *rationally entitled* to treat our RSEs as cognitively reliable. It may seem strange to discuss "rational entitlement to assume an answer to the reliability question" instead of answering the reliability question itself, directly. But the evidential and conceptual complexity of the first-order reliability question is such that we really do not know the whole answer and can answer only bits and pieces of it.

In what follows, I first identify key assumptions that damage rational entitlement to proceed as if RSEs are cognitively reliable. Then I argue that a certain class of RSEs – the evolutionarily stabilized intense experiences – when interpreted appropriately, increase our entitlement to proceed as if RSEs are cognitively reliable. The result has potentially disturbing implications for religious self-awareness, as well as reassuring implications for some people.

Damaging rational entitlement to presume cognitive reliability

RSEs, when thought of as forms of dynamic perceptual engagement, are quite varied in their power to consolidate confidence around ontological questions. As Alston correctly points out, the more the cognitive content of such experiences is contested by groups with standing similar to the one in which we participate, the less compelling are our local religious cognitions. These group-relative religious cognitions will not be trusted very far by anyone with a sufficiently wide vision of the question – *to the extent that they are interpreted literally*. In fact, the arbitrariness of the religious cognitions makes questionable even the existential value of the experiences. Interpreted symbolically, however, the same group-relative religious perceptions can be highly compelling, and their powerful effects in people's lives can be recognized as authentic – and surely authenticity is one kind of reliability.

Such judgments of authenticity are based on the way the beliefs deriving from religious perceptions help people navigate their value-laden ambient environments successfully. They are far from straightforward, because successful navigation typically requires group-relative concepts at least to some degree; for instance, we discern beauty in relation to norms that are at least influenced by culture-level considerations. Judging the truth of religious cognitions deriving from religious perceptions is even more complicated. The symbols used to express the ontological claims about reality coded in those beliefs are typically multivalent, and that makes reconciling conflicting ontological claims tricky. This problem defines a complex philosophical and theological task of interpretation and evaluation, and it is one governed by necessarily flexible standards – which is to say, a problem that requires a kind of artistic sensibility.

It is possible to reconcile the ontological implications of perceptions of a personal deity with the ontological implications of perceptions of the *Dao* in the vibrant depths of natural processes when both are interpreted symbolically. But it is a meaningful reconciliation only when active schemas for interpreting symbolic statements allow the ontological import of the two perceptions to be made relatively precise. Religious and philosophical traditions and their many sub-traditions furnish such schemas, but their implementation is a complex hermeneutical matter that shifts with time and place. It is correspondingly difficult to venture judgments about the truth of religious beliefs. Of course, when the symbolic character of religious cognitions is ignored, then it is relatively easy to make a truth judgment, and the judgment required is that at least one and probably both sets of ontological claims are incorrect. This is devastating to the reliability of RSEs as a cognitively productive mode of perceptual engagement.

Consider an example. Suppose someone says they saw a demon passing into an ancient stone pillar and warns people to stay away from the pillar lest they and their families be cursed. We might grant that a degree of authenticity is present in the action because it expresses compassion and ordinary human concern for mutual safety, regardless of what we think of the assumed ontology. But judging the truth of the ontological claims implied in this testimony is a complicated process fraught with challenges. To the extent that the testimony is intended literally, it involves adjudicating a worldview battle of monumental proportions in human history. Correspondingly, to the extent that the testimony was a self-consciously symbolic one, then we might be able to grant the truth of the implied ontology, if it can be rendered sufficiently determinate to permit evaluation; but it would be a complex judgment, as all such judgments are. Alternatively, we might also question the authenticity of the warning, perhaps on the grounds that it is manipulative, suggesting a view of demons and stone pillars that the putative witness does not in fact hold. Or else we might acknowledge authenticity under the rubric of expediency in an emergency; perhaps the pillar was structurally unstable and this was the only warning that would effectively protect people by keeping them away from the pillar.

How would our assessment of the reliability question unfold in these various alternative scenarios? In the case that the testimony was intended literally, we would immediately point out that other perceptions have contradictory ontological implications, and thus conclude that any case for cognitive reliability is harmed by this data item. We would likely conclude that there is no special exhibition of compassion in this instance, moreover, so that the case for reliability in the sense of authenticity of behavior is neither harmed nor helped. In the case that the testimony is intended symbolically, everything turns on the schema governing the interpretation of the ontological dimensions of the symbols in question. Most likely, the status of both the truth/reliability question and the authenticity/reliability question are left more or less unaltered, on average.

From this example, representative of a large class of religious cognitions, we learn that neglecting the symbolic character of religious cognitions routinely has a large negative impact on the reliability question. We also learn that when we take the symbolism criterion seriously, the reliability question is impacted neither negatively nor positively, subject to the kinds of philosophical arguments that ensue after the ontological implications of the symbolic statements in question are unpacked.

Something similar occurs if we surrender the ecological-semiotic account of perception as dynamic engagement and revert to Alston's Theory of Appearing or another account of perception that entails the simplest forms of direct realism. The damage done to the reliability case by literal interpretation of religious perceptions is done equally well by the ontological over-crispness of direct realism. After all, it matters little for the purposes of undermining *rational entitlement to presume reliability* whether we have two literal and contradictory ontological claims or two clear-cut perceptual situations that imply contradictory ontological claims. In either case, the cognitive faculties that supervised the journey from perception to belief are not to be trusted.

There is a third factor with a similar negative impact on the reliability question, namely, the operation of a supernaturalistic cosmology. In this case the problem derives from the fact that supernaturalism defeats all attempts at public checking and evaluation. As Alston rightly points out, why should a supernatural deity behave in such a way as to ease the epistemological scruples of those who anxiously seek public verification of supernaturalist ontological claims? Yet the removal of a vital basis for public debate and evaluation does negatively impact the reliability question, just because we are rationally justified in vesting great confidence in cognitive procedures that others can check.

So there we have it. The case for the cognitive reliability of RSEs virtually collapses when we give up any one of these three components: a naturalistic cosmology, an ecological-semiotic account of perception as dynamic engagement, or a symbolic account of religious cognitions. Supernaturalists, direct realists (in Alston's sense), or inveterate literalists need not panic, of course. In a slightly adjusted version of what Alston almost correctly argues, people are rationally entitled to explore the world of religious meanings however they see fit, subject to correction based on the consequences of their perceptual experiences. In other words, though supernaturalists, Alstonian direct realists, and literalists adopt assumptions that vitiate their rational entitlement to proceed as if religious perceptions were *actually* reliable, they are still rationally entitled to proceed as if their religious perceptions were *possibly* reliable. This is something. But it is a lot less than these people would want and somewhat less than Alston thinks can be gained.

Enhancing rational entitlement to presume cognitive reliability

The argument about the reliability question to this point has identified three conditions under which the case for reliability is negatively affected. Can we conclude that religious cognitions are reliable when we make them in a framework that holds fast to these three conditions? That is, when RSEs are interpreted in terms of a naturalistic cosmology, an ecological-semiotic account of perception as dynamic engagement, and a symbolic account of the resulting religious cognitions, do we have improved prospects for demonstrating their cognitive reliability?

The answer to this question in relation to the whole diverse tangle of RSEs is, I think, no. As Chapter 3 demonstrates, RSEs are too varied to possess a clear-cut cognitive profile. On the contrary, they correspond to a wide variety of cognitive operations, some of which have been convincingly shown to be quite unreliable, such as superstition, agency detection, and intention attribution (see Gilovich 1991; Vyse 1997; Wildman 2009a). But at this point it is vital to recall that *some RSEs are more universal in our species than others.* In the previous chapter, we identified a class of evolutionarily stabilized RSEs that are also ultimacy experiences. These are the intense experiences, where intensity is understood in a depth-and-breadth way as involving simultaneously strong activation and rich interconnectedness of meanings. In relation to this special and (if the intensity hypothesis is correct) species-wide subset of RSEs, the case for cognitive reliability improves. Of course, we have to uphold the three conditions whose rejection damages rational entitlement to presume reliability, namely, a naturalistic cosmology, an ecological-semiotic account of perception as dynamic engagement, and a symbolic account of religious cognitions. What does that case look like?

At the outset, we once again need to rule out a shortcut. The suite of capacities underlying intense experiences being evolutionarily stabilized – and this is still hypothetical at this point, despite the evidence adduced in the previous chapter – does not mean that they are reliable. I pointed out in Chapter 1 that, in relation to RSEs as a whole, knowing their evolutionary origins by itself does not settle the question of their cognitive reliability. After all, it is adaptive to impute intentionality to a rustling bush and run away even though the wind was doing the rustling, because people lacking that intentionality-attribution instinct will get eaten by lions often enough to impact the human gene pool. Tendencies to certain types of cognitive error are thus demonstrably adaptive. Adaptiveness is a very different issue from cognitive reliability.

Shortcut not taken, we can consider the matter with the appropriate complications firmly in mind.

In a fully naturalistic framework (the first of the three conditions), there is no supernatural realm, no divine beings, and no discarnate entities such as demons or angels. There is enormous richness of value in the structures and process of nature, however, from heart-rending beauty to complexly ambiguous moral possibilities, and from glorious mathematical patterns to staggeringly counterintuitive physical transactions. These depths of nature have important existential implications and are subject to phenomenological, existential, philosophical, and theological renderings (see, for example, Heidegger [1927] 1962, or Tillich 1951, 1957, 1963). Thus, it is not surprising that some religious intellectuals have seen in these depths of nature the proper ontological referent for words such as "God" and "*Dao*," both thought of as ground of being, with different overtones in the corresponding cultural contexts. This kind of value-sensitive naturalism leads directly and easily to a religious naturalism, in a way that flattened out, value-averse types of materialism do not. Religious naturalism is a religiously and theologically potent outlook on life and coexists with other viewpoints within all of the world's major religious traditions. People who cannot bear the superstition-like aspects of supernatural religious beings typically appreciate one or another variation of religious naturalism and engage the spiritual dimensions of reality in its terms.

What, we must now ask, are intense experiences in the context of naturalism, understood in this religiously potent way? They are nothing less and nothing more than perception of the depth structures of nature in all of their intricate differentiation and grading, which I argued in Chapter 4 involves the qualities of depth, horizon, scale, complexity, and mystery. Intense experiences are the means by which we engage the valuational richness of reality, just as sense perception is the way that we engage the sensible aspects of our ambient environment. We need an ecological-semiotic account of perception as dynamic engagement to appreciate fully the parallels between the cognitive-emotional underpinnings of intense experiences and the cognitive capacity for sense perception. These are two levels of a seamless form of engagement consisting in the interested navigation of an environment with the aid of conceptual mediation and cultural traditions, taking in whatever our cognitive apparatus permits us to absorb, powering the action–perception dialectic, and responding to correction as necessary. There is enormous richness in reality's value structures that the capacity for intense experiences enables us to engage.

This richness of value is often mind-boggling and frequently defies normal cognitive processing to the point that we suffer various kinds of aphasia as we struggle to express what we have in fact engaged. Symbolic structuring of such experiences, and symbolic modes of talking about them, are therefore crucial. These symbolic resources liberate us into realms of speech that are different from the literalized speech of daily life yet not even a tiny bit contrived and no more complicated than is demanded by the subject matter that appears in the cognitive aspects of intense experiences. The culturally traditioned character of perceptual experience furnishes the schemas according to which we can give more formal philosophic expression to the beliefs that flow from intense experiences, after which philosophers and theologians carefully consider their consistency. However, because the object of intense perceptual experiences is the valuational depth structures of reality, and because the cognitive medium in question is equally universal, the problem of religious pluralism does not take the form of a spectral horror in the way that it does for Alston. Indeed, the prospects for cross-cultural consensus on the valuational depth structures of reality are quite good, and certainly infinitely better than the insurmountable problem posed by the contradictions that arise within Alston's supernaturalistic, direct-realism, literal belief framework.

This reading of the species-wide capacity for intense experiences is evolutionarily important. The suite of neural capacities underlying intense experiences is an elaboration of the ordinary cognitive process of sense experience itself. It is directly linked to the need for perception to manifest ever more intricate affordances in the environment. Thus, it was probably selected right along with sense experience and for much the same reasons. At worst, it was a side-effect that followed close on the heels of ordinary sense perception, because it is a more or less direct elaboration of ordinary sense perception rather than a new cognitive process. In either case, it was almost certainly adaptive in the original ancestral environment because then, as now, it is a vital skill in social settings that prize high alertness, high awareness of environment, and high sensitivity to emotional nuance. Note that little of this is true for the full diversity of RSEs in general; it applies only to the species-wide suite of capacities for intense experiences.

Recall that a cognitive capacity can be valuable or not valuable – and in this case reliable or not reliable – regardless of its evolutionary origins. So how does this evolutionary account of the emergence of a species-wide capacity for intense experiences help us evaluate the reliability of that capacity? The evolutionary framework serves to delimit relatively precisely the relationship between the capacity for intensity and ordinary sense perception: the former is an elaboration and amplification and intensification of the latter. This grounds our expectation that there will be regions of high reliability and regions of malfunction in the cognitive capacity for intensity, just as these regions exist in the capacity for sense perception. And it also grounds our expectation that we are entitled to evaluate the cognitive elements of intensity perception in the same way that we do sense perception: we look for rational coherence in the consequences of our engagement with the environment on the terms of these modes of perception. In the context of naturalism, there is high rational coherence in the cognitive consequences of intensity perception, as I have said (this has not been shown here, though it has been hinted at in a variety of efforts within comparative theology; see Neville 2001).

Thus, our rational entitlement to presume the cognitive reliability of intense experiences is increased, so long as we maintain the three basic conditions: a naturalistic cosmology, an ecological-semiotic account of perception as dynamic engagement, and a symbolic account of religious cognitions. The rational entitlement to presume the cognitive reliability of RSEs in general is also increased, but only insofar as these experiences are rooted in intense experiences, and only if the three basic conditions are in place.

CONCLUSION

This chapter has answered the question about the cognitive reliability of RSEs at the level and to the extent possible when we resolutely refuse short-circuited approaches that arbitrarily neglect complexities. In the process, a framework for interpreting the cognitive elements of RSEs has been proposed and defended, one that takes with due seriousness the cognitive immediacy criterion, the conceptual mediation criterion, the epistemic tradition criterion, the rational coherence criterion, the symbolism criterion, and the value criterion. The argument has also situated RSEs, as well as ordinary sense perception, within an ecological theory of dynamic engagement.

That much achieved, it is also important to repeat the limitations of the argument. No general answer has been given to the question of the wholesale reliability of RSEs in all their diversity. Indeed, several common answers to this larger question have been ruled out. Moreover, in those cases where I argued that there is strong rational entitlement to presume cognitive reliability, it was only in relation to the significant subset of intense experiences, not RSEs in general, and only when the three basic conditions – a naturalistic cosmology, an ecological-semiotic account of perception as dynamic engagement, and a symbolic account of religious cognitions – are in place. In most other situations, the rational grounds for presuming cognitive reliability are relatively weak. This may strike some as a rather bleak conclusion. But it is far from bleak for the religious naturalist.

In concluding we need to ask whether these three basic conditions are actually true. In the course of this chapter I have argued for the second and third conditions – an ecological-semiotic account of perception as dynamic engagement and a symbolic account of religious cognitions. But I have not argued for the first condition, a naturalistic cosmology. I will return to that question in Chapter 8. For now, it is enough to note that a naturalistic cosmology, in conjunction with other conditions, positively impacts rational entitlement to presume cognitive reliability, while a supernaturalistic cosmology negatively impacts this same entitlement. I have argued that this need not unduly worry supernaturalists, because they are still entitled to presume the *possible reliability* of RSEs, though not their *actual reliability*. This argument's support for religious naturalism is indirect, and supernaturalism is in no serious danger from it. This ancient and vital contention, which is so important for interpreting RSEs, must be resolved in other ways.

CHAPTER 6

The brain-group nexus: the social power of religious and spiritual experiences

INTRODUCTION

Time and Mind: The Journal of Archaeology, Consciousness, and Culture was recently launched with great fanfare, thanks to a controversial article in its very first issue. Benny Shanon, a Professor of Psychology at the Hebrew University of Jerusalem, published a speculative hypothesis about "biblical entheogens" (Shanon 2008). This hypothesis involves Moses ingesting mind-altering entheogens containing a psychedelic chemical also found in the plants from which "the powerful Amazonian hallucinogenic brew Ayahuasca is prepared" (51). Shanon claims that this chemical is found on the Sinai peninsula in a type of acacia tree and a type of bush that flourish in that arid environment. He conjectures that the psychoactive chemicals in these plants produced Moses' visions and inspired his production of a powerful religious outlook that proved to be socially revolutionary for a fledgling Israelite nation.

I am not interested in exploring Shanon's hypothesis; as far as I can tell, his assumptions about ancient Israelite history (i.e. Moses leading an enslaved Israelite people out of Egypt into decades of wandering in the wilderness) are not widely shared by Ancient Near Eastern historians anyway, so I am not confident that his speculative theory even has a stable historical referent. But I am interested in the marketing strategy employed here to generate publicity and subscribers for a new journal.

This article was discussed in the mass media, which is how I found out about it. Part of the reason it was picked up by news agencies was probably the link it assumes between individual religious experiences and large-scale social change. It is quite amazing when relatively small events somehow survive the noise of human activity and end up leveraging vast, civilization-sized effects. It is still news when such a link is proposed – and all the more shocking news when an entire network of religious beliefs is claimed to be based on hallucinations and probable cognitive error.

In our time, we readily accept that Shanon's claims *could* be correct, even if his claim is not borne out by the evidence. Whether it is banned entheogens, physically and psychically dangerous rituals, rhythmic frenzies, or suburban prayer services, we know that RSEs sometimes have potent social effects, influencing political movements, economic practices, and cultural habits. Indeed, under special circumstances, these social effects can be virtually incalculable in their significance.

This chapter is about the complex network of causal linkages joining an individual's RSEs outwards to their social effects – that is, in Shanon's example, the linkage from Moses' supposed religious experiences in the Sinai desert outwards to a moral and legal framework for Israelite community life. I am equally concerned with the linkage in the other direction, from social conditions inwards to the ways that RSEs are sought, experienced, interpreted, and embedded in individual beliefs and behaviors. Both the inward and outward journeys through this causal linkage require that we take account of the social embedding of RSEs, which is just as salient as their neuropsychological embedding for a sound interpretation of the nature, functions, and value of RSEs. Neuropsychological embodiment and social embedding – brains and groups – these are the two major factors governing the interaction between belief and behavior in human beings. Somewhere in this tangled *brain-group nexus* there is a compelling interpretation of the social power of individual RSEs, as well as the impact on individuals of socially widespread patterns of belief and behavior.

For example, from the outside in, both the benefits and the deficits for mental and physical well-being of RSEs appear to be socially mediated, which means we need to understand the brain-group nexus to explain these health benefits and deficits. And from the inside out, socially embedded assumptions condition the way we attach meanings to RSEs. This is demonstrated by the terrifying connection between religious fanaticism and dramatic violence, and the wondrous connection between religious compassion and socially revolutionary altruism.

In addition to providing a theoretical analysis of RSEs in terms of the brain-group nexus, I have a practical goal. I want to raise awareness about the way the brain-group nexus facilitates power dynamics within groups by means of the social embedding of RSEs. This kind of self-awareness is becoming increasingly important for the future of human civilization.

To get at these dynamics, we need a serviceable model of the brain-group nexus that allows us to tease apart its inner workings and thereby trace the linkage from RSEs outwards to social effects and back inwards again. To that end, I present in this chapter a mostly speculative dynamical systems account of the brain-group nexus. At the end of this chapter I consider the brain-group nexus with reference to its ideological character and its moral qualities, which is crucial for grasping the power dynamics operative in the social embedding of RSEs.

A DYNAMICAL SYSTEMS APPROACH TO THE BRAIN-GROUP NEXUS

The central thesis of this chapter is that the brain-group nexus is a dynamical system that migrates through a landscape of possibilities for social arrangements. This dynamical system exhibits self-organization consisting of several equilibrium states and characteristic ways of transitioning between them. Equilibrium states are stable forms of social organization within this landscape of social possibilities that are stable relative to the cognitive capacities of brains and prevailing environmental conditions. RSEs play crucial roles both in the maintenance of equilibrium social arrangements and in the sometimes revolutionary transitions between them.

To understand the social embedding of RSEs, ideally we would want to know how RSEs developed along with the migration of human beings through the landscape of social possibilities. To achieve that goal, however, we first need to understand the brain-group nexus itself. The basic problem with this is that all early hominid societies are gone and only modern humans remain. This leaves a vast gulf between groups of chimpanzees and macaques, which are our closest surviving evolutionary relatives, and the few remaining groups of Stone-Age hunter-gatherer humans, who are not genetically or cognitively significantly different from other human beings. Fortunately, primatologists and anthropologists have carefully studied these two landmarks in the evolutionary story. Despite intricate analyses of archeological and fossil evidence, however, there is a lot that we just do not and probably cannot know about intervening changes in the brain-group nexus.

The tasks in this section are (i) to explain the brain-group nexus as a complex dynamical system; (ii) to define a low-energy stable equilibrium state for the brain-group nexus and show how it probably arose in the era of evolutionary adaptation; (iii) to understand the effects of perturbing that equilibrium state both gently and violently; (iv) to identify higher-energy states of equilibrium with narrower operating parameters into which the brain-group nexus can transition when perturbation forces are large enough or the system is sufficiently fine-tuned; and (v) to isolate the roles that RSEs play both in equilibrium maintenance and in equilibrium transition dynamics. To prepare for a more detailed discussion, I begin with an analogy to which we can refer in what follows.

The self-organized landscape of social possibilities

Picture the landscape of social possibilities as a plain rising gradually from the ocean into a bank of hills. Stable equilibrium states are akin to depressions in the ground where water might puddle, or a rolling bowling-ball might come to rest. Some are broad and very stable with wide operating parameters. Others, particularly on the hillside, are smaller. Imagine gently pushing the bowling-ball after it has come to rest in one of these depressions in the ground. It will wobble around a bit but still stay in its local depression. If you shove the ball hard enough, it might move out of its local depression and fall into another one nearby, perhaps further up the slope. In this landscape analogy, the size of the depression – a deep hole or a shallow dimple – expresses the stability of the equilibrium social arrangement. The height of the depression above the plain corresponds to the energy required to create and maintain the corresponding equilibrium social arrangement. The distance to the right from the ocean expresses the cognitive complexity required to realize that equilibrium possibility.

The evolution of the brain-group nexus is all about migrating across this landscape, first across the gently rising plain, and eventually up the energy–cognitive-complexity hillside in a kind of puddle-jumping process that moves groups from one equilibrium state to another. Each non-human animal has a species-specific social arrangement that remains more or less static relative to given environmental conditions. Humans, by contrast, migrated rightwards across the plain, and did so more or less together, allowing for some bilocation in times of transition between equilibrium states. Once humans reached the base of the energy–cognitive-complexity hillside, they were evolutionarily equipped with the same basic cognitive functionality that we still have today. This defines the lowest energy equilibrium state for modern human beings: the one produced by environmental pressures and social conditions in the hunter-gatherer era of evolutionary adaptation.

After that point, the emergence of complex cultures boasting nested and parallel group structures and widely shared civilizational ideals produces the possibility of higher-energy equilibrium states for the brain-group nexus. Each of these higher-energy equilibrium states is less stable

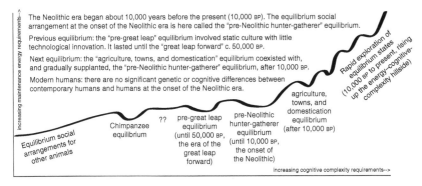

The Neolithic era began about 10,000 years before the present (10,000 BP). The equilibrium social arrangement at the onset of the Neolithic era is here called the "pre-Neolithic hunter-gatherer" equilibrium.

Previous equilibrium: the "pre-great leap" equilibrium involved static culture with little technological innovation. It lasted until the "great leap forward" c. 50,000 BP.

Next equilibrium: the "agriculture, towns, and domestication" equilibrium coexisted with, and gradually supplanted, the "pre-Neolithic hunter-gatherer" equilibrium, after 10,000 BP.

Modern humans: there are no significant genetic or cognitive differences between contemporary humans and humans at the onset of the Neolithic era.

increasing maintenance energy requirements→

Equilibrium social arrangements for other animals

Chimpanzee equilibrium

?? pre-great leap equilibrium (until 50,000 BP, the era of the great leap forward)

pre-Neolithic hunter-gatherer equilibrium (until 10,000 BP, the onset of the Neolithic)

agriculture, towns, and domestication equilibrium (after 10,000 BP)

Rapid exploration of equilibrium states (10,000 BP to present, rising up the energy–cognitive-complexity hillside)

increasing cognitive complexity requirements-->

Figure 6.1. The self-organizing landscape of social possibilities for the brain-group nexus.

than the low-energy equilibrium state in the sense that each has narrower operating parameters and thus is easier to unsettle. After the low-energy equilibrium state where the plain meets the hillside, there have been lots of human groups in diverse social arrangements, so we should picture many groups of puddle jumpers in different places on the hillside of this landscape of social possibilities. Cognitive evolution drives humans rightwards across the plain. Cultural evolution draws them up the energy–cognitive-complexity hillside.

Let's fill out this map by placing several key landmarks on it. First, at the point where the plain meets the hills, we need an indentation corresponding to the first social arrangement of genetically and cognitively modern humans. This social arrangement is a stable equilibrium with wide operating parameters, so the indentation in the ground is broad and deep. Like the social arrangements that preceded it, this social arrangement involves hunter-gatherer tribes, loosely linked by unsystematic interactions among tribes, with geographical boundaries of mountains, rivers, and oceans being the principal conditions governing the extent of this interaction, along with proximity to food and water sources. But this equilibrium social arrangement also had features that distinguish it from earlier hunter-gatherer societies, such as cave painting, flexible use of varied stone tools, and hunting techniques such as drop-holes and driving animals off cliffs, all of which suggest greater aesthetic and cognitive sophistication than in previous eras. Virtually all human hunter-gatherer groups were in this social arrangement 10,000 years before the present, when the Neolithic era began. Human groups fell into this equilibrium roughly 50,000 years ago, long before the Neolithic, and a few have stayed in it all the way up to today. This is the "pre-Neolithic hunter-gatherer" equilibrium, or just the "pre-Neolithic" equilibrium for short, in honor of its dominance at the onset of the Neolithic. This is the default system for the brain-group nexus of genetically and cognitively modern humans. It was spontaneously generated in the evolutionary process, and survivors would revert to something like this equilibrium state should human beings induce a massive collapse of civilization with a corresponding loss of all technological knowledge.

Second, the Neolithic era, beginning around 10,000 years ago, was distinguished by the invention of agriculture and the domestication of animals. This in turn produced settled villages with local economies coexisting with nomadic-subsistence social arrangements that emphasized hunting and gathering. The new social arrangement is the second one for genetically and cognitively modern humans. I call it the "agriculture, towns, and domestication equilibrium" and locate the corresponding indentation a small way up the energy–cognitive-complexity hillside, to express the higher cognitive complexity needed for this social arrangement to be possible and the higher energy needed to maintain its stability. But we will make it smaller and shallower to reflect its relative instability and the ease with which a perturbation could move groups further up the hill into new social arrangements or back downwards to nomadic hunter-gatherer lifestyles. Note that being higher on the energy–cognitive-complexity hillside does not require evolutionary changes in human cognitive capacities. As near as anyone can tell, all human beings after the Neolithic began 10,000 years ago display cognitive functions on a spectrum of capabilities that has changed at most in minor ways. As we shall see, however, moving up the energy–cognitive-complexity hillside does require energy expenditure to stabilize social arrangements that capitalize on existing but unrealized capacities for cognitive complexity.

Third, looking further up the hill, we see dozens of indentations of various sizes corresponding to the numerous social arrangements since the Neolithic. Human cognition in the early Neolithic was such that the dynamical system achieved a critical level of complexity that permitted an explosion of social experimentation, driven by technological innovations and imaginative visions of social life. These factors permitted larger forms of human togetherness, from empires to sovereign nation-states, and from communities with shared interests transcending genetic relatedness to the global village of instant communication, convenient travel, and international trade. Social change has far outpaced biological evolution, so we inhabit these new equilibrium states of the self-organizing brain-group nexus equipped with cognitive abilities and social impulses that were forged by the time of the pre-Neolithic equilibrium, down at the base of the hill.

The indentations corresponding to these new social arrangements are further and further up the hill because each of these regimes of the brain-group nexus requires more energy to maintain its stability – energy both in terms of natural resources and in terms of culture-level forming of individuals to enable them to function within the appropriate equilibrium state. Modern human beings are cognitively equipped by evolution to deal with tribal societies quite naturally. For them to function effectively within cosmopolitan economic and cultural environments requires a great deal of education, which is a high-energy activity; without strong investment in educational processes the equilibrium social arrangement collapses. Despite their high energy requirements and lower stability relative to the Neolithic equilibrium, each of these novel equilibrium states is sufficiently stable to be recognized as a form of social order, and perhaps to get a name, such as the city-state, the Roman empire, the Ming dynasty, medieval Christendom, the global village, or the new world order.

Fourth, let's place the chimpanzee social equilibrium in a large and stable indentation half-way across the plain as it gently rises to meet the base of the hills. From there back toward the ocean are the large and stable indentations corresponding to the social arrangements of less cognitively complex animal species. Like chimps, these animals do not have the cognitive abilities to explore the space of social possibilities in the way that modern humans do, so they always stay in the same species-specific, low-energy equilibrium social arrangement.

Fifth, between the chimpanzee equilibrium half-way across the plain and the pre-Neolithic equilibrium at the base of the hills is the great unknown territory of equilibrium social arrangements during the drawn-out period of hominid evolution. Presumably there are a few broad indentations scattered across this half of the plain because the evolution of new cognitive capabilities would have made possible different kinds of social arrangements. For example, we can be fairly confident that there was another broad indentation on the plain close to but lower than the pre-Neolithic equilibrium's indentation; this corresponds to a much more static and unimaginative form of human social life than the colorful pre-Neolithic equilibrium, with its cave paintings and novel hunting techniques. The last human puddle jumpers seem to have left this indentation between 40,000 and 50,000 years ago, heading for the pre-Neolithic equilibrium. This transition marks the most recent significant evolutionary change in human cognition, sometimes called the "great leap forward" (see Diamond 1991), so I refer to the equilibrium prior to this transition as the "pre-great leap" equilibrium. All transitions since the one from the pre-great leap equilibrium to the pre-Neolithic equilibrium have been culturally rather than evolutionarily driven.

Complex dynamical systems and self-organization

With this landscape analogy for the brain-group nexus in place, we need to step back and discuss the conceptual architecture of the dynamical system so described, starting with mathematics. The mathematical concept of a complex dynamical system has become widely known under the misleading name of chaos theory, thanks to beautiful pictures of fractal geometry, which is one of the features of dynamical systems. A complex mathematical dynamical system is the sort of thing needed to produce those beautiful pictures. This is a mathematical feedback system that evolves with time subject to operating conditions or tuning parameters. Feedback means just what it says: the output of the system at one moment is fed back into the system as input for the next moment.

The fact that a complex mathematical dynamical system evolves with time means that it can display behavior patterns. One of these behavior patterns is stable equilibrium. This means that the system falls into a steady operating state such that a small bump in operating conditions or tuning parameters causes a temporary wobble, followed by the system gradually settling back into the same operating state that it was in before the bump. A stable equilibrium is like a smooth bowling-ball resting at the base of an equally smooth glass depression; a push in any direction and the ball moves but eventually it settles back down toward the stable equilibrium point. A stable equilibrium can be more and less stable: it would take a lot more energy to knock the ball out of a large depression than a small dimple.

Equilibrium states are not always stable; unstable equilibriums exist in these mathematical systems also. Think of a smooth bowling-ball at rest on the very top of a frictionless knoll; one tiny push will send the ball rolling away from its unstable equilibrium position. Equilibrium behaviors are diverse in other ways besides stability. The equilibrium state might be a constant sameness, as in the bowling-ball illustration, or it might be periodic cycling, a kind of dynamic sameness. And equilibrium states can also subsist within a special type of system behavior called chaos, which is an eventually unpredictable form of system behavior even in the deterministic context of mathematical equations ("eventually unpredictable" is the terminology used in Wildman and Russell 1995; equivalent terms are used in both mathematical presentations of chaotic dynamical systems such as Devaney 1989 and popular presentations such as Gleick 1987; Lorenz 1993; and Stewart 2002). In the case of chaotic behavior, all of the equilibrium states mentioned so far often coexist, as does another type of equilibrium known as a strange attractor because of the way the chaotic system hovers around it in many modes of operation.

Complex mathematical dynamical systems display other behavior patterns as well. The most important of these for present purposes is transitions between equilibrium states. Suppose a dynamical system has two stable equilibrium states that are close to one another, like two depressions nearby with a bowling-ball rolling around near the bottom of one of them. If we give the bowling-ball a big enough heave in the right direction, then it may roll right out of one depression into the other. That is, if we perturb the system in just the right way, it can transition between equilibrium states. The mathematics of transitions in complex dynamical systems is just as fascinating and useful as the mathematics of equilibrium states (see Devaney 1989; Feigenbaum 1978; Kadanoff 1983).

So far we have been talking just about feedback systems in mathematics. In the idealized framework of mathematics, all of the intricacy of complex dynamical systems is available for study, unimpaired by noisy real-world environments. This matters because some states of complex dynamical systems are so delicate that even tiny changes in environmental conditions cause transitions in behavior. This makes modeling real-world dynamical systems using mathematical dynamical systems very challenging. The most exquisitely delicate parts of the mathematics typically do not apply in modeling because of energy noise in nature. But the coarser parts of mathematical systems, especially equilibrium states and transition behaviors, have proved to be invaluable for modeling physical systems. Heart rhythms, chemical reactions, animal populations, turbulence, the outbreak of war, traffic, and the stock market have been effectively modeled using the coarser parts of complex dynamical systems (see Arecchi *et al.* 1982; Gollub and Swinney 1975; Guevara *et al.* 1981; Libchaber 1982; May and Oster 1976; Peters 1991; Saperstein 1984; Simoyi *et al.* 1982; Testa *et al.* 1982). For current purposes, it is especially interesting that the neurosciences have made excellent use of modeling using complex dynamical systems, and at many different levels, from tiny clusters of neurons to large assemblies of neuronal clusters.

These modeling efforts have triggered an explosion of research on complex physical systems that exhibit self-organizing behavior (an early work was Prigogine and Stengers 1984; since then works in complexity theory and the analysis of self-organizing systems have multiplied with topics studied varying from the biochemical origins of life in Küppers 1990 and Kauffman 1995, to the social sciences in Byrne 1998 and Kiel and Elliott 1996; other key works are Camazine *et al.* 2003; Haken 2006; Holland 1995; Jensen 1998; Lewin 1992; Nicolis and Prigogine 1977, 1989; Pelesko 2007; Sole and Bascompte 2006; Waldrop 1992). *A self-organized system is a dynamic physical system whose internal architecture permits the spontaneous production of patterned behavior.* The more interesting the patterned behavior, the more impressive the self-organization and the more fascinating the internal architecture. In aggressive forms (Bak 1996; Kelso 1995), theories of self-organization regard every level of behavior in nature as the systemic self-organization of component systems under constraints deriving from (i) operating conditions and tuning variables, and (ii) the functionality for the sake of which the self-organized system develops.

For example, in relation to the mathematical dynamical systems just discussed, the feedback process establishes a dynamical system that operates subject to constraints in the form of operating parameters and tuning variables, producing emergent behaviors with higher-order functionality. In the case of the brain, tiny clusters of neurons interact thanks to brain wiring, and the resulting dynamical system is constrained by environmental conditions and by the task that the brain is attempting to perform. The result is effective assemblies with high-order behavioral features built dynamically out of lower-order clusters as components. Those assemblies then function as components for higher-level dynamical systems to organize, again subject to operating constraints and the task that the brain is attempting to perform, producing still higher-level behavioral properties, say, at the level of nerve signals that cause muscle movements.

This recurring, multilevel self-organization approach promises a mathematical modeling strategy that is becoming increasingly useful across levels in nature from the simplest to the most complex. It also points to the underlying secret of emergence in complex natural systems: there is a constant reuse of lower-level components and constraints in dynamical systems to generate higher-level forms of behavior. The details vary from level to level, depending on the evolved structures that are available to serve as components, the relevant operating constraints, and the new evolutionary problems to be solved and functions to be performed (see the vital distinction between three types of emergence in Deacon 2003, 2006).

Recall the central thesis of this chapter, that the brain-group nexus is a dynamical system exhibiting self-organization consisting of several equilibrium states and characteristic ways of transitioning between them. This is a dynamical system of a very high order, built out of components that we will analyze presently. We might satisfy ourselves with applying a dynamical systems approach to the self-organization of the brain-group nexus merely as an *analogy*, using this analogy to organize a variety of disciplinary perspectives in a convenient and illuminating way. That would certainly be appropriately modest, considering the degree of theoretical speculation involved. Nevertheless, I am proposing the more aggressive hypothesis that the brain-group nexus is *literally* a complex dynamical system exhibiting self-organization. I deploy the conceptuality of dynamical systems literally in what follows, knowing that much modeling work would be necessary to bear out this hypothesis about the brain-group nexus.

Components and constraints: brains in groups

To say the brain-group nexus is a self-organizing dynamical system is to commit to identifying (i) components that are organized, (ii) the basic system that causes component interactions to have emergent dynamics, and (iii) the constraints on the system, including (iiia) the tasks for which the dynamical system is functional and (iiib) operating parameters and tuning variables.

To illustrate the most basic level of the brain-group nexus, consider a tribe of hunter-gatherers in the pre-Neolithic equilibrium, with no significant interaction with humans beyond the tribe. In this case, (i) the components are embodied brains; (ii) the social interaction of these embodied brains is the basis for emergent system dynamics; (iiia) the tasks for which this dynamical system must be functional are primarily those directly related to survival and reproduction: hunting, gathering, reproducing, and rearing offspring; (iiib) the constraints on the dynamical system arise at both environmental and component levels. Environmental constraints include food availability, weather, disease, predators, and accidents. Component constraints include the degree of achieved intelligence, compassion, tolerance, strength, endurance, and immunity.

The brain-group nexus so described will – indeed, *did* – self-organize. The result is an array of higher-level behaviors. Kin groups form, modes of economic exchange spontaneously appear, and sex roles emerge. It would be virtually impossible to predict in advance what sorts of equilibrium social arrangements the dynamical system would support so we have to look and see what self-organization actually produces. It would be illuminating, however, to produce models that explain the actual diversity of social functions that historians and anthropologists describe.

Several higher or more intricate levels of emergent self-organization are also present in the brain-group nexus. First, the components (embodied brains) are not static, but transform over time under the impact of group practices. This is an exceptionally important feature of any system involving components that are inherently adaptive, such as brains. The mutual transformation of brains and groups is challenging to analyze. This dynamic process of mutual transformation within the brain-group nexus is indirectly described with enormous subtlety and the right level of flexibility in the sociology of knowledge, and at a very different level in evolutionary cognitive neuroscience. We will consider both below.

Second, the brain-group nexus spontaneously forms subgroups, each of which is a limited brain-group nexus, lacking the functional independence of the tribe. For example, the spontaneous formation of kin groups produces nuclear and extended families with levels and layers of loyalty, intimacy, trust, and tension. A family could not easily survive in isolation, because the loss of a key member could lead to annihilation. Thus, it is correct to view the tribe as the evolutionarily basic unit of the brain-group nexus, with families and wider kin groups derivative from it (note that this does not settle the question of selection units within evolutionary biology). Other subgroups that form spontaneously are related to tasks such as hunting (usually adult males) and gathering (usually adult females and children). These two sex-based subgroups are functionally dependent on the larger tribal group, but they do have some of the characteristics of a brain-group nexus.

Third, in practice, any instance of the brain-group nexus at the tribe level is in more or less constant interaction with other instances (other tribes). Thus, there are inter-group problems to solve, which each group does on the basis of its available resources of imagination, empathy, justice, courage, sneakiness, predilection for violence, and so on. There is usually enough arbitrariness in the operating parameters of the brain-group nexus that individual tribes quickly consolidate (that is, achieve stable equilibrium) around *different* behavioral patterns and social practices. For example, the practice in one group may be that most of their men must find women from outside the tribe to mate with, whereas another group may seek to protect its women from outsiders. These differences make inter-group problems frequently difficult to resolve, and violence is often the result. In the final analysis, there may be a new level of self-organizing complexity at the inter-group level, with tribes as components, mutual interaction as the dynamic engine of the system, managing inter-group differences as the goal, and individual group survival and flourishing as the major constraint on the system. In that case, inter-tribal conventions and laws would be the emergent features of the dynamical system.

Fourth, and finally, there are even larger scales of human social organization. The first three considerations above are those most pertinent for understanding the brain-group nexus during the era of evolutionary adaptation, in the pre-Neolithic equilibrium, after human cognitive functions were largely evolutionarily stabilized. But the last 10,000 years or so has seen the rapid development of new forms of social organization driven first by settled agriculture in the Neolithic and then by the complex needs and desires of collectives of human beings in towns and cities. This sometimes brought to light other forms of diversity in human groups, such as race and religion, culture and language. Subsequently, larger forms of human togetherness were devised, from empires to internet-based interest groups.

This kind of social change has far outpaced biological evolution, as noted above, so we inhabit these new social forms with cognitive equipment and social impulses that were in place by the time of the pre-Neolithic equilibrium state of the brain-group nexus. These are emergent equilibrium states of the brain-group nexus, nonetheless: social arrangements with extremely surprising and unpredictable features. The difficulty in the case of contemporary globalized society is identifying the components of the system. The evolutionarily basic unit of the tribe is rapidly vanishing, races are mingling at the margins, religions are merging around the edges, kin groups are breaking down, and even nuclear family structures are changing, in many parts of the planet. How can this degree of social complexity and variability fit within the dynamical systems account of the brain-group nexus?

Fortunately, a lot is known about the transitions between post-Neolithic equilibrium social arrangements, from a socioeconomic point of view. Sometimes such transitions involve violent revolutions, sometimes peaceful transformations of imagination, and often technology has been a factor. For example, the invention of iron smelting and forging produced possibilities for new equilibrium states of the brain-group nexus. The dawning of the Iron Age, with its far-reaching military and political consequences, illustrates the way that some equilibrium states of the brain-group nexus are vulnerable to even slight changes in some very particular operating parameters of the dynamical system. Other possible technological improvements at the very same time – say, the invention of the pooper-scooper or of lens grinding – would probably not have had an effect deserving of such a portentous name as "Iron Age" because the brain-group nexus was not sensitively dependent on the associated operating parameters. Information about such social transformations enhances the multileveled model of the brain-group nexus by identifying the factors on which the model should display sensitive dependence.

Religious experiences in the landscape of social possibilities

How do RSEs fit into this evolutionarily framed account of the brain-group nexus with its landscape of equilibrium social arrangements? The main point here builds on a result of earlier chapters, namely, that RSEs are extremely diverse and involve a host of cognitive functions that have evolutionarily distinguishable histories. Thus, the capacity for the various types of RSEs depends on the corresponding cognitive and emotional functions becoming available. Scholars in evolutionary cognitive neuroscience and evolutionary psychology debate when those functions appeared in our evolutionary history. These considerations impact theories of the evolutionary origins of religion as well as theories of the emergence of the various types of RSEs.

For example, judging from its presence in other animals, one of the earliest established aspects of human cognition is the network of cognitive skills needed to form action plans in response to possible danger. These pattern-recognition, intention-attribution, and causation-detection skills produce as side-effects a readiness to embrace beliefs about intentional supernatural beings who act in the world and influence our lives. Thus, we can reasonably assume that a supernatural mindset was ready to go very early in human evolution, and would have been applied to RSEs as soon as cognitive capacities made one or another type of them possible. We can also conclude that any equilibrium social arrangement that refuses to condone supernatural interpretations of RSEs will be committed to a vast expenditure of energy to override the default cognitive functions of (adaptively over-active) pattern recognition, intention attribution, and causation detection. This is why anti-supernatural interpretations of RSEs tend to take hold only within highly educated enclaves of people committed to correcting what they see these days as their evolutionarily bequeathed cognitive biases.

As another example, consider intense experiences. We have described them as an evolutionarily stabilized and thus species-wide subset of ultimacy experiences involving strong and broad neural activation, corresponding to existential potency and wide awareness. They evolved as an intensification of ordinary sense perception and thereby permit perception of, and imaginative engagement with, the aesthetic and moral depths of nature. Intense experiences, *properly interpreted* (recall the three basic conditions from Chapter 5), are almost as reliable as sense perception itself, and they do not have the cognitive liabilities that plague other types of RSEs. How do intense experiences fit into the landscape of social possibilities?

The suite of capacities underlying ordinary perceptual experience is evolutionarily ancient. Even aesthetically charged perceptual experiences are evolutionarily much older than human beings, judging from the aesthetic capabilities of chimpanzees. But chimps appear not to have the breadth-and-depth quality of intense experiences; that requires a kind of neural connectivity that is present in human brains but not in chimp brains. The human brain has a larger cortex and a few new structures relevant to social interaction and language. The human brain also has pervasive differences from the chimpanzee brain in the form of distinctive synaptic connections and neural networking. It is very likely these kinds of connectivity that make the depth-and-breadth quality of intense experiences possible for the first time in earth's evolutionary history. The aesthetically rich and emotionally dense quality of intense experiences is probably the precondition for Paleolithic cave art (see Van Huyssteen 2006). That helps to date the evolutionary emergence of the capability for intense RSEs to no later than roughly 50,000 years ago. That dating further suggests that at least some of the suite of cognitive capacities required for intense experiences is correlated with the onset of the sophisticated imagination and creativity of the hunter-gatherer equilibrium social arrangement that dominated human life from then until the beginning of the Neolithic, 10,000 years ago.

Thus, I think it is reasonable to suppose that intense experiences arrive late on the scene of human evolution as integrated elaborations of the evolutionarily most ancient cognitive capacity: sense perception. Intense experiences originated as side-effects of more complex neural connectivity that profoundly enhanced human cognition. Once established, intense experiences helped drive human exploration of the energy–cognitive-complexity hillside, pock-marked with diverse equilibrium social arrangements. Many of these social arrangements were constructed with enormous effort in the name of realizing visions of just and satisfying social life – visions conjured by potent intense experiences that disclose the value structures and possibilities in the depths of nature. At the very least, therefore, to the extent that they are also intense experiences, RSEs have been essential in creating the explosively diverse sociality of human civilization. Whether this is finally evolutionarily adaptive or disastrous remains to be seen.

DESCRIBING ALL EQUILIBRIUM SOCIAL ARRANGEMENTS SINCE THE NEOLITHIC

The next phase of presenting a model of the brain-group nexus as a dynamical system involves describing the Neolithic equilibrium in some detail. The best way to do this is to relate it to existing models of the relationship between individuals and social groups. Obviously, there is a vast ocean of research on this topic in the human sciences (for classic examples, focusing just on representative works that include extensive discussions of religion, see Bellah *et al.* 1991; Berger and Huntington 2002; Durkheim [1912] 1915; Huntington 1996; Mead 1934; Nietzsche [1883–85] 1954, [1901] 1968). Three conceptually powerful, complementary models of this kind have been produced within the sociology of knowledge, the epidemiology of representations, and social neuroscience. I shall discuss each of these in what follows, before discussing the evolutionary background of the pre-Neolithic equilibrium.

Sociology of knowledge

The sociology of knowledge is much older than the neurologically related disciplines. It describes the mutual conditioning of individuals and social groups in such a way as to make sense of the social construction of reality, the social conditioning of individual imaginations, and a host of other group-related phenomena (see Berger 1967; Berger and Luckmann 1966). In the dynamic systems framework of this chapter, the sociology of knowledge describes the pre-Neolithic equilibrium state of the brain-group nexus achieved by the end of the era of evolutionary adaptation. Indeed, the origins of sociology of knowledge lie in sociologist Émile Durkheim's studies of native Australians, who were at that time living in Stone-Age tribal societies, and thus a population as close to early Neolithic humans as then existed (Durkheim [1912] 1915 relates all of this especially to the sociology of religion). It is difficult to imagine the sociology of bi-directional individual–group influence in the time of so-called mito-chondrial Eve, 150,000 years ago, or of earlier hominid groups. But the sociology of knowledge appears to be a sound description of the mutual conditioning of individuals and social groups before 10,000 years ago, in the pre-Neolithic equilibrium. Fortunately, it has proved robust and flexible enough to make sense of equilibrium states in the brain-group nexus from the low-energy base state of the pre-Neolithic equilibrium all the way up the energy–cognitive-complexity hillside. This means that the sociology of knowledge has successfully isolated aspects of the brain-group nexus that recur in every equilibrium state at least since the Neolithic and probably since the great leap forward 50,000 years ago.

The sociology of knowledge portrays the dynamic interaction between individual experience and social reality in terms of a cyclical process of externalization, objectivation, and internalization. Externalization refers to human self-expression in the social and cultural realms, such as the creation of cultural ideas and artifacts, the development of styles of inter-personal behavior, the public expression of dreams and desires, and the construction of political and legal systems. Objectivation refers to the way our social expressions take on a life of their own, as when traffic laws and authorities that we create cause us to be punished when we break driving rules. There is an ontological question about what it means for social constructions to have objective status, but to answer that we really need to discuss the epidemiology of representations, to which we will come presently. Internalization refers to the way we come to take for granted objectivated social reality – to the point that we accept its benefits and limitations unconsciously and without realizing that there may be other options. So we teach our children how to behave according to norms of interpersonal behavior that we internalize, we speak the language we grew up with, and we categorize the world around us the way everyone else in our social group does. It is out of the fecund particularity of this internalized social reality that we externalize ourselves, expressing our inner worlds for others to share. Sometimes our cultural products are novel, perhaps just for fun. Sometimes they are calculated to help the social system adapt to changing circumstances, causing the cycling system to mutate slightly in the name of maintaining equilibrium. This dynamic cycle of externalization, objectivation, and internalization is the meaning of the social construction of reality.

This model of the pre-Neolithic equilibrium's fundamental rhythmic dynamics is particularly useful for explaining phenomena related to how an achieved equilibrium state is maintained. An equilibrium state of the brain-group nexus is maximally stable so long as the cycle of externalization, objectivation, and internalization is not questioned or challenged. Stability is achieved most effectively when (i) the cycle is transparent to individuals, (ii) the individual is existentially invested in *not questioning or challenging* the cycle, and (iii) the cost of questioning or challenging the cycle is high. The maintenance of these conditions keeps the brain-group nexus in the lowest energy level possible for its current equilibrium state, which is the meaning of optimizing stability. When one or more of these three conditions breaks down, the entire system can become destabilized, and more or less dramatic social change may then occur.

Transparency is achieved through internalization and persists so long as cognitive dissonance does not arise. Cognitive dissonance has many sources, including suffering that the social system cannot explain away, overbearing authority meant to protect the social system but betraying its underlying vulnerability, and encounters with other cultural systems that operate differently (cultural pluralism). Cognitive dissonance perturbs the equilibrium state with varying degrees of force. Effort is required to reestablish stability. Effort is most commonly expended in order to restore stability of the familiar equilibrium state; this is the conservative impulse. Effort can also be bent to revolutionary purposes, in which case the entire system can sometimes be thrown into a transitional phase, perhaps coming to rest in another equilibrium state altogether. In the new equilibrium, the cycle of externalization, objectivation, and internalization is quickly re-established, usually within a generation, and the brain-group nexus settles back down to the lowest energy expenditure possible for that new equilibrium state.

The most ingenious aspect of this equilibrium-maintenance system is the way it enlists individuals in supporting it. The individual wants the cultural system to meet basic needs. Some of these are material, such as the food and security needed to survive and to raise children safely. Some are conceptual and emotional, such as feeling at home in the world and mitigating existential anxiety. Any destabilization of the equilibrium threatens the ability of the social system to meet those needs. So individuals invest in the system, commit to its stability, resist acknowledging its arbitrary aspects, overlook inconsistency where possible, and fight destabilization – at least most individuals do this. It is not just habitual compliance or fear of being shunned by neighbors and punished by social authorities that inspires this investment; it is backed by evolutionarily forged social instincts. Investment in the system is also felt to be existentially vital, partly because the smooth running of the brain-group nexus reduces anxiety and satisfies many life goals, and partly because the social system helps individuals buy into the cosmic moral significance of their lives and the cultural system to which they belong.

Religion is particularly important at this point. As Durkheim showed, and Berger later emphasized, religion cosmologizes the operating principles of the social group, first writing them on the sky and then reading them off as supernaturally commanded moral laws, unquestionable because of their transcendent origins. To challenge the cultural system is thus to challenge the gods themselves, who imposed it and who command its maintenance and stability. Religion is thus a major component of social control, both in terms of the cosmic threat that it presents to anyone challenging the cultural system, and in terms of its ability to comfort people whose suffering has plunged them into the cognitive dissonance of existential anxiety and despair.

The sociology of knowledge leaves many questions unanswered, including why human beings have the drives they do and why they are willing to buy into the supernatural authorization of a cultural system. Evolutionary approaches to cognition are needed to answer those questions. But the general framework offers a plausible and fruitful account of the dynamics operative within equilibrium states of the brain-group nexus, of their destabilization, and of transitions between equilibrium states.

The roles of RSEs in this account of the Neolithic equilibrium and of all social arrangements since then are not difficult to see. These roles are essentially of two types: conservative and revolutionary, which is also to say priestly and prophetic. On the one hand, the conservative, priestly role of RSEs helps to maintain the stability of social arrangements. Imagine a person who has powerful feelings of spiritual and moral orientation in groups whose values are aligned with those of the wider society. That person is effectively enlisted in the maintenance of the stable equilibrium. When someone hears a disembodied voice, the implicit or explicit claims to supernatural authority present in social explanations for the status quo are typically ramified because the experience appears to confirm the reality of supernatural beings. On the other hand, the revolutionary, prophetic role of RSEs inspires deliberate destabilization of social arrangements in the name of values such as compassion or fairness that may be under threat in the existing social equilibrium. An encounter with someone suffering needlessly because of the neglect of the surrounding society can be a profound spiritual experience that utterly evacuates the narratives legitimating such social realities of their plausibility. Such experiences of the suffering Other can also nurture an unstoppable resolve to transform social conditions, even if that transformation is extremely disruptive and provokes fierce resistance.

Epidemiology of representations

The social construction of reality is the functional heart of the brain-group nexus. But what kind of a thing, we might ask, is a "social reality"? Where are social realities located? Thinking of social reality as having an existence in some supra-personal realm certainly is possible. But the sociology of knowledge conceives social reality as internalized, as inscribed in the embodied brains of selves within groups, so we need to account for the objectivity of social reality in terms of its internalization in individuals.

The most intelligible answer to these questions is furnished by the epidemiology of representations (see Sperber 1996). According to this view, social reality is a complex collection of representations of group life widely shared among members of the group. Such representations may be explicit beliefs or unconceptualized habits, but their locus is individual brains. These representations spread from mind to mind, much like a disease (thus, "epidemiology"), though with both constructive and destructive consequences. They spread either through mimesis, which is reflexive repetition, sometimes promoted by mirror-neuron structures in brains; or through one person convincing another by ideas, arguments, or stories. Understanding the evolved cognitive capabilities of the human brain enables us to explain why some representations spread more rapidly than others, why some representations tend to mutate less as they spread, and thus why some representations are present in similar ways in most individuals of a group. This is the basis for the objectivity of social reality and for the possibility of internalization.

These facts of life surrounding the transmission of representations of social reality are also essential for understanding why some social arrangements can become equilibrium states for the brain-group nexus while others cannot. Picture a social arrangement that requires individuals to commit to something that seems implausible, is hard to remember, or fails to meet essential needs – some utopian social schemes have this character. In that case, the energy cost required to maintain that social arrangement will be too high, most people will not be able to commit to it, and it cannot become an equilibrium state of the brain-group nexus, except perhaps for a short while in tiny groups of highly intentional individuals. By contrast, the many possible equilibrium social arrangements that can be stable both require and take advantage of a close match between social arrangement and human cognitive makeup.

Once such a match exists, some equilibrium states will be more stable and others less, depending on energy requirements and resilience to perturbations. The exploration of the space of social possibilities for the brain-group nexus is an intricate process played out on a global historical scale. It involves competition and cooperation among groups in different equilibrium states, the sometimes savage protection of established equilibrium arrangements, and often violent revolutionary transitions between equilibrium states. Doubtless there are many more equilibrium states yet to be explored. But the dynamical system's exploration of this space of possibilities in search of equilibrium states is strongly constrained by evolved cognitive capacities that determine what representations of social reality can be transmitted with minimal energy and absorbed with minimal distortion. Without these characteristics, a social arrangement can never be objectivated and then internalized, the cyclical dynamic depicted in the sociology of knowledge can never take hold, and the social arrangement can never be stably realized.

The evolved features of human cognition most important for the rapid and accurate transmission of representations of social reality are those directly related to satisfying the evolutionary drives of survival and reproduction. For example, as we saw in earlier chapters, it is evolutionarily important that our intention-attribution, causation-detection, and action-plan-formation functionalities are biased toward safety, so that we run away from potentially dangerous situations even if they later prove to be harmless. Representations of social reality that leverage our default cognitive setup of functional paranoia and mild vigilance will spread faster and more accurately than those that require completely rational and accurate discernment of causes and intentions. Moreover, human beings, and particularly children, who matter most in the cultural spread of ideas, are predisposed to remember minimally counterintuitive beliefs more accurately and more strongly than other beliefs (see Atran 2002; Boyer 2001). That is, we remember best ideas that violate folk physics and folk psychology in one memorable way. Comic books bear this out: beings that are like humans in every way except that they are invisible or super-strong or have X-ray vision make for much better stories than regular people. And the differences have to be limited: a superhero lacking human emotions and physical vulnerability is boring and hard to relate to.

These features of human cognition imply that representations of social reality that violate our folk beliefs just enough to draw our attention but not enough to seem ridiculous will be easier to remember and will transmit faster and more accurately than those that are too elaborate or too boring. This in turn defines the parameters for effective supernatural anthropomorphic cosmologies: they should be memorable and colorful and make for good stories, but they should not be silly, either by violating too many folk beliefs or by making the stories too easy to falsify. In addition, they should meet our psychological needs for intelligibility on a human scale (see Epley *et al.* 2007, 2008). Together, these cognitive functionalities of embodied human brains mean that we are primed to believe supernatural accounts of the origins of social arrangements, to submit more completely to authorities that claim supernatural authorization, and to feel more deeply that our existential fate is connected with supernatural powers.

RSEs have twofold significance in relation to this illustration. On the one hand, this cognitive predisposition leads people to interpret vivid RSEs in terms of supernatural agents and intentions. On the other hand, any experience that seems difficult to explain in naturalistic ways reinforces the supernaturalist cognitive reflex. In this way a cycle is established whereby vivid RSEs and a supernaturalist framework of interpretation mutually reinforce one another. This is why most religious people are supernaturalist in their view of significant events and their causes, and why most religious stories deploy the memorable category of invisible supernatural actors. It is also why religious naturalism is impossible without extensive education to overcome the supernaturalist cognitive tendency and thereafter heavy energy investments to maintain a perpetually countercultural view of the world and its religious significance.

There are many other examples of the way that evolved cognitive capacities constrain representations of social reality in such a way as to make some social arrangements feasible and others fragile or fantastic. But enough has been said to indicate the way that the epidemiology of representations functions to fill in gaps around the sociology of knowledge's description of dynamic equilibrium states within the brain-group nexus. To go further, we need to incorporate insights from social neuroscience.

Social neuroscience

In recent times, a field of research known as social neuroscience has emerged with promises of making sense of human social interactions from the point of view of species-wide brain structures and functions (see Brothers 1997; Cacioppo and Berntson 2005; Cacioppo *et al.* 2005; Easton and Emery 2005; Frith and Wolpert 2004; Harmon-Jones and Winkielman 2007). This field builds on psychological studies that have detected regular patterns of social behavior in human beings (see, for example, Bargh and Chartrand 1999; Bargh *et al.* 1996). As with the sociology of knowledge, social neuroscience describes modern humans, and thus the neuroscience of social interactions that apply in the pre-Neolithic equilibrium onwards.

Social neuroscience and sociology of knowledge operate at different levels. In spelling out the mutual conditioning of individuals and social groups, the sociology of knowledge tends to regard individual human beings as evolutionarily settled components of social groups, attributing to individuals a basic suite of cognitive capacities (memory, belief, learning) and an internal dynamism of acting to satisfy felt needs – all complicated by a distinction between conscious awareness and unconscious drives. This proves to be a sound set of assumptions for making sense of the large-scale dynamics of social control, social change, and existential angst. Meanwhile, social neuroscience tends to take the social context more or less for granted, makes fewer assumptions than the sociology of knowledge does about human beings, and takes much more seriously the formidable array of human cognitive and also non-cognitive capacities that spawn an unending variety of social behaviors. This approach is ideal for making sense of more intricate aspects of the brain-group nexus such as the way human beings influence one another, how they read intentions by observing faces and behavior, how prejudice is expressed in the brain, how to tell between truth-telling and lying, or how to assess the probability that someone will become aggressive. Thus, the sociology of knowledge and social neuroscience are complementary levels of description of the brain-group nexus, and both fit well with the epidemiology of representations.

Social neuroscience is particularly helpful for addressing the central paradox of the brain-group nexus. We are in some strong sense isolated as individual embodied brains in groups. Yet the social fabric of human life is intricate and strong and pervades every aspect of human cognition and behavior. How is it possible for both propositions to be true simultaneously? We might be tempted to appeal to disembodied souls that can communicate independently of the bodily houses that they control; this solution argues that we are not as isolated as our individual brains would suggest. We might also be tempted to stress our mutual isolation to the point that we come to see the social fabric of human life not as an intricately woven and strong fabric but as a tattered rag to which we cling, desperate for solace and meaning; certainly the amount of projection and misinterpretation that goes on in human relationships tends to support this.

In the final analysis, these mitigations of the central paradox seem extreme and incompatible with our experience of generally effective communication between basically isolated brains. Social neuroscience is explaining how both sides of the paradox are true simultaneously through experimental analysis of the significant brain resources that are devoted to assessing the intentions of other people, convincing others of our sincerity, expressing emotions such as love and hate, deriving comfort from physical contact, anticipating the thoughts and actions of others, and so on. Much of this depends on creating internal neural representations of others' behavior using mirror neurons so that we can form in our own brains a sense for the contents of other minds.

Our behavior can seem nonsensical to ourselves, at times, particularly when strong emotions arise for reasons we do not grasp and then spark behaviors that are difficult to control. Social neuroscience can disclose the underlying causal architecture that both explains how strong emotions can be triggered from subtle causes that are difficult to detect, and also why the resulting behavioral impulses can be so irresistible. For example, social neuroscience has made significant strides in understanding the neurological networks underlying romantic infatuation. It has also helped to detect the neurological linkage between feelings and behavior that make addiction so destructive.

Social neuroscience is also beginning to trace out how the brain mediates the health effects of social interaction, negatively and positively. How do capacities for dissociation and hypnotizability create possibilities for improved mental and physical health? What is it about involvement in positive community activities that helps elderly people not only improve their quality of life but also live longer? How does group enthusiasm about healing, often involving self-deception and denial about disease, serve to improve health and extend life? How does socially borne rhetoric of violence produce violent behavior? Why does scapegoating violence alleviate widespread anxiety in a social group? In relation to all of these questions, social neuroscience is pressing beyond noting the correlations between brain and behavior in the brain-group nexus, and striving to explain the underlying causal linkages in the brain. These causal linkages define the neural architecture of the brain-group nexus in its default pre-Neolithic equilibrium – neural architecture that human beings subsequently carried with them into every type of social arrangement.

RSEs play roles at many points in the causal architecture of the brain-group nexus as described in social neuroscience. Consider a religious ritual context in which a person is swept up in a trance-like state of blissful surrender while sweeping or rhythmic music plays and people sway and sing or swirl and dance. The fact that one person experiences such a state increases the likelihood that others will be similarly swept up, as eyes and ears read minds and bodies and emotions bubble up and spill over. The likelihood of the phenomenon spreading increases when such experiences are narrated within the group in such a way as to break down natural resistance to outlandish social behavior. Group authority figures will scour sacred texts for wisdom about how to criticize, regulate, or encourage such experiences, which they will then do by means of teaching group members about the putative meaning of the trance state with reference to sacred texts and revered commentators that convey supernaturally authorized information and instructions. People who have gone through this experience may feel more closely bonded to one another, and perhaps even spiritually superior to others. Other group members may feel deeply curious about the meaning of this trance state, and may perhaps resolve to experience it for themselves. Some will push themselves into such a state in a way that amounts to well-intentioned fabrication, and will subsequently wonder how authentic the experience was, both for themselves and for others. People will talk about the experiences and study each other's faces and reflexively analyze voice tones and shifting body parts in an attempt to detect sincerity, insecurity, power moves, and saintly humility.

This kind of complex transaction between a group and its individual members is common in the history of religions, from the Great Awakenings and Pentecostal faith healing to fire-walking and snake-handling. And every phase of it crucially depends on the inter-brain causal linkages that underlie empathic understanding, communication, and shared experience – the capacities that social neuroscience describes.

EVOLUTIONARY ORIGINS OF THE PRE-NEOLITHIC EQUILIBRIUM

We now have in hand a multidisciplinary account of the brain-group nexus, particularly as it took shape in the pre-Neolithic equilibrium. This account covers social dynamics, brain architecture, and the rules governing whether a social arrangement has potential to be a stable equilibrium state. Now we need to consider the "how we got there" question in relation to the Neolithic equilibrium, because this, too, influences our interpretation of the function and value of RSEs.

Learning from behavior patterns

Evolutionary approaches to the brain-group nexus investigate the evolutionary processes by which the cognitive-behavioral-social capacities of human beings were encoded in neurological structures. This evolutionary account is the necessary back story for the theories of the sociology of knowledge, the epidemiology of representations, and social neuroscience discussed above. Finding out about the cognitive-behavioral brain functions of modern human beings that make possible the pre-Neolithic equilibrium does not always require an evolutionary framework. For some inquiries it is enough to identify the way the brain-group nexus works even without knowing the evolutionary reasons why. But the evolutionary framework is indispensable as a consistency check on theories of cognitive-behavioral function, because it calls for a connected explanatory narrative that accounts for all of those functions at once. Evolutionary narratives are inevitably speculative, to varying degrees, but the consistency constraints that they impose on cognitive-behavioral theories enhance their coherence (see, for example, Trivers 2002; and in relation to the role of religion, see Atran 2002; Boyer 2001; Pyysiäinen 2001).

This rapidly developing area of research has several disciplinary specialties. The newest is evolutionary cognitive neuroscience, which focuses on evolutionary conditioning of neurological structures and functions that affect social interaction (see Platek *et al.* 2006). Slightly older is evolutionary psychology, which first developed just as intensive research in social neuroscience was becoming tractable (see Barkow *et al.* 1992; Buss 2007; Dunbar and Barrett 2007). Unsurprisingly, Darwin's own evolutionary reasoning about the brain-group nexus anticipates these developments. In principle, though not always in practice, evolutionary psychology and evolutionary cognitive neuroscience can accommodate and coordinate numerous perspectives on brain dynamics and organization – neural Darwinism (see Edelman 1987), brain modularity (see Carruthers 2006, and also Carruthers *et al.* 2005, 2006, 2008), parallel processing (see Rumelhart *et al.* 1986), connectionism (see Bechtel 1991), computational models (see Churchland and Sejnowski 1994), and the like.

Evolutionary cognitive neuroscience stands to cognitive science generally as evolutionary psychology stands to cognitive psychology generally; both evolutionary disciplines are seeking to discover an evolutionary back story – for the human brain and the human mind, respectively. Evolutionary cognitive neuroscience conceives of itself as inheriting the mantle of evolutionary psychology, as it seeks to integrate neuroscience methods more and more into the research questions of evolutionary psychology, and to reframe those questions in neuroscience terms where possible. Evolutionary cognitive neuroscience and evolutionary psychology will probably persist as complementary research efforts, as cognitive neuroscience and cognitive psychology generally do at present.

The back story to the pre-Neolithic equilibrium

Evolutionary approaches suggest an intriguing background to the pre-Neolithic equilibrium of the brain-group nexus. As is often the case with evolutionary origins stories, the following rendition is cartoon-like and lacks detail. In fact, the entire topic is extremely controverted – partly because archeological evidence relevant for interpreting social arrangements of pre-human hominid species is scarce, and partly because extant evidence is difficult to interpret. But the effort surfaces evolutionary pressures that are crucial for understanding the social embedding of RSEs, and for showing how the various levels of social embedding that we have discussed in this chapter can cohere.

Primate studies is the controlling discipline for the early part of the narrative of human evolution, as it gives the clearest picture of what the brain-group nexus might have been like for hominid species prior to the arrival of human beings about 200,000 years ago. The question is how the dynamical system migrated from there through the space of possible social arrangements that early humans could have occupied by virtue of the cognitive features of human brains, all the way to the Neolithic equilibrium, about 10,000 years ago, which we can describe in some detail because anthropologists have been able to observe it in living Neolithic cultures.

In the period of evolutionary adaptation that we are now considering, available equilibrium states depended primarily on evolutionary changes in human cognition rather than imaginative constructions of a social reality. Similarly, transitions between equilibrium states were relatively gentle because social arrangements were comparatively simple and stable, with few sensitive dependencies to operating parameters, even compared to the Neolithic equilibrium. So we should not be thinking of an explosive exploration of numerous possible high-energy equilibrium states driven by cultural creativity, such as we have seen since the Neolithic. Rather we should think of the series of lowest-energy equilibrium states that allowed human groups to migrate from something akin to the equilibrium state of chimpanzee societies to the Neolithic equilibrium state, with transitions driven almost exclusively by the evolution of new cognitive capabilities.

It follows that a useful strategy is to identify the differences in cognitive abilities between chimpanzees or bonobos or macaques, which are genetically closest to human beings among the ape species, and early Neolithic humans, who appear to be cognitively like contemporary humans in every way except for cultural and social context. Chimpanzees cannot participate in the social construction of reality in the way that Neolithic humans do but they do have a social reality. Chimpanzees use tools. They practice deception, which suggests that they have a theory of other minds. They are capable of loyalty and compassion as well as occasional violence. They are sharply aware of kin and hierarchy relationships, and they appear to have long memories for slights and acts of kindness from other chimps. They already have in place many of the cognitive capacities that Neolithic humans have, therefore, and the question becomes one of salient cognitive differences.

Charles Darwin's famous association between humans and apes has been one of the hottest points of controversy in the reception of Darwinian evolution – witness the publicity surrounding the so-called Scopes Monkey Trial of 1925. Was Darwin correct to say that human beings were big-brained apes? Though obviously he was correct that human beings are ontogenetically closer to apes than to any other animal, it does appear that Darwin overstated the continuities. Chimpanzees grow at a different speed from humans. Human beings in all environmental and cultural settings have slow growth between weaning and puberty whereas chimpanzees do not; this probably is a genetic accommodation to the need in humans to focus energy resources on cognitive rather than physical development in the early years (Walker *et al.* 2005). This suggests that something importantly different is going on neurologically in human beings. Indeed, brain differences between chimpanzees and modern humans are significant.

The human brain is not merely an enlarged chimpanzee brain with a massive frontal cortex; as mentioned above, it also displays different kinds of connectivity between brain cells throughout the brain and novel neural structures relative to all animal brains, including chimpanzees. These pervasive brain differences correspond to pervasive differences in cognitive abilities, even in areas where chimpanzees and other animals have been shown to have cognitive abilities that are also present in human beings (see Premack 2007). For example, some animals teach their young to hunt but the teaching and learning skills are confined to food, whereas in humans this cognitive ability is unleashed from this narrow field of application to make education possible in every sphere of activity. The same is true for cognitive functions related to short-term memory, causal reasoning, planning, deception, transitive inference, theory of mind, and language. These animal–human differences point to a neurological transformation in the human brain relative to prior species that markedly increases human adaptability to changing circumstances. The key is freeing cognitive abilities from the narrow domains of their initial application and development and allowing those cognitive functions to roam freely across the landscape of human experience.

The social-cognition and language areas are particularly interesting. "Virtually all the newly discovered human [brain] singularities are located in areas associated with either complex social cognition [theory of mind] … or language" (Premack 2007: 13861). While in many areas human cognition differs from animal cognition in degree of sophistication and breadth of application, in social cognition and language human beings also have novel neural structures. Neurological changes in these areas evidently facilitated exactly the kind of complex social arrangements that we have been describing in the Neolithic equilibrium. By imaginatively subtracting these neurological capacities, we can picture both pre-Neolithic and even pre-human equilibrium social arrangements as well as the evolutionary pressures that might have forced transitions to equilibrium states in the brain-group nexus that are closer to the Neolithic equilibrium.

For example, weaken human language skills and make human beings less imaginative and less adept at planning and problem solving, and we can imagine long periods of static technology with stone tools that rarely vary in design or function. And that is precisely what the archeological record shows prior to about 50,000 years ago. After that time – the "great leap forward" – humans display marked increase in creativity, from new hunting methods to cave painting (see Diamond 1991). Something happened around that time in one or a few human brains under the constant evolutionary pressure to survive and reproduce. There were probably a few exceptional human beings that were far more imaginative than average. These exceptional few could probably dream about the future and picture possibilities better than others, they could imagine new solutions to old problems and teach the new techniques to others, they could easily navigate the intricacies of their social environment, they were better friends and companions, better at child rearing, and so much more attractive as mates. This guaranteed that their genetic heritage would be passed along and that their style of cognition would soon dominate the species.

The predominance of humans with greater foresight, subtler imaginations, and better problem-solving skills also would have meant that much more complexity was possible and inevitable in the stable equilibrium state of the brain-group nexus, so their arrival would have triggered a transition to a richer and more fluid social life with more exploratory and creative cultural expressions. The next major transition was probably the Neolithic development of agriculture and domestication of animals, which required exceptional pattern-recognition skills and the ability to formulate, test, and correct hypotheses about animals, plants, seasons, and weather.

Though evolutionary anthropologists know much less about the evolutionary back story of the brain-group nexus than everyone would like, important provisional conclusions are possible. Most importantly, it does appear that the evolutionary back story supports the dynamical systems hypothesis that the evolution of cognitive functionalities determines what can count as a stable equilibrium state of the brain-group nexus. Almost as crucially, the evolutionary back story offers an explanation for human cognitive and behavioral predispositions, both the ones that are useful and the ones that are counterproductive.

The evolution of religious and spiritual experiences

The evolution of RSEs must be understood against the complex theoretical vista that emerges as we knit together insights from the many research ventures discussed in this chapter. This disciplinary diversity reinforces the diversity of RSEs and of the cognitive and emotional capacities on which RSEs depend. There will not be just one chapter to the story of the evolution of RSEs. Rather, many chapters will be required to accommodate the likelihood that some aspects of RSEs are selected while others are side-effects of traits selected for a non-religious function (see McNamara 2006a and Wildman 2006b for a review).

In Chapter 4, I argued that the "great leap forward" about 50,000 years ago probably crucially involved a novel kind of neural connectivity that made intense experiences of the depth-and-breadth kind possible. The attendant flowering of aesthetic activities such as cave art and problem-solving abilities such as creative hunting techniques produce the archeological evidence that draws our attention to this era as an especially notable phase of human evolution. As I have said, moreover, the adaptiveness of this kind of neural connectivity seems straightforward in light of sexual-selection pressures toward sensitive and alert mates as partners in the harrowing process of child-rearing. Many intense experiences have religious significance, so here we have one line of analysis concerning the evolution of RSEs, and in this case RSEs appear to be a side-effect of capacities for intense experiences. This merely begins the story, however.

Another domain of RSEs that may depend on adaptive traits is the capacity for dissociation and suggestibility. Scholars of shamanism have pointed out that people with a high capacity for dissociative and hypnotic states are more vulnerable to suggestion in certain ritual processes. They further conjecture that this vulnerability to suggestion may confer therapeutic benefits in properly tuned ritual processes. This in turn may improve health and eventually increase the frequency in the population of the genes underlying the capacities for dissociation and hypnotizability (see McClenon 2001, 2006). Again, just as intense experiences are not all of RSEs, so shamanic activities are not all of RSEs. But a theory of this kind can play a valuable role in accounting for another class of RSEs, and this time as adaptive given particular social settings.

We thus have one example of RSEs as possibly an evolutionary side-effect and another of RSEs as possibly adaptive. Sometimes both qualities occur together. For example, the strong consensus in the cognitive psychology of religion is that human readiness to believe in supernatural agents and actions derives from pattern-recognition, causation-detection, and intention-attribution skills that are tuned to survival and thus are slightly overactive. This makes RSEs bearing on encounters with supernatural beings and discarnate entities an evolutionary side-effect of cognitive traits that first developed for reasons unrelated to supernatural beings or religious and spiritual interests. Once in place, however, these traits can have secondary adaptive functions. The discussion above about the epidemiology of representations indicated that minimally counterintuitive ideas are more memorable and get passed most efficiently down the generations. The fact that supernatural cosmologies are perfect for generating such minimally counterintuitive beliefs and narratives suggests that the human cognitive bias toward superstition and supernaturalism can have spectacular and large-scale social consequences. This religious side-effect of a pre-existing cognitive bias allows for the forging of strongly adaptive corporate life that is necessary for the sociology of knowledge's account of human life to make sense. Moreover, people capable of spectacular supernatural experiences may win prestige in the right social context, which may make them more attractive as friends and mates and partners in child-rearing. In short, RSEs may depend on cognitive and emotional capacities that began life as evolutionary side-effects but eventually became adaptive in a new social context.

These considerations begin to show how complex the question of the evolution of RSEs must be. And this is merely a fragment of the wider question concerning the evolutionary origins of religion (on this, see Atran 2002; Boyer 2001; McNamara 2006a; Wilson 2002). It seems inevitable that RSEs must depend on a rich suite of capacities, some of which arise as evolutionary adaptations, many of which are evolutionary side-effects, and a number of which in particular contexts are both.

BEHIND THE IDEOLOGICAL CURTAIN

The discussion of the brain-group nexus to this point is akin to a coroner's report dictated during an autopsy. We have examined the innards of the causal linkage between brains and groups while the body is dead. Just as people have colorful lives prior to their final meeting with a coroner, however, so the brain-group nexus in any given instance is a vital reality that imposes itself and enables endless varieties of energetic activity. Here we shall consider a couple of the living features of the brain-group nexus and how they relate to RSEs: power dynamics and moral reasoning.

Power dynamics

One of the most notable features of the brain-group nexus is the way power is accumulated, often leading to accidental mishandling or deliberate abuse. These dynamics of power are deadly and destructive as often as they are creative and constructive. The responsible wielding of power typically improves some lives, so members of a group that benefits often issue a relatively positive report on the power dynamics in question. But a wider point of view discloses that these benefits are usually gained by unjustly or ignorantly imposing great costs on others, from whose point of view a very different assessment of the relevant power dynamics would be appropriate. Obviously power dynamics in the brain-group nexus are far from straightforward. Some of the most urgent practical questions confronting human beings concern how power dynamics work, how they can be regulated, and how they can be turned in just and good directions. My particular concern is also important: what does the social embedding of RSEs have to do with power dynamics in the brain-group nexus?

The dynamical systems approach to the brain-group nexus opens up these questions in a helpful way. Our account of the sociology of knowledge above made clear that people invested in social arrangements are vigilant about protecting them. There is real danger when cognitive dissonance arises or the externalization-objectivation-internalization cycle loses its transparency. Such perturbations can cause the entire social arrangement to wobble out of equilibrium and plunge into chaos. The collapse of social arrangements into chaotic violence has happened too often to count in recorded human history. Such chaos might be the accompaniment of a transition to another social arrangement, but, even so, it is still chaos and it is dangerous to people and their children. It thus flies in the face of every innate evolutionary impulse that human beings possess and it will be feared and resisted accordingly.

It makes sense that people invested in protecting social arrangements will vest authority in specialized representatives who will work to prevent the disaster of chaos from ever occurring; these are the priests and politicians. They will also vest authority in specialized representatives who will control chaos if and when it does occur, even if violent means are necessary to achieve this; these are the warrior police. There is nothing hidden about the power dynamics of physical threats and violence from the warrior police. By contrast, power dynamics among the priests and politicians are often extremely subtle. Their greatest priestly and political resource is narratives that make the existing social arrangement unquestionable, that render the social construction of reality invisible, that enlist individuals in the maintenance of the social equilibrium, that convey threats to prevent dissent and promises to induce cooperation, that rationalize whatever social injustices and sufferings occur, and that legitimate whatever aspects of the power dynamics cannot be disguised or finessed.

These political and religious narratives are woven together from threads of ideas that are present in people's minds in the way that the epidemiology of representations suggests. They will be potent, memorable ideas that will appeal to the deep needs and longings of most people, such as gods that know and love us, or means for liberation from alienation and suffering described by bodhisattvas who sacrifice their fulfillment out of compassion for us. The resulting narratives will be glorious in their subtlety and sophistication, their comprehensiveness and comprehensibility. Claims stated or implied in the narratives may or may not be wholly or simply true, but a high-quality narrative has the power to make those truth claims compelling and effective, nonetheless.

The deliberate deployment or reflexive use of shared ideas and compelling narratives to rationalize, regulate, and revolutionize equilibrium social arrangements is what I mean by "ideology." This is a descriptive and neutral use of the word (following Eagleton 1991; Freeden 2003). It contrasts with usages that require the claims embedded in rationalizing narratives to be false, known to be false, and craftily employed to deceive. The sociology of knowledge shows that ideology in this neutral sense is an essential and valuable aspect of the brain-group nexus. It is a kind of mind-control, to be sure. But the people who construct or retell these narratives usually are even more convinced by them than those who hear them in the various cultural channels through which they spread. Radically cynical priests and politicians are rare.

Unfortunately, neither the sociology of knowledge nor the epidemiology of representations offers many insights into how to handle the devastating side-effects of ideologies that legitimate sometimes brutal and unjust power dynamics. For example, if an equilibrium social arrangement makes use of slaves, you can be certain that there will be priests and politicians sincerely narrating the nature of the slave and the nature of the slave holder in such a way as to legitimate the power dynamics of slavery in that social context. The sociology of knowledge tells us why this happens, and the epidemiology of representations tells us why the narratives work when they do. This is ideology at its worst. It often takes an outbreak of violence to perturb the equilibrium enough to transition into a different kind of equilibrium social arrangement – outbreaks that have their own legitimating political and religious narratives. Moreover, the legitimating ideological narratives of the status quo quickly adapt to new circumstances. We need stories almost as badly as we need air, food, water, and sex, and we have a great willingness to buy into the conditions necessary to get all five basic resources for human life.

RSEs leverage power dynamics within the brain-group nexus by supplying basic ideas for legitimating ideologies, and also by ramifying fundamental claims made within such narrative structures. Consider the RSEs associated with fervent anti-abortion groups and fervent pro-choice groups. These experiences are sometimes religious in character, and sometimes they are spiritual experiences that are hostile to organized religion. But they are so compelling that they make members of both groups absolutely certain about their assessments of who is evil and depraved, and who is a brave warrior standing up for goodness and truth.

Two dynamics are at work here. On the one hand, RSEs function as touchstones for rendering believable the narratives that legitimate the way each side regards opponents. The same process makes RSEs extremely useful for consolidating confidence in narratives that legitimate ingroup–outgroup differentiation, prestige hierarchies, and purity judgments, to

which we shall return below. On the other hand, RSEs function to catalyze commitment to action in the name of reforming a social system, on
behalf of the rights either of pregnant women or unborn potential children, which is a personally costly activity. In the same way, RSEs routinely
inspire revolutionary counter-narratives that demand social change in the
name of whatever moral vision is nurtured by the RSEs in question.

To understand these socially encoded power dynamics is to become
more alert to the ideological loading of our RSEs and also to take greater
responsibility for the social effects of those experiences. Ideology is most
dangerous, and also most useful, when it is not recognized. When we
learn to detect it, we partially disempower its positive aspects, which can
disrupt equilibrium-maintaining processes within the brain-group nexus.
But we also defang its negative aspects, and that can be tremendously
important for the causes of justice and peace.

Moral reasoning

The sociology of knowledge shows that both equilibrium and transition
dynamics within the brain-group nexus require narrative legitimation.
The epidemiology of representations describes how narratives spread and
what kinds of narrative elements work best to capture imaginations and
enlist committed support. Social neuroscience ought eventually to be
able to explain what social domains require narratives most urgently and
why narrative moves are effective or ineffective. To a significant extent,
this knowledge is not yet in hand. Meanwhile, empirical psychology illu-
mines the phenomena that social neuroscience needs to explain. A premier instance is the domain of moral reasoning.

The arising of the sensitivities needed to engage the valuational depths
of reality is, as I have been urging, a decisive turning point in the evolutionary history of human beings and the engine of the equilibrium and
transition dynamics of the brain-group nexus. The values that open up
to us when we have the neural architecture sufficient to perceive them
are varied. They run the transcendental gamut from goodness to truth
to beauty, of course, but there are also individual differences in axiological sensitivities. Some people develop a taste for subtle forms of inference
and some for complex combinations of flavors, some for exquisite shapes
and movements and some for social possibilities. Most human beings
awaken to moral values, though to profoundly different degrees, and with
diverse behavioral and social consequences. Most have a taste for justice
and care about arguments related to justice. Most have a taste for prestige

and authority and care about their position in hierarchies that confer and protect privilege.

In recent years, empirical psychologists have identified relatively distinct domains of moral reasoning, each with its presumed evolutionary back story. While it is the task of social neuroscience and evolutionary psychology to answer the associated "how we got this way" questions, empirical psychology has carefully documented the way we are, morally speaking. Moral reasoning takes on new importance in the light of this research. Rather than a rational process of inquiry, which is typically how it is framed and understood, moral reasoning appears to be a form of narrative construction that explains and legitimates instinctive moral reactions. There is compelling evidence that the moral instincts come first and reasoning follows later (see Haidt 2001; Hauser 2006).

The connections among domains of moral reasoning and behavior, as well as the links between them and religion, have been extensively studied both in the psychological sciences and in connection with evolutionary psychology (see Alport and Ross 1967; Berg *et al.* 1995; Bouckaert and Dhaene 2004; Croson 1996; Croson and Buchan 1999; Fehr and Gachter 2000, 2002; Fehr and Rockenbach 2004; Fershtman and Gneezy 2001; Gachter *et al.* 2004; Glaeser *et al.* 2000; Irons 1996, 2001; Isaac and Walker 1988; Isaac *et al.* 1984; King-Casas *et al.* 2005; McCabe *et al.* 2002, 2003; Palfrey and Prisbrey 1997; Saroglou *et al.* 2005; Shariff and Norenzayan 2007; Sosis 2003, 2004, 2006; Sosis and Alcorta 2003; Sosis and Ruffle 2003, 2004). But some lines of recent research in empirical psychology offer a more systematic and theoretically powerful approach.

Jonathan Haidt (2007a) distinguishes five domains of moral reasoning, using slightly different terminology in different publications. I shall refer to these five as the compassion, fairness, ingroup, prestige, and purity domains of moral reasoning. The compassion domain refers to feelings of concern and care for others, fairness to reciprocity relationships and distributive justice, ingroup to discriminating "us" from "them" in the host of ways this occurs, prestige to the exercise of authority and the conferring of privilege in group hierarchies, and purity to taboos and cleanliness.

Each of these five domains boasts characteristic moral instincts, and we recognize them easily. For example, the rise of compassion is unmistakable, as are indignation about an injustice, the blend of fear and loyalty that defines ingroup–outgroup divisions, the deference and confidence that accompany hierarchy behaviors, and the aversion and disgust that accompany being in the presence of the impure. Likewise, each domain has distinctive narrative resources on which moral reasoning draws. Compassion draws on pure-hearted beings such as bodhisattvas and self-sacrificial heroes, fairness draws on good monarchs and Robin Hood avengers of the oppressed, ingroups draw on racial, cultural, or family archetypal figures and on local gods with strong loyalties, prestige draws on powerful supernatural figures whose relationships with human beings map onto human hierarchies, and purity draws on categories of access to holiness and protection from the perverted.

It is not difficult to speculate about the evolutionary origins of these five domains of moral instincts, nor about the reasons why the corresponding domains of moral reasoning make such hearty use of the narrative resources they do. Presumably these details will be filled out in time, hopefully in such a way as to shed light on the neurology of moral reasoning.

My particular interest here is to note the way that RSEs function in the domains of moral reasoning. Expressed simply and directly, *moral instincts are intense experiences*, in the special sense that phrase has in this book. It follows that instinctive moral experiences are spiritual experiences bearing meaning for human individual and social existence, and that they may or may not also be religious, depending on the naming conventions of particular social and personal contexts. It also follows that reasoning about moral instincts involves narrative resources and strategies that are inextricably tangled in the legitimation of social orders. This can be difficult to notice, because we reflexively use moral reasoning to legitimate social arrangements and we reflexively embrace social legitimation arguments to justify moral behaviors.

In some equilibrium social arrangements, all five types of instinctive moral reactions are trusted and welcomed, and this is legitimated with narrative devices emphasizing divine creation or the supernatural equipping of human beings with innate capacities for moral awareness. This amounts to blessing these particular intense experiences uniformly. In other equilibrium social arrangements, some domains of instinctive moral reaction are trusted more or less implicitly, while others are intentionally resisted, with this resistance narrated in terms of the challenge to overcome socially adverse side-effects of our evolutionary heritage, or perhaps in terms of a divine command to rise above sinful impulses. In effect, this discriminates between certain intense experiences that should be welcomed as reliably indicating the morally good and other intense experiences that should be resisted because they mask the morally good and too easily lend themselves to convenient rationalization.

Haidt illustrates these contrasting reactions to moral instincts with reference to the moral differences that arise between cosmopolitan and sheltered social environments. Cosmopolitan environments routinely involve social encounters and economic transactions with strangers, and only the domains of moral reasoning that are least impacted by cultural diversity will prove functional in those contexts. In particular, ingroup, prestige, and purity instincts will have to be arrested to some degree in order for cosmopolitan social arrangements to function smoothly. These restrictions do not apply to relatively sheltered and culturally monochromatic social environments where encounters with strangers are rare and most people agree on quite subtle and sophisticated moral norms. In such environments, there can be broad consensus on ingroup, prestige, and purity norms, at least among dominant groups. In relatively cosmopolitan social contexts, welcoming the least culturally variable moral domains – compassion and fairness – while limiting the others – ingroup, prestige, and purity – is legitimated using compelling narratives about justice for oppressed minorities, consciousness of the other, and subversive reversals of past wrongs. In relatively sheltered social contexts, the embrace of all five domains of moral reasoning is legitimated using motifs of god-given conscience, veneration of ancestral ways, or the natural inevitability and rightness of social roles.

The conflicting moral instincts of liberals and conservatives are limned in this contrast (see Haidt 2008; Lakoff 2002). Yet we all start with the same array of moral instincts and the same need to narrate their meanings and regulate their social effects. Manifest in and through the complexities of moral reasoning, therefore, is the axiological ambiguity of reality. Intense RSEs open up to us a wealth of moral and other valuational possibilities. All of them are available as resources for the dreaming and realizing of social orders, for the maintenance of their equilibrium states, and for the revolutions that drive social change. As in individual life, so in the social construction of reality: the way we pull the pieces together is itself a matter of art.

These reflections on moral reasoning have another implication for the wider argument. To achieve greater self-awareness of one's own patterns of moral reasoning is simultaneously to understand one's neighbor, precisely at the point where human disagreements often seem most intractable. The particular intense experiences that we know as moral instincts can seem so completely internally incorrigible that we cannot imagine ever holding another moral opinion or sympathizing with someone who has a different moral point of view. But research on moral reasoning helps us build sympathy for moral and political and religious opponents. To acknowledge such insights at all immediately challenges the apparently self-authenticating character of the intense experiences that are moral instincts, and it can be disturbing to have to learn to regard such experiences with some degree of analytical suspicion. Many people value the benefits of understanding opponents so highly, however, that learning new approaches to moral reasoning seems a small price to pay.

If this can happen with intuitive moral judgments, which are often enough also RSEs, then why not with other RSEs? Indeed, why would we not welcome greater awareness regarding every functional aspect of the brain-group nexus? Painful cognitive dissonance will follow, to be sure, but the feared social chaos may not. We can learn to flourish amid uncertainty, aware of our own role in constructing social reality, so long as we end our habitual insistence that RSEs should deliver perfect assurance about every spiritual and moral issue, and savor the thrill of self-determination instead.

CONCLUSION

In concluding this chapter, I note three ironies about the social embedding of RSEs.

First, RSEs function both to support the status quo and also to revolutionize it, and thereby often work at cross purposes. This does not mean that they are merely ubiquitous accompaniments of most kinds of human social activity, like language or emotions. On the contrary, RSEs are essential power sources for both priestly conservatism and prophetic revolution. Their distinctive usefulness in both applications lies in their ability to structure imaginations and thereby to leverage staggering displays of commitment to cultural and political projects – projects of both the conservative and revolutionary kinds.

Second, if people become aware of the social conditioning of RSEs, the first thing they tend to worry about is cognitive reliability. This was the topic of a previous chapter, and we noted there how anxious people can get about the cognitive reliability question and how difficult it is to settle. But the practical importance of RSEs for the brain-group nexus lies less in the putative truth of their cognitive content and more in the way they help to construct, maintain, and transform social realities. This suggests that we would do well to worry at least as much about the social consequences of RSEs as we do about their cognitive reliability.

Third, when the ideological curtain is drawn back so that we can behold the inner workings of the brain-group nexus, RSEs can no longer depend for their power on our ignorance of their social embedding. The result is complicated. On the one hand, we would probably insist that self-awareness about the social embedding of RSEs is important for the future of human civilization, especially now that unthinkable destructive power can find its way into the grasping hands of religious and political fanatics with no interest in building a better human future for everyone. On the other hand, drawing aside the veil of ignorance – not just in safe and socially buffered intellectual havens but broadly within the general public – seems potentially disastrous. Based on the way the brain-group nexus has worked in the past, this would wreck the transparency of the externalization-objectivation-internalization cycle and undermine the legitimation narratives that protect the stability of equilibrium social arrangements – all this at a time when our evolved cognitive capacities seem to require those devices to remain firmly in place for the smooth functioning of social systems.

This third point is more than a curious irony; it has the proportions of a terrible conundrum, because it is directly relevant to the continuation of the human project as it puddle-jumps around on the energy–cognitive-complexity hillside. In the next chapter, I will suggest that we need to venture into less credulous social arrangements, where participants understand rather than remain ignorant of the mechanisms of stability, ideology, and social change. In that yet-to-be-realized equilibrium social arrangement, we will have to adopt a discriminating attitude to the various kinds of RSEs. We will have to educate ourselves to the point that we do not rely on a great many such experiences but rather treat them with care as sometimes pleasurable but also potentially misleading life events. Yet, even in this less credulous social arrangement, the cognitively most reliable RSEs – the intense experiences – will continue to play vital roles in constructing social reality, orienting human beings, binding us to our most precious goals, and helping us picture a future worth building.

CHAPTER 7

Make it start, make it stop! Religious and spiritual experiences in the future

INTRODUCTION

From the earliest traces of human history to the present there have been technologies of religious and spiritual experience. This chapter is about the form these technologies are likely to take in the near and longer-range future, assuming continuous growth in scientific and cultural understanding rather than civilizational collapse and reversion to less technologized forms of life. Whether we welcome it or fear it, the era in which we can induce, prevent, and effectively control many kinds of religious behaviors, beliefs, and experiences is fast approaching. This presents us with an ethical quandary of enormous proportions. What does this level of control say about the authenticity of religious behaviors, beliefs, and experiences?

In relation to some forms of religiously relevant experience, this era is already upon us. We are able to measure such experiences, describe them, distinguish them, and evaluate their social functions, behavioral consequences, and health effects. We are also more and more able to start them, stop them, alter them, and even exert control over the way people interpret them. For example, religious experts have long known that bright lights, emotional passion, and repetitive motions make people vulnerable to suggestion, which is often a key component of religious conversion (as well as health changes; see McClenon 2001, 2006). In addition, certain entheogens reliably produce experiences that seem suffused with profound existential significance for those who ingest them. In fact, we know that social conditioning, pharmacological substances, ritual practices, and genetics all play roles in the mediation of religious behaviors, beliefs, and experiences, and details are starting to yield to neurological inquiry. Our technological control over RSEs may be coarse at this point, but it is rapidly becoming more refined. Soon we will know a great deal more about the functional and anatomical neurology of many aspects of RSEs, thereby exposing the relevant brain functions and structures to selective inhibition and enhancement. Capacities for control that today come to us only in dreams and nightmares, in science fiction and fantasy, will in short order be familiar aspects of life.

The future is the best context in which to raise the question of the meaning and value of RSEs because it frees us from the mistaken impression that RSEs lie beyond human control and understanding – whether as a result of putatively supernatural origins or for any other reason. A proper awareness of the technologies of RSEs, past, present, and future, injects sober realism into the interpretation of their meaning and value and resists idealistic blind spots and wishful thinking of interpretations inspired by allegiance or allergy to traditional religious worldviews.

We begin here with a survey of the technologies of RSEs in the past, noting how some are undergoing rapid change right now. We then discuss several unprecedented technologies. This presentation of existing and emerging technologies of RSEs is accompanied by case studies that make the discussion practical. It is at this meaningful level of everyday events and unavoidable decisions where moral quandaries and value questions are often felt most sharply. Thus, it is at this level that we can best raise the vital question of the meaning and value of RSEs in light of these considerations about technologies of control.

PAST TECHNOLOGIES, TRANSFORMED IN THE PRESENT, HURTLING INTO THE FUTURE

In the past, technologies of RSEs were of three overlapping kinds: botanical, psycho-social, and meditative. The reason these three overlapping spheres of technology surrounding RSEs are so widespread and ancient within human cultures is that groups of human beings will inevitably encounter them. We need to eat, so we must explore the possibilities for food and medicine afforded by our botanical environment. We have to function in groups, so we spontaneously explore the space of psycho-social possibilities in the brain-group nexus. And each of us struggles to understand and control our own thoughts and feelings, and so we naturally explore the space of psychological possibilities. In all three areas, as we explore we also inquire, detecting patterns, drawing inferences about causation, formulating promising hypotheses to test, and learning from successes and failures.

These three types of technology remain important today and will remain important in the future. The way each is important, however, changes dramatically as scientific understanding discloses the causal architecture that links RSEs to their existential potency, their social functions, their behavioral consequences, and their health effects. These changes have been notable in the last century, during which RSEs have been the object of scientific study, and especially dramatic in the last decade or so with the rapid increase in our knowledge of neurophysiology, neuropsychopharmacology, and the neurology of social behavior. It appears that we are not near the end of this period of rapidly expanding knowledge about RSEs, but rather closer to the dawn of a research-based transformation in our understanding. This transformation will place into our hands refined control over RSEs that has been unthinkable in past generations.

In what follows I shall discuss this dawning transformation, first in relation to these three longstanding types of technology, and subsequently in relation to unprecedented technologies that our growing understanding of RSEs makes possible.

Botanical techniques

Human beings and other animals get drunk from fermented fruit fallen from trees. Some foods are poisonous. Brackish water makes us ill. When there is any confusion about effects of foods, we can compare reports from multiple sources and use trial and error to find out which food is responsible. Our sense of taste guides us to foods that contain all-important glucose, but it also draws us to explore the marvelous aesthetic world of tastes. Our enjoyment of food leads us to explore more widely, in search of foods with special powers that are more important to us than how pleasant things taste. All species explore their botanical environment for food. Human beings do so in a more systematic and experimental way than other species, and we have been doing it for thousands of years.

It is in this way that, long ago in the uncharted past, human beings discovered foods that induced altered states of consciousness replete with religious and spiritual significance. These foods are known as entheogens, as are the naturally occurring or artificially prepared substances that have similar religiously potent psychoactive properties. The botanicals producing these effects were recorded in the oral lore of medical and shamanic traditions, passed down the generations. Corporate rituals often developed around plants with psychoactive properties, perhaps as a way simultaneously to sequester the authority that such experiences can confer on those who have them, to regulate negative side-effects, and to control potentially disruptive religious interpretations of the resulting altered states of consciousness. Medical anthropologists and ethno-biologists have identified hundreds of plants believed by ancient cultures to have mind-altering effects. Here are several well-known examples.

First, the peyote cactus has been used for millennia in medicinal and ritual practices among people native to the southwest of the North American continent. This cactus is best known for its specifically religious use within the so-called Native American Church, which has been the subject of protracted legal battles over its religious ritual involving a brew made from the cactus buttons.

Second, the psilocybin mushroom also has a multimillennial history. It was made famous in recent times by Timothy Leary and Richard Alpert, who founded Harvard University's Psilocybin Project in 1960. The formal research project ended within a couple of years, and the two men were fired from the university in 1963 after a highly public scandal and an aborted state investigation.

Third, *ayahuasca* is a vine widespread in the Amazonian rainforests. By itself it is not psychoactive because the human digestive system breaks down the psychoactive chemicals quickly. When combined with certain other plants, however, the breakdown of *ayahuasca*'s psychoactive ingredients is inhibited, and the resulting brew can be extremely potent. Many other plants have similar properties, including certain acacia trees, as noted in an earlier chapter. The fact that there are so many recipes for *ayahuasca* brews illustrates the deliberate experimentation needed to produce potent psychoactive substances, which in turn indicates the different skill levels that would have been present within shamans. Several contemporary religious groups use one or another form of *ayahuasca* brew in religious rituals, including Santo Daime, which integrates shamanistic elements with Christianity. Santo Daime was founded by Mestre Irineu in Brazil in the first half of the twentieth century, and has since spread to many parts of the world. The usage of *ayahuasca* in religious rituals has been the subject of numerous court rulings in the last two decades.

The difference between the past and the future in regard to botanicals is the scientific discovery of the psychoactive chemicals within these plants that are primarily responsible for the entheogenic effects. This allows us to determine better than ancient shamans could precisely how to produce an effective and safe dose from the botanicals in question. For example, we know that peyote cacti are rich in mescaline, among other things, and we know what dosage of mescaline produces a strong psychoactive effect. Thus, we can avoid the unpleasant bitterness of the peyote brew and the associated vomiting if we so choose, and we can manage dosing safely, by ingesting mescaline directly. Again, we know that the psilocybin mushroom's active ingredient is psilocybin, though there are also a few other psychoactive triptamines involved. Psilocybin is broken down during digestion into the psychoactive alkaloid psilocin, which is structurally similar to serotonin, and probably affects serotonin receptors in brain synapses. With regard to *ayahuasca*, we know that the main psychoactive ingredient is N,N-dimethyltriptamine, or DMT. This small psychoactive chemical is broken down very quickly by monoamine oxidase, or MAO, so DMT has to be ingested along with MAO-inhibitors in order to ensure that DMT has an effect on the brain. Psychedelic researcher Rick Strassman argues that the human brain actually has receptors that specifically draw DMT through the blood–brain barrier. He also argues that DMT is endogenous, being synthesized in the pineal gland (Strassman 2001).

Such knowledge shows precisely what it is within each botanical that yields psychoactive effects. Experience and testing then indicate the relationship between dosage and both quality and strength of the induced RSEs. Unregulated use of these psychoactive chemicals can be dangerous, which is why governments ban most of them. But religious groups have successfully argued that ingesting traditional brews made from the plants themselves should not be illegal. This is knowledge that ancient shamans would have found deeply mysterious, and they would have kept such powerful wisdom secret, yet we regard such knowledge as part of medical science (for example, see Wasson *et al.* 1998).

We have something else that ancient shamans lacked, namely, a rich comparative database of psychedelic experiences. We know the different qualities of the hallucinations produced by various psychoactive chemicals, the conditions under which ingesting them produces positive rather than negative experiences, which chemicals enhance feelings of community, and many other things. This database is a vital resource for neuro-psychopharmacology, and helps guide researchers in their quest to understand neurotransmitter functions in the human brain. Despite the near cessation of psychedelic research, this body of knowledge can play a role in customizing and controlling RSEs using various botanicals more intentionally and effectively than ever was possible in the past.

Psycho-social techniques

For a long time human beings have instinctively understood that rhythmic music and movement in tight-knit group contexts can be hypnotic, inducing susceptibility to suggestion and surrender to dissociative states. These experiences can liberate us from tired conventions, they can bond us closely to others, they can catalyze commitment and courage, they can stimulate bodily changes that alter the conditions for mental and physical health, they can render people psychologically fragile, and they can change beliefs and behaviors more or less radically. In our time it is not only rock-music concert designers and nightclub planners that know about this. Most rapidly growing religious movements make use of such techniques to facilitate conversion to a favored religious outlook.

These psycho-social techniques are rarely deployed in religious contexts specifically with the aim of cynical manipulation. Typically religious leaders believe in the spiritual significance of such experiences at least as much as participants do. It seems crucial for everyone involved to be able to attribute the RSEs that occur in such settings to the work of spiritual powers of enlightenment or divinity. Because understanding how psycho-social conditioning and suggestion operate in such social settings might interfere with that attribution, religious leaders de-emphasize these conditioning factors and offer theological rationalizations for the ways they organize such social gatherings. For example, we sing repetitive songs while swaying and holding hands. Why? Not to induce semi-hypnotic suggestibility but to worship God. We dance around flickering firelight. Why? Not to induce semi-hypnotic suggestibility but to summon the spirits. The music and handholding and swaying, or the rhythmic dancing and flickering lighting are represented not as causes but as the tools of supernatural powers. These ingroup theological interpretations are so persuasive and pervasive that people rarely become aware of the physiological aspects of the emotions and thoughts they have in such settings. Not understanding how embodied human brains work in group settings helps to conjure a veil of mystery around such experiences. This makes more compelling the ruling theological interpretations of the effects that arise.

Such psycho-social techniques are unquestionably effective. But they are not so universally or overwhelmingly effective that they could not be made more potent through careful research and by customizing sensory experiences to individual backgrounds and brains. In fact, rhythms and lights and music and togetherness are coarse tools in the way they are usually deployed. Loud noises are painful to some people, rhythmic movement does not work well for people with arthritis, flashing lights make some people nauseous, and some people grow anxious in crowds. While the precise kinds of rhythms and lights that work best for most people are not currently well understood, it is conceivable that the sensory conditions most likely to render an individual susceptible to suggestion will be understood much more clearly in the future, and that specific physiological tests such as blood tests and brain scans could disclose individual variations quickly and easily. The result would be the possibility of a customized social environment for hosting RSEs.

Imagine a socially and emotionally intense religious gathering fifty years from now – something like a Billy Graham Crusade or an evening with the Dalai Lama, but with a twist. The advertising describes the event as a customized religious experience in a diverse group of loving fellow believers – more realistic than holodeck theaters and more meaningful than coarse forms of human togetherness such as live sporting events and music concerts. Upon entering, each person signs an informed consent document and is quickly analyzed using a microscopic drop of blood and a brain scan. These non-invasive and painless procedures happen in mere seconds, and the analysis allows a program to set optimal sensory parameters and physical location within the auditorium. The guest then moves to an assigned hi-tech seat that is automatically programmed with customized parameters. The location of the seat and its unobtrusive sensory equipment adapt the experience of the event to the individual's specific physiological profile.

The result is an individually customized social experience. It takes full advantage of whatever capacity for suggestiveness, learning styles, and neurological distinctiveness exist in each individual. In this environment, the music, public addresses, lighting, and surroundings produce an optimally potent experience. People leave the event stronger than ever in their religious beliefs, confident in their moral orientation, happier and healthier, and determined to live more wholesomely and compassionately. They came understanding the technology involved and hoping that this would happen. They willingly paid the exorbitant entrance fee to support this important religious event and to make use of the technology for their own purposes. And they returned home satisfied and inspired.

At this point we should also pause to consider the possibilities for abuse of such technologies. Abuses can arise in the transition period, when some people understand these technologies and others do not. Differential understanding creates opportunities for economic and political exploitation. For example, people may not know that the organizers of a social event or the promoters of subliminal-message advertising are taking specific advantage of them with the aim of influencing their thoughts and behavior. In due course, however, presumably most people would know how these technologies work and would accept them and their regulation as ordinary parts of social and religious life.

Abuses can also arise even when everyone understands how things work, and yet technologies of RSEs are deployed as means of explicit social control. In that case a host of miserable scenarios arises, some of which are depicted in dystopian novels such as Aldous Huxley's *Brave New World* and George Orwell's *1984*. We are right to worry about mind control, because it is a reflexive temptation to which those seeking to gain and protect power easily fall prey. Such control can be enhanced using customized psycho-social technologies to manipulate suggestibility in a religious framework. The dystopias that could result from this go beyond even what Huxley and Orwell imagined in their disturbing futurist nightmares.

Meditative techniques

Meditative techniques derive from the fact that some individuals can deploy thoughts, actions, postures, foods, and surroundings in various combinations with concentration, focused attention, or relaxation to induce desired altered states of consciousness. Some of these states yield changes in behavior, mood, and physical and mental health, and some are so illuminating and moving that they are said to have profound spiritual significance. Meditative techniques that proved to be widely effective were shared, practiced, refined, and encoded in traditions.

Despite extensive research into meditation, mentioned in earlier chapters, there are numerous open questions. In particular, what varied effects on consciousness can different types of meditation produce? What are the biochemical triggers and accompaniments of these effects? What key brain regions and functions are implicated in particular meditation effects? Unfortunately, the comparative meditation database linking techniques and effects on states of consciousness is far less developed than the botanical database linking plants with consciousness effects. But it ought to be possible in principle and in practice to construct such a database using existing correlational data, such as Kristeller's (2007) multimodal scheme of meditation effects and Benson's (1975) relaxation response mentioned in previous chapters, along with traditional knowledge about particular styles of meditation and the types of cognitive and emotional effects they produce. While that database is being built, another linking meditation styles to neurochemistry and neural activation sites is also being enriched.

Before many decades have passed, it will be possible to picture the following scenario.

Imagine in two decades coming across a Web advertisement for biofeedback-enhanced meditation experiences. You know that biofeedback has been used in stress management, lie detection, and pain management, among other applications. But the ad explains that a wealth of information about the physiological conditions and effects of meditation now make possible a new type of biofeedback that reduces the time required to master a meditation technique from decades to hours. The ad points out that traditional meditation practitioners have been protesting this turn of events, claiming that a decades-long cultivation of meditation skills is the only authentic approach. But the ad likens this attitude to a refusal to fly across oceans in airplanes in favor of the traditional method of rowing. The traditional meditation student is immediately lost in the forests of the mind, with almost no relevant guidance. Almost all are confined forever to the domain of low-level changes of consciousness and only a few lucky students manage to get very far, thanks to in-built feedback mechanisms that allow them to make purposeful modifications during meditation. But now, the ad insists, you can have the same benefits that these special brains offer their lucky hosts. Through the miracle of biofeedback joined with advancing knowledge of the physiology of meditation, you can use externally generated information about the state of your embodied mind, information that you cannot produce internally, to guide your meditation practice.

The ad invites you to think of regularly visiting a biofeedback meditation location near you in the same way that you think of going to the gym. Both are about fitness. When you arrive for the first time, you will be asked to select one of two dozen meditation styles, each of which is associated with particular biochemical and neurological characteristics, and also with particular typical outcomes in terms of states of consciousness and behavioral changes. Expert counselors will be on hand to help you make this vital decision. Once you know what you want, you will be situated in a beautiful and comfortable location where non-invasive equipment is used to produce the relevant biofeedback. Your task is then to deploy the biofeedback information with the aim of training your mind to produce the target state of consciousness. You will have to work hard, like every student of meditation. But you will no longer be guessing about what works, constantly being overwhelmed with frustration. At last you can have the information you need to make the most of your brain's ability to produce transformative states of consciousness.

UNPRECEDENTED TECHNOLOGIES

We have tried to picture the future of familiar technologies of RSEs: the botanical, psycho-social, and meditative technologies that have been important in human cultures for millennia. But there are new technologies that offer unprecedented levels of control over states of consciousness, pointedly challenging traditional understandings of the meaning and value of RSEs.

Neuropsychopharmacology

Neuropsychopharmacology isolates psychoactive ingredients within entheogenic plants, thereby potentially assuming the role that these botanicals have played in human civilizations to this point. But neuropsychopharmacology goes well beyond this.

The human brain, like other animal brains, saves space by using overlapping circuitry. This is not immediately easy to grasp, because our normal models of electrical circuits have only one transmitter of electricity – namely, electrons – and distinct circuits do not interpenetrate except through on–off switching gates. The brain is quite different. Though the brain's neurons send electrochemical signals along their length in much the same way regardless of the type of neuron, each interface between the axon of one neuron and the dendrite of another, called the synapse, uses at least one (sometimes several) of a wide variety of chemical transmitters. Thus, the very same neuronal architecture can contain numerous active circuits, and some neurons can participate in numerous circuits, depending on which neurotransmitters are active and which are inhibited. This ingenious system not only saves space; it also allows for intricate overlaps between neural systems. This is one reason why mapping brain circuitry is so difficult and why conscious experience is so interesting.

There are several ways in which neurotransmitter activity can be affected, all based around the neurochemistry of transmitter release, reception, and reuptake. Here are five of the most common ways, with examples related specifically to entheogens. First, a neurochemical can stimulate the release of a neurotransmitter from an axon terminal. This happens with MDMA or ecstasy, which prompts the release of the neurotransmitter serotonin. Second, a neurochemical can dock with receptors thereby simulating a neurotransmitter's function. This happens with DMT, mescaline, and psilocybin, all mentioned above, and also with LSD. Each of these chemicals simulates the effects of the neurotransmitter serotonin.

Third, a neurochemical can inhibit the breakdown of a neurotransmitter, thereby allowing it to remain active. This happens with MAO inhibitors, mentioned above, which prevent the breakdown of monoamine neurotransmitters as well as neurochemicals such as DMT, thereby enhancing DMT's effect on the serotonin system. Fourth, a neurochemical can block receptors in several different ways so that the appropriate neurotransmitter function cannot be performed and signaling is suppressed. This happens with PCP, which docks with receptors for the neurotransmitter MDMA and prevents MDMA circuits from functioning. Fifth, a neurochemical can inhibit the reuptake pumps on the axon thereby leaving the corresponding neurotransmitters active within the synapse for longer than would otherwise be the case. This happens with SSRIs, or selective serotonin reuptake inhibitors, which are a common antidepressant that prevent the reuptake of serotonin and thus leave it active within the synapse, where it can change mood and sometimes produce entheogenic effects.

The brain maintains a strong defense against the many and varied chemicals in the blood. This defense is called the blood–brain barrier and consists of tightly packed cells in capillaries within the brain. This system effectively blocks most chemicals, only allowing those for which there are specific transport mechanisms to cross over into the brain. Of course, some small molecules can diffuse into the brain despite the blood–brain barrier's defenses. Most need an invitation. The blood–brain barrier poses problems for administering psychotropic substances in general, including those with entheogenic effects, but new techniques using nanotechnology may make the blood–brain barrier traversable more or less at will. This may be one of the most important transformations in the neuropsychopharmacological technology of entheogens.

Already at this point, neuropsychopharmacologists know which chemicals both enhance and suppress many neurochemical systems by virtue of operating on specific receptors and neurotransmitters. They have some grasp of the dangers, also, including addiction, modification of synaptic receptor density, and structural damage to the brain. It is not for nothing that many psychotropic substances are illegal to possess or consume. Most importantly they have a lot of information about what kinds of effects can be expected from modifying neurotransmitter functions. Though we are not there yet, it is not stretching credulity to imagine a meaningful menu of psychoactive substances directly productive of a variety of specific types of RSEs – something like the near-future neuropsychopharmacological equivalent of the Chinese herbalist with intriguing shelves of substances and a lifetime of accrued wisdom.

What is more difficult to picture is the social context within which such a menu of neuropsychopharmacological enhancements of RSEs could be presented and orders taken. It may remain underground, like the religious groups that use psychoactive substances such as LSD as their sacrament. Or it may eventually become a common part of life, spawning new industries at the intersection of neuropsychopharmacology and religion akin to the psychiatry industry that thrives at the intersection of medicine and human emotional life.

Transcranial brain stimulation

In previous chapters we discussed the claim of neuroscientist Michael Persinger and others that stimulation of the brain using targeted magnetic fields from outside the cranium might be able to induce specific types of RSEs, particularly the feeling of an invisible presence. I pointed out the controversy surrounding Persinger's work and also mentioned the Shakti and Koren helmets that market this purported technology to eager spiritual cybernauts.

The prima facie likelihood that transcranial electrical or magnetic stimulation of the brain could produce any meaningful experiential or behavioral effects seems small, given the complex ways in which the brain realizes anything as high-level as states of consciousness and behaviors. Nevertheless, presumably this type of technology will gradually be more deeply understood and could eventually become more precise and powerful. While most states of consciousness would remain immune to any amount of transcranial stimulation, a few might prove to be reliably affected – hopefully without the side-effects associated with electroshock therapy for persistent severe depression, and without the controversy surrounding Persinger's work. This represents a brave new world of technology, going far beyond the scalp massages and clubs to the head that have defined the state of the art in transcranial influence on brain states for millennia.

Controlling the health effects of religious and spiritual experiences

Another controversial domain of research pertains to the health effects of religious behaviors, beliefs, and experiences. There have been numerous studies identifying correlations between religiousness and improved physical and mental health outcomes (see Aukst-Margetic *et al.* 2005; Baetz *et al.* 2002; Bartlett *et al.* 2003; Beit-Hallahmi and Argyle 1997; Bosworth *et al.* 2003; Braam *et al.* 2004; Burker *et al.* 2004; Carlson *et al.* 2004; Compton and Furman 2005; Comstock and Partridge 1972; Contrada *et al.* 2004; Daniels *et al.* 2004; Daugherty *et al.* 2005; Ellison *et al.* 1989; Gillings and Joseph 1996; Harrison *et al.* 2005; Hill *et al.* 2005; Hixson *et al.* 1998; Idler 1987; Idler and Kasl 1992; Kinney *et al.* 2003; Koenig 2000, 2001a, 2001b, 2001c, 2001d, 2001e, 2002; Koenig *et al.* 1998, 1999a; Kune *et al.* 1993; Levin and Vanderpool 1989; Levin *et al.* 1995; Masters *et al.* 2004; Murphy *et al.* 2000; Newlin *et al.* 2003; Oman *et al.* 2002; Steffen *et al.* 2001; Strawbridge *et al.* 1997, 2001). There have also been a few studies that found correlations between religiousness and *decreased* physical and mental health (see King *et al.* 1999), or no effect in contrast to other studies that found an effect (see Idler and Kasl 1992 versus Koenig 2001e; Musick *et al.* 2000; Strawbridge *et al.* 1997). There have been a number of pointed and persuasive methodological criticisms of research in this area focusing mainly on design and interpretation challenges that all correlational studies must confront (see, for example, Lawrence 2002; Sloan 2006; Sloan and Bagiella 2002; Sloan and Ramakrishnan 2006; Sloan *et al.* 1999, 2000; and the reply to some of these criticisms in Koenig *et al.* 1999b; and see the methodological discussions in the National Institute for Healthcare Research Consensus Report in Larson 1998 and in Idler *et al.* 2003). Nevertheless, the associations between positive health outcomes and religiosity are persistent and impressive (see judicious conclusions to this effect in Eckersley 2007 and Williams and Sternthal 2007; for reviews, see Hufford 2005; Miller and Thoresen 2003; Thoresen and Harris 2002).

Some of these studies examined extrinsic features of religiosity such as religious participation (see meta-analytic studies in Coruh 2005; George 2002; Powell 2003; Townsend *et al.* 2002). Others focused on intrinsic features such as strength of religious belief and fervor of personal prayer or meditation (see Batson *et al.* 1993; Beit-Hallahmi and Argyle 1997; McNamara *et al.* 2003; Watson *et al.* 1984; Worthington *et al.* 1996). It is important to keep in mind that RSEs in the broad sense used in this book encompass both extrinsic and intrinsic types of religiosity. Ultimacy experiences, and the special subset of them that I call intense experiences, are of the intrinsic type. But at this point it is the full range of RSEs that is of interest.

This domain of research perfectly illustrates the challenges involved in tracing the connections between religious behaviors, beliefs, and experiences and their bodily conditions and effects. Brains and bodies are extraordinarily complicated individually; their causal interactions are vastly complex and poorly understood. Correlational studies gradually build up a database of the possible health effects of RSEs, which is a huge advance on the impressionistic wisdom of the past. But disclosing the underlying causal mechanisms that mediate those effects promises a far greater degree of refined control at some point in the future.

Just as neuropsychopharmacology promises customized dispensing of psychotropic substances for targeted spiritual purposes, so knowledge of the health effects of religiosity eventually promises scientifically explicable customized advice for those with particular health problems. The relaxation response (Benson 1975) appears to be especially good for lowering blood pressure, recovering from heart surgery, and a range of other health challenges relating to stress and healing. Consistent involvement in a religious group (or some other group that delivers similar social connectivity and existential meaning) appears to extend significantly the quality and length of life. In due course, it is reasonable to expect a long list of such correlations, with increasing detail and precision as knowledge of causal mechanisms begins to appear.

Multimodal therapeutic spiritual direction

Picture a new breed of spiritual director twenty years from now. This new type of specialist blends the analytical insight and prescribing authority of the psychiatrist with the spiritual sensitivity of the traditional spiritual director. Let us call this person a neuro-spiritual director. Once spiritual goals are set, a neuro-spiritual director can advise a client to make use of neuro-customized psycho-social experiences or to explore biofeedback meditation exercises, as depicted above, or they might recommend magnetic brain stimulation therapy or conventional psychotherapy. They might also augment such recommendations with a medication regimen designed to facilitate desired goals.

For example, a client might present with difficulties trusting and cooperating with others because of a persistent inability to achieve a normal level of empathy. This problem is devastating, leaving the client feeling lonely and spiritually empty. The neuro-spiritual director might prescribe a course of low-dose empathogens such as MDMA derivatives or oxytocin that are well suited to compensate for natural difficulties with empathy and to stimulate awareness of the degree to which most people normally feel attached to others. The memories of the empathic experiences that result can be used within a therapeutic process permanently to produce behavior changes toward realizing the client's goal of greater empathy and social connectedness.

Alternatively, a client might present as religiously tone deaf, firmly believing that the doors of their spiritual perception capabilities are locked shut. The neuro-spiritual director might prescribe low doses of an entheogenic hallucinogen – not one that produces visions and auditions bearing no relation to experience, as some hallucinogens do, but rather one that enhances the emotional richness and perceptual texture of ordinary experience. The experiences from this short course would be accompanied by intensive therapeutic discussions of the significance of seeing ordinary experience in a more intense way. Biofeedback-guided meditation exercises would then make this richer type of experience a more consistent part of the client's everyday life.

CONCLUSION

We have been looking ahead to an era when the biological and psycho-social mechanisms of RSEs are well understood. Thought experiments about the future of RSEs help us detect the criteria that matter when we try to decide questions of their meaning and value, authenticity, and reliability. At this point we need to step back from these reasonable speculations and attempt to draw some conclusions about the meaning and value of RSEs in light of these technological scenarios. I mention seven such conclusions here.

First, affirmation of the meaning and value of RSEs has often silently depended on ignorance of their neural and psycho-social workings. Many of these affirmative interpretations have relied on supernatural accounts of the origins and mechanisms of RSEs. When we discover the technologies that allow us to start, stop, and regulate such experiences, we naturally wonder why we still need hypotheses about supernatural causes and mechanisms. To the extent that we assigned meaning and value to RSEs based on their putative supernatural origins, we may feel foolish and conclude that they have no value after all. The lesson here is that we should avoid interpretations of the meaning and value of RSEs that make us uncomfortable with eventual discoveries about how they actually work.

Second, knowing the mechanisms of RSEs need not interfere with people's willingness to claim cognitive reliability, moral value, and existential authenticity on behalf of such experiences. This is true even when artificial means are deployed to trigger RSEs. Many thoughtful people interpret their RSEs as colorful and cognitively deceptive side-effects of a big-brain cognitive system, yet deem them exquisitely valuable despite this. The analogy here is with wonderful food and glorious music, which are evolutionary side-effects of our neurological makeup rather than experiences for which we are specifically adapted. Whether or not we are adapted for RSEs, a strong case can be made for their meaning and value.

Now, let's suppose that we get past the shock of realizing that ignorance has often supported positive assessments of the meaning and value of RSEs. Let's further suppose that we are fully aware that both positive and negative cases can be made about their meaning and value. To what criteria can we appeal when deciding on the meaning and value of RSEs? This question leads to several other conclusions.

So, third, the more the mechanisms of RSEs are understood, the more we are rationally obliged to relate judgments of their meaning and value, their authenticity and reliability, to deliberate, regulated deployments, and the less we can attach significance to spontaneous, unsought occurrences. It is common for someone to report a mystical experience and to attach enormous significance to the fact that it seems to strike them from nowhere, completely unexpectedly. This linkage between spontaneity and significance merely masks ignorance of biological and psychosocial causes, and thus we must refuse to uphold it. If we cannot attach meaning and value to RSEs that we ourselves induce in any of the ways discussed in this chapter, then we should not attempt to attach meaning and value to such experiences because of their apparent spontaneity.

Fourth, the more mechanisms of RSEs are understood, the more judgments of their meaning and value, their authenticity and reliability, depend on effects and the less such judgments depend on their putative causes. This is a case of "by your fruits shall you know them" – no matter how RSEs come to us, what they produce in our lives and in wider social contexts is what matters most.

Fifth, an integrative interpretation of RSEs in relation to everything we know about religion and the sciences, about human nature and the spiritual depths of life, is crucial in any argument on behalf of their meaning and value, their authenticity and reliability. Such integrative interpretations must link up the many relevant components of our knowledge into a persuasive causal narrative that explains how the neural embodiment and social embedding of RSEs relate to our moral choices, our value judgments, and our behavior. I have presented one such integrated interpretation in this book, and will survey the results of my effort in the next and concluding chapter.

Sixth, integrative interpretations are most plausible when they do not require supernatural agents with special causal powers. We saw something similar in assessing the cognitive reliability of RSEs. Our speculations about the future of RSEs drive the point home forcefully: supernatural agents were once thought essential for explaining RSEs, but we have no need of that hypothesis any longer. By itself, this does not rule out supernatural agents, of course, because we can still say that they spark RSEs through the processes whose causal mechanisms we are learning to trace. But a hypothesis of this supernatural sort comes to seem increasingly exorbitant and implausible when it is repeatedly shown to be superfluous for explaining the meaning and value of RSEs.

Seventh, the brave new world of technologized and regulated RSEs that I have sketched in this chapter should not be a reason solely for alarm and anxiety. Some of the case studies show the ways in which the technology of RSEs might be welcome and helpful, even exciting and engaging. There are corresponding risks, obviously, but that is true of every era, commensurate with the types and sophistication of technology in existence at the time. The future I have described can seem either bleak or welcoming for those who prize RSEs. The key to the way we respond is largely the extent to which we welcome self-knowledge. Are we willing to draw aside the veil of ignorance covering the neural embodiment and social embedding of RSEs? Are we ready to see the ideological elements of religious behaviors, beliefs, and experiences that mask destructive power transactions? Are we open to understanding ourselves as we truly are, wondrous embodied brains equipped to perceive both reality's sense-accessible features and its intricate and spiritually potent valuational depths?

CHAPTER 8

Brains in bodies, persons in groups, and religion in nature: an integrative interpretation of religious and spiritual experiences

INTRODUCTION

We have come to the end of a long journey of exploration, filled with rich disciplinary vistas. The journey has been complicated by the recurring challenges of absorption and synthesis forced upon us by the multidisciplinary framework of the inquiry. In this concluding chapter, having arrived back home, so to speak, I attempt to fulfill the obligations of an integrative interpreter of many disciplinary perspectives on RSEs by weaving together the main strands of the inquiry into the theoretical equivalent of a tapestry that recalls where we have traveled. The tapestry records the many ways the interpretation has been knotted tightly to relevant data, and illustrates the affiliations among valid insights that might otherwise seem unrelated or even opposed. In fact, most of the tapestry was finished on the journey, but it is important to pause at the end, step back, and see what we have wrought.

I proceed first by crystallizing five controversies that the unfolding argument has held in suspension and indicating their bearing on my conclusions. Subsequently, I shall summarize the argument by restating the five affirmations that express in the most substantive way the interpretative conclusion of the book about the nature, functions, and value of RSEs.

FIVE KEY CONTROVERSIES

Five controversial themes run through the argument of this book. These are: Definitive proof versus hypothesis correction; Ideological extremity versus multidisciplinary balance; Supernaturalism versus naturalism; Instinctive innocence versus self-critical responsibility; and Natural law versus social engineering. The argument comes to rest on the second item in each pair, though perhaps sometimes in unexpected ways. I intend this discussion of controversies to clarify points from the unfolding argument that may require explicit discussion, to head off misunderstandings, and to expose central arguments to proper scrutiny.

Definitive proof versus hypothesis correction

Following a theory of inquiry influenced by the early American pragmatist philosophical tradition (laid out in Wildman 2010), the argument of this book has eschewed definitive proof as a rational ideal and embraced the hypothetico-corrective method instead. The hypothetico-corrective method seeks the refinement by all possible means of hypotheses formulated creatively within an epistemologically fallibilist framework. The aim in all cases is to improve promising interpretations by placing them into conversation with the best ideas from as wide a range of disciplinary partners as may be relevant to the inquiry.

This approach to inquiry can be disturbing to people wedded to epistemologically foundationalist ideas of certainty, and a relief to those who see foundationalist ideals as vain. Instead of demonstrating the validity and soundness of an argument with the aim of attaining a definitive conclusion, the hypothetico-corrective approach to multidisciplinary comparative inquiry operates by steadily eliminating rational and evidential flaws in promising hypotheses. This involves simultaneously elaborating, comparing, and evaluating competing hypotheses, and looking for telltale shifts in plausibility that indicate the superiority of one hypothesis over others. Very often, the conclusion of an inquiry takes the form of "hypothesis A is superior in respect of criterion X, while hypothesis B is superior in respect of criterion Y; But criterion X is a weightier consideration than criterion Y, so hypothesis A is the most robust of the alternatives for now, subject to further correction in the future" (the logic of comparative analysis and inference to best explanation argumentation is laid out in Wildman 2006a). Consider two examples from this book.

First, in Chapter 2, we considered the neural mediation hypothesis. This area is philosophically well traveled so there are numerous competing alternative hypotheses of the mind–brain relationship. A number of extreme views were ruled out as highly implausible because of empirical failures, and several less extreme views were ruled out as less plausible than the two most compelling classes of interpretations: di-polar monism theories and dualist theories. I then presented an argument that the di-polar monist class is significantly more plausible than the dualist class in every respect except that of being consistent with worldviews boasting discarnate supernatural entities. Thus, subject to supernatural world-views being mistaken, di-polar monist interpretations are more plausible interpretations than the competition. This is an example of an inference-to-best-explanation argument whose conclusion has an "if-then" form, which clearly manifests the conditions under which the conclusion is maximally sound, as well as the most effective way of overthrowing that conclusion. While the very opposite of a definitive argument, this plausibility-weighing approach matches the way we actually reason and weigh evidence, and it properly responds to the reality that plausibility structures and contexts matter in evaluating philosophical arguments.

Second, in Chapter 6, we were dealing with the relation of RSEs to the evolution of the brain-group nexus. In this case, the territory is not as well traveled and there are no existing hypotheses that comprehensively integrate the relevant disciplinary perspectives and pertinent evidence into a coherent interpretation. Accordingly, the task was one of hypothesis construction, rather than analysis and comparison and evaluation. The plausibility of the brain-group nexus hypothesis derives from its ability to register relevant data in the right respects rather than from its superiority to competitors.

Ideological extremity versus multidisciplinary balance

The argument attempted to appreciate insights where possible, even in extreme views that express sharply opposed evaluations of RSEs. The so-called new atheists are confident that RSEs are cognitively misleading side-effects of the brain's amazing simulation software with the potential to cause great psychological and social harm (see, among others, Dawkins 2006; Harris 2006; Hitchens 2007; Mills 2006). But they do not evaluate the possibility that even an obviously flawed cognitive system may be able to foster authentic engagement with ultimacy conceived without superstition or supernaturalism. Meanwhile, a number of religious writers defend the reliability of cognitions and the value of behaviors that derive from RSEs (see, among others, Alston 1991; Davis 1989; Forman 1999; Gellman 1997; Plantinga 1993, 2000; Runehov 2007; Swinburne 1979; Yandell 1993). Most mount this defense within a particular subtradition (typically personalist theism) of a particular religion (typically Christianity) and pay insufficient attention to the impact of such a determinate outlook on the force of the argument.

This list of one-sided interpretations in the area of RSEs can be extended more or less indefinitely. Contextualist philosophers get context dependence of interpreting RSEs correct but finesse the question of whether empirical evidence might actually be able to support the claim of "sameness" in some sense across religious traditions. Perennialist philosophers are in love with an admittedly grand vision of reality having tremendous potential to transcend religious conflict but are insufficiently responsive to evidence about contexts and conditions affecting interpretations of RSEs. Some neuroscientists are certain that understanding how the brain produces RSEs confirms a dualist, body–soul ontology, while others are certain that the same understanding confirms that RSEs are cognitive delusions.

Despite these disagreements, I have argued that there is a way to combine the most persuasive evidence from a host of disciplines into a coherent and compelling interpretation of RSEs. I have not ignored inconvenient evidence. The journey on which this book reports has involved many wrong turns and many corrections of initial hypotheses. The result is as complex as the phenomena demand. It is not expressible in slogans, because it requires particular interpretative frameworks to stabilize the concepts on which the conclusions depend. This conclusion will be wholly consistent with none of the many one-sided interpretations of RSEs, even as it accommodates the evidence and persuasive elements of each.

Supernaturalism versus naturalism

No issue impacts interpretation of RSEs more than the conflict between supernaturalism and naturalism. I have argued that naturalist worldviews are supportive of the meaning and value, the authenticity and reliability of RSEs. I argued that our growing understanding of RSEs makes supernatural worldviews increasingly implausible. I also indicated that it is not possible to resolve the dispute within the confines of a book of this sort.

To recall, supernaturalism affirms disembodied intentionality, in beings such as demons and angels, spirits and ghosts, bodhisattvas and ancestors, and deities major and minor, all with centers of consciousness and awareness, memory and thought, and possessing causal powers that operate either beyond or through the regularities of nature. These entities are the heart and soul of religious narratives by which the large majority of people guide their lives. That majority understands these entities to be the objects and causes of at least some kinds of RSEs. According to supernatural worldviews, it is through our capacity for such RSEs that communication and interaction can exist between embodied creatures like us and disembodied beings of the supernatural sort.

Meanwhile, religious naturalism affirms that intentionality is always embodied and emergent from a world of natural possibilities. In sufficiently neurologically and socially complex beings, engagement with value structures and flows in the depths of nature becomes possible. These axiological depths fund exploration of the space of aesthetic and moral possibilities. Intense experiences (in the depth-and-breadth sense of this book, a significant subset of RSEs) manifest these depths in much the same way that sense experience manifests the sensible elements of our environment. Once encountered and engaged, the axiological depths of reality power the construction of meaning on which individual lives and cultural projects crucially depend. Religious naturalism is compatible with ground-of-being views of ultimate reality, from the mystics' God beyond God to the *Dao* That Cannot Be Daoed, and from *Nirguṇa Brahman* to *śūnyatā*.

How does growing knowledge of RSEs push the plausibility scale in the direction of religious naturalism and away from supernaturalism? Consider an analogy from medicine. I may say that it was God's will that my child died of dysentery, in an understandable attempt to handle the unremitting pain of such a tragedy by attributing it to supernatural divine action. But in taking this psychologically intelligible approach, I may fail to notice that the dysentery was a direct result of poor public health in my community and was in fact a thoroughly avoidable tragedy having a lot more to do with economic justice than divine providence. As we learn more about how the world works, we are better able to take our fate into our own hands and thereby prevent future tragedies of this kind. We still need meaning in our lives, but we no longer require supernatural narratives to generate or sustain that meaning.

It is impossible definitively to rule out supernatural explanations of RSEs. Just as with disease and medical treatments, however, supernatural accounts of the causal origins of RSEs will become steadily less plausible as such experiences can be produced on demand. And the meaning of those experiences will become increasingly tied to their consequences rather than to the sheer fact of their occurrence. Moreover, people will become less credulous about the cognitive content of their RSEs, knowing that they are socially conditioned and never transparently self-interpreting events.

Yet, even as supernaturalism necessarily becomes less plausible in the presence of a detailed understanding of the mechanisms underlying RSEs, our need for existential meaning and moral orientation persists and religion remains important. Thus, our interpretation of RSEs will shift from a supernatural encounter model not to an outright rejection of RSEs but to a religious naturalist engagement model. That is, more and more people will want to give up the idea of RSEs as serendipitous encounters with supernatural beings sending us inspiration and information, and intervening to guide our lives. Instead they will understand their RSEs as forms of engagement with the wondrous and dangerous and morally ambiguous depths of natural reality. This change will not come quickly, and it will not come at all if a collapse of civilization prevents humanity from moving to the less stable social equilibria that this change entails, with their higher energy requirements and educational demands. The point, however, is that this change can come, and thus that a religiously supportive naturalistic framework for interpreting RSEs as potentially authentic is socially realizable on a wider scale than merely the minority of people who work hard to overcome their supernaturalist impulses.

Instinctive innocence versus self-critical responsibility

Another recurring theme is the contrast between instinctive human self-understandings that are innocent of knowledge about the causes and conditions of RSEs, on the one hand, and human self-understandings that take such knowledge fully into account and seek to exercise full responsibility for the existential and social effects of RSEs, on the other. We noted that the sociology of knowledge offers an interpretation of the social construction of reality in which ignorance of the processes of construction and legitimation is essential to their smooth and effective operation. We also saw that confidence in the cognitive reliability of RSEs often silently depends in practice on questionable beliefs about their causes and conditions, and that self-awareness of the mechanisms of the brain-group nexus decreases the stability of social equilibria and requires correspondingly large investments of energy in education and rituals to create stable social transactions. In all of these cases, self-awareness disrupts the "normal" operation of social processes.

This theme is picked up with enormous power in Fyodor Dostoevsky's *The Brothers Karamazov* (see Dostoevsky [1880] 1990). In one of that book's finest allegories, the Grand Inquisitor is forced to deliver a monologue by the silence of the supernaturally returned but now arrested Jesus Christ. Using this device, Dostoevsky presents a perspective on the human condition and the form of political organization necessary to control and develop it – of course, with his immediate context fully in mind. This political solution requires deception of the masses by the few burdened by the responsibilities of their powerful leadership positions. Dostoevsky confronts this perspective with the deafening silence of Christ, whose presumed viewpoint the Grand Inquisitor himself expresses in his criticisms. The ultimate judgment – to burn Christ on the next day – turns especially on the danger to human happiness that Christ represents. Christ raises questions, magnifies options, and increases confusion, which amounts to a thoughtless form of exquisite cruelty in the eyes of the Grand Inquisitor, and one that must be resisted absolutely for the sake of the people. Christ believes that that we have nothing to lose and everything to gain by telling the truth about social reality and its ultimate meaning. The Inquisitor proposes instead to conceive of political and social arrangements as means to limit the enormous pain of the world's disappointments and tragedies, and thereby to minimize futile human writhing in the grip of vain hopes and deluded beliefs about the world's workings and its ultimate meaning.

Could the happy hopes of the innocent majority who trust their instinctive reactions to RSEs be wiser and truer than the sincere austerity of the self-critical, self-aware, self-regulating minority? I have argued that the scientific study of religion, including the scientific study of RSEs, has produced overwhelming evidence that the answer to this poignant question must be in the negative.

Natural law versus social engineering

Should we trust the cognitive and emotional resources for interpretation that nature furnishes the human species, or embrace the necessity of social engineering to battle instinctive interpretative and behavioral responses? In arguing for the latter, I am acknowledging the full force of the mass of evidence that scientists have produced bearing on the problems of cognitive error and emotional instability in human interpretation and behavior. Human beings are remarkably adept at generating serviceably accurate interpretations of their physical surroundings and social contexts – accurate, that is, for the coarse purposes of evolutionary adaptation. But the exquisitely complex cultural forms of modern humans, when combined with the investigative resources of empirical psychology and neurosciences, have manifested many stretched seams in what once appeared to be a seamless cognitive-emotional garment. We interpret the world as best we can, but some people are better than others at this task. Moreover, extensive training is necessary to avoid elementary errors that can be shown to be such. This mixed story of basically useful but subtly flawed inferential and interpretative equipment in the human species is a vital component of any adequate interpretation of RSEs.

Some people may never seek accurate interpretations of complex subject matters, but extensive training can help limit errors of interpretation for those who make use of it. This helps would-be social engineers determine both the guiding social vision and the specific pedagogical agenda. We see this impulse fully present in contemporary anti-religion writers who criticize religious education of children as cruel indoctrination. Their idea of social engineering begins with eliminating such religious education and stressing instead enlightened scientific education that helps people overcome the deficits of their reflexive ways of interpreting complex subject matters by training them to think critically and in full awareness of where they are most likely to make inferential or interpretative errors. One must be brave to embrace any social engineering project this enthusiastically, given how badly the most aggressive of such projects in the last century have turned out; enthusiasm has bred suppression with alarming speed, in religious and anti-religious contexts alike.

A gentler approach to education is more responsible and truer to our considerable ignorance about the religious and spiritual meanings of reality. To educate at all, particularly in critical thinking skills that directly influence people's self-interpretations and behavior, is still social engineering, and there is nothing to be gained by attempting to evade this terminology. But education in critical thinking and self-awareness, driven by experimental data and empirically based theories of human cognition and emotion, need not be haughty, need not suppress other kinds of education, and need not be tightly controlled. Let reality speak in its manifold voices and let people listen in their manifold ways. This leads to creative confusion, to be sure, but it also functions as a hedge against dangerous over-confidence of the self-appointed social engineers who are quick to dream of a better future and slow to doubt their own wisdom.

I characterized the view opposing mine as reflexive trust in the cognitive and emotional resources for interpretation that nature furnishes the human species. In most forms, this view entails an affirmation of natural law: we are made (by God, perhaps) and equipped with all of the powers we need to determine the morally good, the aesthetically beautiful, and the cognitively true – and also, in religious contexts, to achieve spiritual fulfillment through recognizing revelation and accepting salvation or enlightenment. The view I defend refuses the static and intentional categories in this form of natural-law thinking. Our cognitive and emotional resources may be set in our era by our evolutionary heritage, and our cognitive and emotional potential may be limited by our particular genetic endowment, but there is nothing sacred about the way these resources function. We routinely seek to improve the functional efficacy of our evolutionary and genetic endowments through education and skill development. To do this is in fact to act naturally, in the sense of "in accord with nature's own ways."

It follows that my religious naturalist argument on behalf of increasing critical awareness of problems surrounding reflexive interpretation of RSEs is itself a kind of natural law. But it is a modified natural-law approach, in at least three senses. It refuses divine intentions and analogous devices used to legitimate arbitrary demarcations between the natural and the non-natural. It affirms the dynamism of natural capacities and embraces the challenge of greater self-awareness even when the new insights that result confound established wisdom. And it refuses simple axiological visions that suppose the good, the true, and the beautiful are ultimately as simple as a moment of pure awareness. Thus, this viewpoint is completely in accord with nature as the religious naturalist understands it.

FIVE KEY AFFIRMATIONS

The five key affirmations that express the resting point of the argument of this book are: the neural mediation hypothesis, the intensity hypothesis, the brain-group nexus hypothesis, the religious naturalism hypothesis, and the conditional value hypothesis. All but the last of these has received extensive discussion. The conditional value hypothesis, which conveys my philosophical, theological, and ethical evaluation of RSEs in light of everything we have discussed, has been mostly implicit in the argument, and now becomes explicit.

The neural mediation hypothesis

Chapter 2 presented a case for the neural mediation hypothesis, namely, that *the mind does nothing we can detect that is not exhaustively mediated by and expressed in the brain.* While so obvious as to be hardly worth discussion to some, it is important to remember that exhaustive neural mediation has been a minority viewpoint in every era, including today. This case capitalized on basic framework evidence, functional neuroimaging evidence, electrical activity evidence, localized lesion evidence, neurochemical and genetic evidence, and direct experimental evidence.

I pointed out that clinching the neural mediation hypothesis does not settle basic ontological questions about the mind–brain problem; mind–body dualists can affirm the neural mediation hypothesis with as much conviction as di-polar monists (these are, roughly, physicalists who affirm that values and physicality are jointly rooted in the ontological depths of reality). But there is an important difference here: dualists can live with or without the neural mediation hypothesis, whereas di-polar monists require it. Put differently, dualists can win the philosophical argument decisively by showing that the neural mediation hypothesis is mistaken, whereas di-polar monists can only win gradually by showing over a long period of time that the dualist theory does no useful explanatory work. This point is obscured by interpretations of RSEs that overestimate the evidential value of neurological discoveries or pay little attention to nuances of argumentation in the philosophy of mind.

Chapter 2 discussed a number of challenges facing the neurological study of RSEs. These problems are more tractable in the presence of the neural mediation hypothesis than in its absence. In particular, focusing on the qualitative features of states of consciousness related to RSEs opens up new avenues of research. Most important among these are the generation of constraints on cognitive models of RSEs, and subsequently, in league with neuroimaging and brain-lesion studies, on neural models of RSEs. These cognitive and neural models are the keys to meaningful, testable theories about the neural embodiment and social effects of RSEs. They also promise effective resolution of the chaotically diverse perspectives within the phenomenology of religion by producing a stable suite of categories and processes that can be used to map the species-wide features of RSEs.

None of these new ventures makes much sense in isolation from the neural mediation hypothesis. After all, if there is some immediate source of RSEs with non-natural causal properties that somehow bypasses the brain by communicating directly with a putative disembodied soul, then cognitive and neural models are not especially relevant to understanding the actual causality of RSEs, no matter how much those experiences may eventually find partial expression in the brain.

I affirm di-polar monism for philosophical and theological reasons as well as because it has a more constructive relationship with promising scientific research programs. Much of the book's argument falls apart if the neural mediation hypothesis is mistaken. But most of the argument survives, regardless of preferred ontological framework (dualism or di-polar monism) *as long as the neural mediation survives.*

The intensity hypothesis

Chapter 3 presents a phenomenological description of the terrain of RSEs with quite distinctive features. I construe experience in terms of states of consciousness in beings whose existential interests, social relationships, and natural environments are partly constitutive of those experiences. Within the endlessly rambling territory of human experiences, I focused on a small region defined as the union of three groups of experiences: the especially strange (called "anomalous" experiences); the especially meaningful (called "ultimacy" experiences); and the experiences people are willing to call "religious." While the first two groups can be given relatively stable definitions and demarcations, the third crucially depends on cultural and individual usage of the contested word "religious." The map allows for the definition of spiritual experiences as including all of the especially meaningful (ultimacy) experiences and whatever portion of the territory of religious experiences is also called "spiritual" in a particular social context.

These features are theoretically valuable because they make the phenomenological map responsive both to species-wide aspects of RSEs and to cultural, traditional, and personal considerations, while keeping the existential meaningfulness of some RSEs clearly in mind. This approach to mapping the territory of RSEs also clearly embraces mundane religious experiences such as Seder meals and committee meetings along with the especially meaningful ultimacy experiences. These features overcome difficulties in existing maps of the territory of RSEs, many of which oversimplify the territory without due notice.

Despite the fact that RSEs constitute only a small part of human experience as a whole, this way of mapping embraces a staggering diversity of RSEs. This presents a problem. There are so many levels of meaning, varieties of emotion, and social impacts implicated that it is impossible to speak of RSEs as having a single distinctive type of neural representation, a unique type of social significance, or a singular value. Moreover, if we narrow our view to small groups of experiences, we forgo the opportunity to look for patterns that yield understanding of meaning and value, and we ignore the fact that many aspects of RSEs must depend on evolutionarily stabilized, which is to say species-wide, cognitive and emotional brain processes. In squarely facing this problem, I sought to identify a maximal subclass of RSEs that depends only on virtually species-wide brain features for its neural representation. These were called the "intense experiences." While intense experiences constitute only a fraction of the territory of RSEs as a whole, they are the closest we can come to an extensive species-wide class of experiences. This makes them essential for assessing the meaning and value of RSEs.

This, then, is the *intensity hypothesis*: that there is such a maximal subclass of RSEs, that it can be conceived as a subclass of ultimacy experiences, that it includes experiences that some people may be willing to call religious and other experiences that few would call religious, that this class depends on evolutionarily stabilized aspects of human neurology, and that the neural and social capacity for intense experiences is a key defining factor in evolutionarily modern human beings. The evidence for the intensity hypothesis is more speculative than for the neural mediation hypothesis because it involves claims about the evolutionary past and about species-wide features of human neurology. Nonetheless, the evidence is compelling.

The idea of a maximal subclass of RSEs that draws on species-wide neural capacities is relatively unproblematic. The deeper difficulty is identifying the boundaries and characteristics of this class and arguing that the class is large enough to play a significant role in assessing the meaning and value of RSEs. The intensity hypothesis asserts that this subclass, while small relative to the entire territory of RSEs, is large enough to have distinctive phenomenological characteristics and to play a vital role in the evaluation of RSEs. And this is what makes the intensity hypothesis both important and controversial. Portions of the argument – especially Chapter 5 on the cognitive reliability of RSEs and parts of Chapter 6 on the social embedding of RSEs – depend significantly on the intensity hypothesis and would have to be reframed if it proved to be fatally flawed. The remainder of the book focuses on the wider domain of RSEs and does not depend crucially on the intensity hypothesis.

Chapter 4 attempts to identify the territory of intense experiences with more precision, and also to isolate the phenomenological components of intense experiences. Intensity is not the neurologist's high-pitched activation alone; it also involves breadth of activation that produces subjective experiences of great meaningfulness, connecting normally distinct parts of life together in one complex state of conscious awareness, often difficult to put into words. I concluded that there were at least five distinct "faces" of depth-and-breadth intensity, probably corresponding to five partially overlapping but distinguishable species-wide neurological capacities: depth, horizon, scale, complexity, and mystery. This is not a typology in the sense that intense experiences are asserted to come in one or another of five flavors. Rather, intense experiences combine these five neurologically rooted elements in various proportions and modalities to produce existentially gripping and memorable events that sometimes give rise to stunning changes in beliefs and behaviors.

Chapter 4 also makes a preliminary, speculative attempt to identify the species-wide neurological processes giving rise to the five faces of intensity. I argued that each of the five is evolutionarily intelligible as an intensification of the familiar capacities for sensory perception and inference. The upshot of this is that the types of experiences that are rooted in the capacities for intensity – both religious and non-religious varieties – are highly meaningful, produce great cultural exertions and artistic creativity, and yield formative practical and aesthetic convictions that orient and guide individual and collective human life. On this view, therefore, RSEs are far broader in their application and effects than those authorized and encouraged within organized religious traditions, and thus are far more richly related to human culture and existence than religious experiences alone.

The theological import of this is immediate: we should look for theologically significant experiences both within and outside the culturally variable domains of religion, and we should expect to find ultimacy not just in religious practices and beliefs and communities, but lying at the intense root of every aspect of human life. Insofar as intense experiences engage us with the depth, horizon, scale, complexity, and mystery of life, these experiences are effective means of exploring the valuational dynamics and structures of reality itself, and are thus an indispensable opening for understanding ultimate reality and our place within it.

Chapter 5 pursues these insights in search of an answer to one of the most perpetually urgent issues surrounding RSEs, namely, their cognitive reliability. That is, do RSEs reliably produce true beliefs? In conversation with the complex philosophical and theological literature on this topic, this chapter furnished an answer to this question. But answering for all of RSEs is impossible, such is their diversity, so I focused on the cognitive reliability of intense experiences. This approach takes advantage of the circumscribed character of intense experiences while extending the reliability case beyond strictly religious experiences; it capitalizes on the fact that intense experiences appear in evolutionary perspective to be intensifications of ordinary sense experience, which inspires an ecological-semiotic theory of religious perceptual engagement; and it escapes the unhelpfully narrow religious-tradition-specific character of almost all existing arguments about the cognitive reliability of religious experiences.

My conclusion was not supportive of the reliability of tradition-specific beliefs that people typically trace back to RSEs. For example, "I felt God's presence with me, comforting me, and communicating with me" describes an experience that can give rise to beliefs such as "God exists," "God cares about me," "God is an intentional personal being with awareness and will who communicates." I concluded that the complex cognitive-emotional journey from intense experience to interpretation to belief formation is not generally reliable. At the same time, I argued that observing three basic conditions – a naturalistic cosmology, an ecological-semiotic account of perception as dynamic engagement, and a symbolic account of religious cognitions – increases rational entitlement to presume cognitive reliability of RSEs, insofar as they are intense experiences or derive substantially from intense experiences. If we weaken any of these three conditions, we damage entitlement to presume cognitive reliability. By contrast, if we uphold all three, we increase this entitlement while also significantly constraining the kinds of interpretation that can reasonably attach to RSEs.

Here we see the value of the intensity hypothesis. While not confirming the cognitive reliability of religious experiences in a way that many philosophers and theologians would want, it isolates precisely that domain of RSEs that can in fact produce reliable cognitions under certain specifiable conditions. Theologically embedded in this is a rational approach to analyzing the various roles that RSEs play in making sense of the problem of religious pluralism. Also on offer is a way of speaking theologically about the profound sanctity of everyday life. Wherever intense experiences engage us authentically with the valuational depths of reality – whether in a glorious sunset, a traumatic episode, a thought-provoking idea, or a captivating curve – there we find the holy, and it is sanctified through being manifested as holy in that experience of intensity. Finally, I noted that even cognitively unreliable experiences can still foster authentic transformational engagement, which may be the most important consideration in evaluating the functional effects of RSEs.

The brain-group nexus hypothesis

Chapter 6 attempts to answer the double question of the evolutionary origins of RSEs and the social significance of these experiences. While these questions are not normally asked together, in an evolutionary perspective they immediately entail one another. My answer to these questions takes the form of the *brain-group nexus hypothesis*, which asserts that brains and groups are mutually conditioning realities, that the brain-group nexus can be represented as a dynamical system with regions of stability and transition dynamics that move the system between equilibrium states, and that the brain-group nexus so modeled is the optimal framework for interpreting both the evolutionary origins and social effects of RSEs.

The dynamical-system model of the brain-group nexus draws heavily on the typically disconnected disciplinary insights of the sociology of knowledge, the epidemiology of representations, and social neuroscience. It posits a pre-Neolithic equilibrium state for human social life that held sway from the so-called "great leap forward" about 50,000 years ago until the advent of agriculture and animal domestication about 10,000 years ago. This is the fundamental equilibrium state for modern humans, the one requiring the least maintenance energy, and the one to which we would return should there be a complete loss of civilizational knowledge and habits of behavior. The argument is that, since the Neolithic, human groups migrated back and forth between the pre-Neolithic hunter-gatherer equilibrium lifestyle and the agriculture, towns, and domestication equilibrium lifestyle, with more and more groups inhabiting the latter. Town life requires special forms of cooperation, as do agriculture and domestication, so the associated social equilibrium has higher maintenance-energy demands. But post-Neolithic lifestyles are still relatively simple and low-energy, requiring few people to read and write or know arithmetic, and relying on brutality to keep order where necessary. It is the civilizations and social experiments that come after the agriculture, towns, and domestication equilibrium that begin to make truly formidable energy demands on the brain-group nexus.

This is the way of human social life, according to the dynamical systems model of the brain-group nexus: it has involved a fanning out across an energy–cognitive-complexity hillside seeking stable equilibria to inhabit and from which to explore the depths of reality and possibilities for society. Cognitive evolution drives hominid species and finally human beings toward the pre-Neolithic equilibrium; cultural evolution drives groups of human beings, with their pre-Neolithic equilibrium cognitive capacities and potential, up and across the energy–complexity hillside. As they fan out, exploring a host of equilibrium social arrangements, they dream social visions and then commit ever larger amounts of energy to create and stabilize them – energy in the form of educational practices, cultural expression, political organization, and social control. The sociology of knowledge describes how brains in groups invest energy in constructing a social reality. The epidemiology of representations describes how ideas survive and spread, including especially ideas necessary for stable social life. Social neuroscience describes the intricate architecture that links individual brains in the elaborate network that is a social group and explains how the brain makes possible the mutual influence of individuals and groups.

This network of theories constitutes a tremendously fruitful environment for the interpretation of the evolutionary origins of RSEs and for their social effects. I argued that the capacity for depth-and-breadth intensity helps to define modern humans because it requires a degree of intricate neural connectivity not present in our closest surviving evolutionary relatives. The full flowering of this neural connectivity probably dates to the "great leap forward" of 50,000 years ago, with its explosion of cultural expression and hunting creativity. The capacity for intense experiences opened human beings up to the valuational depths of reality, helping them construct social arrangements as lattice-like structures above a vast abyss of meaning and power. This drove them to ritual practices in an effort to explore and control the abysmal depths they could now sense, with the effect of structuring human social life in the way the sociology of knowledge describes. If the intensification of sense experience in early modern humans allowed them to perceive formerly hidden valuational worlds of meaning and to picture new forms of social life, then their ritual attempts to control this awesome reality, and to regulate access to it, created an energy source that was capable of powering the realization of new possibilities for social life they were picturing. Intense RSEs lie at the heart of this energy source because they serve to commit individuals to corporate identities and social engineering projects.

This framework for interpreting the dynamical systems model of the brain-group nexus is built around a powerful fact: beginning in the pre-Neolithic equilibrium, cognitive evolution was massively outpaced by cultural evolution. So the cognitive equipment in place in the modern human version of the hunter-gatherer lifestyle is much like what we operate with now. Our tendencies to supernatural beliefs and superstition derive from the overactive pattern-recognition, intention-attribution, and cause-detection skills that were adaptive in the pre-Neolithic equilibrium. Indeed they may be adaptive now in some settings, particularly if they foster cooperation through facilitating hard-to-fake signs of sincerity that costly signaling theory analyzes.

Merely to notice this is enough to condemn all religious experiences, according to the new atheist writers. They explain toxic expressions of religion in terms of our undiagnosed and unresisted tendencies to supernaturalism and superstition, and then quickly reduce all forms of religious experience to these most toxic manifestations. But the intensity engine at the heart of human social creativity belongs to every part of human life, not just religion, as do our thoroughly documented cognitive liabilities and our tendencies to jump to conclusions, resort to insults, and escalate spats into violence. Marx was essentially correct that religion could not be eliminated directly because it compensated people for suffering and misery, and also essentially correct that religion would become less desperately important as socio-economic justice became a more prominent feature of human life. But he, too, ignored the fact that the most basic power source for religion is not its role in legitimating ideology and exercising social control. Rather, religion's power source is also the power source for cultural creativity more generally: the human sensitivity to the intense valuational landscape of reality.

This axiological sensitivity was made possible by our capacity for intense religious experiences and for intense non-religious but spiritual experiences related to aesthetic sensitivities and circumstantial extremities. This capacity for intense awareness cannot be eliminated, and we would not want to eliminate it, because doing so would destroy everything about cultural life that we highly regard. The best we can do is to understand the brain-group nexus in enough detail so that we can efficiently deploy our energy-intensive educational resources to combat toxic expressions of our stunning capacity for self-sacrificial commitment to ideas and values and possibilities. Thus, as we puddle-jump up and across the energy–cognitive-complexity hillside, a better future consists not in eliminating religion or in regulating RSEs, but rather in helping everyone toward a shared understanding of the brain-group nexus and how our taste for depth-and-breadth intensity powers our exploration of its manifold possibilities. After that, RSEs may well persist, as would religious traditions and groups. But those same traditions and groups would then have better resources for preventing the turn to toxicity than the variable moral rules they deploy now. And individuals would accept and savor their strange and wonderful RSEs without falling prey to socially supported credulity in interpreting them.

This vision for the future of RSEs is tested in Chapter 7. Focusing on technologies for producing RSEs, the chapter imagines how knowledge of their neural embodiment and social embedding would impact their role in human life some decades from now. I argue that the contemporary enhancements of traditional botanical, psycho-social, and meditation techniques, as well as novel technologies arriving only now, will profoundly change the way we regard RSEs. To have such fine-tuned control over them may not be a problem for the religious naturalist, for whom this does not threaten the possibility of authentic RSEs, but many religious people will vigorously resist such developments. Indeed, when an interpretative framework insists that the possibility of authenticity of RSEs depends on the fiction that fine-tuned control is impossible, that framework is deeply questionable. Which frameworks fall under this criticism? This remains to be seen, as fine-tuned technologies of control become widely available, but I suspect that supernatural frameworks for interpreting RSEs will take the heaviest hits. It is those frameworks, after all, that make the most pointed assumptions about the causal architecture of RSEs, and fine-tuned technologies of the sort imagined in this chapter effortlessly show that such supernaturalist assumptions play no useful role in explaining the production and regulation of RSEs.

The religious naturalism hypothesis

At several points in the book, I stressed that metaphysical arguments such as those between naturalism and supernaturalism cannot be resolved in knock-down fashion, but that cumulative weight of evidence can slowly shift plausibility structures in such a way as to leave a metaphysical theory struggling for life. I pointed out that the graveyard of metaphysical ideas demonstrates that this happens, and often enough to make the graveyard rather large. Despite this defense of the partial tractability of metaphysical disputes, I freely acknowledge that the battle between pro-religious naturalism and pro-religious supernaturalism is an ancient one in all cultures and surely one of the most intractable metaphysical debates of all. Certainly it shows no signs of ending any time soon. The world continues to be dominated by human imaginations and groups tuned to supernatural instincts. Religious beliefs and practices are infused with supernatural worldviews. And RSEs are taken by many to be the fundamental wellspring of evidence for supernaturalism. I have criticized every part of this flimsy association of cognitive and emotional habits of mind, but I am clearly in a minority. It is an honorable, ancient, and prestigious minority, to be sure, but a minority nonetheless.

To make matters worse for this perpetually beleaguered minority, there are new and sharp divisions in the naturalist camp (for a debate that surfaces some of these divisions, see Haidt 2007b). Throughout the argument I have engaged my naturalist compatriots and pressed those whose views neglect to give a serious account of the axiological depth structures and flows of reality. The idea of a religious naturalism appears to some naturalists as a wistful and ultimately foolish compromise with toxic institutional forces devoted to keeping human beings in an easily controlled state of ignorance. Some go so far as to label religious naturalists the greatest evildoers of all, consorting with the religious enemy and failing to take a stand where a stand must be taken for the sake of justice and the future of the human project. I have tried to show how deeply mistaken this criticism is. RSEs are not going anywhere, and so neither is one of the primary power sources of religion. The naturalist's challenge, rightly framed, is not to posture at eliminating such experiences and all traces of their existential and social effects, toxic or otherwise, but rather to understand, appreciate, savor, and manage RSEs.

The book's argument has shown how religious naturalism is better suited to a comprehensive interpretation of all relevant disciplinary insights into RSEs – better suited than both anti-religious naturalism and any form of supernatural worldview. Some elements of this argument have been philosophically subtle, as when Chapter 5 traced the logical force of religious naturalism in arguments over the cognitive reliability of RSEs. Others have been obvious, as when Chapter 7 pointed out the dependence of supernaturalist frameworks on credulity regarding the degree to which RSEs can be induced and regulated using existing and emerging technologies. I judge the combined effect of these aspects of the argument to be compelling. Reality does have axiological depth, and some of our RSEs make us aware of it and give us purchase on it. But we do not need supernaturalism to explain it, and supernaturalism gets in the way of a properly rich understanding of it. It is not a knock-down case. But it is strong enough to shift plausibility away from pro-religious supernaturalism and toward pro-religious naturalism.

The conditional value hypothesis

Implied in the whole sweep of the book's argument is an assertion of the conditional value of RSEs. There are many points at which I have criticized common interpretations of RSEs, as well as some reigning views of their meaning and value within organized religious traditions. These criticisms have not been wholesale dismissals; they have typically taken the form of pointing out one-sidedness in interpretation or failure to account for some basic evidence. On the whole, existing interpretations, even those operating within just one or two disciplines, are loaded with relevant insights, as are the religious traditions whose practices encode longstanding and extensively tested wisdom about the management and interpretation of RSEs.

In their less contentious moments, most people – from eliminative materialists to rabid anti-religious naturalists, from atheistic Buddhists to passionate supernaturalistic theists, and from the excessively educated to the desperately undereducated – can agree on the wonder and perils of life. Almost everyone is highly attuned to one or another form of aesthetic possibility, whether it is exquisitely organized patches of color on canvas or exotically blended tastes from the kitchen, a staggering athletic accomplishment or the simplicity of self-giving acts of compassion. There was a time in the evolutionary past when the human species was blind to almost all of this. We could see and hear, we could taste and smell and touch, but we could not access the wondrous valuational depths of reality. Then something happened and we could. However this is explained – and I have offered a significantly speculative explanation in this book – this new-found capacity marks the beginning of the era of modern humans and simultaneously the birth of the capacity for central types of RSEs. Everything is different with this degree of axiological depth perception now available to human beings; it is better than switching from monocular to binocular vision, and better than trading in black-and-white television for high-definition color.

Once the capacity for RSEs exists, they prove prodigiously useful and quickly produce a host of side-effects. Social life becomes more complex, cultural expression becomes more refined, and the possibility of regulating the mysterious axiological chasm now manifested as lurking in the midst of human life becomes a sacred imperative. Thus, the birth of the capacity for RSEs also marks the beginning of elaborate mechanisms of social enabling and control – and they have their own side-effects, such as intricate webs of interpretation that perpetuate cognitive delusion, and ideological rationalizations of dangerous and ignorant acts that define human life at its most toxic and self-defeating.

To be obsessed with solving the problematic aspects of RSEs is completely understandable. To eliminate them or the religions to which some of them help to give rise is utterly impossible. Even if religions disappear or become quaint elements in personal identity rather than the roaring tsunamis of social power that they are now, RSEs will persist – differently framed to be sure, but still the power source and the means of access to a great deal of what is wonderful in the human purchase on reality. Eliminating these experiences is not only futile and impossible; it would also drain the very lifeblood from the human project. So far from regulating access to the axiological chasm in our midst, therefore, the sacred task of the religious naturalist is to understand RSEs, to criticize manipulation of them, to raise consciousness about them, and to treasure everything that they tell us, in their indirect and intriguing way, about ultimate reality.

I have been describing a new world of understanding, in which the causal factors powering RSEs are understood, in which their cultural conditioning and social effects are recognized, and in which ignorance of the cognitive liabilities that produce mistaken interpretations of RSEs is no longer needed in order to appreciate them as meaningful and valuable features of human life. In that new world, we draw strength from RSEs not because they confirm the existence of a supernatural world beyond this one, but because they testify to the beauty and complexity of the world we treasure and strive to enrich. We derive moral orientation from those experiences not because they convey moral commands from supernatural beings in a position to make demands upon us but because those experiences help us detect the potential for the good and the true and the beautiful in our amazing surroundings. We find meaning in RSEs not because of what they supposedly reveal about other spiritual worlds but because they open up to us the value-laden depths of this world.

It is through engaging the richness of nature that we can understand and feel its depths, internalize the stunning vision of our natural environment that its axiological structures and fluxing intensities reveal, and thus decide how to comport ourselves in relation to it. For the religious naturalist, these only ever partially plumbed depths of nature are the true referent of religious talk about deities and salvation, liberation and enlightenment. Properly understood, and carefully disentangled from our cognitive reflex to construct supernaturalist explanations, RSEs, particularly in respect of their intensity, are the means by which we become aware of this profound spiritual reality – a reality that defies the grasping tentacles of religious understanding. They are some of the ways by which we learn to engage that reality with every fiber of our beings, if we so choose.

This new world may not be fully with us for decades or even centuries. But it will arrive, as surely as the sun rises, unless civilizational disaster blots out the sun and destroys this fragile future. Regardless of its future prospects, this new future is available right now for those who have the eyes to see the dawn. There are things to fear about the new day and many adjustments in religious self-understanding are required. But there is great promise as well. RSEs will always be with us, because that is our evolutionary heritage, our birthright, and the best means we have to engage the spiritual depths of reality. The question before us now, and increasingly in the years to come, is whether we require ignorance of the workings of RSEs to appreciate their meaning and value. If so, then we will resist new knowledge with a fury born of desperation – desperation commensurate with the catastrophic failure of supernatural worldviews. Or we will reject both supernaturalism and RSEs and pitifully pretend that our world has no spiritual depths out of grief and fear of the uncertainties that result when these experiences no longer enjoy supernatural authorization. Alternatively, if we learn to appreciate the meaning and value of RSEs, even after knowledge overcomes ignorance of their workings and supernaturalism fades away, then a whole new adventure begins.

Our cognitive deficits are almost irresistible, so a collapse of civilization would cause us to revert to default supernaturalist readings of RSEs. But if enlightened religious wisdom traditions persist, if science remains balanced by humanities and the arts, and if we continue to educate one another about what we discover about all dimensions of social and natural reality, then we can learn to control the cognitive liabilities that continually give rise to supernaturalism and superstition. At the same time, we will be warranted in affirming the meaning and value of RSEs, and particularly spiritually intense versions of ordinary experience that help us to detect the dimensions of depth, horizon, scale, complexity, and mystery within natural reality. Such experiences are indicators of the aesthetic, moral, conceptual, and spiritual richness of human life in its wondrous natural environment.

What I have described is a possible future for human beings. It is a future that promises greater awareness of cognitive error surrounding the interpretation of RSEs. It is a future that promises a decisive decline in the extreme violence and toxic irrationality that RSEs so easily spark and rationalize. It is a future in which RSEs can increase appreciation of the wonders of our natural environment and of experiential and religious diversity. At this point in human history, we may be able only barely to imagine a world in which we can be critically appreciative of RSEs regardless of our personal religious or anti-religious convictions. Yet the flourishing of the human project, and perhaps its very continuation, may require that we both imagine such a future and succeed in realizing it.

Glossary of key terms

CHAPTER 1

supernaturalism the affirmation of disembodied intentionality.

supranaturalism the affirmation of ultimate reality as a personal being with awareness and purposes and powers to act in the world.

super/supranaturalism the affirmation of both supernaturalism and supranaturalism; the dominant viewpoint within most religious traditions.

religious naturalism a religiously positive form of naturalism that rejects both supernaturalism and supranaturalism; an ancient view that persists within all religious traditions as a minority voice, usually on the underside of dominant super/supranaturalism.

CHAPTER 2

mind–body problem (a.k.a. the "hard problem") the problem of relating mental phenomena as we experience them to the physical processes of the body as described by the natural sciences, especially neuroscience.

eliminative materialism a radical approach to the mind–body problem that insists that mental phenomena as described by common sense or "folk psychology" do not exist, and thus can be eliminated from descriptions of human thought and behavior.

epiphenomenalism an approach to the mind–body problem that allows for the existence of mental phenomena but denies them causal efficacy; thus the qualitative aspect of thought is an "epiphenomenon" – an inconsequential by-product – of material processes (sometimes likened to steam from a boiling kettle).

dualism an approach to the mind–body problem that affirms the existence of mental phenomena and grants them causal efficacy, while affirming that material and mental processes belong to distinct parts of reality, indicating a major "ontological divide" (see below) in nature. Some forms of dualism (e.g. Descartes') allow for causal interaction between material and physical processes;

266

others – sometimes called psychophysical parallelism – assert correlation without causation.

emergentism   an approach to the mind–body problem that looks for the emergence of mental phenomena from material processes of sufficient complexity.

di-polar monism   an approach to the mind–body problem that asserts that mental and material properties are aspects of a single "stuff"; monism embraces the existence and causal efficacy of both material and mental phenomena while at the same time denying any kind of ontological divide between them.

ontology   for this discussion, ontology refers to theories about the kinds of entities that exist; dualism asserts an ontological divide insofar as it insists that there are two fundamentally distinct kinds of entities – mental and physical.

epistemology   theories about knowledge and the branch of philosophy that deals with such theories. Dualism creates special epistemological problems, because in order to know the physical world minds must somehow cross an ontological divide. Thus ontology is directly relevant to epistemology.

functional naturalism   a functional naturalism (a.k.a. methodological naturalism) considers only causes of mental phenomena that are experimentally tractable within current methods of neurology.

naturalistic ontology   a naturalistic ontology asserts that there are no ontological divides. Eliminative materialism and di-polar monism are both categories of naturalistic ontology, but quite different with respect to inclusiveness.

neural mediation hypothesis   the mind does nothing we can detect that is not exhaustively mediated by and expressed in the brain.

functional magnetic resonance imaging (fMRI)   tracks oxygen usage in the brain by means of the magnetic properties of oxygenated blood; this oxygen usage is then correlated with neural activity.

positron emission tomography (PET)   tracks short periods of metabolic process associated with brain activity by tagging basic chemicals of cell metabolism with radioactive substances and injecting them into the bloodstream.

single photon emission computed tomography (SPECT)   similar to PET, permits tracking of metabolic processes over longer periods of time.

magnetoencephalography (MEG)   measures magnetic fields caused by electrical activity near the brain's surface.

electroencephalography (EEG)   measures voltage differences caused by electrical activity near the brain's surface. EEG readings have good temporal resolution but poor spatial resolution. Quantitative EEG (qEEG) produces localization and connectivity information from detailed EEG results using computer analysis.

modularity   a theory of functional localization in the brain; strong versions of modularity assert that the brain is an aggregate of functionally independent and domain-specific modules.

Phenomenology of Consciousness Inventory (PCI)   a method of retrospective phenomenological analysis, a PCI gives a quantitative profile of the contents and qualities of personal consciousness during a past event along twenty-six measures, grouped into twelve major dimensions. Each of these profiles is an individual quantitative signature of a particular conscious experience.

general quantitative signature (GQS)   a pattern of individual quantitative signatures that indicates general characteristics of particular kinds of experiences. For example, individual quantitative signatures of experiences of deep grief may all exhibit a common pattern that can be extracted as a GQS.

CHAPTER 3

religious experiences   used in a broad way to encompass the experiences that people have by virtue of being religious or being involved in religious groups; reflects common usage.

spiritual experiences   encompasses all ultimacy experiences and some of the domain of religious experiences that are not of ultimate significance for people; reflects common usage.

RSEs   the combined domains of the usage-determined categories of religious experiences and spiritual experiences.

vivid experiences   spectacular experiences extending beyond the borders of the officially religious into a wealth of existentially significant (ultimate) and strange (anomalous) experiences.

ultimacy experiences   the domain of existentially significant experiences which engage us with our ultimate concerns.

anomalous experiences   out-of-the-ordinary, where ordinary is defined partly by organism-in-environment habits and partly by social convention.

decentering   a neurocognitive process whereby an individual suspends a self-construct's control over attention and behavior in order first to search semantic memory for alternate self-models better suited to the individual's needs, and subsequently to integrate that superior self into attention and behavioral goals.

CHAPTER 4

intense experiences   a subset of ultimacy experiences involving: (i) strong and broad neural activation, corresponding to existential potency and wide awareness, involving both strength of feeling and interconnectedness of ideas, memories, and emotions in such a way as to engage a person with ultimate existential and spiritual concerns and leverage significant personal or social effects; (ii) brain connectivity not present in other species and probably not in humans prior to 50,000 years ago, and the so-called "great leap forward"; and (iii) an intensification of ordinary sense perception that permits (without guaranteeing) cognitively reliable perception of, and imaginative engagement with, the aesthetic and moral depths of reality.

intensity hypothesis a mixture of empirical claims, theoretical interpretations, and descriptive elements pertaining to intense experiences. Centrally, the neural capacity for intensity in the depth-and-breadth sense is the driving force of human spirituality and one of several essential evolutionary building blocks of religion. Along with pattern-recognition, intentionality-attribution, dissociability, and suggestiveness capacities in human beings, the capacity for intensity prepared the way for the emergence of complex forms of religious experience. *Significance*: the intensity hypothesis paves the way for a species-wide theory of religious and theological experiences, beneath their intricately varying cultural and circumstantial embeddings. In particular, it furnishes an optimal basis for evaluating the cognitive reliability of RSEs and for studying RSEs across cultures.

CHAPTER 5

cognition refers to all of the processes that pertain to knowledge and information processing in animals, including human beings. This involves perception and memory, reasoning and imagination, as well as knowledge and belief.

reliability question to the extent that RSEs tend to produce true beliefs, we judge the experiences to be cognitively reliable. To the extent that those experiences tend to produce false beliefs, we think of the experiences as cognitively unreliable.

CHAPTER 6

brain-group nexus the system of interacting brains-in-groups that is characteristic of many social animal species, including human beings.

brain-group nexus hypothesis the brain-group nexus is a dynamical system that migrates through a landscape of possibilities for social arrangements. This dynamical system exhibits self-organization consisting of several equilibrium states and characteristic ways of transitioning between them. Equilibrium states are social arrangements within this landscape of possibilities for social arrangements that are stable relative to the cognitive capacities of brains and environmental conditions. RSEs play crucial roles both in the maintenance of equilibrium social arrangements and in the sometimes revolutionary transitions between them.

self-organized system a dynamic physical system whose internal architecture permits the spontaneous production of patterned behavior.

epidemiology of representations the theory of the way that ideas spread through populations (like diseases spread); it assumes that human cognitive abilities make some ideas more "catchy."

minimally counterintuitive beliefs beliefs that violate folk physics and folk psychology in one memorable way; e.g. beings that are like humans in every way except that they are invisible.

ideology (in the neutral, descriptive sense) the crafty deployment or reflexive use of shared ideas and compelling narratives to rationalize, regulate, and revolutionize equilibrium social arrangements.

CHAPTER 7

sociology of knowledge describes the mutual conditioning of individuals and social groups in terms of a cyclical process of externalization, objectivation, and internalization.

externalization refers to human self-expression in the social and cultural realms, such as the creation of cultural ideas and artifacts, the development of styles of interpersonal behavior, the public expression of dreams and desires, and the construction of political and legal systems.

objectivation refers to the way our social expressions take on a life of their own so that they bite back, as when traffic rules that we create cause us to get a ticket when we break them.

internalization refers to the way we come to take for granted objectivated social reality – to the point that we accept its benefits and limitations unconsciously.

maximum stability an equilibrium state of the brain-group nexus is maximally stable when the externalization-objectivation-internalization cycle is not challenged. This occurs when (i) the cycle is transparent to individuals; (ii) individuals are existentially invested in not questioning or challenging the cycle; and (iii) the cost of questioning or challenging the cycle is high.

social function of religion religion cosmologizes operating principles of its social group, treating them as supernaturally commanded moral laws, unquestionable because of their divine origins. To challenge the cultural system is thus to challenge the gods themselves, who imposed it and who command its maintenance and stability. Religion is thus a vital resource for social control.

References

Allport, G. W. and Ross, J. M. 1967. "Personal Religious Orientation and Prejudice." *Journal of Personality and Social Psychology* 5/4: 432–43.

Alper, Matthew. 2001. *The "God" Part of the Brain: A Scientific Interpretation of Human Spirituality and God.* New York: Rogue.

Alston, William P. 1991. *Perceiving God: The Epistemology of Religious Experience.* Ithaca, NY: Cornell University Press.

Alter, M. G. 1999. "Christian Experience Inventory." In Hill and Hood 1999 (160–62).

Ames, Edward Scribner. 1910. *The Psychology of Religious Experience.* Boston and New York: Houghton Mifflin.

Andresen, Jensine (ed.). 2001. *Religion in Mind: Cognitive Perspectives on Religious Belief, Ritual, and Experience.* Cambridge University Press.

Angelini, F. J., Kumar V. K., and Chandler, L. 1999. "The Harvard Group Scale of Hypnotic Susceptibility and Related Instruments: Individual and Group Administrations." *International Journal of Clinical and Experimental Hypnosis* 47/3 (July): 236–50.

Arecchi, F. T., Meucci, R., Puccioni, G., and Tredicce, J. 1982. "Experimental Evidence of Subharmonic Bifurcations, Multistability, and Turbulence in a Q-Switched Gas Laser." *Physical Review Letters* 49/17: 1217–20.

Arnot, Robert, Finger, Stanley, and Smith, C. U. M. 2003. *Trepanation: History, Discovery, Theory.* Lisse, The Netherlands: Swets & Zeitlinger.

Ashbrook, James B. 1984. *The Human Mind and the Mind of God: Theological Promise in Brain Research.* Lanham, MD: University Press of America.

Ashbrook, James B. and Albright, Carol Rausch. 1997. *The Humanizing Brain: Where Religion and Neuroscience Meet.* Cleveland: Pilgrim Press.

Atran, Scott. 2002. *In Gods We Trust: The Evolutionary Landscape of Religion.* Oxford University Press.

———. 2003. "Genesis of Suicide Terrorism." *Science* 299 (March 7): 1534.

———. 2004. "Religion's Evolutionary Landscape: Counterintuition, Commitment, Compassion, Communion." *Behavioral and Brain Sciences* 27/6: 713–730. (Discussion of this article appears on pp. 731–70.)

Aukst-Margetic, B., Jakovljevic, M., Margetic, B., Biscan, M., and Samija, M. 2005. "Religiosity, Depression and Pain in Patients with Breast Cancer." *General Hospital Psychiatry* 27/4: 250–55.

Austin, James. 1998. *Zen and the Brain: Toward an Understanding of Meditation and Consciousness*. Cambridge, MA: MIT Press.

Ayer, Alfred Jules. [1936] 1946. *Language, Truth, and Logic*, reprinted with new introduction. London: Victor Gollancz; New York: Oxford University Press.

Azari, Nina P., Nickel, J., Wunderlich, G., Niedeggen, M., Hefter, H., Tellmann, L., *et al.* 2001. "Neural Correlates of Religious Experience." *European Journal of Neuroscience* 13/8: 1649–52.

Baetz, M., Larson, D. B., Marcoux, G., Bowen, R., and Griffin, R. 2002. "Canadian Psychiatric Inpatient Religious Commitment: An Association with Mental Health." *Canadian Journal of Psychiatry* 47/2: 159–66.

Bagger, Matthew C. 1999. *Religious Experience, Justification, and History*. Cambridge and New York: Cambridge University Press.

Bak, Per. 1996. *How Nature Works: The Science of Self-Organized Criticality*. New York: Springer.

Bargh, J. A. and Chartrand, T. L. 1999. "The Unbearable Automaticity of Being." *American Psychologist* 54/7: 462–79.

Bargh, J. A., Chen, M., and Burrows, L. 1996. "Automaticity of Social Behavior: Direct Effects of Trait Construct and Stereotype Activation on Action." *Journal of Personality and Social Psychology* 71/2: 230–44.

Barkow, Jerome, Cosmides, Leda, and Tooby, John (eds.). 1992. *The Adapted Mind: Evolutionary Psychology and the Generation of Culture*. Oxford University Press.

Barrett, Nathaniel and Wildman, Wesley J. 2009. "Seeing Is Believing? How Reinterpreting the Direct Realism of Perception As Dynamic Engagement Alters the Justificatory Force of Religious Experience." *International Journal for Philosophy of Religion* 66/2: 71–86.

Bartlett, S. J., Piedmont, R., Bilderback, A., Matsumoto, A. K., and Bathon, J. M. 2003. "Spirituality, Well-Being, and Quality of Life in People with Rheumatoid Arthritis." *Arthritis & Rheumatism – Arthritis Care & Research* 49/6: 778–83.

Batson, C. Daniel, Shoenrade, P., and Ventis, W. Larry. 1993. *Religion and the Individual: A Social-Psychological Perspective*. New York: Oxford University Press.

Bear, David M. 1979. "Temporal Lobe Epilepsy – A Syndrome of Sensory-Limbic Hyperconnection." *Cortex* 15/3: 357–84.

Bear, David M. and Fedio, P. 1977. "Quantitative Analysis of Interictal Behavior in Temporal Lobe Epilepsy." *Archives of Neurology* 34/8: 454–67.

Bear, David M., Levin, Kenneth, Blumer, Dietrich, Chetham, Diedre, and Ryder, John. 1982. "Interictal Behaviour in Hospitalised Temporal Lobe Epileptics: Relationship to Idiopathic Psychiatric Syndromes." *Journal of Neurology, Neurosurgery, and Psychiatry* 45/6: 481–88.

Beauregard, Mario 2007. "Mind Does Really Matter: Evidence from Neuroimaging Studies of Emotional Self-Regulation, Psychotherapy, and Placebo Effect." *Progress in Neurobiology* 81/4: 218–36.

Beauregard, Mario and O'Leary, D. 2007. *The Spiritual Brain: A Neuroscientist's Case for the Existence of the Soul.* New York: HarperOne.

Beauregard, Mario and Paquette, Vincent. 2006. "Neural Correlates of a Mystical Experience in Carmelite Nuns." *Neuroscience Letter* 405/3: 186–90.

Bechtel, William. 1991. *Connectionism and Mind.* Oxford: Blackwell Publishers.

Beit-Hallahmi, B. and Argyle, M. 1997. *The Psychology of Religious Behavior, Belief, and Experience.* New York: Routledge.

Bellah, Robert N., Madsen, Richard, Sullivan, William M., Swidler, Ann, and Tipton, Steven M. 1991. *The Good Society.* New York: Knopf.

Benson, Herbert. 1975. *The Relaxation Response.* New York: Morrow.

1996. *Timeless Healing: The Power and Biology of Belief.* New York: Scribner.

Berg, J., Dickhaut, J., and McCabe, K. 1995. "Trust, Reciprocity and Social History." *Games and Economic Behavior* 10/1: 122–42.

Berger, Peter L. 1967. *The Sacred Canopy: Elements of a Sociological Theory of Religion.* Garden City, NY: Doubleday.

Berger, Peter L. and Huntington, Samuel P. (eds.). 2002. *Many Globalizations: Cultural Diversity in the Contemporary World.* New York and Oxford: Oxford University Press.

Berger, Peter L. and Luckmann, Thomas. 1966. *The Social Construction of Reality: A Treatise in the Sociology of Knowledge.* Garden City, NY: Doubleday.

Bloch, Maurice. 1992. *Prey into Hunter: The Politics of Religious Experience.* The Lewis Henry Morgan Lectures. Cambridge and New York: Cambridge University Press.

Boan, D. M. 1999. "Religious Expression Scale." In Hill and Hood 1999 (320–26).

Booth, J. N., Koren, S. A., and Persinger, M. A. 2005. "Increased Feelings of the Sensed Presence and Increased Geomagnetic Activity at the Time of the Experience During Exposures to Transcerebral Weak Complex Magnetic Fields." *International Journal of Neuroscience* 115/7: 1053–79.

Bosworth, H. B., Park, K. S., McQuoid, D. R., Hays, J. C., and Steffens. D. C. 2003. "The Impact of Religious Practice and Religious Coping on Geriatric Depression." *International Journal of Geriatric Psychiatry* 18/10: 905–14.

Bouckaert, J. and Dhaene, G. 2004. "Inter-Ethnic Trust and Reciprocity: Results of an Experiment with Small Businessmen." *European Journal of Political Economy* 20/4: 869–86.

Boyer, Pascal. 2001. *Religion Explained: The Evolutionary Origins of Religious Thought.* New York: Basic Books.

Braam, A. W., Hein, E., Deeg, D. J. H., Twisk, J. W. R., Beekman, A. T. F., and van Tilburg, W. 2004. "Religious Involvement and Six-Year Course of Depressive Symptoms in Older Dutch Citizens: Results from the Longitudinal Aging Study Amsterdam." *Journal of Aging and Health* 16/4: 467–89.

Breasted, James Henry. 1991. *The Edwin Smith Surgical Papyrus: Published in Facsimile and Hieroglyphic Translation and Commentary in Two Volumes.* Chicago: Oriental Institute of the University of Chicago.

Brinton, Howard H. 1996. *Quaker Journals: Varieties of Religious Experience among Friends*, 3rd edn. Wallingford, PA: Pendle Hill Publications.

Brothers, Leslie. 1997. *Friday's Footprint: How Society Shapes the Human Mind*. New York: Oxford University Press.

Brown, Warren and Caetano, Carla. 1992. "Conversion, Cognition, and Neuropsychology." In H. N. Maloney and S. Southard (eds.), *Handbook of Religious Conversion*. Birmingham, AL: Religious Education Press.

Bryant, Ernest and O'Connell, Daniel. 1971. "A Phonemic Analysis of Nine Samples of Glossolalic Speech." *Psychonomic Science* 22: 81–83.

Burhenn, H. 1995. "Philosophy and Religious Experience." In Hood 1995 (144–60).

Burke, Edmund. 1757. *A Philosophical Inquiry into the Origin of Our Ideas of the Sublime and the Beautiful* [published anonymously]. London: R. and J. Dodsley.

Burker, E. J., Evon, D. M., Sedway, J. A., and Egan, T. 2004. "Religious Coping, Psychological Distress and Disability among Patients with End-Stage Pulmonary Disease." *Journal of Clinical Psychology in Medical Settings* 11/3: 179–93.

Buss, David. 2007. *Evolutionary Psychology: The New Science of the Mind*, 3rd edn. Boston: Allyn & Bacon.

Byrne, David. 1998. *Complexity Theory and the Social Sciences: An Introduction*. New York: Routledge.

Byrne, Peter. 2000. "Perceiving God and Realism." *Philo* 3/2: 74–88.

Cacioppo, J. T. and Berntson, G. G. 2005. *Social Neuroscience*. Hove, UK: Psychology Press.

Cacioppo, John T., Visser, Penny S., and Pickett, Cynthia L. (eds.). 2005. *Social Neuroscience: People Thinking about People*. Cambridge, MA: MIT Press, 2005.

Callahan, Sidney. 2003. *Women Who Hear Voices: The Challenge of Religious Experience*. New York: Paulist Press.

Camazine, Scott, Deneubourg, Jena-Louis, Franks, Nigel R., Sneyd, James, Theraulaz, Guy, and Bonabeau, Eric (eds.). 2003. *Self Organization in Biological Systems*. Princeton University Press.

Campbell, Joseph. 1959. *The Masks of God*, vol. i, *Primitive Mythology*. New York: Viking Press.

—— 1962. *The Masks of God*, vol. ii, *Oriental Mythology*. New York: Viking Press.

—— 1964. *The Masks of God*, vol. iii, *Occidental Mythology*. New York: Viking Press.

—— 1968. *The Masks of God*, vol. iv, *Creative Mythology*. New York: Viking Press.

Cardeña, Etzel, Lynn, Steven Jay, and Krippner, Stanley (eds.). 2000. *Varieties of Anomalous Experience: Examining the Scientific Evidence*. Washington D.C.: American Psychological Association.

Carlson, L. E., Speca, M., Patel, K. D., and Goodey, E. 2004. "Mindfulness-Based Stress Reduction in Relation to Quality of Life, Mood, Symptoms of Stress and Levels of Cortisol, Dehydroepiandrosterone Sulfate

(DHEAS) and Melatonin in Breast and Prostate Cancer Outpatients." *Psychoneuroendochrinology* 29/4: 448–74.

Carruthers, Peter. 2006. *The Architecture of the Mind.* New York and Oxford: Oxford University Press.

Carruthers, Peter, Laurence, Stephen, and Stich, Stephen (eds.). 2005. *The Innate Mind,* vol. I, *Structure and Contents.* New York and Oxford: Oxford University Press.

2006. *The Innate Mind,* vol. II, *Culture and Cognition.* New York and Oxford: Oxford University Press.

2008. *The Innate Mind,* vol. III, *Foundations and the Future.* New York and Oxford: Oxford University Press.

Casey, Aggie and Benson, Herbert. 2005. *The Harvard Medical School Guide to Lowering Your Blood Pressure.* New York: McGraw-Hill.

Caston, Victor. 1997. "Epiphenomenalisms, Ancient and Modern." *Philosophical Review* 106/3: 309–63.

Cattoi, Thomas and McDaniel, June (eds.). In press. *Mystical Sensuality: Perceiving the Divine through the Human Body.* Basingstoke: Palgrave Macmillan.

Chalmers, David J. 1995. "Facing Up to the Problem of Consciousness." *Journal of Consciousness Studies* 2/3: 200–19.

1996. *The Conscious Mind: In Search of a Fundamental Theory.* New York: Oxford University Press.

Chudler, Eric H. 2007. "Brain Facts and Figures," http://faculty.washington. edu/chudler/facts.html (accessed December 10, 2007).

Churchland, Patricia Smith. 1986. *Neurophilosophy: Toward a Unified Science of the Mind-Brain.* Cambridge, MA: MIT Press.

Churchland, Patricia Smith and Sejnowski, Terrence J. 1994. *The Computational Brain.* Cambridge, MA: MIT Press.

Churchland, Paul M. 1988. *Matter and Consciousness,* rev. edn. Cambridge, MA: MIT Press; first published 1984.

2007. *Neurophilosophy at Work.* Cambridge University Press.

Churchland, Paul M. and Churchland, Patricia Smith. 1998. *On the Contrary: Critical Essays, 1987–1997.* Cambridge, MA: MIT Press.

Compton, M. T. and Furman, A. C. 2005. "Inverse Correlations between Symptom Scores and Spiritual Well-Being among African American Patients with First-Episode Schizophrenia Spectrum Disorders." *Journal of Nervous and Mental Disease* 193/5: 346–49.

Comstock, George W. and Partridge, K. B. 1972. "Church Attendance and Health." *Journal of Chronic Disease* 25/12: 665–72.

Comstock, George W. and Tonascia, J. A. 1977. "Education and Mortality in Washington County, Maryland." *Journal of Health and Social Behavior* 18/1: 54–61.

Contrada, R. J., Goyal, T. M., Cather, C., Rafalson, L., Idler, E. L., and Krause, T. J. 2004. "Psychosocial Factors in Outcomes of Heart Surgery: The Impact of Religious Involvement and Depressive Symptoms." *Health Psychology* 23/3: 227–38.

Cornwall, M., Albrecht, S. L., Cunningham, P. H., and Pitcher, B. L. 1999. "Dimensions of Religiosity Scale." In Hill and Hood 1999 (278–79).

Corrington, Robert S. 1992. *Nature and Spirit: An Essay in Ecstatic Naturalism*. New York: Fordham University Press.

1994. *Ecstatic Naturalism: Signs of the World*. Bloomington and Indianapolis: Indiana University Press.

1996. *Nature's Self: Our Journey from Origin to Spirit*. Lanham, MD: Rowman & Littlefield Publishers.

1997. *Nature's Religion*. Lanham, MD: Rowman & Littlefield Publishers.

2000. *A Semiotic Theory of Theology and Philosophy*. Cambridge and New York: Cambridge University Press.

Coruh, B., Ayele, H., Pugh, M., and Mulligan, T. 2005. "Does Religious Activity Improve Health Outcomes? A Critical Review of the Recent Literature." *Explore* 1/3: 186–91.

Croson, R. 1996. "Partners and Strangers Revisited." *Economic Letters* 53/1: 25–32.

Croson, R. and Buchan, N. 1999. "Gender and Culture: International Experimental Evidence from Trust Games." *American Economic Review Papers and Proceedings* 89/2: 386–91.

Csíkszentmihályi, Mihaly. 1990. *Flow: The Psychology of Optimal Experience*. New York: Harper & Row.

Currie, R., Klug, L. F., and McCombs, C. R. 1982. "Intimacy and Saliency: Dimensions for Ordering Religious Experiences." *Review of Religious Research* 24/1: 19–32.

Dalai Lama. 2003. "A Collaboration between Science and Religion." Speech of January 14, 2003, www.dalailama.com/page.102.htm (accessed December 30, 2007).

Damasio, Antonio R. 1994. *Descartes' Error: Emotion, Reason, and the Human Brain*. New York: G. P. Putnam.

Daniels, M., Merrill, R. A., Lyon, J. L., Stanford, J. B., and White, G. L. 2004. "Associations between Breast Cancer Risk Factors and Religious Practices in Utah." *Preventative Medicine* 38/1: 28–38.

d'Aquili, Eugene G. 1972. *The Biopsychological Determinants of Culture*. Reading, MA: Addison-Wesley Modular Publications.

1975. "The Biopsychological Determinants of Religious Ritual Behavior." *Zygon* 10/1: 32–58.

1978. "The Neurobiological Bases of Myth and Concepts of Deity." *Zygon* 13/4: 257–75.

1983. "The Myth-Ritual Complex: A Biogenetic Structural Analysis." *Zygon* 18/3: 247–69.

1993. "Apologia pro Scriptura Sua, or Maybe We Got It Right after All." *Zygon* 28/2: 251–66.

d'Aquili, Eugene G., Laughlin, Charles D., and McManus, J. 1979. *The Spectrum of Ritual: A Biogenetic Structural Analysis*. New York: Columbia University Press.

d'Aquili, Eugene G. and Newberg, Andrew B. 1993. "Religious and Mystical States: A Neuropsychological Model." *Zygon* 28/2: 177–200.

1998. "The Neuropsychological Basis of Religions, or Why God Won't Go Away," *Zygon* 33/2: 190–91.

1999. *The Mystical Mind: Probing the Biology of Religious Experience.* Minneapolis: Fortress Press.

2000. "The Neuropsychology of Aesthetic, Spiritual and Mystical States." *Zygon* 35/1: 39–52.

Darwin, Charles. 1871. *The Descent of Man.* London: John Murray.

Daugherty, C. K., Fitchett, G., Murphy, P. E., Peterman, A. H., Banik, D. M., Hlubocky, F., *et al.* 2005. "Trusting God and Medicine: Spirituality in Advanced Cancer Patients Volunteering for Clinical Trials of Experimental Agents." *Psycho-Oncology* 14/2: 135–46.

Davidson, Donald. 1970. "Mental Events." In Lawrence Foster and J. W. Swanson (eds.), *Experience and Theory.* Amherst, MA: University of Massachusetts Press. Reprinted in Davidson, *Essays on Actions and Events*, 2nd edn. Oxford University Press, 2001.

Davidson, Richard and Harrington, Anne. 2001. *Visions of Compassion: Western Scientists and Tibetan Buddhists Examine Human Nature.* New York and Oxford: Oxford University Press.

Davis, Caroline Franks. 1989. *The Evidential Force of Religious Experience.* Oxford University Press.

Dawkins, Richard. 2006. *The God Delusion.* London: Houghton Mifflin.

Deacon, Terrence. 1997. *The Symbolic Species: The Co-Evolution of Language and the Brain.* New York: Norton.

2003. "The Hierarchic Logic of Emergence: Untangling the Interdependence of Evolution and Self-Organization." In Bruce H. Weber and David J. Depew (eds.), *Evolution and Learning: The Baldwin Effect Reconsidered* (273–308). Cambridge, MA: MIT Press.

2006. "Emergence: The Hole at the Wheel's Hub." In Philip Clayton and Paul Davies (eds.), *The Re-Emergence of Emergence: The Emergentist Hypothesis from Science to Religion* (111–50). New York and Oxford: Oxford University Press.

DeJong, G., Faulkner, J., and Warland, R. 1999. "Cross-Cultural Dimensions of Religiosity." In Hill and Hood 1999 (270–76).

Dennett, Daniel C. 1991. *Consciousness Explained.* Boston: Little, Brown and Co.

2006. *Breaking the Spell: Religion As a Natural Phenomenon.* New York: Penguin Books.

Descartes, René. [1649] 2003. *Treatise of Man [Les passions de l'âme],* trans. Thomas Steele Hall: Amherst, NY: Prometheus Books.

Desmond, William. 1995. *Being and the Between.* Albany: State University of New York Press.

2001. *Ethics and the Between.* Albany: State University of New York Press.

2008. *God and the Between.* Albany: State University of New York Press.

Devaney, Robert L. 1989. *An Introduction to Chaotic Dynamical Systems,* 2nd edn. Redwood City, CA: Addison-Wesley.

Dewhurst, K. and Beard, A. W. 1970. "Sudden Religious Conversions in Temporal Lobe Epilepsy." *British Journal of Psychiatry* 117: 497–507.

Diamond, Jared, 1991. *The Third Chimpanzee: The Evolution and Future of the Human Animal.* New York: HarperCollins.

Donovan, P. 1979. *Interpreting Religious Experience.* New York: Seabury Press.

Dostoevsky, Fyodor. [1880] 1990. *The Brothers Karamazov,* trans. Richard Pevear and Larissa Volokhonsky. New York: Farrar, Straus, and Giroux.

Dreyfus, Hubert L. 1992. *What Computers Still Can't Do: A Critique of Artificial Reason,* 3rd edn. Cambridge, MA: MIT Press.

Dreyfus, Hubert L. and Dreyfus, Stuart E. 1986. *Mind over Machine: The Power of Human Intuition and Expertise in the Era of the Computer.* New York: Free Press.

Dunbar, Robin and Barrett, Louise (eds.). 2007. *The Oxford Handbook of Evolutionary Psychology.* New York and Oxford: Oxford University Press.

Durkheim, Émile. [1912] 1915. *The Elementary Forms of the Religious Life,* trans. Joseph Ward Swain. Glencoe, IL: Free Press.

Eagleton, Terry. 1991. *Ideology: An Introduction.* London and New York: Verso.

Easton, A. and Emery, N. (eds.). 2005. *The Cognitive Neuroscience of Social Behavior.* Hove, U.K.: Psychology Press.

Eckersley, R. 2007. "Culture, Spirituality, Religion and Health: Looking at the Big Picture." *Medical Journal of Australia* 186 (Suppl. 10): S54–S56.

Edelman, Gerald M. 1987. *Neural Darwinism: The Theory of Neuronal Group Selection,* 2nd edn. New York: Basic Books.

Edwards, K. J. 1999. "Religious Experience Questionnaire." In Hill and Hood 1999 (218–20).

Eliade, Mircea. 1954. *Cosmos and History: The Myth of the Eternal Return.* New York: Harper.

1960. *Myths, Dreams, and Mysteries.* New York: Harper.

1961. *Images and Symbols.* New York: Sheed & Ward.

Ellison, C. G., Gay, D. A., and Glass, T. A. 1989. "Does Religious Commitment Contribute to Individual Life Satisfaction?" *Social Forces* 68/1: 100–23.

Epley, Nicholas, Akalis, Scott, Waytz, Adam, and Cacioppo, John T. 2008. "Creating Social Connection through Inferential Reproduction: Loneliness and Perceived Agency in Gadgets, Gods, and Greyhounds." *Psychological Science* 19/2: 114–20.

Epley, Nicholas, Waytz, Adam, Akalis, Scott, and Cacioppo, John T. 2008. "When We Need a Human: Motivational Determinants of Anthropomorphism." *Social Cognition* 26/2: 143–55.

Epley, Nicholas, Waytz, Adam, and Cacioppo, John T. 2007. "On Seeing Human: A Three-Factor Theory of Anthropomorphism." *Psychological Review* 114/4: 864–996.

Faulkner, J. E. and DeJong, G. 1999. "Five-Dimensional Scale of Religiosity." In Hill and Hood 1999 (295–300).

Fehr, E. and Gachter, S. 2000. "Cooperation and Punishment in Public Goods Experiments." *American Economic Review* 90/4: 980–94.

2002. "Altruistic Punishment in Humans." *Nature* 415 (January 10): 137–40.
Fehr, E. and Rockenbach, B. 2004. "Human Altruism: Economic, Neural and Evolutionary Perspectives." *Current Opinion in Neurobiology* 14: 784–90.
Feigenbaum, Michael J. 1978. "Quantitative Universality for a Class of Nonlinear Transformations." *Journal of Statistical Physics* 19/1: 25–52.
Fenton, G. W. 1981. "Psychiatric Disorders of Epilepsy: Classification and Phenomenology." In E. Reynolds and M. Trimble (eds.), *Epilepsy and Psychiatry* (12–26). New York: Churchill Livingstone.
Fershtman, C. and Gneezy, U. 2001. "Discrimination in a Segmented Society: An Experimental Approach." *Quarterly Journal of Economics* 116/1: 351–77.
Fetzer Institute. 1999. "Multidimensional Measurement of Religiousness/Spirituality for Use in Health Research: A Report of the Fetzer Institute/National Institute on Aging Working Group," www.fetzer.org/PDF/Total_Fetzer_Book.pdf (accessed January 1, 2008).
Fischer, Roland. 1971. "A Cartography of Understanding Mysticism." *Science* 174 (November 26): 897–904.
Fodor, Jerry A. 1983. *Modularity of Mind: An Essay of Faculty Psychology.* Cambridge, MA: MIT Press.
2000. *The Mind Doesn't Work That Way: The Scope and Limits of Computational Psychology.* Cambridge, MA: MIT Press.
Forbes, E. J. and Pekala, Ronald J. 1993. "Predicting Hypnotic Susceptibility via a Phenomenological Approach." *Psychological Reports* 73/3 (2): 1251–56.
Forman, Robert K. C. 1999. *Mysticism, Mind, Consciousness.* Albany: State University of New York Press.
Forman, Robert K. C. (ed.). 1990. *The Problem of Pure Consciousness: Mysticism and Philosophy.* New York: Oxford University Press.
Fowler, James. 1981. *Stages of Faith: The Psychology of Human Development and the Quest for Meaning.* San Francisco: Harper and Row.
Frazer, James George. 1900. *The Golden Bough: A Study in Magic and Religion,* 2nd edn. London: Macmillan.
Freeden, Michael. 2003. *Ideology: A Very Short Introduction.* Oxford University Press.
Freud, Sigmund. [1913] 1918. *Totem and Taboo: Resemblances between the Psychic Lives of Savages and Neurotics,* authorized English trans. A. A. Brill. New York: Moffat, Yard, and Company.
[1920] 1922. *Beyond the Pleasure Principle,* authorized English trans. from 2nd German edn. C. J. M. Hubback. London: The Hogarth Press and the Institute of Psycho-Analysis.
[1927] 1928. *The Future of an Illusion,* trans. W. D. Robson-Scott. New York: H. Liveright and the Institute of Psycho-Analysis.
1930. *Civilization and Its Discontents,* authorized English trans. Joan Riviere. New York: J. Cape & H. Smith.
1939. *Moses and Monotheism,* trans. Katherine Jones. London: The Hogarth Press and the Institute of Psycho-Analysis.

Frisina, Warren G. 2002. *The Unity of Knowledge and Action: Toward a Nonrepresentational Theory of Knowledge*. Albany: State University Press of New York.

Frith, C. D. and Wolpert, D. 2004. *The Neuroscience of Social Interaction: Decoding, Imitating and Influencing the Actions of Others*. New York and Oxford: Oxford University Press.

Gachter, S., Herrmann, B., and Thoni, C. 2004. "Trust, Voluntary Cooperation, and Socio-Economic Background: Survey and Experimental Evidence." *Journal of Economic Behavior & Organization* 55/4: 505–31.

Gadamer, Hans Georg. 1975. *Truth and Method*, trans. and ed. Garrett Barden and John Cumming. New York: Seabury Press.

Gale, Richard M. 1994a. "Swinburne's Argument from Religious Experience." In Alan G. Padgett (ed.), *Reason and the Christian Religion* (39–63). Oxford University Press.

——— 1994b. "Why Alston's Mystical Doxastic Practice Is Subjective." *Philosophy and Phenomenological Research* 54/4: 869–83.

Gavrilyuk, Paul, and Coakley, Sarah (eds.). In press. *Perceiving God: The Spiritual Senses in the Western Christian Tradition*. Cambridge University Press.

Gellman, Jerome I. 1997. *Experience of God and the Rationality of Theistic Belief*. Ithaca, NY and London: Cornell University Press.

George, L. 1995. *Alternative Realities: The Paranormal, the Mystic, and the Transcendent in Human Experience*. New York: Facts on File.

George, L., Ellison, C., and Larson, D. 2002. "Explaining the Relationship between Religious Involvement and Health." *Health Services Research* 13/3: 190–200.

Geschwind, Norman. 1979. "Behavioural Changes in Temporal Lobe Epilepsy." *Psychological Medicine* 9/2: 217–19.

——— 1983. "Interictal Behavioral Changes in Epilepsy." *Epilepsia* 24 (Suppl. 1): 523–30.

Gibson, James J. 1950. *The Perception of the Visual World*. Boston: Houghton Mifflin.

——— 1966. *The Senses Considered As Perceptual Systems*. Boston: Houghton Mifflin.

——— 1979. *The Ecological Approach to Visual Perception*. Boston: Houghton Mifflin.

Gillings, V. and Joseph, S. 1996. "Religiosity and Social Desirability: Impression Management and Self-Deceptive Positivity." *Personality and Individual Differences* 21/6: 1047–50.

Gilovich, Thomas. 1991. *How We Know What Isn't So: The Fallibility of Human Reason in Everyday Life*. New York: Free Press.

Glaeser, E., Laibson, D., Sheinkman, J., and Soutter, C. 2000. "Measuring Trust." *Quarterly Journal of Economics* 115/3: 811–46.

Gledhill, Ruth. 2007. "We'd Be Better Off without Religion." Report on speech by Richard Dawkins. Times Online, March 28, 2007, http://timescolumns. typepad.com/gledhill/2007/03/wed_be_better_o.html (accessed September 10, 2007).

Gleick, James. 1987. *Chaos: Making a New Science*. New York: Penguin Books.

Glock, C. and Stark, R. 1999. "Dimensions of Religious Commitment." In Hill and Hood 1999 (279–92).

Gollub, J. P. and Swinney, Harry L. 1975. "Onset of Turbulence in a Rotating Fluid." *Physical Review Letters* 35/14: 927–30.

Good, James M. M. 2007. "The Affordances for Social Psychology of the Ecological Approach to Social Knowing." *Theory and Psychology* 17/2: 265–95.

Goodman, Felicitas D. 1972. *Speaking in Tongues: A Cross-Cultural Study in Glossolalia*. University of Chicago Press.

Gorsuch, R. L. and Smith, C. S. 1999. "Nearness to God Scale." In Hill and Hood 1999 (408–9).

Granqvist, Pehr. 2005. "Reply to 'A Response to Granqvist *et al*. "Sensed Presence and Mystical Experiences Are Predicted by Suggestibility, Not by the Application of Transcranial Weak Magnetic Fields"'." *Neuroscience Letter* 380/3: 348–50.

Granqvist, Pehr, Fredrikson, M., Unge, P., Hagenfeldt, A., Valind, S., Larhammar, D., *et al*. 2005. "Sensed Presence and Mystical Experiences Are Predicted by Suggestibility, Not by the Application of Transcranial Weak Complex Magnetic Fields." *Neuroscience Letters* 379/1: 1–6.

Grant, J. E. 2004. "Dissociative Symptoms in Kleptomania." *Psychological Reports* 94/1: 77–82.

Griffin, David Ray. 1997. *Parapsychology, Philosophy, and Spirituality: A Postmodern Exploration*. Albany: State University of New York Press.

Griffith-Dickson, Gwen. 2000. *Human and Divine: An Introduction to the Philosophy of Religious Experience*. London: Duckworth.

Guevara, Michael R., Glass, Leon, and Shrier, Alvin. 1981. "Phase Locking, Period-Doubling Bifurcations, and Irregular Dynamics in Periodically Stimulated Cardiac Cells." *Science* 214 (December 18): 1350–53.

Haidt, Jonathan. 2001. "The Emotional Dog and Its Rational Tail: A Social Intuitionist Approach to Moral Judgment." *Psychological Review* 108/4: 814–34.

——— 2007a. "The New Synthesis in Moral Psychology." *Science* 316 (May 18): 998–1002.

——— 2007b. "Moral Psychology and the Misunderstanding of Religion." With comments by David Sloan Wilson, Michael Shermer, Sam Harris, P. Z. Myers, and Marc D. Hauser; and with a reply by the author, www.edge.org/3rd_culture/haidt07/haidt07_index.html (accessed September, 2008).

——— 2008. "What Makes People Vote Republican?" With comments by Daniel Everett, Howard Gardner, Michael Shermer, Scott Atran, James Fowler, Alison Gopnik, Sam Harris, and James O'Donnell; and with a reply by the author, www.edge.org/discourse/vote_morality.html (accessed September, 2008).

Haken, Hermann. 2006. *Information and Self-Organization: A Macroscopic Approach to Complex Systems*, 3rd edn. Berlin: Springer.

Hamer, Dean. 2004. *The God Gene: How Faith Is Hardwired into Our Genes.* New York: Doubleday.

Hand, J., Pekala, Ronald J., and Kumar, V. K. 1995. "Prediction of Harvard and Stanford Scale Scores with a Phenomenological Instrument." *Australian Journal of Clinical and Experimental Hypnosis* 23/2: 124–34.

Happel, Stephen and Walter, James. 1980. *Conversion and Discipleship: A Christian Foundation for Ethics and Doctrine.* Philadelphia: Fortress Press.

Hardwick, Charley. 1996. *Events of Grace: Naturalism, Existentialism, and Theology.* Cambridge, MA and London: Harvard University Press.

Hardy, Alister C. 1979. *The Spiritual Nature of Man: A Study of Contemporary Religious Experience.* New York: Oxford University Press.

Harmon-Jones, Eddie and Winkielman, Piotr (eds.). 2007. *Social Neuroscience: Integrating Biological and Psychological Explanations of Social Behavior.* New York: Guildford Press.

Harris, Sam. 2006. *Letters to a Christian Nation.* New York: Knopf.

Harrison, M. O., Edwards, C. L., Koenig, H. G., Bosworth, H. B., Decastro, L., and Wood, M. 2005. "Religiosity/Spirituality and Pain in Patients with Sickle Cell Disease." *Journal of Nervous and Mental Disease* 193/4: 250–57.

Hassan, Nasra. 2001. "An Arsenal of Believers: Talking to the 'Human Bombs'." *New Yorker* 77/36 (November 19): 36–41.

2004. "Al-Qaeda's Understudy." *Atlantic Monthly* 293/5: 42–44.

Hauser, Mark. 2006. *Moral Minds: How Nature Designed Our Universal Sense of Right and Wrong.* New York: HarperCollins.

Haynes, Renée. 1982. *The Society for Psychical Research, 1892–1982: A History.* London: Macdonald.

Heidegger, Martin. [1927] 1962. *Being and Time*, trans. J. Macquarrie and E. Robinson. New York: Harper & Row.

Hick, John. 2004. *An Interpretation of Religion: Human Responses to the Transcendent*, 2nd edn. New Haven: Yale University Press.

Hill, Peter C. and Hood, Ralph W., Jr. (eds.). 1999. *Measures of Religiosity.* Birmingham, AL: Religious Education Press.

Hill, T. D., Angel, J. L., Ellison, C. G., and Angel, R. J. 2005. "Religious Attendance and Mortality: An Eight-Year Follow-Up of Older Mexican Americans." *Journals of Gerontology, Series B – Psychological Sciences and Social Sciences* 60 (Suppl. 2): S102–S109.

Hitchens, C. 2007. *God Is Not Great: How Religion Poisons Everything.* New York: Twelve Books.

Hixson, K. A., Gruchow, H. W., and Morgan, D. W. 1998. "The Relation between Religiosity, Selected Health Behaviors, and Blood Pressure among Adult Females." *Preventative Medicine* 27/4: 545–52.

Holland, John H. 1995. *Hidden Order: How Adaptation Builds Complexity.* New York: Perseus Books.

Holmes, H. Rodney. 1993. "Thinking about Religion and Experiencing the Brain: Eugene d'Aquili's Biogenetic Structural Theory of Absolute Unitary Being." *Zygon* 28/2: 201–15.

Hood, Ralph W., Jr. 1999. "Mysticism Scale." In Hill and Hood 1999 (363–67).

Hood, Ralph W., Jr. (ed.). 1995. *Handbook of Religious Experience*. Birmingham, AL: Religious Education Press.

Hood, Ralph W., Jr. and Rosegrant, J. 1999. "Religious Experience Episodes Measure." In Hill and Hood 1999 (220–24).

Hook, Sidney. 1961. *Religious Experience and Truth: A Symposium*. New York: New York University Press.

Hsieh, T. T. Y. 1999. "Word–Spirit Orientation Scale." In Hill and Hood 1999 (225–27).

Huang, Milton P., Himle, Joseph, and Alessi, Norman E. 2000. "Vivid Visualization in the Experience of Phobia in Virtual Environments: Preliminary Results." *CyberPsychology and Behavior* 3/3: 315–20.

Hufford, D. 2005. "Beliefs and Health." *Journal of Science and Healing* 1/6: 464–73.

Huntington, Samuel P. 1996. *The Clash of Civilizations and the Remaking of World Order*. New York: Simon & Schuster.

Hutchinson-Phillips, Susan, Jamieson, Graham A., and Gow, Kathryn. 2005. "Differing Roles of Imagination and Hypnosis in Self-Regulation of Eating Behaviour." *Contemporary Hypnosis* 22/4: 171–83.

Huxley, Aldous. 1945. *The Perennial Philosophy*. New York: Harper & Brothers.

Huxley, Thomas H. 1874. "On the Hypothesis That Animals Are Automata, and Its History." *Fortnightly Review* 16: 555–80. Reprinted in *Method and Results: Essays by Thomas H. Huxley*. New York: D. Appleton and Company, 1898.

Idler, E. L. 1987. "Religious Involvement and the Health of the Elderly: Some Hypotheses and an Initial Test." *Social Forces* 66/1: 226–38.

1992. "Self-Assessed Health and Mortality: A Review of Studies." In S. Maes, H. Leventhal, and M. Johnston (eds.), *International Review of Health Psychology* (33–54). New York: Wiley.

Idler, E. L. and Kasl, S. V. 1992. "Religion, Disability, Depression, and the Timing of Death." *American Journal of Sociology* 97/4: 1052–79.

Idler, E. L., Musick, M. A., Ellison, C. G., George, L. K., Krause, N., Ory, M. G., *et al.* 2003. "Measuring Multiple Dimensions of Religion and Spirituality for Health Research: Conceptual Background and Findings from the 1998 General Social Survey." *Research on Aging* 25/4: 327–65.

Irons, William. 1996. "Morality, Religion, and Human Nature." In W. Mark Richardson and Wesley J. Wildman (eds.), *Religion and Science: History, Method, and Dialogue* (375–99). New York: Routledge.

2001. "Religion As a Hard-to-Fake Sign of Commitment." In R. Neese (ed.), *Evolution and the Capacity for Commitment* (292–309). New York: Russell Sage Foundation.

Isaac, R. M. and Walker, J. 1988. "Group Size Effects in Public Goods Provision: The Voluntary Contributions Mechanism." *Quarterly Journal of Economics* 103/1: 179–200.

Isaac, M., Walker, J., and Thomas, S. 1984. "Divergent Expectations on Free Riding: An Experimental Examination of Possible Explanations." *Public Choice* 43/2: 113–49.

Jaber, Hala. 1997. *Hezballah: Born with a Vengeance.* New York: Columbia University Press.

James, William. 1902. *The Varieties of Religious Experience: A Study in Human Nature.* New York: Longmans, Green, & Company.

[1909] 1996. *A Pluralistic Universe.* Omaha: University of Nebraska Press.

[1912] 2003. *Essays in Radical Empiricism.* New York: Dover Publications.

Jaynes, Julian. 1976. *The Origin of Consciousness in the Breakdown of the Bicameral Mind.* Boston: Houghton Mifflin.

Jensen, Henrik Jeldtoft. 1998. *Self-Organized Criticality: Emergent Complex Behavior in Physical and Biological Systems.* Cambridge and New York: Cambridge University Press.

Johanson, M., Valli, K., Revonsuo, A., Chaplin, J. E., and Wedlund, J. E. 2008. "Alterations in the Contents of Consciousness in Partial Epileptic Seizures." *Epilepsy & Behavior* 13/2: 366–71. Epub, June 5, 2008.

Kadanoff, Leo P. 1983. "Roads to Chaos." *Physics Today* (December): 46–53.

Kant, Immanuel. [1781/1787] 1933. *Critique of Pure Reason,* trans. Norman Kemp Smith, 2nd edn. New York and London: Macmillan.

Kapstein, Matthew T. (ed.). 2004. *The Presence of Light: Divine Radiance and Religious Experience.* Chicago and London: University of Chicago Press.

Kason, Y. 1997. *A Farther Shore: How Near-Death and Other Extraordinary Experiences Can Change Ordinary Lives,* 2nd edn. New York: HarperCollins.

Katz, Steven T. (ed.). 1978. *Mysticism and Philosophical Analysis.* New York and Oxford: Oxford University Press.

1984. *Mysticism and Religious Traditions.* New York and Oxford: Oxford University Press.

1992. *Mysticism and Language.* New York and Oxford: Oxford University Press.

2000. *Mysticism and Sacred Scripture.* New York and Oxford: Oxford University Press.

Kauffman, Stuart A. 1993. *The Origins of Order: Self-Organization and Selection in Evolution.* New York and Oxford: Oxford University Press.

1995. *At Home in the Universe: The Search for Laws of Self-Organization.* New York and Oxford: Oxford University Press.

Kaufman, Gordon D. 1993. *In Face of Mystery: A Constructive Theology.* Cambridge, MA: Harvard University Press.

Kelso, J. A. Scott. 1995. *Dynamic Patterns: The Self-Organization of Brain and Behavior.* Cambridge, MA and London: MIT Press.

Kiel, L. Douglas and Elliott, Euel (eds.). 1996. *Chaos Theory in the Social Sciences: Foundations and Applications.* Ann Arbor: University of Michigan Press.

Kierkegaard, Søren. [1843] 1983. *Fear and Trembling; Repetition*, ed. and trans. with introduction and notes by Howard V. Hong and Edna H. Hong. Princeton University Press.

Kildahl, John P. 1972. *The Psychology of Speaking in Tongues*. New York: Harper & Row.

King, M., Speck, P., and Thomas, A. 1999. "The Effect of Spiritual Beliefs on Outcome from Illness." *Social Science & Medicine* 48/9: 1291–99.

King, M. B. and Hunt, R. A. 1999. "Religious Variables: Ten Scales." In Hill and Hood 1999 (333–39).

King-Casas, B., Tomlin, D., Anen, C., Camerer, C., Quartz, S., and Montague, P. R. 2005. "Getting to Know You: Reputation and Trust in a Two-Person Economic Exchange." *Science* 308 (April 1): 78–83.

Kinney, A. Y., Bloor, L. E., Dudley, W. N., Millikan, R. C., Marshall, E., Martin, C., *et al.* 2003. "Roles of Religious Involvement and Social Support in the Risk of Colon Cancer among Blacks and Whites." *American Journal of Epidemiology* 158/11: 1097–107.

Klein, Richard G. 2002. *The Dawn of Human Culture*. New York: John Wiley & Sons.

Knepper, Timothy D. 2005. "How to Say What Can't Be Said: Techniques and Rules of Ineffability in the Dionysian Corpus." Ph.D. dissertation, Boston University.

Koenig H. G. 2000. "Religion and Medicine I." *International Journal of Psychiatry in Medicine* 30/4: 385–98.

2001a. *Handbook of Religion and Health*. New York and Oxford: Oxford University Press.

2001b. "Religion and Medicine II." *International Journal of Psychiatry in Medicine* 31/1: 97–109.

2001c. "Religion and Medicine III." *International Journal of Psychiatry in Medicine* 31/2: 119–216.

2001d. "Religion and Medicine IV." *International Journal of Psychiatry in Medicine* 31/3: 321–36.

2001e. *The Healing Power of Faith: How Belief and Prayer Can Help You Triumph over Disease*. New York: Simon & Schuster.

2002. *The Link between Religion and Health: Psychoneuroimmunology and the Faith Factor*. New York and Oxford: Oxford University Press.

Koenig, H. G., George, L. K., Hays, J. C., Larson, D. B., Cohen, H. J. and Blazer, D. G. 1998. "The Relationship between Religious Activities and Blood Pressure in Older Adults." *International Journal of Psychiatry in Medicine* 28/2: 189–213.

Koenig, H. G., Hays, J. C., Larson, D. B., George L. K., Cohen, H. J., McCullough, M. E., *et al.* 1999a. "Does Religious Attendance Prolong Survival? A Six Year Follow-Up Study of 3,968 Older Adults." *Journal of Gerontology: Medical Sciences* 54A/7: M370–M376.

Koenig H. G., Idler, E., Kasl, S., Hays, J. C., George, L. K., Musick, M., *et al.* 1999b. "Editorial: Religion, Spirituality, and Medicine: A Rebuttal to Skeptics." *International Journal of Psychiatry in Medicine* 29/2: 123–31.

Koenig, Laura B. Bouchard, Jr., and Thomas, J. 2006. "Genetic and Environmental Influences on the Traditional Moral Values Triad – Authoritarianism, Conservatism, and Religiousness – As Assessed by Quantitative Behavior Genetic Methods." In McNamara 2006a (31–60).

Kokoszka, A. 1992. "Occurrence of Altered States of Consciousness among Students: Profoundly and Superficially Altered States in Wakefulness." *Imagination, Cognition, and Personality* 12/3: 231–47.

Körner, Stephan. 1974. *Categorical Frameworks*. Oxford: Basil Blackwell.

Kris, J. D., Friedman, R., Lassermman, J., Zuttermeister, P., and Benson, H. 1999. "Index of Core Spiritual Experiences." In Hill and Hood 1999 (360–63).

Kristeller, Jean. 2004. "Meditation: Multiple Effects, a Unitary Process?" In Mark Blows, Yutaka Haruki, Peter Bankart, Johanna Blows, Michael DelMonte, and Saroja Srinivasan (eds.), *The Relevance of the Wisdom Traditions in Contemporary Society: The Challenge to Psychology* (21–37). Delft, The Netherlands: Eburon Publishers.

2007. "Mindfulness Meditation." In P. Lehrer, R. L. Woolfolk, and W. E. Sime (eds.), *Principles and Practice of Stress Management*, 3rd edn. (393–427). New York: Guilford Press.

Kukla, Andre. 1983. "Toward a Science of Experience." *Journal of Mind and Behavior* 4/2: 231–46.

Kumar, V. K., Marcano, G., and Pekala, Ronald J. 1996a. "Behavioral and Subjective Scoring of the Harvard Group Scale of Hypnotic Susceptibility: Further Data and an Extension." *American Journal of Clinical Hypnosis* 38/3: 191–99.

Kumar, V. K. and Pekala, Ronald J. 1988. "Hypnotizability, Absorption, and Individual Differences in Phenomenological Experience." *International Journal of Clinical and Experimental Hypnosis* 36/2: 80–88.

1989. "Variations in Phenomenological Experience As a Function of Hypnosis and Hypnotic Susceptibility." *British Journal of Clinical and Experimental Hypnosis* 6: 17–22.

Kumar, V. K., Pekala, Ronald J., and Cummings, J. 1996b. "Trait Factors, State Effects, and Hypnotizability." *International Journal of Clinical and Experimental Hypnosis* 44/3: 232–49.

Kune, G. A., Kune, S., and Watson, L. F. 1993. "Perceived Religiousness Is Protective for Colorectal Cancer: Data from the Melbourne Colorectal Cancer Study." *Journal of the Royal Society of Medicine* 86/11: 645–47.

Küppers, Bernd-Olaf. 1990. *Information and the Origin of Life*. Cambridge, MA: MIT Press.

Lakoff, George. 2002. *Moral Politics: How Liberals and Conservatives Think*. University of Chicago Press.

Lakoff, George and Johnson, Mark. 1980. *Metaphors We Live By*. University of Chicago Press.

1999. *Philosophy in the Flesh: The Embodied Mind and Its Challenge to Western Thought*. New York: Basic Books.

Larson, D. B., Sawyers, J. P., and McCullough, M. E. 1998. *Scientific Research on Spirituality and Health: A Consensus Report.* Rockville, MD: National Institute for Healthcare Research.

Lawrence, R. J. 2002. "The Witches' Brew of Spirituality and Medicine." *Annals of Behavioral Medicine* 24/1: 74–76.

Lenski, G. 1999. "Religious Orientation and Involvement." In Hill and Hood 1999 (330–33).

Lévi-Strauss, Claude. [1962] 1963. *Totemism*, trans. Rodney Needham. Boston: Beacon Press.

Levin, J. S., Taylor, R. J., and Chatters, L. M. 1995. "A Multidimensional Measure of Religious Involvement for African Americans." *Sociology Quarterly* 36/1: 157–73.

Levin, J. S. and Vanderpool, H. Y. 1989. "Is Religion Therapeutically Significant for Hypertension?" *Social Science & Medicine* 29/1: 69–78.

Levine, J. 1983. "Materialism and Qualia: The Explanatory Gap." *Pacific Philosophical Quarterly* 64: 354–61.

Lewin, Roger. 1992. *Complexity: Life at the Edge of Chaos.* New York: Macmillan.

Libchaber, A., Laroche, C., and Fauve, S. 1982. "Period Doubling Cascade in Mercury, a Quantitative Measurement." *Le Journal de Physique-Lettres* 43: L211–L216.

Lieberman, David A. 1979. "Behaviorism and the Mind: A (Limited) Call for a Return to Introspection." *American Psychologist* 34/4: 319–33.

Lieberman, Philip. 1991. *Uniquely Human: The Evolution of Speech, Thought, and Selfless Behavior.* Cambridge, MA: Harvard University Press.

Lorenz, Edward N. 1993. *The Essence of Chaos.* Seattle: University of Washington Press.

Main, Stephen Thomas. 1998. "Abyss without a Ground: Nietzschean Spirituality and Self-Healing." Ph.D. dissertation, University of Chicago.

Maitz, E. A. and Pekala, R. J. 1991. "Phenomenological Quantification of an Out-of-the-Body Experience Associated with a Near-Death Event." *OMEGA* 22/3: 199–214.

Manmiller, Jessica L., Kumar, V. K., and Pekala, Ronald J. 2005. "Hypnotizability, Creative Capacity, Creativity Styles, Absorption, and Phenomenological Experience During Hypnosis." *Creativity Research Journal* 17/1: 9–24.

Marx, Karl. 2002. *Marx on Religion*, ed. John Raines. Philadelphia: Temple University Press.

Marx, Karl and Engels, Friedrich. [1846] 1970. *The German Ideology, Part One*, ed. C. J. Arthur. New York: International Publishers.

Maslow, Abraham H. 1964. *Religions, Values, and Peak Experiences.* New York: Viking Press.

1970. "Religious Aspects of Peak Experiences." In William A. Sadler Jr. (ed.), *Personality and Religion.* New York: Harper & Row.

1971. *The Farther Reaches of Human Nature.* New York: Viking Press.

Masson, J. M. 1980. *The Oceanic Feeling: The Origins of Religious Sentiment in Ancient India*. Dordrecht: D. Reidel.

Masters, K. S., Hill, R. D., Kircher, J. C., Lensegrav-Benson, T. L., and Fallon, J. A. 2004. "Religious Orientation, Aging, and Blood Pressure Reactivity to Interpersonal and Cognitive Stressors." *Annals of Behavioral Medicine* 28/3: 171–78.

Mathes, E. W., Roter, P. M., Joerger, S. M., and Zevon, M. A. 1982. "Peak Experiences Scale." In L. H. Janda (ed.), *Psychologist's Book of Personality Tests: 24 Revealing Tests to Identify and Overcome Your Personal Barriers to a Better Life* (195–206). New York: John Wiley & Sons.

Maurer, R. L., Sr., Kumar, V. K., Woodside, L., and Pekala, Ronald J. 1997. "Phenomenological Experience in Response to Monotonous Drumming and Hypnotizability." *American Journal of Clinical Hypnosis* 40/2: 130–45.

Maxwell, Meg and Tschudin, Verena (eds.). 1990. *Seeing the Invisible: Modern Religious and Other Transcendent Experiences*. London: Penguin Books.

May, Robert M. and Oster, George F. 1976. "Bifurcations and Dynamic Complexity in Simple Ecological Models." *American Naturalist* 110 (July–August): 573–99.

McCabe, K., Rigdon, M., and Smith, V. 2002. "Sustaining Cooperation in Trust Games." Unpublished manuscript.

2003. "Positive Reciprocity and Intentions in Trust Games." *Journal of Economic Behavior & Organization* 52/2: 267–75.

McClenon, James. 2001. *Wondrous Healing: Shamanism, Human Evolution, and the Origin of Religion*. De Kalb: Northern Illinois University Press.

2006. "The Ritual Healing Theory: Therapeutic Suggestion and the Origin of Religion." In McNamara 2006a (135–58).

McCloskey, M. S., Kumar, V. K., and Pekala, Ronald J. 1999. "State and Trait Depression, Physical and Social Anhedonia, Hypnotizability and Subjective Experiences during Hypnosis." *American Journal of Clinical Hypnosis* 41/3: 231–52.

McKinney, Laurence O. 1994. *Neurotheology: Virtual Religion in the 21st Century*. Cambridge, MA: American Institute for Mindfulness.

McNamara, Patrick, 2009. *The Neurology of Religious Experience*. Cambridge and New York: Cambridge University Press.

McNamara, Patrick (ed.) 2006a. *Where God and Science Meet*, vol. I, *Evolution, Genes, and the Religious Brain*. Westport, CT: Praeger Publishers.

2006b. *Where God and Science Meet*, vol. II, *The Neurology of Religious Experience*. Westport, CT: Praeger Publishers.

2006c. *Where God and Science Meet*, vol. III, *The Psychology of Religious Experience*. Westport, CT: Praeger Publishers.

McNamara, Patrick, Andresen, Jensine, and Gellard, Judit. 2003. "Relation of Religiosity and Scores on Verbal and Non-Verbal Fluency to Subjective Reports of Health in the Elderly." *International Journal for the Psychology of Religion* 13/4: 259–71.

McNamara, Patrick and Durso, Raymon. 2006. "Neuropharmacological Treatment of Mental Dysfunction in Parkinson's Disease." *Behavioral Neurology* 17/1: 43–51.

McNamara, Patrick, Durso, Raymon, and Brown, Ariel. 2006. "Religiosity in Patients with Parkinson's Disease," *Neuropsychiatric Disease & Treatment* 2/3: 341–48.

Mead, George H. 1934. *Mind, Self, and Society from the Standpoint of a Social Behaviorist*. University of Chicago Press.

Meissner, William W. 1984. *Psychoanalysis and Religious Experience*. New Haven: Yale University Press.

Mesulam, M.-Marsel. 1981. "Dissociative States with Abnormal Temporal Lobe EEG: Multiple Personality and the Illusion of Possession." *Archives of Neurology* 38/3: 176–81.

Miller, W. R. and Thoresen, C. E. 2003. "Spirituality, Religion, and Health: An Emerging Research Field." *American Psychologist* 58/1: 24–35.

Mills, David. 2006. *Atheist Universe: The Thinking Person's Answer to Christian Fundamentalism*. Berkeley, CA: Ulysses Press.

Mills, Watson E. 1986. *A Guide to Research on Glossolalia*. Grand Rapids, MI: William B. Eerdmans Publishing Company.

Moacanin, Radmila. 1986. *Jung's Psychology and Tibetan Buddhism: Western and Eastern Paths to the Heart*. London: Wisdom Publications.

Moehle, D. 1983. "Cognitive Dimensions of Religious Experiences." *Journal of Experimental Social Psychology* 19/2: 122–45.

Mungas, Dan. 1982. "Interictal Behavior Abnormality in Temporal Lobe Epilepsy." *Archives of General Psychiatry* 39/1: 108–11.

Murphy, P. E., Ciarrocchi, J. W., Piedmont, R. L., Cheston, S., Peyrot, M., and Fitchett, G. 2000. "The Relation of Religious Beliefs and Practices, Depression, and Hopelessness in Persons with Clinical Depression." *Journal of Consulting and Clinical Psychology* 68/6: 1102–6.

Musick, M. A., Traphagan, J. W., Koenig, H. G., and Larson, D. B. 2000. "Spirituality in Physical Health and Aging." *Journal of Adult Development* 7/2: 73–86.

Nagel, Thomas. 1974. "What Is It Like to Be a Bat?" *Philosophical Review* 83: 435–50.

——— 1986. *The View from Nowhere*. New York and Oxford: Oxford University Press.

Neville, Robert Cummings. 1981. *The Axiology of Thinking*, vol. 1, *Reconstruction of Thinking*. Albany: State University of New York Press.

——— 1996. *The Truth of Broken Symbols*. Albany: State University of New York Press.

Neville, Robert Cummings (ed.). 2001. *The Comparative Religious Ideas Project*, 3 vols. Vol. 1, *The Human Condition*; vol. 11, *Ultimate Realities*; vol. 111, *Religious Truth*. Albany: State University of New York Press.

Newberg, Andrew B. 2006. *Why We Believe What We Believe: Uncovering Our Biological Need for Meaning, Spirituality, and Truth*. New York: Free Press.

2009. *How God Changes Your Brain: Breakthrough Findings from a Leading Neuroscientist.* New York: Ballantine Books.

Newberg, Andrew B., Alavi, A., Baime, M., Mozley, P. D., and d'Aquili, E. 1997. "The Measurement of Cerebral Blood Flow during the Complex Cognitive Task of Meditation Using HMPAO-SPECT Imaging." *Journal of Nuclear Medicine* 38: 95P.

Newberg, Andrew B., Alavi, A., Baime, M., Pourdehnad, M., Santanna, J., and d'Aquili, E. 2001a. "The Measurement of Regional Cerebral Blood Flow during the Complex Cognitive Task of Meditation: A Preliminary SPECT Study." *Psychiatry Research* 106/2: 113–22.

Newberg, Andrew B. and d'Aquili, Eugene. 1994. "The Near-Death Experience As Archetype: A Model for 'Prepared' Neurocognitive Processes." *Anthropology of Consciousness* 5/4: 1–15.

2000. "The Creative Brain/The Creative Mind." *Zygon* 35/1: 53–68.

Newberg, Andrew, d'Aquili, Eugene and Rause, Vince. 2001b. *Why God Won't Go Away: Brain Science and the Biology of Belief.* New York: Ballantine Books.

Newberg, Andrew B. and Iversen, J. 2003. "The Neural Basis of the Complex Mental Task of Meditation: Neurotransmitter and Neurochemical Considerations." *Medical Hypotheses* 61/2: 282–91.

Newberg, Andrew B., Wintering, Nancy A., Morgan, Donna, and Waldman, Mark R. 2006. "The Measurement of Regional Cerebral Blood Flow during Glossolalia: A Preliminary SPECT Study." *Psychiatry Research: Neuroimaging* 148/1: 67–71.

Newlin, K., Melkus, G. D., Chyun, D., and Jefferson, V. 2003. "The Relationship of Spirituality and Health Outcomes in Black Women with Type 2 Diabetes." *Ethnicity & Disease* 13/1: 61–68.

Nicolis, Gregoire and Prigogine, Ilya. 1977. *Self-Organization in Nonequilibrium Systems: From Dissipative Structures to Order through Fluctuations.* New York: John Wiley & Sons.

1989. *Exploring Complexity: An Introduction.* San Francisco: W. H. Freeman & Company.

Nietzsche, Friedrich. [1883–85] 1954. *Thus Spake Zarathustra,* in *The Portable Nietzsche,* ed. and trans. Walter Kaufmann. New York: Penguin Books.

[1901] 1968. *The Will to Power,* ed. and trans. Walter Kaufmann and R. J. Hollingdale. New York: Vintage Books.

Norenzayan, Ara and Hansen, Ian. 2006. "Belief in Supernatural Agents in the Face of Death." *Personality and Social Psychology Bulletin* 32/2: 174–87.

Núñez, Rafael and Freeman, Walter J. (eds.). 1999. *Reclaiming Cognition: The Primacy of Action, Intention and Emotion, Journal of Consciousness Studies* 6/11–12. Bowling Green, OH: Imprint Academic.

Oman, D., Kurata, J. H., Strawbridge, W. J., and Cohen, R. D. 2002. "Religious Attendance and Cause of Death Over 31 Years." *International Journal of Psychiatry in Medicine* 32/1, 69–89.

Otto, Rudolf. [1917] 1925. *The Idea of the Holy: An Inquiry into the Non-Rational Factor in the Idea of the Divine and Its Relation to the Rational,* 3rd English edn., trans. John W. Harvey from 9th German edn. London and New York: Oxford University Press.

Oxman, T. E., Rosenberg, S. D., Schnurr, P. P., Tucker, G. J., and Gala, G. 1998. "The Language of Altered States." *Journal of Nervous and Mental Disease* 176/7, 401–8.

Palfrey, T. and Prisbrey, J. 1997. "Anomalous Behavior in Public Goods Experiments: How Much and Why?" *American Economic Review* 87/5, 829–46.

Pargament, Kenneth I. 1997. *The Psychology of Religion and Coping: Theory, Research, Practice.* New York: Guilford Press.

Pearson, R. S. 2005. *The Experience of Hallucinations in Religious Experience.* Seattle: Telical Books.

Peirce, Charles S. 1931–35. *Collected Papers of Charles Saunders Peirce,* 6 vols., ed. Charles Hartshorne and Paul Weiss. Cambridge, MA: Harvard University Press.

____ 1955. *Philosophical Writings of Peirce,* ed. Justus Buchler. New York: Dover; originally published in 1940.

____ 1958. *Charles S. Peirce: Selected Writings,* ed. Philip P. Wiener. New York: Dover.

Pekala, Ronald J. 1991. *Quantifying Consciousness: An Empirical Approach.* New York and London: Plenum Press.

____ 1995a. "A Short, Unobtrusive Hypnotic-Assessment Procedure for Assessing Hypnotizability Level: I. Development and Research." *American Journal of Clinical Hypnosis* 37/4: 271–83.

____ 1995b. "A Short Unobtrusive Hypnotic Induction for Assessing Hypnotizability: II. Clinical Case Reports." *American Journal of Clinical Hypnosis* 37/4: 284–93.

____ 2002. "Operationalizing Trance II: Clinical Application Using a Psychophenomenological Approach." *American Journal of Clinical Hypnosis* 44/3–4: 241–55.

Pekala, Ronald J. and Forbes E. J. 1997. "Types of Hypnotically (Un)Susceptible Individuals As a Function of Phenomenological Experience: Towards a Typology of Hypnotic Types." *American Journal of Clinical Hypnosis* 39/3: 212–24.

Pekala, Ronald J., Forbes E. J., and Contrisciani, P. A. 1989. "Assessing the Phenomenological Effects of Several Stress Management Strategies." *Imagination, Cognition, and Personality* 8/4: 265–81.

Pekala, Ronald J. and Kumar V. K. 1984. "Predicting Hypnotic Susceptibility by a Self-Report Phenomenological State Instrument." *American Journal of Clinical Hypnosis* 27/2: 114–21.

____ 1987. "Predicting Hypnotic Susceptibility via a Self-Report Instrument: A Replication." *American Journal of Clinical Hypnosis* 30/1: 57–65.

____ 1988. "Phenomenological Variations in Attention across Low, Medium, and High Hypnotically Susceptible Individuals." *Imagination, Cognition, and Personality* 7/4: 330–14.

____ 1989. "Phenomenological Patterns in Consciousness during Hypnosis: Relevance to Cognition and Individual Differences." *Australian Journal of Clinical and Experimental Hypnosis* 17: 1–20.

Pekala, Ronald J., Kumar V. K., Maurer R., Elliott-Carter, N. C., and Moon, E. 2006. "'How Deeply Hypnotized Did I Get?' Predicting Self-Reported Hypnotic Depth from a Phenomenological Assessment Instrument." *International Journal of Clinical and Experimental Hypnosis* 54/3: 316–39.

Pekala, Ronald J. and Nagler, R. 1989. "The Assessment of Hypnoidal States: Rationale and Clinical Application." *American Journal of Clinical Hypnosis* 31/4: 231–36.

Pekala, Ronald J., Steinberg, J., and Kumar, V. K. 1986. "Measurement of Phenomenological Experience: Phenomenology of Consciousness Inventory." *Perceptual and Motor Skills* 63/2: 983–89.

Pelesko, John A. 2007. *Self-Assembly: The Science of Things That Put Themselves Together*. Boca Raton, FL: Chapman & Hall/CRC.

Pelikan, Jaroslav. 1996. *Mary through the Centuries: Her Place in the History of Culture*. New Haven: Yale University Press.

  1999. *Jesus through the Centuries: His Place in the History of Culture*. New Haven: Yale University Press.

Penrose, Roger. 1994. *Shadows of the Mind*. Oxford and New York: Oxford University Press.

Persinger, Michael A. 1983. "Religious and Mystical Experiences As Artifacts of Temporal Lobe Function: A General Hypothesis." *Perceptual and Motor Skills* 57/3: 1255–62.

  1987. *Neuropsychological Bases of God Beliefs*. New York: Praeger Publishers.

  1994a. "People Who Report Religious Experiences May Also Display Enhanced Temporal-Lobe Signs," *Perceptual and Motor Skills* 58/3: 963–75.

  1994b. "Propensity to Report Paranormal Experiences Is Correlated with Temporal Lobe Signs." *Perceptual and Motor Skills* 59/2: 583–86.

  1994c. "Striking EEG Profiles from Single Episodes of Glossolalia and Transcendental Meditation." *Perceptual and Motor Skills* 58/1: 127–33.

Persinger, Michael A. and Healey, F. 2002. "Experimental Facilitation of the Sensed Presence: Possible Intercalation between the Hemispheres Induced by Complex Magnetic Fields." *Journal of Nervous and Mental Disease* 190/8: 533–41.

Persinger, Michael A. and Koren, S. A. 2005. "A Response to Granqvist *et al.* 'Sensed Presence and Mystical Experiences Are Predicted by Suggestibility, Not by the Application of Transcranial Weak Magnetic Fields'." *Neuroscience Letters* 380/3: 346–47.

Peters, Edgar E. 1991. *Chaos and Order in the Capital Markets: A New View of Cycles, Prices and Market Volatility*. New York: Wiley & Sons.

Phillips, Dewi Z. 1993. *Wittgenstein and Religion*. New York: St. Martin's Press.

Plantinga, Alvin. 1993. *Warrant and Proper Function*. New York and Oxford: Oxford University Press.

  2000. *Warranted Christian Belief*. New York and Oxford: Oxford University Press.

Platek, Steven M., Keenan, Julian Paul, and Shackelford, Todd K. (eds). 2006. *Evolutionary Cognitive Neuroscience*. Cambridge, MA: MIT Press.

Porush, David. 1993. "Finding God in the Three-Pound Universe: The Neuroscience of Transcendence." *Omni* 16/1: 60–62.

Powell, L. H., Shahabi, L., and Thoresen, C. E. 2003. "Religion and Spirituality. Linkages to Physical Health." *American Psychologist* 58/1: 36–52.

Premack, David. 2007. "Human and Animal Cognition: Continuity and Discontinuity." *Proceedings of the National Academy of Sciences of the USA* 104/35: 13861–67.

Prigogine, Ilya and Stengers, Isabelle. 1984. *Order out of Chaos*. New York: Bantam Books.

Proudfoot, Wayne 1985. *Religious Experience*. Berkeley: University of California Press.

Pyysiäinen, Ilkka. 2001. *How Religion Works: Towards a New Cognitive Science of Religion*. Boston: Brill.

Rahner, Karl. 1978. *Foundations of Christian Faith: An Introduction to the Idea of Christianity*. New York: Seabury Press.

Ramachandran, Vilayanur S. and Blakeslee, Sandra. 1998. *Phantoms in the Brain: Probing the Mysteries of the Human Mind*. New York: William Morrow.

Ramachandran, Vilayanur S., Hirstein, W. S., Armel, K. C., Tecoma, E., and Iragul, V. 1997. "The Neural Basis of Religious Experience." Paper presented at the 27th Annual Meeting, Society for Neuroscience, New Orleans, LA, October 25–30.

Randi, James. 1982. *Flim-Flam: Psychics, ESP, Unicorns, and other Delusions*. Amherst, NY: Prometheus Books.

Rappaport, R. A. 1979. *Ecology, Meaning and Religion*. Berkeley, CA: North Atlantic Books.

Redwood, Daniel. 2007. "Interview with Richard Davidson," http://healthy.net/scr/interview.asp?id=306 (accessed December 10, 2007).

Revonsuo, Antti. 2006. *Inner Presence: Consciousness As a Biological Phenomenon*. Cambridge, MA: MIT Press.

Rizzuto, Ana-Maria. 1979. *The Birth of the Living God: A Psychoanalytic Study*. University of Chicago Press.

Rock, Adam J., Abbott, Gavin R., Childargushi, Hatun, and Kiehne, Melanie L. 2008. "The Effect of Shamanic-Like Stimulus Conditions and the Cognitive-perceptual Factor of Schizotypy on Phenomenology." *North American Journal of Psychology* 10/1: 79–97.

Rohrbaugh, J. and Jessor, R. 1999. "Religiosity Measure." Hill and Hood 1999 (307–10).

Rumelhart, David E., McClelland, James L., and PDP Research Group. 1986. *Parallel Distributed Processing: Explorations in the Microstructure of Cognition*, 2 vols. Cambridge, MA: MIT Press.

Runehov, Anne L. C. 2007. *Sacred or Neural? The Potential of Neuroscience to Explain Religious Experience*. Religion, Theology, and Natural Science 9. Göttingen: Vandenhoek & Ruprecht.

Sagan, Carl. 1996. *The Demon-Haunted World: Science As a Candle in the Dark*. New York: Random House.

Samarin, William J. 1972. *Tongues of Men and Angels: The Religious Language of Pentecostalism*. New York: Macmillan.

Saperstein, Alvin M. 1984. "Chaos – A Model for the Outbreak of War." *Nature* 309 (May 24): 303–5.

Saroglou, V., Pichon, I., Trompette, L., Verschueren, M., and Dernelle, R. 2005. "Prosocial Behavior and Religion: New Evidence Based on Projective Measures and Peer Ratings." *Journal for the Scientific Study of Religion* 44/3: 323–48.

Schachter, Stephen. C. 2006. "Religion and the Brain: Evidence from Temporal Lobe Epilepsy." In McNamara 2006b (171–88).

Schaeffer, Annette. 2007. "Inside the Terrorist Mind." *Scientific American Mind* (December 2007–January 2008): 72–79.

Schleiermacher, Friedrich D. E. [1799] 1893. *On Religion: Speeches to Its Cultured Despisers*. London: K. Paul, Trench, Trübner.

[1820–21] 1928. *The Christian Faith*, trans. of 2nd German edn., 1830–31, H. R. Mackintosh and J. S. Stewart. Edinburgh: T. & T. Clark.

Schopenhauer, Arthur. [1819] 1977. *The World As Will and Idea*, 2 vols. bound in 3, trans. R. B. Haldane and J. Kemp. New York: AMS Press.

Schuon, Fritjof. [1948] 1953. *The Transcendent Unity of Religions*, trans. Peter Townsend. New York: Pantheon.

Searle, John R. 1984. *Minds, Brains and Science*. Cambridge, MA: Harvard University Press.

1992. *The Rediscovery of the Mind*. Cambridge, MA: MIT Press.

2004. *Mind: A Brief Introduction*. New York and Oxford: Oxford University Press.

Sells, Michael A. 1994. *Mystical Languages of Unsaying*. University of Chicago Press.

Shanon, Benny. 2008. "Biblical Entheogens: A Speculative Hypothesis." *Time and Mind: The Journal of Archaeology, Consciousness and Culture* 1/1: 51–74.

Shariff, A. F. and Norenzayan, A. 2007. "God Is Watching You: Priming God Concepts Increases Prosocial Behavior in an Anonymous Economic Game." *Psychological Science* 18/9: 803–9.

Sharpe, Eric J. 1986. *Comparative Religion: A History*, 2nd edn. La Salle, IL: Open Court.

Shermer, Michael. 2002. *Why People Believe Weird Things: Pseudoscience, Superstition, and Other Confusions of Our Time*, revised and expanded edn. New York: Henry Holt.

Simoyi, Reuben H., Wolf, Alan, and Swinney, Harry L. 1982. "One-Dimensional Dynamics in a Multicomponent Chemical Reaction." *Physical Review Letters* 49/4: 245–48.

Skinner, Burrhus F. 1974. *About Behaviorism*. New York: Knopf.

Sloan, Richard P. 2006. *Blind Faith: The Unholy Alliance of Religion and Medicine*. New York: St. Martin's Press.

Sloan, Richard P. and Bagiella, E. 2002. "Claims about Religious Involvement and Health Outcomes." *Annals of Behavioral Medicine* 24/1: 14–21.

Sloan, Richard P., Bagiella, E., and Powell, T. 1999. "Religion, Spirituality, and Medicine." *The Lancet* 353 (February 20): 664–67.

Sloan, Richard P., Bagiella, Emilia, VandeCreek, Larry, Hover, Margot, Cassalone, Carlo, Hirsch, Trudi Jinpu, et al. 2000. "Should Physicians Prescribe Religious Activities?" *New England Journal of Medicine* 342/25: 1913–16.

Sloan, Richard P. and Ramakrishnan, R. 2006. "Science, Medicine, and Intercessory Prayer." *Perspectives in Biology and Medicine* 49/4: 504–14.

Smith, Huston. 1992. *Forgotten Truth: The Common Vision of the World's Religions*, 2nd edn.; 1st edn., 1965. San Francisco: HarperSanFrancisco.

2000. *Why Religion Matters: The Fate of the Human Spirit in an Age of Disbelief*. San Francisco: HarperOne.

Smith, Jonathan Z. 1993. *Map Is Not Territory: Studies in the History of Religions*. University of Chicago Press.

Sole, Ricard V. and Bascompte, Jordi. 2006. *Self-Organization in Complex Ecosystems*. Princeton University Press.

Sosis, R. 2003. "Why Aren't We All Hutterites? Costly Signaling Theory and Religious Behavior." *Human Nature* 14/2: 91–127.

2004. "The Adaptive Value of Religious Ritual." *American Scientist* 92/2: 166–72.

2006. "Religious Behaviors, Badges, and Bans: Signaling Theory and the Evolution of Religion." In McNamara 2006a (61–86).

Sosis, R. and Alcorta, C. S. 2003. "Signaling, Solidarity and the Sacred: The Evolution of Religious Behavior." *Evolutionary Anthropology* 12/6: 264–74.

Sosis, R. and Ruffle, B. 2003. "Religious Ritual and Cooperation: Testing for a Relationship on Israeli Religious and Secular Kibbutzim." *Current Anthropology* 44/5: 713–22.

2004. "Ideology, Religion, and the Evolution of Cooperation: Field Experiments on Israeli Kibbutzim." *Research in Economic Anthropology* 23: 87–115.

Speckhard, Anne. 2006. "Understanding Suicide Terrorism: Countering Human Bombs and Their Senders." *NATO Security through Science Series E* 9: 158–75.

Sperber, Dan. 1996. *Explaining Culture: A Naturalistic Approach*. Oxford: Blackwell Publishers.

Spilka, B., Hood, R., Jr., Hunsberger, B., and Gorsuch, R. 2003. *The Psychology of Religion: An Empirical Approach*. New York: Guilford Press.

Spinhoven, P., Vanderlinden, J., Ter Kuile, Moniek M., Corry, A., and Linssen, G. 1993. "Assessment of Hypnotic Processes and Responsiveness in a Clinical Context." *International Journal of Clinical and Experimental Hypnosis* 41/3: 210–24.

St.-Pierre, L. S. and Persinger, M. A. 2006. "Experimental Facilitation of the Sensed Presence Is Predicted by the Specific Patterns of the Applied Magnetic Fields, Not by Suggestibility: Re-Analyses of 19 Experiments." *International Journal of Neuroscience* 116/9: 1079–96.

Stace, Walter T. 1960. *Mysticism and Philosophy*. Philadelphia: Lippincott.

Stark, Rodney. 1965. "A Taxonomy of Religious Experience." *Journal for the Scientific Study of Religion* 5/1: 97–116.

Steffen, P. R., Hinderliter, A. L., Blumenthal, J. A., and Sherwood, A. 2001. "Religious Coping, Ethnicity, and Ambulatory Blood Pressure." *Psychosomatic Medicine* 63/4: 523–30.

Stenger, Victor J. 2007. *God: The Failed Hypothesis. How Science Shows That God Does Not Exist.* Amherst, NY: Prometheus Books.

Stewart, Ian. 2002. *Does God Play Dice? The New Mathematics of Chaos*, 2nd edn. Malden, MA and Oxford: Wiley-Blackwell.

Strassman, Rick J. 1996. "Human Psychopharmacology of N, N-dimethyltryptamine." *Behavioral and Brain Research* 73/1–2: 121–24.

2001. *DMT: The Spirit Molecule. A Doctor's Revolutionary Research into the Biology of Near-Death and Mystical Experiences.* Rochester, VT: Park Street Press.

Strawbridge, W. J., Cohen, R. D., Shema, S. J., and Kaplan, G. A. 1997. "Frequent Attendance at Religious Services and Mortality over 28 Years." *American Journal of Public Health* 87/6: 957–61.

Strawbridge, W. J., Sherma, S. J., Cohen, R. D., and Kaplan, G. A. 2001. "Religious Attendance Increases Survival by Improving and Maintaining Good Health Behaviors, Mental Health, and Social Relationships." *Annals of Behavioral Medicine* 23/1: 68–74.

Swinburne, Richard. 1979. *The Existence of God.* Oxford: Clarendon Press.

Szabó, C. 1993. "The Phenomenology of the Experiences and the Depth of Hypnosis: Comparison of Direct and Indirect Induction Techniques." *International Journal of Clinical and Experimental Hypnosis* 41/3: 225–33.

Szára, Stephen. 1989. "The Social Chemistry of Discovery: The DMT Story." *Social Pharmacology* 3: 237–48.

Taylor, Jill Bolte. 2008. *My Stroke of Insight: A Brain Scientist's Personal Journey.* New York: Penguin Viking.

Teresa of Avila. [1577] 1979. *The Interior Castle*, trans. Kieran Kavanaugh and Otillo Rodriguez. Classics of Western Spirituality. Mahwah, NJ: Paulist Press.

Teske, J. 1996. "The Spiritual Limits of Neuropsychological Life." *Zygon* 31/2: 209–34.

Testa, James, Pérez, José, and Jeffries, Carson. 1982. "Evidence for Universal Chaotic Behavior of a Driven Nonlinear Oscillator." *Physical Review Letters* 48/11: 714–17.

Thoresen, C. E. and Harris, A. H. S. 2002. "Spirituality and Health: What's the Evidence and What's Needed?" *Annals of Behavioral Medicine* 24/1: 3–13.

Tillich, Paul. 1951. *Systematic Theology*, vol. I. University of Chicago Press.

1952. *The Courage to Be.* New Haven: Yale University Press.

1957. *Systematic Theology*, vol. II. University of Chicago Press.

1963. *Systematic Theology*, vol. III. University of Chicago Press.

Townsend, M., Kladder, V., Ayele, H., and Mulligan, T. 2002. "Systematic Review of Clinical Trials Examining the Effects of Religion on Health." *Southern Medical Journal* 95/12: 1429–34.

Trivers, Robert. 2002. *Natural Selection and Social Theory: Selected Papers of Robert Trivers*. Evolution and Cognition Series. Oxford and New York: Oxford University Press.

Tsang, E. W., Koren, S. A., and Persinger, Michael A. 2004. "Electrophysiological and Quantitative Electroencephalographic Measurements after Treatment by Transcerebral Magnetic Fields Generated by Compact Disc through a Computer Sound Card: The Shakti Treatment." *International Journal of Neuroscience* 114/8: 1013–24.

Tucker, David, Novelly, Robert, and Walker, Preston. 1987. "Hyperreligiosity in Temporal Lobe Epilepsy: Redefining the Relationship." *Journal of Nervous and Mental Disease* 175/3: 181–84.

Twiss, Sumner B. and Consser, Jr., Walter H. (eds.). 1992. *Experience of the Sacred: Readings in the Phenomenology of Religion*. Hanover, NH: Brown University Press.

Tyler, Edward Burnett. 1874. *Primitive Cultures: Researches into the Development of Mythology, Philosophy, Religion, Art, and Custom*, 2 vols. London: John Murray.

Ullman, Chana. 1989. *The Transformed Self: The Psychology of Religious Conversion*. New York: Plenum Press.

Van der Leeuw, Gerardus. [1933] 1964. *Religion in Essence and Manifestation*, 2nd edn., foreword by Ninian Smart, trans. Hans H. Penner. Princeton University Press.

Vanderlinden, J., Spinhoven, P., Vandereycken, W., and van Dyck, R. 1995. "Dissociative and Hypnotic Experiences in Eating Disorder Patients: an Exploratory Study." *American Journal of Clinical Hypnosis* 38/2: 97–108.

Van Huyssteen, J. Wentzel. 2006. *Alone in the World? Human Uniqueness in Science and Theology*. Grand Rapids, MI: William B. Eerdmans Publishing Company.

Varela, Francisco J., Thompson, Evan, and Rosch, Eleanor. 1991. *The Embodied Mind: Cognitive Science and Human Experience*. Cambridge, MA: MIT Press.

Varga, K., Józsa, E., Bányai, E. I., Gösi-Greguss, A. C., and Kumar, V. K. 2001. "Phenomenological Experiences Associated with Hypnotic Susceptibility." *International Journal of Clinical and Experimental Hypnosis* 49/1: 19–29.

Velmans, Max. 2000. *Understanding Consciousness*. New York: Routledge.

Venkatesh, S., Raju, T. R., Shivani, Y., Tompkins, G., and Meti, B. L. 1997. "A Study of Structure of Phenomenology of Consciousness in Meditative and Non-Meditative States." *Indian Journal of Physiology and Pharmacology* 41/2: 149–53.

Vyse, Stuart A. 1997. *Believing in Magic: The Psychology of Superstition*. New York and Oxford: Oxford University Press.

Waldrop, M. Mitchell. 1992. *Complexity: The Emerging Science and the Edge of Order and Chaos*. New York: Simon & Schuster.

Walker, Robert, Hill, Kim, Burger, Oskar, and Hurtado, A. Magdalena. 2005. "Life in the Slow Lane Revisited: Ontogenetic Separation between

Chimpanzees and Humans." *American Journal of Physical Anthropology* 129/4: 577–83.

Wasson, R. Gordon, Hofmann, Albert, and Ruck, Carl A. P. 1998. *The Road to Eleusis: Unveiling the Secret of the Mysteries.* Los Angeles: Hermes Press.

Watson, John B. 1913. "Psychology As the Behaviorist Views It." *Psychological Review* 20: 158–77.

Watson, John B. and William McDougall. 1929. *The Battle of Behaviorism.* New York: Norton.

Watson, P. J., Hood, R. W., Morris, R. J., and Hall, J. R. 1984. "Empathy, Religious Orientation, and Social Desirability." *Journal of Psychology* 117: 211–16.

Weber, Max. [1920] 1930. *The Protestant Ethic and the Spirit of Capitalism,* trans. Talcott Parsons. London: Allen & Unwin.

Weinberg, Steven. 2001. *Facing Up: Science and Its Cultural Adversaries.* Cambridge, MA: Harvard University Press.

Whitehead, Alfred North. [1929] 1978. *Process and Reality: An Essay in Cosmology,* corrected edn., ed. David Ray Griffin and Donald W. Sherburne. New York: Free Press.

Wildman, Wesley J. 1998. *Fidelity with Plausibility: Modest Christologies in the Twentieth Century.* Albany: State University of New York Press.

1999. "Strategic Mechanisms within Religious Symbol Systems." In Lieven Boeve and Kurt Feyaerts (eds.), *Metaphor and God-Talk* (273–91). Bern: Peter Lang.

2001."Slipping into Horror." *Soundings: An Interdisciplinary Journal* 84/1–2: 143–55.

2002. "Consciousness Expanded." In Sangeetha Menon, A. Sinha, and B. V. Sreekantan (eds.), *Science and Metaphysics: A Discussion on Consciousness and Genetics* (125–41). Bangalore: National Institute of Advanced Studies.

2006a. "Comparative Natural Theology." *American Journal of Theology and Philosophy* 27/2–3: 173–90.

2006b. "The Significance of the Evolution of Religious Belief and Behavior for Religious Studies and Theology." In McNamara 2006a (227–72).

2009a. "Cognitive Error and Contemplative Practices: The Cultivation of Discernment in Mind and Heart." *Buddhist-Christian Studies* 29: 59–79.

2009b. *Science and Religious Anthropology: A Spiritually Evocative Naturalist Interpretation of Human Life.* Farnham, UK: Ashgate Publishing.

2010. *Religious Philosophy As Multidisciplinary Comparative Inquiry: Envisioning a Future for the Philosophy of Religion.* Albany: State University of New York Press.

Wildman, Wesley J. and Brothers, Leslie A. 1999. "A Neuropsychological-Semiotic Model of Religious Experiences." In Robert J. Russell, Nancey Murphy, Theo C. Meyering, and Michael A. Arbib (eds.), *Neuroscience and the Person: Scientific Perspectives on Divine Action* (347–416). Vatican City: Vatican Observatory; Berkeley, CA: Center for Theology and the Natural Sciences.

Wildman, Wesley J. and McNamara, Patrick. 2008. "Challenges Facing the Neurological Study of Religious Belief, Behavior and Experience." *Method and Theory in the Study of Religion* 20/3: 212–42.

2010. "Evaluating Reliance on Narratives in the Psychological Study of Religion Experiences." *International Journal for the Psychology of Religion* 20/4.

Wildman, Wesley J. and Russell, Robert John. 1995. "Chaos: A Mathematical Introduction with Philosophical Reflections." In Robert John Russell, Nancey Murphy, and Arthur R. Peacocke (eds.), *Chaos and Complexity: Scientific Perspectives on Divine Action* (49–90). Vatican City: Vatican Observatory; Berkeley, CA: Center for Theology and the Natural Sciences.

Williams, D. R. and Sternthal, M. J. 2007. "Spirituality, Religion and Health: Evidence and Research Directions." *Medical Journal of Australia* 186 (Suppl. 10): S47–S50.

Wilson, David Sloan. 2002. *Darwin's Cathedral: Evolution, Religion, and the Nature of Society*. University of Chicago Press.

Wisneski, Leonard A. and Anderson, Lucy. 2009. *The Scientific Basis of Integrative Medicine*, 2nd edn. New York: CRC Press.

Worthington, E. L., Kurusu, T. A., McCullough, M. E., and Sandage, S. J. 1996. "Empirical Research on Religion and Psychotherapeutic Processes and Outcomes: A 10-Year Review and Research Prospectus." *Psychological Bulletin* 119/3: 448–87.

Yandell, Keith E. 1993. *The Epistemology of Religious Experience*. Cambridge and New York: Cambridge University Press.

Yao, Xinzhong and Badham, Paul. 2007. *Religious Experience in Contemporary China*. Cardiff: University of Wales Press.

Yoganada, Paramhansa. 1954. *Whispers from Eternity*, 7th edn. Los Angeles: Self-Realization Fellowship.

2004. *Conversations with Yoganada; Stories, Sayings, and Wisdom of Paramhansa Yoganada*, ed. Swami Kriyananda. Nevada City, CA: Crystal Clarity Publishers.

Zaehner, Robert Charles. 1957. *Mysticism, Sacred and Profane: An Inquiry into Some Varieties of Praeternatural Experience*. Oxford: Clarendon Press.

Index

40872693R00184